Fort, Millwall.

An A to Z of

Football Collectibles

Pitch Publishing Ltd
A2 Yeoman Gate
Yeoman Way
Durrington
BN13 3QZ

Email: info@pitchpublishing.co.uk
Web: www.pitchpublishing.co.uk

First published by Pitch Publishing 2019
Text © 2019 Carl A. Wilkes

1

A CIP catalogue record for this book is available from the British Library.

13-digit ISBN: 9781785315602
Design and typesetting by Olner Pro Sport Media - www.olnerpsm.com
Printed in India by Replika Press Pvt. Ltd.

An A to Z of

Football Collectibles

Precious Football Cards and
Sought-After Soccer Stickers

CARL WILKES

Dedicated to Joss

This book would not be were it not for the initial gifts of tea cards, and stickers given by Nan, in the early 1970s; and the 1974 World Cup FKS album given by Mom; Bee's collectibles gene; Potter's style, enthusiasm and Roxy support (Ferry grateful); Owl's weekly flights to Aston Villa (and hoots at Aldridge cricket club); and Berk's daft but endless empathy, and his highly entertaining lessons in how to grow up without following the quotidian. Pippa Moth & pencil-top fruitmen Gra. Fine memories of West Brom toy fairs and steam rollers! J&G.

This writer knew many of the great card collectors of the Twentieth Century, wonderful characters, one and all: former soldiers, erstwhile secret agents (no kidding), former models (women, not men), stars (pop and film) and statisticians (the non-football type); gentlemen of leisure and lounge lizards too. It's to them that this book is co-dedicated, in particular, to the original smoking man, Don Mayne, a personal hero in cards; and to Harry Richards, artist at large in a small loft; and to all who contributed to the journal, Football Card Collector Magazine, during the 1990s, including John (RIP), Roy Davies (Wolves), Peris Hatton (FKS), Neville (Cambrian), Peter (Burnley), Bill (Baines) and Alan Jenkins (FCIE).

In acknowledgement of the artists and photographers, without whom the cards we enjoy would not be, this writer is thankful to the players of the past. With gratitude, their images are respectfully included in this book. Thanks to the publishers of the cards of yore, and the issuers of the stickers of yesteryear. It's now nigh on impossible to trace the original artists of cards made in the 1950s, not to mention the 1880s. Photographers of images from cards of the 1960s are often long gone, and those behind the cards of the 1920s have departed without trace, but they are celebrated herein. This writer has tried to contact the various issuers of cards shown in this book but most firms are long since defunct. Thanks to those from whom positive and encouraging replies were received.

This writer grew up with a passion for film and media, and he studied these things at university, and well beyond; into television news and the press, specialising in picture research. From news to design this writer eventually landed in publishing and issued Football Card Collector Magazine. Thanks to Garry Daynes for keeping that journal alive for the last twenty years. Thanks to Tim Davidson; to Programme Monthly and everyone who helped share publicity for this book. Highest regards to Rey Bowen, this writer's first published author (Kamite eschatology & valve record players); The Lioness; Jeremy Cantwell, playwright; and to Gibby, World Serpent; Andy at Fosse Films; Sunflower, Red Skelton bridge; Robert for Murtology and Tudor wear-em, scare-ems; to Blue (the search for ephemera and antiques goes on) and to dear Poin, now sailing a star but never far. The book is dedicated to Joss. She knows why.

Special thanks to Martin Routledge, author of The Beautiful Badge, for the introduction to Pitch Publishing. Thanks to Jane and Paul for publishing this book; and thanks to Duncan, Matt and Ciaran, at Olner Pro Sport Media, for its beauty.

Carl Wilkes

Hell and stickers, season 1981/82

Goodies of Bristol, 1973, World Cup cards, uncut sheet, detail

Introduction

This is the first book of its kind. It seems a little odd, to be the first, because what this book is about – football cards – have been around for almost 150 years.

Footballers have been pictured on trade cards since the 1880s, and on stickers since the 1910s. Little, sticky pictures of soccer stars and cards of footer teams have found their way into most homes in Europe, and the Americas, at some time or other. The cards included in this book are mostly from Great Britain and Western Europe, however, it also includes soccer cards of note from countries further afield. So, this is not only the first illustrated history of soccer cards from around the world, it is also the first price guide for football cards. While some cards have been shown in other publications, those books have been about other things, like memorabilia; or particular themes, like one-club histories; or books on the story of contemporary stickers. This book's focus is on trade cards, including cigarette cards, trading cards and stickers, from around the world, issued from 1880 until 1980.

So, what is a trade card, and is it the same thing as a trading card? You may have heard of trading cards. You are less likely to have heard of trade cards, even though you probably owned them at some time or other. A trade card is a card that is given with a product, a thing that is issued by one of the trades. It's that simple. You may know what a cigarette card is. Cigarette cards are but one type of trade card. They are issued by the tobacco trade. Whether it is tobacco (cigarettes, rolling tobacco, cigars, snuff, etc.), confectionery (chocolates, sweets, gum, etc.), print media (magazines, comics, newspapers, etc.), toys (games, football figurines, lucky bags, etc.), foodstuffs (breakfast cereals, gravy granules,

cheese, etc.) or beverages (beer, tea, coffee, etc.), all are trades, and all issue trade cards with their various produce and brands.

In the past, trades gave away cards to entice and to encourage the purchase of their products. They were often aimed at children because the young have a powerful influence over the old: '*I want one!*' Trade cards are still made. They are given away, freely, because they are very useful little advertising tools. They implant the name of a brand into a young and impressionable person's head, where it stays for life. When seen they remind adults about a particular marque, or a brand. Trade cards have come to be collected but collecting was never their reason for being. Trade cards are, therefore, very different to trading cards.

Trading cards, in contrast to trade cards, were designed for collecting, and swapping – or trading, as it's known in America. Such cards are not usually sold with products, though a packet of trading cards, or a packet of stickers, may be given away with a magazine, or a newspaper, to advertise the release of a new series of such cards. Stickers that are sold in packets, like the ones made by Panini, are synonymous with trading cards. Though stickers are designed to be glued into an album, sticker doubles, or swaps, are traded with other sticker collectors. Trade cards cost little to make. They are good little earners for their issuers.

Modern trading cards, and stickers, tend to be made in much higher numbers than trade cards. This is partly due to product and popularity, but mostly it's due to distribution. The major brands of trading cards and stickers are distributed nationally, with blanket coverage in all areas, even in the remotest corners of the land. The multinationals, which now own the brands of yesterday, also own distribution networks. They

may also own some media, like newspapers, TV news or internet platforms. It wasn't always so. In the past there was more competition. Manufacturers vied for a patch, for influence, and for distribution. One publisher might have good distribution in the west, another in the north, while others popped up here and there, all over the place. In the 1970s there were many different firms making diverse collections of football stickers, and cards. It's a scene that is unlikely to be enjoyed again. Like the game of Monopoly made clear: winner takes all. Capitalism ends with one or two super rich players having the lot. The rest, the majority, have to lump it. So much for the lullaby of competition bringing down prices and offering more choice!

Trading cards are still collected by the packet but nowadays stickers are often bought by the carton – a box full of 100 packets! Generally there are more trading cards in circulation than trade cards, and trade cards are often rarer, and more valuable than trading cards. Not always, but mostly. Whereas contemporary trading cards are collected for the sake of collecting, trading cards of the 1890s were very different ephemera. Some cards were designed for playing games, while others were gambled away in the hope of winning prizes. Victorian trading cards were sent back to the issuer for prize draws and competitions. Lucky collectors would receive footballs or sports clothing, in return for their cards. Unlucky collectors simply lost their collections, and the issuer would reuse the forfeit cards, in newly sealed packets, to be sold anew from his shop, or from his horse-drawn wagon. Imagine that! A door-to-door football cards service. A man, a horse and a cart, with a monkey, to boot, selling cards. And we think we have it all!

The values in this book have been arrived at by assessing sales data collected over the last 25 years. The data has been collected, first and foremost, by recording prices paid in hundreds of public and postal auction sales, since 1995. Secondly, the prices paid in thousands of internet auctions have also been recorded, since 2010. Thirdly, values have been recorded from so-called *wants lists*. These are wish lists made by collectors, with prices they offer for cards they require. Collectors make such lists because finding rare cards needs a lot of help. Wants lists often include offers for cards that remain on the run, at large, and otherwise unavailable. One collector, in particular, presently promises prices in the thousands, for cards he requires.

The values are given in ranges, for example, £5 to £10, or £20 to £30, because cards from the same set, though issued at the same time, may have very different values. This is partly due to team and player popularity, with bigger clubs having more collectors, but it is also to do with certain collecting habits that suit some sellers, like the sale of rookie cards, the first cards to feature a famous player, from early in his or her career.

Collectors collect all sorts of cards. Some seek brands, others search for marques. Most football card collectors chase teams or particular players. Others buy end-number cards (card number 1, and whatever the last number card in a set happens to be), or rookies. Accordingly, sellers price such cards to suit the market. To some extent value is in the eye of the coveter even more than that of the possessor. It seems this way with rare cards. Every sale seems to increase values.

The manufacturing of card consumers, the shaping of how buyers buy, is a money-making machination that suits some sellers. Good advice is, collect and buy what appeals to you, and don't believe you ought to buy rookie cards, or other commercial conceits like slabbed cards, no matter what sellers tell you will be best for the future. Their future?

While this book may encourage a storm of sales, a new wave of collectors, or a surge in values, it ought to be remembered that prices may go down, as well as up. This author asserts that rare cards are valuable assets but having the right cards is the key. How do you find the right cards? The appendices at the end of this book include tips for buyers, and sellers. Garry Daynes sells cards by post; Loddon Auctions and Tim Davidson Auctions both sell and buy cards by auction; and Alan Jenkins is your man for sharing cards information about modern cards and cards of aulde. Contact details for this super league of gentlemen will be found in the appendices at the back of this book. For cards by internet, sales and purchases, see the websites below.

The images included in this book are from this writer's private collection, except where credited otherwise. Many more images of cards not seen here can be viewed at www.rarecards.co.uk and at www.footballsoccercards.com

Over 100 years old, British football cards

1972 BAB sticker of Derek Dougan

Joe Baker on an Italian gum card. It cost about a penny, it's now worth up to £100

Introduction to football cards

The football card has been a thing of fascination for well over 100 years. It's also an asset of some worth. Football cards have been collected, swapped, traded and resold, not only as beautiful and historical collectibles, but as investments too.

This writer's first footballer cards were given with bubblegum, circa 1971, when packets of gum cost tuppence (see: A&BC Gum). Cards bought for two pennies in 1971 have become worth up to £5 each! The discarded packets from those cards are now worth up to £50 each, and the box from which they were distributed, the container that sat on the shelf in the newsagent's shop, is now worth £250! Not bad for squandered pocket money, wasted in the best of George Best ways, as wailed bemoaning parents of those days.

These prices are peanuts when compared to what collectors in America have been paying for their sports cards. Since the 1990s American sports cards regularly sell for up to, and well over, a million US dollars each! In Europe prices remain much lower, at least for now. In the British Isles prices still enjoy a quaintly old fashioned affordability. This is also known as 'the early days'. Inexpensive British and European cards are now attracting more and more buyers from America, as well as Monaco and the oil-rich Middle Eastern states. Very rare cards are one of the assets they seek. While rare cards may be available today, this may not be the case for long. Prices are expected to rise, and quite sharply in some cases. Very rare cards are already in limited

Avant-garde, women's football stickers were issued in France, in 1978

supply, and many simply cannot be bought, no matter how much money a buyer is prepared to pay! There remains a window of opportunity for acquiring very rare soccer cards of yesteryear, but it's a closing aperture. However, it comes with a warning: defenestration is possible.

A so-called limited edition card from the 1990s is a readily available resource when compared to vintage cards of genuine rarity, like an A&BC Gum checklist, with Liverpool, from 1964; a Batger football clubs colours trade card, of Manchester City, from 1900; or a scarce News Chronicle card of a Heart of Midlothian player, from the 1950s. Vintage and antique cards like these are much rarer than any contemporary conceit, no matter the marketing claims of sharp executives and the glossy public relations ads they buy to tempt you to believe. There are dealers holding stocks of recently made so-called limited edition cards but there are no dealers holding stocks of an antique card of great rarity. You'll see very costly cards of Messi and Zidane, cards that are called 'mega-rare', but you won't see a 1905 Baines card of Billy Meredith, or a 1900 Sharpe's card of Steve Bloomer, to name but two great players of their day. For every one 1896 Charles Fry you'll see 1,000 rookie stickers of Mbappe for sale (and there are probably many more behind closed doors).

Cards and stickers made since 1980 may become rare, in time. Before 1980 no one thought such things would become worth a lot of money. Cards were neither contrived as limited editions, nor as collectibles. They were considered as marketing gimmicks, or as cheap toys. When a 1970s series of cards was out of date the remaining stock was destroyed. That no longer

happens. The great divide is the 1980s. Cards from before the 1980s are generally rarer, and often worth more, than cards from after the 1980s. Not always but mostly. This book evaluates cards from the earlier period, from before the 1980s. Further back in time, before World War Two, cigarette cards were collected, typically by adults. Due to millions of cigarette cards being well cared for, and passed on by parents to children, many have survived until today, and they are quite easily available. Trade cards, on the other hand, were issued in much smaller numbers, and were played with by children. They were issued as early as the 1880s yet were not typically collected by adults until the 1950s. Trade cards have been less well understood than cigarette cards because of the number and types of trade cards issued. They were made by all sorts of publishers, small and large, far and wide. They were harder to collect because they were issued with diverse products, from comics to ice cream, from gravy powder to sweets, from gum to newspapers, meaning it was not possible to know by whom, where, or when, or how often they were published. Tobacco cards were easier to track, and to collect. They came from one source, the tobacconist, by whom smokers were kept informed of newly issued collections. Conversely, most trade cards were destined for youngsters. Those that were not acquired with toys or sweets were often bought by mothers, the housewives of family homes in those days, and thus found their way into children's hands, from food products opened in the kitchen, thence played with, damaged, lost or destroyed. Cards that survived such rigours are now sought by serious collectors, many of whom are willing to pay highly for cards they seek.

The cards shown and evaluated in this book are bought by people from across the wealth divide. The buyers of cards are often collectors of football club ephemera and memorabilia but recently a new market has emerged. People are now buying cards as alternative assets.

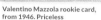

Valentino Mazzola rookie card, from 1946. Priceless

1978 Panini, Gilbert Gress, looking very...1970s!

A 1920s Celtic Tango Toffee card. It's now worth £200

1920s Spanish football card

In 2016 the highest selling cigarette card in history made over $3million! In 2014 a rare postage stamp sold for around $10million! A rare coin also topped $10million, in 2013. The rarest postcard sold for considerably less, but still, at $30k it's not to be sniffed at. The rarest trade cards are as rare, and probably much rarer, than many rare postcards. So, it's not surprising that trade and tobacco cards are in popular demand, and prices are rising sharply in some cases.

There are more soccer fans than stamp collectors, yet, until now, most football fans have not realised that relics from their favourite sport may be worth as much, or more, than rare stamps. Stamps sell for thousands, daily. You can check the figures on internet auction sites. There are endless choices of rare stamps on Ebay, up to prices of a million each! The rarest football cards are just as scarce as rare stamps, and they may even be rarer! Only now are people starting to realise this.

For some, collecting cards is primarily about lost-in-time images, forgotten social history, having rare ephemera, and supporting a football team which is reflected in those cards. The miniature pictures give visual pleasure, and contentment comes through their acquisition. It takes time to compile a collection. Rare cards cannot simply be bought. They take effort and patience. Given a million pounds to find a Wood Brothers card in the next 24 hours most, probably all people would fail to buy one. There are not many things you simply cannot buy. No matter how much money you have rare cards are in that exquisite category and they take guile to acquire.

Some buyers worry about putting money into paper goods. Like keeping books, or any kind of collection, scarves, bags, stamps, clothing, records,

or jewels, there are risks. Other than metal coins most collectibles are all too easily damaged or lost in destructive accidents. Then again burglars take coins, and jewellery, and maybe even stamp albums, but not many burglars would give a thought to carrying off heavy albums full of soccer cards. Most people do not appreciate the value of such things.

The savour of capture and the pleasure of acquisition is what collecting is all about. Collecting is a contemporary form of hunting and that's what human beings are: hunters and gatherers. When it's not essential to hunt for food, or for shelter, the innate hunting instinct in humankind is turned to other things. Commerce knows this. At leisure we gather art, antiques, old toys and collectibles but multinationals and corporations prefer we spend our money on them, on their gadgets, their new cars, on handbags with expensive labels, the latest phone, etc. Collectibles and antiques trump those things because collectibles and antiques have more value, over time, than gizmos, gadgets and new consumer products, which lose half their value on the day you buy

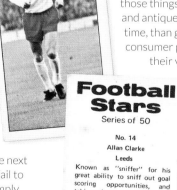

them. The maxim, buy what you like and not what you expect to go up in value, is a good one, but buying cleverly is part of the trick. Buy so you can at least get the ticket price back, or so that you can make a trade for similar or better value, if need be.

Antique cards are historical

artefacts. History is not what's found in the results generated by a search engine. History is found in objects that date from a time in the past, in beautiful things that cannot be reproduced, and in the lies the victor writes. Victors and vanquished aside, antiques are popular for good reason. Once anything has limited availability it accrues value, a little like gold. It could be argued that cards cannot do anything, that they can't be used as food or as energy. The same goes for gold. It's still worth a lot. Limited supply garners value. When something is limited there is always someone who wants some of it.

Hobbies and interests, especially those that demand a certain application of mind, patience and wit, are also very good for you. Some say they are as good as medicine. People who pursue interests like collecting often live longer and healthier lives than people who retire with nothing to do. Younger people, who start collections early, often end up with assets of enormous worth. Cards bring pleasure, peace of mind, a little Zen, and endless fun. It's about what makes you feel good, and, in this stressful world, a moment of calm is priceless.

This book does not offer investment advice. This writer wishes to make clear that though he has not lost a penny with vintage cards it's a chancy game of fortune, and it is possible to lose, and prices do fluctuate. Modern cards are a gamble, and older cards can be bought unwisely by the unlearned. However, buying the right antique cards seems a lot more sensible than buying today's throw-away culture knick knacks, and similar show-the-neighbour-how-I-wasted-my-money mass market consumer products. These things will end up on an unwanted table at next year's jumble sale.

Allan Clarke, 1974 sweet cigarettes card

Southampton

Manager: Ted Bates
Address: The Dell, Milton Road, Southampton SO9 4XX
Telephone: Southampton 23408
Ground Capacity: 30,000
Record Attendance: 31,044 v. Tottenham H., Div.1 October, 1969
Year Formed: 1885
Colours: Red and white striped shirts black shorts
Nickname: Saints
Turned Professional: 1894
Playing Area: 110 x 72

PLACE SUPERSTAR
RON DAVIES
STAMP HERE

g First Division club, Southampton struggled for the first two seasons after gaining champions of the Third Division in 1960, they gained further promotion in 1966 for producing their own players, especially forwards, skipper Terry Paine, Martin ree recent examples. Southampton have never won the F.A. Cup, but were semi- nchester United, the eventual winners, at Villa Park. Two years ago the Saints p but were unable to make much progress in the competition. Last season again bid to bring European soccer to the Dell.

Tottenham Hotspur

Manager: W. E. Nicholson
Coach: Eddie Baily
Address: 748 High Road, Tottenham N.17
Telephone: 01 808 1020
Ground Capacity: 58,000
Record Attendance: 75,038 v. Sunderland F.A. Cup March 1938
Year Formed: Approx. 1882
Colours: White shirts, blue shorts
Nickname: Spurs
Turned Professional: 1895

PLACE SUPERSTAR
ALAN MULLERY
STAMP HERE

Last season's League Cup winners. Tottenham's great League and Cup double in 1961 has stood as a testimony to a magnificent team. Twice League Champions, in 1951 and 1961, they have also won the F.A. Cup on five occasions in 1901, 1921, 1961, 1962 and 1967, and have the enviable record of never having lost a Wembley final after beating Aston Villa 2-0 in the League Cup last season. In addition, they became the first English club to win a major European trophy, being victorious in the Cup Winners Cup in 1963. Always on the lookout for new players, Tottenham built a reputation as the biggest spenders in the Football League, but the introduction of some of their own discoveries into the side over the past few seasons has proved that they can produce their own stars.

Stoke City

Manager: Tony Waddington
Coach: Alan A'Court
Address: Victoria Ground, Stoke-on-Trent
Telephone: Stoke-on-Trent 44660
Ground Capacity: 50,500
Record Attendance: 51,380 v. Arsenal Div. 1 March 1937
Year Formed: 1863
Colours: Red and white striped shirts white shorts
Nickname: Potters

PLACE SUPERSTAR
GORDON BANKS
STAMP HERE

n, Stoke lost an equalising penalty to Arsenal in the last minute of their aten 2-0 in the replay. Division Two champions in 1963, Stoke have been buy established stars. Under their manager Tony Waddington this system ood mixture of youth and experience in the Stoke City team. An attractive ng anyone on their day, and one of the highlights of last season was a 5-1 With some impressive displays, Stoke showed that they will be one of the

W.B.A.

Manager: Don Howe
Address: The Hawthorns, West Bromwich
Telephone: 021-553 0095
Ground Capacity: 50,000
Record Attendance: 64,815 v. Arsenal F.A. Cup, 6th Rd., March 1937
Year Formed: 1879
Colours: Blue and white striped shirts, white shorts
Nickname: Albion, Throstles, Baggies
Turned Professional: 1885

PLACE SUPERSTAR
JOHN KAYE
STAMP HERE

One of the best Cup fighting sides of recent years, Albion struggled last season, but improved later results saw them move away from the lower regions of the league. League Champions in 1920, they have won the F.A. Cup on five occasions, in 1888, 1892, 1931, 1954 and 1968, when Jeff Astle scored an extra time goal to beat Everton. In addition, they won the League Cup in 1966, and were beaten finalists in 1967 and 1970. In 1969 they entered the European Cup Winners Cup, reaching the quarter-final where they lost 1-0 to Dunfermline at the Hawthorns after a goal-less draw in Scotland. Now under the new management of Don Howe, and with a young side, Albion will soon be back challenging for top honours.

American & British Gum it's not!
It's as British as British can be is A&BC

Britain's best loved gum cards are those by A&BC gum. It's seemly then that the core of this book opens with them. Cigarette card collectors of yore thought A&BC stood for American & British Chewing gum but the initials are, in fact, the surnames of the directors, a group of friends from the 1940s. Soon after World War Two A&BC was incorporated as a limited company, registered in Great Britain, to sell chewing gum, the kind of gum made popular by wartime American G.I.s serving in the British Isles. Gum cards followed soon afterwards.

In the 1950s A&BC gum was sold from vending machines. In went a coin and out popped a ball of gum. A card emerged from an adjacent slot. The earliest cards typically showed film stars and singers, then sportsmen. In the 1960s vending machines were replaced by packaged confections. The cards and gum, wrapped together in colourful paper packets, were sold by newsagents, tobacconists and small grocery shops. By the 1970s A&BC had become the most successful gum cards issuer in British history. But where did it all start, and why gum cards and not stickers?

Gum cards had been issued in Great Britain long before World War Two, but not on the scale of A&BC's output. In the 1920s a chewing-and-card-collecting craze had been encouraged by an English firm called Lacey's. It printed 50 Welsh, Scottish and English footballer picture cards which were given away with its in-house creation, chewing wax [sic]. The fad was revived a few years later with Oh Boy Gum, a brand issued by British Chewing Sweets, a firm born of American gum giant Goudey, also noted for its Oh Boy Gum cards. In England, in 1933, Oh Boy Gum was issued with a fabulous series of 60 footballer cards. It was not long before other manufacturers were on the

scene. In 1938 Klene Confectionery, from Holland, issued Val Footer Gum cards of British footballers. The trend for chewing gum and collecting gum cards would surely have continued into the 1940s but for war. Holland fell in 1940 and paper rationing put paid to all and any issues of domestic cards. British presses would not roll anew for years. It would seem that 20 years of progress in cards had been lost when primitive post-war cards appeared during the 1946/47 season.

Following the destructive hiatus of war Italian, French and German cards also came to be produced once more. In Iberia it had been different. The 1940s was a time of peace in Spain. Spanish cards were more sophisticated than those made elsewhere in post-war Europe. However, American troops had not arrived in Madrid as they had in London, Rome and Berlin. No fashionable Yankee chewing gum had come to fascist Iberia. This resulted in Spanish football cards evolving in a different direction. In Spain cards were becoming soccer stickers.

Football stickers had been published in Scotland before anywhere else in the world. They were first issued with The People's Journal in 1914. The English caught up in 1922 with a collection issued by Sports Fun and Football Favourites magazine. Other sticker collections emerged in the late 1920s and 1930s, typically issued by comics like Adventure and Boys' Magazine. However, it was a certain fraternity from Bilbao with whom the credit for modern soccer stickers rests, for the Spanish birthed FKS, the British Soccer Stars issuer of the ubiquitous paper football stickers of the 1970s.

The Spanish developed the sticker and the packet of stickers while other countries were going to war. After the war, during the 1946/47 season, British producers started reissuing cards.

They were sold in packets of sweets, and they also came stapled together in little booklets to be pulled apart and swapped with friends. Stickers were a long way from a renaissance in Britain! Cigarette cards, whose production had also been paused for war, were struggling to find their next breath. Tobacco cards were squeezed out of production by cost-cutting manufacturers. They were as good as finished by the time A&BC launched its first gum cards, in 1953.

The registry at Companies House in London records four men, Messrs. Aynsz, Braun and two Coakley brothers, as directors of A and BC Chewing Gum, a private company limited by shares. It was incorporated in 1949. The newly formed company allied with an eccentric home-based chemist, Oscar Janser. He'd recently had his Eureka moment. After a year inventing it he'd finally created a decent artificial chewing gum. A&BC paid him royalties for the use of his creation. The gum was similar to American chewing gum but had no need of American ingredients, and no need of ration permits. By 1950, with a ration-busting gum to call its own, A&BC were up and running. Printing cards was soon to follow. From 1953 onwards A&BC's vibrant gum card designs were often as far out as the music of the times. The colourful cards of singers and other youthful themes that graced the Rock'n'roll years morphed into spaced-out weirdness during the flower power high. Whacky designs of sheer lunacy would grace the glam rock era. As well as gum cards A&BC made stickers, tattoos, transfers, games and posters. Then, in 1974 A&BC found itself on the wrong end of a court case and lost it all to the American cards giant, Topps.

Thanks to almost five decades of card collecting, hours of research at The National Archive, and the shared knowledge of card *fiends*

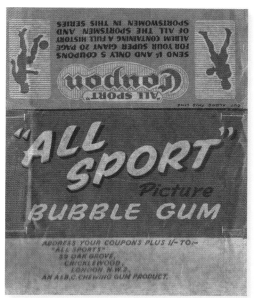

A&BC Gum wrapper 1954

A&BC Gum cards 1954

A&BC Gum card variations 1958

the world over, the story of A&BC's cards is now known, yet, until the 1990s it was a piecemeal tale apocryphally carved out by careless writers who cared little for gum cards, and less still for football. As a remedy, in 1998, this author was the first publisher to print an illustrated article on the packaging and ephemera from A&BC's 21 years of soccer cards. Football Card Collector Magazine presented an incomplete though foundational timeline which laid a framework upon which more knowledge has since accrued. The cards, the different series, the printing anomalies and much more are now common knowledge.

Evaluating A&BC cards, as with all cards, starts with their condition. Quality is king. Near-mint A&BC cards hold a value 100 times greater than damaged cards. Values ascribed throughout this book are for cards in excellent condition. Very good cards are worth a little less, and so on... fair or average condition cards are worth less than good, and poor condition cards are worth little, if anything at all. Only the rarest of Victorian and Edwardian cards retain value in a poor state – and early A&BC wrappers!

A&BC's earliest packets looked *Gospel* but the cards inside were *Rock'n'roll*!

It was 1954 and the first football cards by A&BC appeared in a series called All Sport. The packets had a very sober design, which was no doubt reassuring to parents, and they contained a single card. They were racked and stacked in vending machines across the land. One waxy packet and a ball of gum were dispensed for every halfpenny coin cast into the cumbersome gum machine. Later, in the 1960s, gum vending was done from a glass bubble perched atop a metal stork seated in concrete. It looked a little like a colourful parking meter (to those for whom parking meters still mean anything) but in 1953 the gum machines looked more like oversized condom dispensers. The ugly metal boxes were affixed firmly to walls outside sweet shops. A little window into the box would show cards stacked inside, ready for purchase. Another showed a mountain of gum balls. A sample card on display filled a third glass aperture. There were various slots for coins, and for rejected money [the manufacture of home-made coins that could con the machines was an art form]. A handle to turn, and a dispensing tray presented a satisfying A-Z test that was usually passed with flying colours. Paying-in a coin and turning the handle

encouraged an inner mechanism to entice a ball of gum to drop into a tray, where eager, dirty fingers grabbed at it. [Were those trays ever cleaned?] A pristine card, neatly wrapped in colourful waxy paper, was delivered at the same moment from an adjacent slot. One hand in the tray, the other hand on the bounty made for beautiful symmetry.

The 120 *All Sport* picture bubble gum cards of 1954 had plain backs and dull monotone photos. It didn't matter. A nation's children starved of sports gum cards since 1938 greeted these cards like old friends. Further, the novelty of collecting the coloured tokens of sportsmen, cut from the packaging, to send away for an album made up a little for what the cards lacked in creative design. These days most of the *All Sport* cards are available for less than £5 a card but you will pay plenty for an unused card of the legendary footballer, Puskas. An album with all 120 cards glued in may cost you less than that single Hungarian star. There were many albums completed so a full set glued down is not where the value lies. A single wrapper, at about £100, is the most expensive element in collecting this series, though were an advertising poster to be found, it should be worth well over £1,000!

A&BC Gum card photo variations 1958

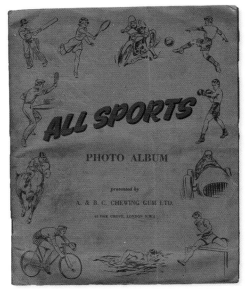

A&BC Gum album 1954

JOHN MOLYNEUX

LIVERPOOL

A&BC Gum card 1959

Accompanying the cards in the vending machines was Oscar Janser's chewy stuff. The British professor's gum would come to form a billion black globs on the country's pavements. The pock-marked patina of British streets lasted for decades. By 1962 A&BC would switch from British to American gum. A deal with Topps's Bazooka gum sealed its fate.

It took four years for A&BC to reprise sports cards. Like the Brothers Grimm the pals at A&BC had been mean with their new fare. Distracted by glamorous subjects, they issued series after series of attractive film stars. When they turned back to sport, in 1958, they found their golden goose in the rugged stars of football. Soccer player cards could be reprinted every year, guaranteeing an annual income for little creativity, low cost design and relatively little artwork. Better still, soccer player cards could be issued seasonally, up to three times a year, every year!

In 1958 Topstars Bubblegum Picture cards arrived in the shops. Much like the *All Sport* cards of 1954 they were packaged singly and issued from gum vending machines. The wrappers displayed a sporting figure which could have been a drop-kicking rugby player, or a Can-Can dancer, so high was the kick! There were two series of 46 cards issued over the 1958/59 football season. However, unbeknown to collectors back then, success caused stock shortages and the first series of 46 cards had to be reprinted – twice! The newly printed cards are slightly different by issue. To collect all of the varieties you'll need 138 cards! The known types include a card with a special offer (with a *Planet* token) and a blue back; and, two

types without tokens but with different size photos and black backs. Thankfully, the cards that followed in series two are easier to find, with only 46 different issues to seek. All of these cards have the *Planet* offer atop. Cut cards are worth very little. Values fluctuate enormously due to the varieties and their availability. In 1992 a series of Topps Stadium Club football cards featured an homage to this series, albeit giving the cards a title they never had, and a value of only 27p each. How times have changed! Entry level prices for the cards nowadays start at £2 each but the most sought after cards may touch £200, as a certain Bobby Charlton card did, in public auction, in 2017. An album for the cards was issued. It had the legend: *Topstars Album of Famous Footballers*. The title seen on the series wrapper is different: *Bubblegum Picture Cards Topstars*. The wrapper would now cost around £200 – were it to come to market.

In autumn of 1959, whilst Asterix was chasing his first Gallic wild boar, A&BC was finding its stride in modern Britain. A new collection of footballers had 96 player cards showing colourful, though stiffly frozen action shots. They were shuffled with two hard to find team cards which served as picture checklists: Wolves and Nottingham Forest. The latter now commands up to £200 for an excellent condition example. There were only meant to be 98 cards in the series but two varieties are known: cards 83 and 84 are available with different backs. So, you'll need 100 cards if you want the lot. On the backs of the cards was a *magical* picture quiz. Rubbing the edge of a coin over the card made a player *appear* out of the ether! Two different wrappers were issued, one of

A&BC Gum checklist team card 1959

which was for multiple cards. It was A&BC's first shop issue packet. The other type was for vending machines. Coloured mostly blue, the wrappers show a player in a bi-sectional kit similar to the Blackburn Rovers strip. The second sub-series of 49 (51) cards is worth more than the first. This is the rule of thumb for all A&BC *Footballer* cards. First series issues, typically released in late August, sold more due to the novelty of a new collection, not to mention summertime lazy days at home, and the start of a new sports season. Wintery second series issues, from Christmastime, often had less success. Third series cards, launched towards Easter, sold fewer still and are the rarest and often the most valuable A&BC cards.

A pop band called The Beatles was strumming its first chords just as A&BC's 1960 *Footballer* cards came out. A design make-over and a return to photographic portraits gave collectors 84 circular photos of soccer players on garishly coloured cards, plus a couple of team checklist cards. The checklist images are at odds with the year of issue. Burnley ought to be included in this series but their 1959 league championship honour was not celebrated by A&BC. Blackpool, having won no honours for the previous six seasons, takes the place of Burnley! The other checklist has Wolves, once again. Wolves had won the FA Cup in 1960 but A&BC used the team image from 1959. The old picture is cropped into an oval frame and there is no mention of Wolves's new Cup, nor any change in the legend, which still reads, 'champions 1957-58, 1958-59'. The wrappers for the 1960 series have the same design as the 1959 issue but they are coloured green instead of blue. Note

the change of address too. The firm had moved from London to Harold Hill in Essex. An original wrapper from this issue would cost £200 or more.

In 1961 Yuri Gagarin was the first man in space but a move backwards in time marred A&BC's launch. Autographed Topstars cards were retro in the wrong way. Even the packet was old fashioned. On the cards a blue facsimile autograph did not make up for boring black and white photos, plain backs, no quiz games, no checklists, no team line-ups and a lack of player biographies to boot! It must have been a very disappointing series to behold. As only 64 cards were made the collection was dropped before 1962, and there was no second issue. The throwback wrapper is coloured green and yellow, just as it was in 1958, with the same Topstars Can-Can high kicker, but with a by-line, *Autographed*. The packets can also be distinguished from the earlier type of Topstars packet by the address at Harold Hill.

The most creative thing A&BC did with this series was to launch a selection of Scottish players. The so-called Scottish *Autographed Topstars* cards consisted of 44 similarly monotone cards, also with blue facsimile autographs. Released in 1962 they were a little smaller than the English cards but the values are now much grander! You'll pay over £10 each player, sometimes much more! Prices may approach £100 for the Celtic, Hearts, Dundee and Rangers team cards. Pricey too is international player Gerry Baker, the brother of Hibernian and Arsenal star Joe Baker. Gerry was the USA's first national soccer player from another country's league. A distinctive wrapper remains unknown and it seems that the English design was

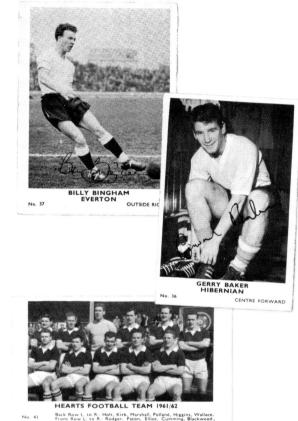

English and Scottish A&BC Gum cards 1961

A&BC Gum card, 1960

A&BC Gum checklist team card, 1960

employed. However, the Scottish packet will be distinguishable by its original folds because these cards are smaller than their English cousins.

With *Bazooka*, *The Chew of Champions*, A&BC was back with a blast and American gum to boot! Following the drab black and white cards of 1961 this series went all out to charm back disenchanted younger collectors. In autumn 1962 these colourful and attractive cards had footballers front and back, photos *and* illustrations. This series features two checklist team line-ups: the England 1962 World Cup squad, and Tottenham Hotspur, which are two of the three most valuable cards in the set. The third card is that of Bobby Moore, which is considered to be one of his rookie cards. The orange and blue wrapper from this issue is perhaps the rarest of A&BC packets and may fetch £250 were it to reappear on the market. Only one example has been seen in the last 25 years!

The 1960s had its fair share of awful design but surely melamine fake wood furniture takes first prize. Sadly, in 1963/64, A&BC succumbed to similar taste and issued two collections with faux wood designs. These *Footballer* cards reprised a 1959 novelty, the *rub-a-coin* 'magic' feature, bringing it back as *Make-a-Photo*, which is how these blue back cards are now known. Taking the edge of a coin to the backs of all 110 cards revealed a hidden gallery of footballers! This series includes three team checklist cards: Manchester United and two of Everton. Artificial curled corners on hard to see action photos, and melamine wood-effect frames has not dulled the value. Prices have been rising, year on year. These cards start at £5 but many of the bigger names sell for £50 each! The wrapper for this set is coloured red and yellow, and shows a jumping goalkeeper catching a high ball. It would sell for over £100. A point-of-sale display box would exceed £1,000.

A&BC Gum card 1963

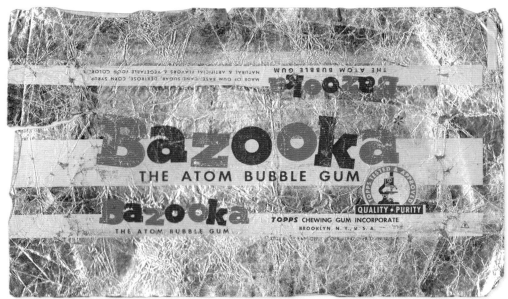

American Bazooka gum wrapper

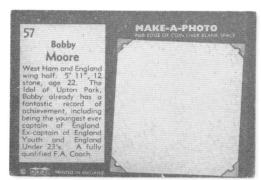

A&BC Gum card backs 1963

A&BC Bazooka Gum cards, 1962

A&BC Gum team checklist card 1962

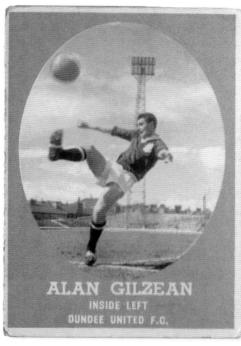

A&BC Gum Scottish checklist team card 1963

A&BC Gum Scottish 1964 card back

A&BC Gum Scottish card 1963

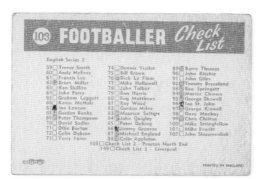

A&BC Gum 1964 team checklist card

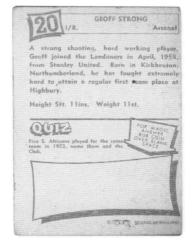

A&BC Gum 1964 English back

Thankfully the Scottish issue of *Make-a-Photo*, in 1964, was not blighted with faux-wood. This attractive series of 81 cards utilised the popular oval design from the fronts of the 1962 English Bazooka series. A&BC added radioactive green to the backs, where a hidden series of images lay in wait for the edge of a coin. Values for these cards start at £25 each though many will exceed £50 and £100 has become the price for a top quality checklist team card of Rangers or Hearts. The wrapper and box are believed to be the same as the English issue of 1963/64.

The Liverpool team card from the 1964/65 English *Footballer* cards collection has been seen to sell for £200! With quiz games to the back, 149 of these cards were issued over three staged launches from autumn 1964 to Easter 1965.

Prices for certain players exceed £25 per card though the regular issues can usually be found for £5 each. The team checklist cards are West Ham United, Preston North End and that costly Liverpool gem. The wrappers usually sell for £40 each and the box is worth about £500. For identification purposes both packet and display box show a pair of tackling footballers, one of whom has gone to ground.

The Scottish *Footballer* cards of 1964/65, the so-called quiz cards, were visited by the awful English design from 1963/64: melamine faux-wood frames and sentimental, artificial curls were added to otherwise decent photos. Rangers and Hearts fans were no doubt disgruntled with the colour of the backs: green again! This series features three team line-up cards: Rangers, Celtic and Dundee.

A&BC Gum 1964 English card

A&BC Gum stamps wrapper 1965

A&BC Gum World Cup stamp 1965

A&BC Gum World Cup stamp 1966

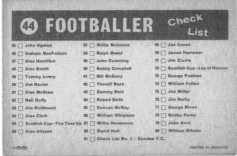

A&BC Gum Scottish team checklist cards 1964/65

A&BC Gum Scottish card back 1964/65

A&BC Gum Scottish card 1964/65

Only the latter two function as checklists though all three command premium prices. The wrapper and box are presumed to be the same as those used in the English series quiz cards series.

Stickers in the style of stamps became a seasonal replacement for football cards during the season of 1965/66. Much of A&BC's other fare, including pop stars and flags, also moved to stamps in 1966. Only two series of cards were made before the autumn. A set of *Rolling Stones* cards had flopped badly. The directors of A&BC also found themselves in court accused of selling obscene images to minors! A series of World War Two *Battle* cards had caused a couple of armchair moralists to file a law suit. Illustrated scenes of

destruction, including a Merry Christmas Mr. Lawrence beheading in Burma, had caused a stir. The series also has at least three scenes of gagged, chained and whipped women. These days the BDSM cognoscenti are on to them and these particular *Battle* cards are keenly sought.

The *World Cup Football* stickers were bought one stamp at a time. The cost was minimal, at just one penny each, but the contents were a little disappointing. A stamp and a stick of gum, and if the stamp featured an unknown international from Patagonia many British kids spent their next penny of pocket money with a rival. These low cost items have risen in value to become some of the most expensive items of A&BC ephemera. Packets

sell for £150 each and the rarest of the stamps, those of Pelé (for there were two, different) may make more than that! The relatively few stamps that survived the decades since have driven up values. Condition is always a big factor in pricing. A poor condition Roger Hunt of Liverpool, without perforations, will sell for £15 but in clean condition, more or less as issued, it could top £75.

The stamps series came in two halves. At the end of 1965 the first selection of 20 British stars and 15 world greats was issued in portrait format. Due to the early date of issue it included players destined to be outside the England squad, like Alan Peacock and Joe Baker. It also included the likes of George Eastham and John Connelly, both of whom

Postcard from Malta, 1966, with variation stamp

A&BC Gum 1966 twinned cards, two series: first series without caption and second series with captions

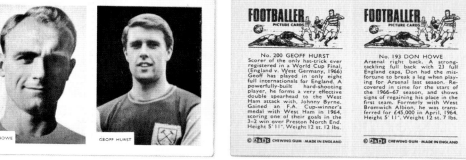

A&BC Gum 1966 twinned card backs

would fail to make the first XI. The 15 stickers of foreign players included one from each nation except North Korea! Two were from Brazil: Pelé and Bellini.

In early 1966 a second run of 15 stamps appeared. These were more colourful and included football flags. They were printed in landscape format. World stars included goalkeeper Lev Yashin from the USSR Eusebio of Portugal and Pelé, once again. North Korea was snubbed for a second time! These days a thing like that could spark an international spat.

A version of the football stamps is believed to have been printed by an A&BC copyist in Valletta, Tony Xuereb. Some collectors and sellers have

ascribed the Malta issues to his firm, Tip-Top, which issued football cards in the 1950s. The stamps are smaller than the originals and only known in landscape format. They are rough in design, and primitive in printing but far rarer than the A&BC issues. Yashin's stamp is very different to the Russian language A&BC issue, having a legend in English which looks like it was set by the official A&BC artist. Only a few of these stamps have been recorded, including one glued to a postcard, alongside postage stamps, mailed from Valletta to England in 1966. *Caveat Emptor*: it is believed that there are modern day copies of these bootleg Maltese stamps. The best place to find the originals is from reputable philatelists – postage stamp sellers.

It seems odd looking back. There were few actual football cards issued during England's World Cup winning season. There were also very few stickers, just 50 A&BC stamps, a handful of comic free gifts and a series of sweet cigarette cards by Barratt, a London firm. Surely victory would change things?

Black and white are hardly colours that come to mind after a World Cup victory, yet A&BC kicked off the celebrations with monotone cards, featuring ostensibly nameless footballers in pairs. Why black and white, in England, in glorious 1966? A cynic might wonder whether the A&BC directors knew they could get away with producing a cheaper series on the back of the

READING LEFT–RIGHT

HOTTGES
OVERATH
HELD
HALLER
WEBER
EMMERICH
SCHULZ
BECKENBAUER
SCHNELLINGER
TILKOWSKI
SEELER

A&BC 1966
English issue
checklist cards

FOOTBALLER PICTURE CARDS
213 West Germany World Cup Runners-Up
CHECK LIST
126. JAMES STORRIE
127. RAY CHARNLEY
128. CAMPBELL FORSYTH
129. JOE KIRKUP
130. WYN DAVIES
131. ALAN SKIRTON
132. EDDIE McCREADIE
133. FRANK WIGNALL
134. ALEX STEPNEY
135. PETER DOBING
136. GARETH SPRAKE
137. MALCOLM BEARD

FOOTBALLER PICTURE CARDS
214 West Germany World Cup Runners-Up
CHECK LIST
138. MIKE HARRISON
139. JOHN BOYLE
140. JOHN HOLLINS
141. CHARLIE COOKE
142. PAT JENNINGS
143. PETER BRABROOK
144. ERIC McMILLAN
145. GEORGE ARMSTRONG
146. ALBERT JOHANNESON
147. GEORGE BEST
148. PETER EUSTACE
149. BOBBY HUNT

FOOTBALLER PICTURE CARDS
215 West Germany World Cup Runners-Up
CHECK LIST
150. FRED ELSE
151. GORDON MILNE
152. RICHARD NORMAN
153. ERNIE HUNT
154. RONNIE REES
155. TERRY HENNESSEY
156. RON FARMER
157. DAVID GIBSON
158. PETER THOMPSON
159. PAT CRERAND
160. BOBBY THOMSON
161. ALAN PEACOCK

FOOTBALLER PICTURE CARDS
216 West Germany World Cup Runners-Up
CHECK LIST
162. BRYAN DOUGLAS
163. DICK LE FLEM
164. JOHN CONNELLY
165. RON HENRY
166. CLIVE CLARK
167. RON YEATS
168. MIKE TREBILCOCK
169. IAN CALLAGHAN
170. ALAN HINTON
171. JIM McCALLIOG
172. PETER OSGOOD
173. CLIFF JONES

FOOTBALLER PICTURE CARDS
217 West Germany World Cup Runners-Up
CHECK LIST
174. RAY CRAWFORD
175. ALEC JACKSON
176. MARTIN PETERS
177. DOMINIC SHARKEY
178. GEORGE KINNELL
179. MIKE SUMMERBEE
180. ALEX YOUNG
181. BRIAN MILLER
182. IVOR ALLCHURCH
183. JIMMY MELIA
184. BILL BROWN
185. GORDON WEST

FOOTBALLER PICTURE CARDS
218 West Germany World Cup Runners-Up
CHECK LIST
186. ANDY McEVOY
187. RAY WILSON
188. FRANCIS LEE
189. JOHN SJOBERG
190. ALAN GILZEAN
191. JOHNNY HAYNES
192. JOHN SLEEUWENHOEK
193. DON HOWE
194. ALEX SCOTT
195. ADAM BLACKLAW
196. ALBERT McCANN
197. CYRIL LEA

FOOTBALLER PICTURE CARDS
219 West Germany World Cup Runners-Up
CHECK LIST
198. KEN SHELLITO
199. BOBBY ROBSON
200. GEOFF HURST
201. JOHN SILLETT
202. MARK PEARSON
203. MEL SCOTT
204. IAN URE
205. MALCOLM LUCUS
206. JOHN TALBUT
207. RON SAUNDERS
208. JIM MONTGOMERY
209. ALAN SUDDICK

FOOTBALLER PICTURE CARDS
220 West Germany World Cup Runners-Up
CHECK LIST
210. SEAMUS BRENNAN
211. GRAHAM SHAW
212. DEREK DOUGAN
213 West Germany World Cup Runners-Up
214 West Germany World Cup Runners-Up
215 West Germany World Cup Runners-Up
216 West Germany World Cup Runners-Up
217 West Germany World Cup Runners-Up
218 West Germany World Cup Runners-Up
219 West Germany World Cup Runners-Up
220 West Germany World Cup Runners-Up

ALEX FERGUSON   DAVID McPARLAND

A&BC 1967
Scottish pairs
and checklists

No. 6 DAVID McPARLAND
Partick Thistle. Wing half.
Signed as an outside left from
Larkhall Thistle in 1953. Has
won representative honours with
the Scottish League. Made 24
League appearances last season
and scored 2 goals.

No. 18 ALEX FERGUSON
Inside left. Rangers. Joined Rangers
this summer from Dunfermline, he has previously been with
St. Johnstone and Queens Park.
Won his first cap against Israel
in May of this year. Has also
represented the Scottish League.
Made 30 league appearances
last season and scored 20 goals.

England win; no matter the design it would sell like hot cakes. The feel-good football fever in England in autumn 1966 would have helped sell even blank football cards! Whatever the reason, A&BC issued its shadowy first series of 110 cards (consisting of 220 images) and left collectors to tear them apart, if not tear them up. The cards, which lack player names to the fronts, have two small pictures and had the possibility of being separated along a barely visible serrated division betwixt the two pix. Cards which have remained in pairs retain a much higher value than singles, especially those from the second launch, a further 110 cards. For the second series A&BC deigned to add player names. Team line-ups of West Germany and England, from the 1966 final, consist of four double cards each and

act as checklist sets. These quads make premium prices! Pairs from the first series sell for around £10 each. Second series pairs can fetch five times that price! Cut cards are worth little. Notably, while a cut card of George Best may struggle to make double figures an un-cut pair with George Best can fetch over £150. A wrapper from this issue has a value of around £75, and a point-of-sale box would sell for about £500. Not the prettiest issue but one of the most valuable series to complete, as pairs, because most cards were torn into singles long ago.

A&BC dared not issue a drab offering in Scotland, not after an England win! A suitable period of time was allowed to pass, then a similar series of paired cards was approved but it was in

glorious colour, and it put the Sassenach series of colourless cards in the shade. The autumnal 1967 series celebrated only 42 players but they can be found in various twinned pairs that these days allow collectors the chance to get a rookie of Alex Ferguson in two varieties! A stunning selection of 12 Celtic cards, a celebration of the European Cup winning team, is an achievement to complete and to behold! The Lisbon Lions cards (24 halves if the cards have been tragically separated) is where the series value lies, for making a set of these is nigh on impossible and the value for a complete Celtic team (and Celtic Park turf, for many of these cards show just that) might cost you around £500! Typically players sell for £40 a pair, up to about £200 for Alex Ferguson's rookie (in a pair). Cut single cards remain low in value. The 1966/67 paired cards were the last A&BC collections to be sold without a novelty insert, or the promise of one.

Launched at the moment the first pulsar star was seen from earth, in autumn 1967, *Star Cards* was an aptly named set. The creative but awkward calligram on these cards shows a trophy-shaped graphic made from the four letters in the word star. A calligram ought to show, in its visual design, the very thing of the noun used to make the picture. A twinkly object would have been proper

A&BC 1967 Star Players

A&BC 1967 Pin-Ups

A&BC 1968 English and Scottish cards

A&BC 1968 Scottish variations, same player but different backs

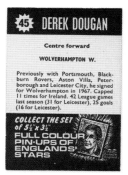

A&BC 1968
Team Pennant

A&BC 1968 Metallised Team Emblems

for this series of stars but a paper poster sufficed as a novelty gift. These were the first in what would become a long tradition of gift inserts. The miniature folded posters, one per pack, were given to protect the *Star Cards* from sticky gum residue. The insert idea had come from USA, where inserts themselves were collected as avidly as the cards. The wrapper for this series is in yellow, black and magenta, with the legend: *EXTRA! England's Stars Pin-Ups*. It's a small series with but 55 cards, most of which are easily available today. George Best made his penultimate appearance for A&BC, and his card commands a premium. The 12 miniature poster inserts are rare and may cost you over £20 apiece. The wrapper fetches £100 and the box, which shows Bobby Charlton, may cost over £300!

By 1968 things were going from good to great. A&BC had massive success not just in soccer. It had launched Superman, Planet of The Apes, Famous Indian Chiefs and a host of other cards that year. The gum tasted better, the cards were attractive, and the inserts were appealing. Insert cards allowed the firm to re-launch a staged collection of cards over time. The 1968/69 *Footballer* cards were initially sold with inserted paper *Team*

Pennants. In the second of the staged releases of this collection metallic foil team emblems were included in place of the pennants. This helped sell the second launch just as well as the first. After some years without a quiz the retro game returned to the backs of the cards, which were coloured yellow. Variations in design on one of the 102 cards resulted in price spikes for that of Joe Baker, whose Nottingham Forest card comes with and without a certain graphic feature. Twenty-six different English teams were featured on the paper pennants. They were designed to be cut out so pennants that remain un-cut fetch higher prices than cut examples. The metallic stickers were a new development in the world of football cards. In Italy, the biggest producers of football cards, Mira and Panini, had recently issued their first shiny stickers, and enjoyed considerable success through them. A&BC hereby followed suit but the shiny fare was restricted to England. The cards and inserts in both British series of 1968 were issued in distinctive and colourful wrappers. Later point-of-sale packaging and wrappers, those advertising the *Metalized Team Emblems*, are the rarest and command higher prices than the *Team Pennants* packets.

176 Scottish cards, also with yellow backs, followed the English release at the end of 1968.

This is a remarkable and rare series. Officially there were only 45 cards but, due to printing varieties, up to four different backs for every player card are known. There are also two team checklist cards: Celtic and Dunfermline. Paying £25 or more per card is the starting point for this series but cards have been known to sell for up to £150 each! This issue was further complicated by packets of cards being packed without the *Team Pennants*. Clear paper bags full of pennants were rushed to shops with instructions to shopkeepers to furnish one pennant for each packet of cards sold. Notably the box for this series was the first A&BC box with a Scottish design. Expect to pay more than £1,000 for it! A pennants distribution bag, which has the A&BC logo in red, has been seen to sell for £150. The Scottish pennants themselves sell for even more!

Unlike the English release there were no foil emblems for Scotland. In some places there were no Scottish *Team Pennants* either! The pennants are so rare that most of them remain unseen by modern-day collectors. At the time of writing, in 2019, Hibs, Celtic and Clyde remain unrecorded – after 52 years! Two of this trio finished at the top of the league and played in Europe. Clyde had been a regularly featured team in Scottish sets since 1961. So, it is almost sure that there is a pennant for each of them and for each team in the Scottish top flight that year. Prices for individual pennants in this rare series have been seen to top £250 each! Their omission from the first packets distributed contributes to their scarcity. Greaseproof paper bags full of late arrival pennants were hurriedly sent to wholesalers but they went mostly undistributed. The stock may still be sitting somewhere in a dusty wholesaler's warehouse, or it went on to a bonfire. A million pounds in paper pennants?

Due to gum firm rivalries of the time, and machinations of a technical nature, both intrigue and variety played parts in the arrogant conceit of A&BC's 1969/70 collection. George Best had demanded a payment 100 times higher than other players were getting. A&BC said no. He walked. Best sold his image to a rival gum firm, Anglo Gum of Halifax. He appeared on Anglo's wrappers and on one of the 84 cards in Anglo's Football Quiz. A&BC met this affront with triple the number of cards Anglo could muster. Two hundred English

players – regulars and irregulars – a phalanx of 36 insert cards and the trusty 90 Scots to the flanks. It was a defining moment in gum cards history. Anglo Confectionery was to cease production of football cards within a year! In the heaven of A&BC were more stars than all and sundry found hanging in the lowly firmament over Halifax. It was back to cheaper cards of club colours, and illustrative hints on playing the game, for Anglo.

The 1969/70 British collections are some of the most appealing A&BC cards to collect, not least due to the technical mysteries surrounding an English issue which contained errors, misprints and doppelganger cards: a handful of players have two cards each! Seeking the entirety of the 1969/70 *Footballer* collection is a worthwhile challenge, not least as values have been rising year upon year. The many variations and errors in the various sub-series make for quite a roller-coaster ride. Once thought to consist of 170 cards there are, in fact, about 200 different cards to seek. Some cards changed photo mid series, others received technical improvements (new stats). Cards of

Frank McLintock, John Sissons, Bobby Moncur, Allan Clarke, David Sadler and Colin Suggett have two cards each. In other cases some players, though listed on checklist cards, don't appear at all! Andy Lochhead of Leicester City should have card number 66 but Coventry City's Chris Cattlin appears at that spot. Certain cards have different players parading under the same number. Look out for cards of Wolves's David Woodfield and Liverpool's Tommy Lawrence. Some checklist cards were quietly upgraded during the course of the season meaning you'll need to find both varieties of one particular checklist. The colourful wrappers of the second and third sub-series of this issue came with the legend, "plus real photograph". This was actually a monotone football card, with a facsimile blue autograph, very much in the style of A&BC's 1961 cards. It came die-cut with wavy edges, also called deckled or rouletted cards. Values for the green backs vary drastically. The rarer variations can make £50 each, or more. Wrappers and ephemera values vary too. Packets sell for £50 upwards and point-of-sale boxes will cost over £300.

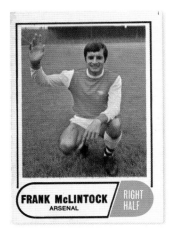
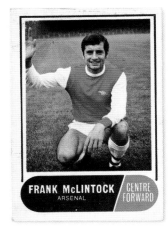
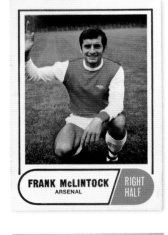

A&BC 1969 English and Scottish cards

A&BC 1969 die-cut insert cards to protect the coloured cards from the gum

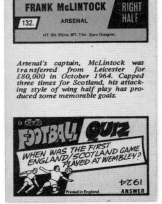

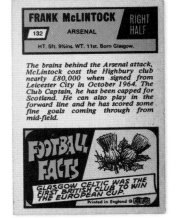
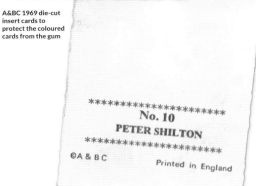

A&BC 1969 English and Scottish cards backs

A&BC 1970, plain and embossed World Cup Souvenir cards

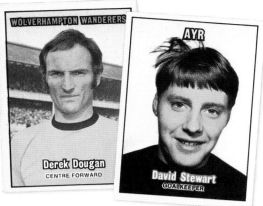

A&BC 1970 Giant Footballer cards, English and Scottish

A&BC 1970
Pin-Up Posters

A&BC 1970 Giant Footballer cards, checklists

A&BC 1970 Action Transfers

In comparison with this phenolic blend the Scottish *Footballer* collection of 1969/70 was a dignified single malt. The 77 cards have blue backs and a football quiz. The series heralded English league players' inclusion in a Scottish set for the first time. Bloodline not club was now the criterion. Henceforth, all Scottish series by A&BC could include cards of players from Sassenach clubs if the players had Scottish roots, albeit the cards would remain in a different style to those cards of said same player in the parallel English series. The cards of English stars in the Scottish series now brag of values between £10 and £70 each. This is partly due to English club collectors keenness to acquire a Scottish version of their man. Fifthteen black and white cards with wavy, die-cut edges complete the issue.

Mexico guaranteed a sunny World Cup in 1970. England had been expected to do well, so A&BC went big time with a series of 37 England player cards and 16 paper fold-outs of teams, called *World Cup Giant Posters*. Values for the posters vary but £10 for a poster is typical, with England and Brazil fetching higher prices. The inserts used in this launch have become more prized than the posters. In each packet was a single gum card. It has a purple back and a gilt-coloured frame. These cards of England hopefuls

now command high prices, up to £50 for rarer types. Originally there were 37 different cards with a Jules Rimet trophy in relief. A re-issue came without the cup in relief. Thus, there are 37 cards with a relief trophy, and 37 with a deflated cup. Were the latter printed after England lost hope? The *World Cup Souvenir Cards*, as they were called on the sales box of the *World Cup Giant Posters*, were not mentioned on the wrappers so it must have been a nice surprise to find one tucked away inside. A wrapper from this issue would cost £100 and a box might make £300.

Following the posters came so-called *Giant Footballer Cards*. They hardly seem gigantic from today's perspective and, in fact, they were no bigger than the 1959 cards by A&BC but sales is sales and 259 slightly larger than typical cards, with orange backs, hit the autumnal streets of England and Wales in 1970. They were issued in the now typical staged release of three sub-series: Autumn, Christmas and Easter. The last of the three sub-series includes the rarest cards which can sell for more than £10 each. Earlier cards, with lower numbers, are easily available. Like the 1969 collection this release also includes misprinted and reprinted cards, so if you want them all you'll have some hunting to do! One particular checklist card is known with different backs, one of which

warns the collector, 'subject to change'. No kidding! Reminiscent of the 1969/70 collection it lists players of whom collectors would see nothing. Variants of checklists, players, point-of-sale boxes, and the three types of wrapper, not to mention the error cards, make chasing this collection a challenge. Moreover, some players from this series were also issued in the Scottish set, with green backs. Ian Ure and Pat Crerand, of Manchester United are but two.

Accompanying the first issue of the *Giant Cards* (the English cards have orange backs) was a series of 14 so-called *Pin-Up Posters*. These came folded, wrapped between the cards and gum.

To further confound the hapless collector it should be noted that some of the English league players on the *Pin-Up Posters* also appear in the Scottish series of pin-ups with differences. Billy Bremner, for example, has two distinct posters to collect.

Late in 1970 the *Pin-Up Posters* were replaced with *Action Transfers* in a bid to excite a tiring marketplace. There was little action, per se, other than rubbing these colourful players' portrait decals (transfers) on to skin or into scrapbooks. These days rarer examples of this series of 72 decals, with original backing papers, can sell for up to £100 each! There was no parallel Scottish issue.

A&BC 1970 Giant
Footballer cards, English
and Scottish backs

A&BC Wrappers for all three
series of 1970/71 cards

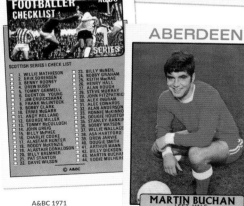

A&BC 1971
Footballer cards

There were 171 so-called *Giant Cards* in Scotland. Their values today are around £5 a card though higher prices are paid for cards that appeal to collectors both sides of the border, for example John Fitzpatrick of Manchester United. In the history of A&BC these are the first Scottish cards that cost less to collect than the parallel issue from south of the border. The wrappers are varied, with many different gift offers, but the generic design has the diving goalie in green, on a red background. The rarest type has the legend: New Superstars Poster. This was a Scottish only issue of re-branded *Pin-Up Posters*. They segued into *New Superstar Posters*. Whereas Scottish pin-ups (the first series) may fetch up to £50 each, the second series, *New Superstar Posters*, will exceed £50 each – sometimes by a long way.

Purple Haze! The 1971/72 collection is a classic, with a twist. 291 *Footballer* cards were issued in England and Wales with backs that teased, 'did you know?' Values now vary wildly for these cards with some higher numbers fetching way over £20 each! Mental health warning: trying to follow the numbering and naming on the checklist cards in this collection may cause more than just hazy consternation! There are many inaccuracies. Some players appear two times, showing up on different cards with different numbers and different images, for example Paul Madeley of Leeds United has two distinct cards. He's not alone! Some players appear in both the English and the very similar Scottish series, which was printed with the same purple colour on the back, making identification of English team players

in the Scottish set something of a challenge. Then there are the checklists! The wrappers seem to have just as many varieties. The boxes differ in design too. The second and third release packaging advertises different series of inserts. Box and wrapper values rise the later they were issued, so adverts for *Superstars* (inserts) make the ephemera worth more than packets and boxes that show the earlier *Club Crests* inserts.

These cards can also be found with intricate, die-cut edges. The die-cut cards seen are generally all from the rarer higher numbers second and third series. These die-cut cards were re-sold during 1973 and 1974, in Lucky Bags, given with sweets and other gifts. The re-cut cards, in the fancy style of the 1973 black and white inserts, helped shift unsold, remaindered stock. Look closely at the edges, at the cut. The cards fit, cut for cut, corner for corner, edge-for-edge within the card silhouette of the 1973 black and white die-cut inserts. This shows they are official releases and, therefore, some of the rarest A&BC cards extant, notwithstanding their erroneous occasional nomenclature as crinkle cards. Crinkled clothing, crinkled crisps, and chips may come crinkle-cut. Not card nor paper; not unless you screw it up into a paper ball. Then it's crinkled. Whatever! *Crinkled* or die-cut, these are some of the hardest to find A&BC issues and prices are rising to reflect this. Expect to pay £20 per card, and more for certain stars.

NB: *Pinked* cards have also been seen but these are recent forgeries made with tailoring pinking shears. If the edge looks like it has diamond-shaped tips, if it has regular points all around, then the card

A&BC 1971 Footballer die-cut
cards re-issued in 1973

A&BC 1971 Club Crests
and Superstar stickers

A&BC 1973 die-cut insert
card, and a later re-issue
with a regular cut

has been sheared by someone to create a 'rarity'. These are worthless.

The 1971/72 purple back cards' earliest inserts were called *Club Crests*. A&BC had been feeling the heat from FKS so it made a foray into the stickers arena. An album was produced with spaces for 23 crests and a further 23 players called Superstars.

Issued with the second and third series of English purple back cards these 46 inserts are not easy to find. Superstars fetch prices around £10 each, with one or two pricier exceptions. An unused album would be worth at least £100, while a full album could more than double that figure. An unused set of 46 sold in auction, in 2018, for over £600!

The 144 Scottish purple back *Footballer* cards of 1971/72 are very similar to the English edition, both types having purple backs. It's worth noting that the Scottish players with Arsenal, Chelsea, Liverpool and other English teams appear in both English and Scottish series but they have different numbers, and some cards also have contrasting designs. Billy Bremner, for example, is numbered 20 in the Scots set while his card in the English series is numbered 155.

The 16 different paper inserts that accompanied the Scottish cards show Scots emblems and were also called Club Crests.

A&BC 1971 sticker album

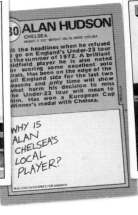

A&BC 1972 Footballer cards,
English issue

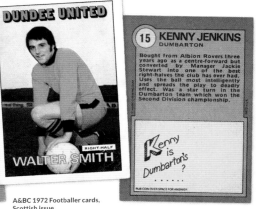

A&BC 1972 Footballer cards,
Scottish issue

A&BC 1972 playing cards

A&BC issued no album in Scotland, nor Superstar stickers. FKS did not issue Scottish stickers so there was little need for A&BC to compete north of the border.

At the height of glam rock, between 1972 and 1973, it would have been par for the course had A&BC shifted up a gear and gone OTT (over the top) by putting even more into its product. It opted for less. A straight series of cards was issued in autumn 1972. Gone was the flamboyance of albums and the profligacy of *Pin-Up Posters*. Missing too were the colourful transfers. Radiant foils were nowhere to be found. Simply streamlined were the 221 new orange back cards. They were launched in two stages, and were as conservative as cards could be. The inserts were as traditional as playing cards (what they were based upon) and rather disappointing as components in a football card game consisting of 22 sober images. The inserts were pretty much ignored by children of the day. Thankfully the master series is not without its varieties, which include Spurs's Roger Morgan. He can be found on two different cards. Norwich City, Nottingham Forest, Huddersfield Town and Birmingham City collectors will be perplexed by checklist cards that differ in number (sets of both 218 and 219 sets are listed) and in names of players shown but not found, and vice versa.

The parallel edition in Scotland was a little more wired! It consisted of 90 blue back cards and a further 50 with the same colour as the English issue: orange. Scottish players from the English league are included, like Bob Wilson of Arsenal who's also present in the English release. The card of Celtic's George Connelly was printed in both Scottish colours: one has a blue back, the other has an orange back! Prices for such varieties fetch premiums. It's a mystery lost to the winds of time why A&BC switched to the confusing two-tone reddish backs, from the clearly and easy to differentiate blue but they probably never imagined the collecting frenzy 40 years later. Toon fans took to drink over Jimmy Smith. This Magpie

was numbered 20 in England but 150 in Scotland – with a different biography to boot! As to what happened to card 164 no one knows. Values for Scottish issues range from £5 up to £50 for the errors and varieties. Should card 164 ever appear it'll break the bank.

The 1973/74 sets of *Footballer* Gum cards is believed to have been the most popular edition in A&BC's history. In England the 260+ cards had beige frames and blue backs. Those from north of the border, 178 cards, were pretty in pink, on magenta. Though the English checklist cards have less than reliable lists, and some Sassenach cards never appeared (they seem not to have been printed) the issue certainly delights collectors. Amongst the unusual fare on offer in this edition is Wales's John Toshack, for Liverpool. He has two cards to seek. His card was withdrawn and reissued with a different picture, and different stats, though no one knows why. AWOL are Johnny Giles of Leeds United and Lou Macari of demoted Manchester United, though both are listed on a checklist. More on this series in a future book, with full listings of the cards and images of Giles and Macari! The wrappers are white, showing three players in an embrace, and are valued at

about £30 each. The cards range in values with error cards fetching prices in double figures. Checklist cards were not free from errors and they too command premium prices for rarer issues.

The Scottish *Footballer* cards of 1973, graced with their pink fronts and magenta coloured backs, are much rarer than the English issue. Values for Scots cards tend to be £5 to £10 each, with Kenny Dalglish in Celtic hoops often making over £50.

Both editions of 1973 were accompanied with die-cut, so-called Autographed Photo cards. These 32 insert cards updated a design from 1969 and blended Scottish and English players into the same series for the first time since 1960. Very rare editions of these cards with straight edges are known. Values reflect the rarity factor, rising from £2 each to £50 each.

The Giant Team Posters of 1973 were one of the least popular issues by A&BC, with a price that was double the usual cost for a packet of cards, at a time of increasing competition from rival firms like BAB, FKS and Panini (in the guise of Top Sellers). The need to fold-out, iron or flatten then pin-up the piece of coloured paper, the likes of which

A&BC 1972
wrappers

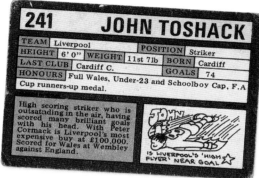

A&BC 1973 Footballer cards,
English issues, variations

A&BC 1973
Footballer cards,
Scottish issues

were being given away freely in football weeklies and monthly magazines, was a misjudgement on the part of A&BC. The result is that the 16 folded paper posters of the English and Scottish teams included have become very rare and prices paid have reached £30 each. The series wrapper fetches £100, the box £500.

The end of A&BC was nigh. The American predators at Topps were waiting. The two series released in autumn 1974, having only 120 players each, sported a mere third of typical output. It was a sign of things turning bad. Further, there were no inserts, though the packets seemed to promise freebies. The misleading legend on the wrappers offered 12 Extra Top Team Photos. These were nothing more than 12 regular cards from the new series, a set of 132 cards. The cards were no improvement on the previous series. The Scottish edition was more of the same: 120 players plus 12 teams, all with yellow borders to the fronts, green backs and extras that turned out to be neither free nor extra. The values of these cards are low, at around £5 each; a wrapper £25 and a box about £200. In late 1974 a series called Cup Winner Bags of Fun was issued by a firm called A&BC Novelties (not A&BC Chewing Gum Limited). Included were 12 small folded posters. The black and white images of Scottish players, on reddish paper, were sold with sweets, cards and small plastic toys in so-called lucky bags, a blind prize pouch which was bought without knowing what was inside. Notably, these were not sold by major retailers like Menzies or Smiths, as A&BC cards had been. The Lucky Bags were only sold at independent news agencies and sweet shops. Inscribed, "a souvenir of the 1974 World Cup in Munich" the posters seemed a little grim. The wrapper from the series shows two footballers in green and blue, and is priced 2½p. A Spilsby Road address, in Harold

Hill, confirms the association with A&BC Gum but it was different, it was of lower quality, cheaper and meaner. It did nothing to aid A&BC's fading star though the posters are now worth upwards of £25 each. The wrapper will sell for more than £150.

Football Hobby Cards was the terminal issue. It was an unofficial release, and the ultimate chapter in the history of A&BC. It is believed that after Topps took control some of the workers at A&BC bagged and sold old cards illicitly, packaging them in new design wrappers. The black and white die-cut cards from 1973 were re-sold herein but they were un-cut, retaining straight edges, making for a valuable addition to an A&BC collection. Values: £50 for single cards and wrappers are £150 each.

By 1975 A&BC Gum had ceased to exist. The business had been acquired by the American cards giant Topps after winning a court battle with the Brits. However, the gum cards marketplace was fast becoming less about gum, less about cards and more about stickers. British FKS and Italian Panini (as Top Sellers) had the ascendancy. By 1978 stickers and albums became *the* way to collect. By the end of the decade gum cards seemed old fashioned. Gum itself was changing. Chewing gum was being marketed differently. There were cooler brands on the shelf and stickers cost less.

A&BC 1973 wrappers

A&BC 1974 Footballer cards, English issues

A&BC 1974 Footballer cards,
Scottish issues

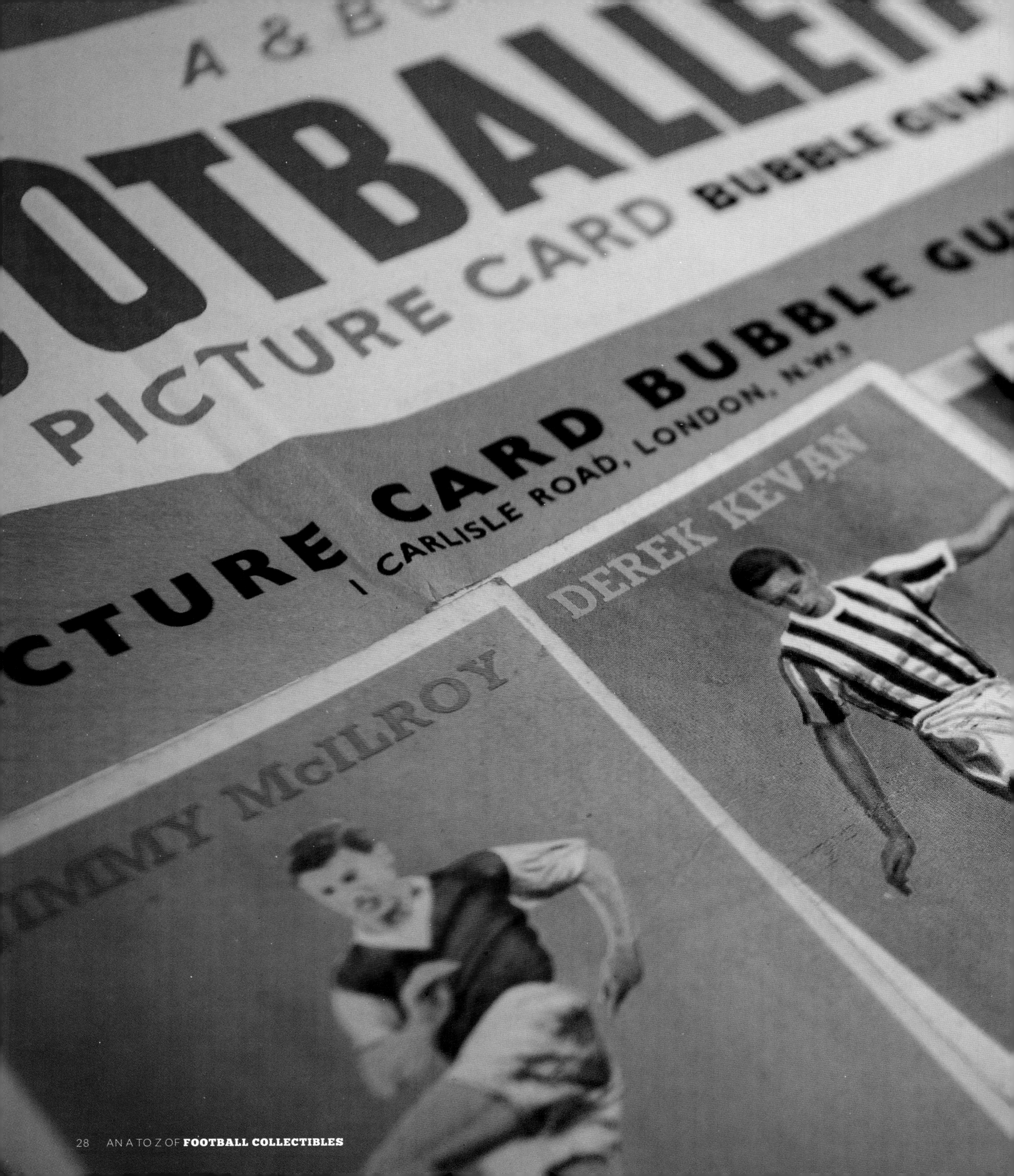

A & BC
FOOTBALLER
PICTURE CARD BUBBLE GUM

PICTURE CARD BUBBLE GUM

CTURE CARD BUBBLE
1 CARLISLE ROAD, LONDON, N.W.9

DEREK KEVAN

JIMMY McILROY

Abdulla's Russian Eggs by Cthulhu for Coco Chanel

Following World War One, around the same time as the first mention of Abdul's *Necronomicon* (in the dark tales of *Cthulhu*, written by H.P. Lovecraft) Abdulla tobacco nestled into the Fabergé Egg shop on London's New Bond Street. Until 1917 the store had been graced by the Czar's jewellers. Their bloody end opened the way for Abdulla, purveyor of *No.1* tobacco. The haunt would later become the London lair of Chanel (*No.5*) whose founder had enjoyed affairs with the Czar's cousin. Abdulla came to fame thanks to successful rebranding. It produced trophy tobacco memorabilia (not just cards but ceramics and other ceremonial cigarette wares) upon which it emblazoned esoteric ciphers and images. Much like Chanel would do, with *No.5*, Abdulla removed its *No.1* brand from general sale and sold it only from its own fashionable domain. It created want, and higher prices. In time Chanel came to reside in the very same shop. Chanel also removed *No.5* from stores worldwide and advertised the newly scarce scent at a hefty price and made a small fortune. So, what does this have to do with football cards? Abdulla and Chanel were experts in product manipulation and myth-making, taking the ordinary and making it something seemingly special. Today's football card manufacturers have learned the skill of creating rarity of something that costs them very little to make. Beware of contemporary cards that claim rarity. Product manipulation is a dark art.

Abdulla's elitist series, *Nationale & Internationale Sport-Recorde* [sic] includes a host of footballers as well as Babe Ruth and Bobby Jones. This pair of baseball and golf cards, alone, will afford a crate of Chanel *No.5* but the footballers are less pricey. So, what of *Cthulhu* and Coco? Well, let's not suggest Chanel obtained her success through occult grimoires but the five-pointed star of Coco's youth certainly touched everything she did. Moreover, few know that Chanel produced trade cards. Coincidentally, from the same French roots and a similar background in Parisian perfume came Maurice Babani. His family made a perfume called *Abdulla*. It would go on to make soccer stickers, in England, as BAB Publishing.

Abissinia Cioccolato [sic] came from the Necronomicon kingdom of Aksum. In days gone by it was fashionable for colonial lords to name a marque of cocoa or tobacco after a newly conquered exotic kingdom. As Arabic tobacco was diffused by Abdulla, Abyssinian chocolate was marketed by Mussolini's chocolatiers. Various series of Italian sports cards were issued with this 1930s confectionery. Elegant soccer star cards, in the format of miniature postcards, helped sell a range of Abissinia Cioccolato treats. Some show the legend *La Portoghese Di Catania*. Stylish and sophisticated, the cards are easily identified by their jagged blue and black borders, and the inscription *Cartolina Postale*. Football greats and World Cup winning internationals are included: Meazza and Piola will cost you!

While Motorhead were writing the first chords to 'The Ace Of Spades' a tobacco firm once thought lost in the smoke of times past turned up *Sporting Aces*. British & American Tobacco (BAT) took recently retired Bobby Charlton and put him back on top at Christmas 1977. *Sporting Aces* was a forerunner of Top Trumps, the cards game bandwagon of 1978 that re-invented the pre-war game *Happy Families* (also known as *Quartets*). BAT's *Sporting Aces* mitigated the implosion of World Cup glory in Argentina, though Kenny

Abdulla No.1 box

Fashionable 1920s Abdulla cigarettes advert

Abissinia Cioccolato card

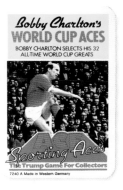

Ace Sporting Aces cards

Acropole stickers

Dalglish was its single nod towards Scotland's 1978 dream. Consisting of 32 footballers *Bobby Charlton's Sporting Aces* game of playing cards is, these days, often found incomplete due to the loss of a single card. Values are generally around £2 each but the elusive Dalglish will sell for much more!

Acropole, from the upper city of Lisbon, also rode the 1978 World Cup carousel. The funicular firm from Portugal produced a series of over 260 World Cup stickers called *Mundial 78*. The interest for collectors lies with national team players, stickers which were not available outside Iberia. Scottish players are included. If you find them you may well pay £20 a head for unused stickers. Notably, players in this series can be found on stickers with mirror images. So, Forest fans should seek two Archie Gemmills, and so on. A beautiful land with a relatively small population, Portugal has produced some of the rarest soccer cards and stickers of the 20th century.

Adams Sports Virginia Cigarettes bequeathed a costly collection to adamant Spireites. A series of cards that spanned various 1920s seasons at Chesterfield FC was printed in various monotones by Arthur Adams, a local tobacco firm. Over 60 different cards are known. They are valued at around £150 each, so it's a bitter-sweet legacy for Chesterfield collectors.

Adkin & Sons issued a collection of *Sporting Cups & Trophies* cigarette cards. Some of these 1914 artefacts recently turned up preserved in a tobacco tin ploughed up on a farm field in the

Somme! The cache of printed sports memorials was found amidst rusty helmets and rotting rifle butts. Soccer silverware forever! Although Adkin cards in top condition can sell for hundreds this series typically fetches £50 a card. Attractive items, these football trophies will decorate any collection with honour.

Admiral. Leicestershire's underwear midshipmen of yore, boasted the earliest advertising emblazoned kits ever seen on football cards. In doing so it beat both FKS and Topps to this dubious honour. Admiral had lost its pants long before it came to brand the smiley shirts at Leeds United, in 1974. The slippery slope down to England's soccer shorts was not far off. Admiral birthed the multi-billion pound replica soccer kit market, and higher prices for everything to do with football soon followed. Keep an eye out for Admiral's 1974 England's Soccer Stars cards, a series of postcard size trade cards printed by Major Sports of Leicester.

Adolph, not Adolf, launched Subbuteo upon an unsuspecting world. During his war service in the Royal Air Force Peter Adolph dreamed up the barmy chalk-and-army blankets affair that came to be Subbuteo. After World War Two Adolph's idea was marketed to great success and it wasn't long before his football game was issuing football cards of its own, some of which boast mighty prices!

For more on the P.A. Adolph football cards see: Subbuteo.

Adkin Cigarettes card

Adolph Subbuteo card

Adventure

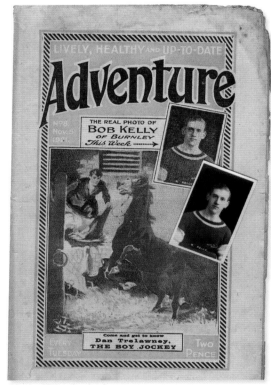

Adventure 1921 comic and card

dventure was a fine name for a newly launched children's comic of the 1920s, the time of *Swallows & Amazons*, Arthur Ransome's junior adventure; and the heroic escapades of Biggles; not to mention the extraordinary tales of Winnie-the-Pooh! Adventure was the first of a new breed of comic. It would come to produce a vast array of football cards, soccer stickers and sports albums in its 40 years of life. It was one of five comics that came to be known as The Big Five, in the inter-war years: Adventure, Rover, Wizard, Skipper and Hotspur.

Adventure was quick off the mark with football cards, launching a series of *Famous British Footballers Real Photographs*. Thirty-four different cards were distributed with the first 18 issues. Today the value of these cards depends upon whether they are Scottish or English. Mostly different cards were issued north and south of the border. Hence, £5 to £50 is the value range for a single card today. However, if you have a card with the original comic it came with you can up the ante to £200 for the complete package. For example, Burnley's Bob Kelly was given with

issue 8, on November 5th 1921, which showed the very same card on the front cover. Top price is the combination of card and comic for England's Sam Chedgzoy, of Everton. He became a noted soccer star in the USA playing for New Bedford Whalers, a team in the original American Soccer League. Sam was remarkable for being responsible for the change of rule that permits a goal to be scored directly from a corner kick. His card often sells to American collectors.

Arcane reference sources have often classed Adventure cards under the name of Thomson. This name is not displayed on a single card issued and it merely serves to confuse new collectors. In this book comic cards will be known by the publication name seen on the card, or attributed to it, and not by the name of an otherwise anonymous publisher. This applies to Rover, Wizard, and to all comics from Champion to Jag, the Hornet, Lion and Tiger, etc.

The second collection of footy cards issued by Adventure comic was the so-called series of *Signed Real Photos*. Not quite signed, as such, they have printed facsimile autographs and came as 36 different black and white glossy photographs

"The second collection of footy cards issued by Adventure comic was the so-called series of Signed Real Photos..."

Adventure 1922 cards

Adventure 1923 coins of footballers & motors

FAMOUS CLUB COLOURS AND PLAYERS

Adventure Famous Club Colours & Players

Adventure Star Footballers twin cards

in early 1922. They are valued today at less than £5 for English issues but over £30 each for the Scottish cards. Fourteen distinct cards were issued in each country, one of which bears the same player, Syd Puddefoot, with different teams: West Ham and Falkirk. Eight cards of players were issued simultaneously in both lands. Photo varieties exist and cards with rarer variations command much higher prices. A card with the original comic with which it was issued will make a premium price.

In 1923 Adventure took a road untravelled and issued free gifts worth having: coins! Twelve metal tokens of footballers, to be precise, with motor cars to the obverse. These are very hard to come by. Numismatists are the best source but charge highly. Valued from £25 to £100 each, value rises with quality. Of the series, six coins were issued with Adventure and six were given with the twin publication, Wizard.

Adventure returned to paper later in 1923 with a stunning gallery of *Famous Club Colours & Players*: 12 coloured supplements, each with nine players. The 108 footballers typically became cut and separated. Values for cut single players are around £5 to £10 each but uncut sheets fetch £100 or more. With an original comic a sheet might top £200. The design of these colourful supplements was influenced by the glorious colour fold-outs once issued in Boys' Own Paper, a magazine from the previous generation.

Coloured Photos of Star Footballers was Adventure comic's next issue. Twin cards featured pairs of footballers in colour. Uncut pairs, as issued, can sell for £50 to £150! Most were cut to singles and their values remain stubbornly below £20 each. A notable inclusion in the series is a certain H.Gallacher for Airdrie. Hughie packs a premium price in a pair.

Between 1924 and 1925 Adventure comic gave away miniature printed albums of footballers. *Star Players of 1924*, *Star Footballers*, *Great Players of Today* and *Cup Fighters 1925* are miniature magazines in the style of pre-printed sticker albums. They were not meant to be cut though they are often found butchered and worthless.

Adventure joined with Vanguard comic for a 1925 promotion. Forty so-called *Football Photos* (photographic trade cards) now sell for between £20 and £500 each! Every week five different cards were released to the public, however, only a single card was issued with a comic. Buying one of each comic would, at best, result in two cards per week. Three cards remained to be had! How children of the time ever collected a full set remains a mystery. The fact that these cards are hard to come by suggests that few succeeded. The card of Everton's Dixie Dean has

Adventure miniature album 1924

Adventure miniature album 1924

Adventure 1929 Mysto Mind Reader teams card

Adventure 1930 Footballers & motors cards

Adventure 1931 Football Towns Crests & Famous Ships

been seen to sell for well over £500. Punctuation differences to the rear of the Dean card mean this card is known in two varieties.

After a pause of some years Adventure comic returned to football cards in 1929 with an occult mystery that sounded like it had been inspired by Sax Rohmer's Fu-Manchu. The *Mysto Mind Reader Mystery* series of soccer clubs collection consisted of 10 trade cards with 100 teams! Valued between £25 and £35 each card the players are miniature so you'll probably need a magnifying glass to see who's who. Occult powers of darkness will baffle your friends and amaze your neighbours as you read their minds with these divinatory ciphers. Well, that's how it was meant to be. The cards certainly stand out for being different!

In 1930 the combination of Footballers & Motor Cars returned, albeit to cards not on coins. Adventure issued a series of 24 cards with images of soccer players to one side, and cars to the other. These 1930 cards are scarce and most are valued at over £20 each, some fetching as much as triple that figure!

Football cards were twinned with coats of arms in 1931. Adventure issued folding cards titled *Football Towns and their Crests*. The cards also showed a parallel series: Famous Ships. These days most quadruplicities of heraldic crests have been cut from the ships so pairs of the 32 uncut cards are rare and their values start at £50 each. Cut cards showing only quads of township emblems, or only ships, are worth a mere £5.

In 1932 Adventure bucked the Great Depression with colourful football cards made of glistening if not precious metal. The *Footballers Cup-Tie Collection* of metal cards brought an unnatural weight to the weekly paper comic. The glistening freebies were considered miraculous at the time. They came in anonymous brown paper sachets, inscribed with the compliments of the editor. Issued in England and Scotland, mostly different cards were made available in each country. The Everton and Portsmouth cards were issued in both countries. Values depend on condition. Many metal cards have not stood the test of time. A rusty example may struggle to make £10 but fine Scottish-only issues can top £100 each.

Late in 1932 Adventure issued one of the earliest known soccer sticker collections: 36 stickers called *Football Snapshots*

were issued in sheets to be cut-and-stuck into a dedicated album. Ten years earlier Sports Fun had been the first English magazine to release a sticker collection. Almost a decade earlier than that, the first footballers on stickers had been issued in Scotland, by The People's Journal. Still, the colourful *Football Snapshots* series is one of the first soccer sticker collections known. The collection also merits a note of its creativity. The images gracing the collection were taken from monotone photographs and were tinted with colour, by hand. Seeing the line-up of Aston Villa players hanging from a set of iron street railings is one for the archives! Quirkily the album doubled as an identity card! Devoting the rear cover of the pocket-size album to the owner's name, address and...his size of football boots, his school cap size, and so on, it also rather worryingly included an entry for the nearest doctor's phone number! Today, an uncut sheet of stickers would fetch £200. A complete album may also fetch a price in three figures. Single cut stickers are worth £10 to £20 each.

Adventure 1932 metal cards and wrapper

Adventure 1932 Football Snapshots sticker album

Adventure 1933 Football Clubs cards strip

Adventure 1934 Hunt The Cup cards

Adventure's so-called *Football Clubs* cards of 1933 were a disappointing way to open the year. There were 16 different cards, each showing four miniature, anonymous players in club colours. Most were cut to singles and few quads remain intact so value lies with uncut cards at £40 each. Cut singles hardly rise past £2 each. There are 64 teams in all but different combinations of quartet mean there are many combinations for each club. These cards were also issued by four of The Big Five. Adventure was joined by Skipper, Rover and Wizard. Hotspur, the fifth, wasn't quite born at the time.

It had been four decades since the FA Cup had been stolen. 1934 seemed a good time for Adventure to mark the unsolved mystery with a new gift, a game known as *Hunt The Cup*. It included 52 double-sided game cards, issued in batches of 13, weekly during the run up to the 1934 final. On one side was a famous star, whilst the reverse featured a game card. These may be found for £10 each, but many of the more elusive cards will cost more.

Adventure comic's second sticker collection, the *Football Stamp Album*, was out by 1936. It consisted of a football-shaped album and 130 stickers of clubs, players and emblems, to be cut from sheets of stickers given weekly. Values: a complete album £125; an uncut sheet £150. Singles of club colours, trophies and nicknames are worth about £2 each but certain players may fetch more than £20 each! This was the last free football gift given by Adventure until the 1950s.

After World War Two Adventure comic finally started giving football gifts anew in 1951. A series called *Famous Footballers* was what's known as a package issue series. Football cards were printed to be cut out. They came printed in both black and blue. These are quite rare, and rarer still are uncut comics displaying the uncut footballers. The aim was to cut them out, collect enough of them and send off for a special offer football. No wonder few uncut comics remain in circulation. Though cut singles are worth little, intact comics are sought after. The value for an uncut comic is £25 but you may pay £50 for an issue with footballers on the back cover.

In 1952 Adventure reprised the inexpensive paper cut out, launching *Famous Goal-getters*, a collection of 24 paper tokens. Though famous footballers are named none are actually shown. The value for these images of generic players is nominal.

Five years down the road, in spring 1957, Adventure finally returned to the quality content that made its pre-war freebies treasured. In tandem with Hotspur comic a selection of British players from Scottish and English leagues were issued in sheets of four. The 48 *Football Stars* issued included the ill-fated Duncan Edwards. The series was a little too early to include the Munich survivor, rookie Bobby Charlton. Uncut strips of four cards can sell for up to £50 each but cut singles struggle to rise above £3. Twelve different sheets were issued, six with Adventure and six with Hotspur comic. Released during the new wave of gum cards, issued by the likes of Colinville Gum and A&BC Gum, the series seems anachronistic.

Adventure 1936
Football Stamp Album

Adventure 1951 Famous Footballers cut-out cards

In World Cup year, 1958, Adventure joined forces with its sister papers, Hotspur, Rover and Wizard, to issue *World Cup Footballers*. They were given weekly, in pairs. It meant having to buy four comics every week for two months to get the set. Value: uncut pairs fetch about £15 but rise to over £100 for a certain pair (a *triplet* in fact. Some of the single cards featured two players). Cut singles are worth around £2 each but the Jimmy Greaves rookie in an uncut pair will fetch a lot!

In 1959 Adventure reprised the sticker collection fad of the 1930s. In May it released *World Footballers of Tomorrow*. Sheets of stickers were issued weekly and a free album was given. Uncut sheets can sell for over £150 now, though cut single stickers fetch only £2 each. A complete album can secure £100 in auction. The collection also included other athletes, like runners and swimmers. There is a notable rookie sticker of Denis Law, and a tribute to the Manchester United Munich team.

Adventure stumbled with *Football Tips & Tricks by The Mystery Trainer*. Garish cards issued in pairs show tips given by an anonymous trainer – or was it just the editor of Adventure in his tracksuit? The 64 cards showed no famous footballers and may have been Adventure's first dud. It was a low point shared with Rover, Hotspur and Wizard, co-sponsors of this series. Uncut pairs of cards are rare but cost only a few pounds each. Most cards were cut to singles and are worth very little indeed.

Adventure 1957 Football Stars cards

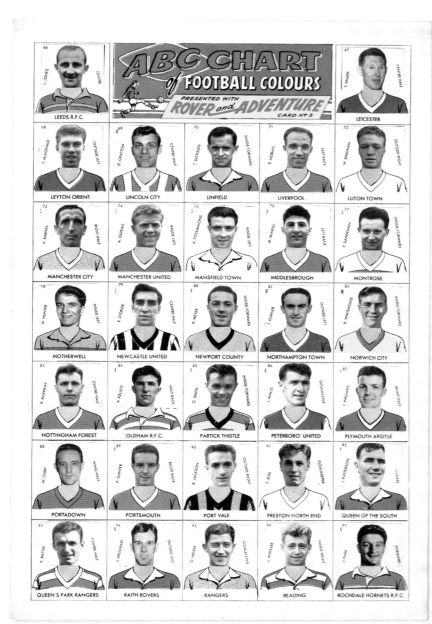

Adventure 1961 ABC Chart of Football Colours

Adventure 1959 Football Tips & Tricks cards

Adventure comic merged with Rover comic in 1961 and disappeared shortly afterwards. *The ABC Chart of Football Colours* was a colourful way to bow out. This deluxe free gift of 130 stickers, and cards upon which to mount them, was based on a Wizard comic gizmo from 1931. The sheets of stickers showed players' faces. These were to be cut and glued to large cards that showed the player colours. Complete sets of unused stickers and cards may cost over £150. Typically the cards have all too often been cut to single players. Cards and stickers that remain uncut are worth a magnitude more.

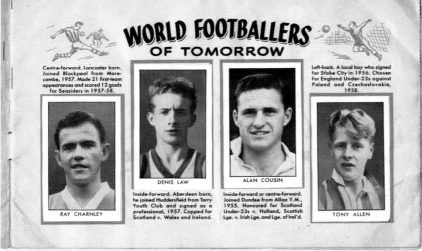

Adventure 1959 World Footballers of Tomorrow

> "Adventure comic merged with Rover comic in 1961 and disappeared shortly afterwards."

African Tobacco

African Tobacco 1939 World of Sport card

AGEducatifs Argentina 78 cards

Fher & APR stickers, L-R: Spanish and Portuguese

African Tobacco was a South African brand that issued a 1939 series of mixed sports cards called *The World of Sport*. The cards are known in two languages, Dutch and English, and also in two sizes, the larger of which measure about 8x6cm. Values start at £10 each. The series includes soccer stars like Ted Drake, of Arsenal. Footballer card values are around £50 each but Babe Ruth out-strikes them at over £1,000!

AG éducatif (or AGEducatifs) was the dominant French soccer stickers issuer of the 1970s. Licensed by Fher in Spain, as was FKS in Great Britain, AGEducatifs issued packets of paper footballers to be glued into albums, much like FKS. The albums, packets and stickers bear a stylistic resemblance to those by its British counterpart. The French firm's output included *Football en Action, Etoiles du Football (Football Stars), Football 1975/76, and Argentina 78*, among others. Prices for complete albums start at over £100 each, rising markedly for the 1974/75 collection due to the inclusion of a sticker believed to be Michel Platini's rookie. Unused the sticker can sell for over £1,000! Rookie

prospectors sift AGEducatifs as anteaters sort soil to devour ants. Finding the rare nugget is a time consuming and tricky game. Values may plummet if too many are mined yet too few in circulation results in high costs.

In 1978 AGEducatifs jumped on to the trumps game bandwagon. It issued two sets of playing cards, in boxes. Both contain world stars of the day, including Scottish players, one of which shows *King* Kenny Dalglish. A cover card with Everton and Arsenal match action must have bemused French fans! Values for cards are around £3 each and complete sets will fetch over £50. More on AGEducatifs in a future issue of this book. In the meantime you can see more at www.footballsoccercards.com

Agencia Portuguesa de Revistas (APR), of Portugal, issued an attractive World Cup collection the year England won the Jules Rimet Trophy. *Campeonato Mundial Futebol 1966* is very similar to a parallel series issued by Fher (Disgra), in Spain. Laying the two album covers side by side the obvious difference is in the spelling of *futebol* (Portuguese) and *fútbol* (Spanish). A full album is valued at £400. Most stickers are very similar to those issued by Fher but there are key

differences, notably in the spellings. For example, Lev Yashin has the legend *Rusia* on Spanish Fher stickers while it shows *Rússia* on the Portuguese APR stickers. For an unused sticker Yashin will net well over £50!

Alba–Tortona issued *Lo Sport Italiano* in 1959. A hundred vending machine gum cards included sub-series for various sports. For easy identification the cards are marked ATD82. Soccer cards from the series may fetch £20 each card, with premium prices paid for all-time greats like Wales's John Charles for Juventus. The card of Gianni Rivera for Alessandria is one of his most sought after rookie cards and may command a value of three figures if the condition is very good.

Alifabolaget of Sweden, a tongue-twister that's as misspelled as the name of ABBA's high heeled sandal-wearing German soldier's daughter, future Countess Plauen, Her Serene Highness, the very red-headed Anni-Frid Synni Lyngstad. Alifabolaget issued a highly prized series in autumn 1958. It shows the World Cup winners. The Pelé card will often top £1,000! Earlier cards by said same producer feature Jesse Owens, the Olympic track & field legend. This card also breaks the bank! Swedish cards are much rarer

Michel LANINI

Jean PALKA

Michel PLATINI

AGEducatifs 1974 stickers

OWENS
U. S. A.

**Alifabolaget
card of Jesse
Owens**

CHARLES - F. C. Juventus

**Alba-Tortona
1959 card of
John Charles**

H.G. BATTEN

**Allen's 1926
British Empire
Sports Stars card**

Supplement to SPORT PICTURES, November 19, 1921.

S. CHEDGZOY.
(EVERTON F.C.)

All Sports 1919 supplement, Everton's Chedgzoy

than Brazilian issues due to the population level. In 1958 Sweden had only a few million people whereas Brazil had 10 times that number, with 60 million! More cards per capita were made in Brazil. Values of Swedish 1958 cards are higher because the cards are much rarer.

Allen's medicinal confectionery, of Australia, issued 54 cards of British Empire sports stars, in 1926. The cards are rare and values exceed £100 each. The 54 cards include 15 British soccer players advertising different products, like *Irish Moss*, *Daphne* and *Cure-Em-Quick* tablets. All of the cards also bear the series title, *Quality Kicks The Goals*. The soccer stars were probably included due to the Football Association's 1925 tour of Australia.

Allen is a surname readers of the seminal 1990s publication *Football Card Collector Magazine* will be familiar with. *Allen's All Stars of Soccer* was a series of very limited edition cards made in the 1980s. Today values exceed £100 each card! John Allen [RIP] made only two or three of each type. Numbered and sealed with an embossed stamp, they were available to subscribers of the *John Allen Football Memorabilia* postal sales lists, issued in the 1980s. John was

a pioneer in the modern craft of homemade soccer cards. He made his cards before the era of desktop computers and printers. They are of exceptionally high grade and each retains a unique quality. He was the first contemporary issuer of his own designs which include series called *London Legends*, a collection of 25 different cards from Brentford to West Ham; and Crystal Palace to Spurs; *Northern Nomads*, which consisted of 25 cards from Glasgow Rangers to Sunderland, and from Liverpool to Aberdeen; and *Heartlands Heroes*, featuring Wolves, Villa, West Brom, Birmingham City and other Midlands players. Limited to a maximum of three cards for each player, being handmade each card was different. Every single card was an original artwork. Long since sold out, they have never been seen for re-sale. Note: these are not to be confused with John's later, general releases like *Sportsmen* cards, which were produced in large numbers and retain only nominal values.

All Sports Illustrated Weekly magazine was a journal that ran from 1919 until 1930. During certain periods of the year it would issue gift souvenirs. The early souvenirs were typically paper supplements, a little like miniature posters,

printed in black or in sepia monotone. The souvenirs are typically rarer than the magazines themselves, often selling for between £50 and £100 each! Amongst known souvenir supplements from the early 1920s are Ducat of Aston Villa, Derby County's Quantrill, Everton's Chedgzoy, Liverpool's Longworth, Manchester United's Mew, Grimsdell of Spurs, Sunderland's Buchan and Morris of West Brom.

All Sports is also credited with a series of 12 large, coloured cards of sportsmen which were issued circa 1930. The series, often known as *Grape Nuts* cards, probably due to an error is association, includes the footballers Cliff Bastin of Arsenal and Harry Hibbs for Birmingham City. Other cards show tennis stars including the British legend, Bunny Austin.

Althea foods of Italy issued four series of die-cut, stand-up footballer cards between 1962–66. Issued with a product called *Cremifrutta* the *Calciatori* cards will sell for at least £25 each if they retain their original card frames. Premium prices will be applied by knowledgeable sellers for Aston Villa's legendary Italian export, Gerry Hitchens.

Amaika, of Spain, sustained the Iberian tradition of sports playing cards with a 1975 deck of 50 boxers, skiers, athletes and footballers, including Neeskens, Rexach, Breitner and Cruyff. The first football playing cards in Spain date back to the 1920s. Most of these cards sell for £2 each but you will pay well over £20 for Cruyff.

Amalgamated Tobacco produced a twilight series of cigarette cards in 1961. *Football Clubs and Badges* includes 25 cigarette cards of football colours and emblems for the top British teams of the day. This was one of the final card issues by a tobacco producer. These pretty cards can be found with other trademarks, and also with plain backs but values are low at around £2 each.

Amatller is a name to remember. This short entry is hereby made to sample its wares. A Spanish producer of the Jazz Age, Amatller made glorious football cards! The earliest known series dates from 1915 and is titled simply *Foot-ball*. This is a stunning series! The 54 cards include many British stars as well as a host of other, early greats. This series of soccer treasures features Plumstead F.C. (Arsenal interest), Cardiff Corinthians, London Nomads, New Crusaders and the English Amateur Team, not to mention action scenes of dashing Brits in Barcelona colours, namely the Wallace brothers: Percy and Charles. These cards are very rare and may sell for over £100 each. For more images see www.footballsoccercards.com

Amatller was the foremost Spanish chocolates football card producer of the time. During the 1920s it issued hundreds of beautiful soccer cards, many featuring Spanish legends like Alcantara, Samitier and Zamora. Such cards command premium prices and may fetch hundreds each!

Americana München was formed in the mid-1960s, in West Germany. Initially it issued cards in lucky bags but became best known in the United Kingdom for its various 1970s football sticker series (see also: Ava Americana). It issued well over 100 series of stickers between 1964 and 1980. To this day its various collections of unbranded issues confound British collectors, notably those issued in 1973 as *Soccer Parade*. It consisted of 351 cards with plain backs, of stars from English Football League Division I (and team emblems). The value for a complete album is around £500 but unused cards demand premium prices and will cost £10 to £50 each!

The *Soccer Parade* collection was optimistically launched into an arena where battle was well underway between Panini (in the guise of Top Sellers), A&BC Gum's *Footballer* cards and FKS's *Soccer Stars stickers*. Americana München issued four cards per packet along with a stick of bubblegum. Thus, it offered much more than some of its rivals but it was let down by poor

distribution. Failing to make a mark in 1973, these attractive cards became rare and they have become very much sought-after today.

Americana München's 1976 *Sport Parade* collection included 388 stickers, many of which now sell for over £10 each, if unused. A complete album will fetch around £750. Premium prices are paid for the football stickers from this pan-sports series. Notable footballers may cost £20 each but Muhammad Ali will fetch over £200 if he remains unused, and in excellent condition. A favourite sticker from this series features two Leeds United fans, adorned with club scarves and rosettes, mulling over the gloomy unfolding of events during a match against Bayern Munich in the European Cup.

In 1978 Americana München launched *Fussball Weltmeisterschaft Argentinien 1978*, consisting of 384 stickers. These can be identified by the mark: EAM/KPA. The complete album is worth around £100 and unused stickers fetch £2 each but premium prices are paid for certain players of note, especially for Kenny Dalglish and fellow Scots, which may top £20 each!

Liverpool appeared in the next Americana München release: *Fussball 79*. It came out in late 1978 with 384 stickers. Most unused stickers from this series cost little, about £2 each, but each of the eight Liverpool players included will be priced over £20 each, as will an unused Paolo Rossi!

All Sports 1930s Grape Nuts card

Althea 1962 stand-up card

Amaika 1975 playing card of Cruyff

Americana München 1973 Soccer Parade cards

Amatller 1915 cards of Cardiff Corinthians and Plumstead

Americana München 1976 Sport Parade stickers

Americana München Fussball 79 stickers

Anglo 1969 Football Quiz card

Americana München World Cup 1978 stickers

Anglo 1970 World Cup card

Anglo 1970 National Team Colours card

Anglo & Bauer, 1971 gum insert (top) and gum card (bottom)

Anglo Confectionery of Halifax was a later incarnation of the 1950s firm known as Anglo American Chewing Gum (for Anglo American Chewing Gum see: Bellboy). By the late 1960s the outfit was still issuing football wares with various brands of bubblegum, notably *Football Quiz*, which came out in 1969. Its 84 colourful cards seemed ready to challenge A&BC Gum's *Footballer* series for a prize spot in the British marketplace. George Best had signed a deal with Anglo and would not appear for its rival. Today, Best's card in top condition will sell for £25 but most of the other cards in this widely distributed set can be collected for a mere £1 each.

Anglo Confectionery made *Monster Bubbly* and *Match* brands of chewing gum, as well as a gum called *Double Kick*. Wrappers of *Match* are known to feature George Best. Each of the five different George Best wrappers sell for about £50.

Anglo released *National Team Colours*, in 1970, an ugly set of bland cards of badly drawn footballers dancing around in gaudy hues. Like many unpopular series of their time, present day values are high: it's over £10 per card for some of these teams. Anglo followed with another international series where each card featured two series: *World Cup 1970* on one side and *Learn The Game* on the other. The 48 cards include Pelé. Values start at £5 each card and rise to £25 for Pelé.

Losing the 1969/70 cards war to A&BC Gum, the Halifax firm returned to waxy paper gum inserts, like those it had issued in the 1950s under the name Anglo American Chewing Gum. In 1971, Anglo's *Ace Gum* came with *World Famous Football Clubs*, a series of 72 paper gum inserts of club colours. Notwithstanding the folds found in all known examples (due to being wrapped with gum) single inserts now fetch prices between £5 and £50. An album was also available. It's now very rare due to being a redemption issue requiring a set of all 72 waxy paper inserts, sent in exchange. The album has all 72 club colours pre-printed. A parallel issue printed as cards, not waxy paper inserts, was available in West Germany, France and Benelux. Issued by a firm called Bauer, being bilingual, it was titled *Weltfussball 1970* and *Football Mondial 1970*. An album is also available for this continental variation.

Anglo Confectionery meandered from cards to inserts to booklets in a quest for a new and original type of gum gift. *Football Hints* was a series of 12 different miniature publications upon football skill and technique. Issued with gum in 1972 they were the final nail in Anglo's casket. Today they can be acquired for a couple of pounds each. The wrappers show Leeds United and Chelsea action and are worth up to £50 each.

gham (...100.000 hbs.), Liverpool (790.000 hbs.), Manchester (703.000 hbs.) Sheffield (513.000 hbs.)

UNIDAD MONETARIA.- Libra esterlina con un valor de 2.80 dólares.

PRINCIPALES PRODUCTOS DE EXPORTACION.- Maquinarias, motores material de guerra, vehículos motorizados, tejidos, aviones y barcos.

IDIOMA.- Inglés

COMO DICEN LOS INGLESES
Hola: Jalou
Amigo: Frend
Adiós: Gud bay
Gracias: Zankiú

INGLATERRA
ESCUDO

HODGKINSON
ARQUERO

141
RON FLOWER
DEFENSA

ARMFIELD
DEFENSA

143
WILSON
DEFENSA

144
TONY KNAPP
MEDIOS

145
MILLER
MEDIOS

CONOLLY
DELANTE

147
J. GREAVES
DELANTERO

148
ROBSON
DELANTERO

149
MUSGROVE
DELANTERO

BYRN
DELANT

Anonymous

Anonymous is a card collecting term that harks back to lost-in-time grammar coined by deceased cigarette card enthusiasts of the 1930s. They considered cards sold with non-tobacco products to be inferior to their collections of Churchman cigarettes *old school ties* and Wills tobacco *wireless telegraphy*. Rather than researching further they categorised unbranded non-tobacco cards thus. Anonymous is also how some card collectors have categorised cards they do not know much about. It's a useless archaic term and it's now time to bring cards into the 21st century. This book proposes the use of unknown and/or unbranded, in place of anonymous.

The discovery of unknown cards is one of the most appealing aspects of collecting. Frankly, finding unknown cards is akin to discovering an unknown species in botany and can be quite exciting. Until you find your first unknown card you may not quite empathise with this level of enthusiasm. When you do, you'll know.

To see more unbranded and unknown cards from modern times and yesteryear, to see stickers and inserts by mysterious issuers, and much more besides, please see the section of this book titled Unknown & Unbranded. There you'll see a raft of rare cards made by producers lost in time, by issuers never known; and for cards quite unlike others; cards rarely, if ever, seen.

Unknown Bobby Moore packet-issue card

Unknown Kenny Sansom sticker

Aquarela 1958 Pele sticker

Arabic 1982 World Cup card

Ardath 1934 card

Aquarela

Aquarela was a publisher in Brazil. The firm's imprint has become legendary to card collectors due to the rare stickers of Pelé, though some Aquarela cards are not actually by Aquarela! 1970s reprints by a firm called 7 Cores (7 Colours) copied the original Aquarela collection. Originals are known with both blue and black numbers. Re-issues have different black digits and different perforations. The former were issued in late 1958, in a very slight album printed to celebrate the victorious Brazilian World Cup squad. The Pelé sticker with a blue number may top £1,000 if it's in top condition, and Garrincha may cost three figures. Other values lie between £25 and £50 each. This collection is considered to be a classic. See also: 7 Cores (Seven Colours).

Arabic cards remain a mystery to most collectors in the west but some are familiar to tea drinkers. During the summer of 1982 footballer cards were issued in Arabic by Lipton Tea! The marketplace was Dubai. The cards were copies of cards first issued by Lipton in Great Britain. Both series feature mostly British Isles players but Ricardo Villa and Ossie Ardiles of Argentina (and Spurs) make notable appearances.

Arabic language *World Cup 1982* cards have become popular with collectors in the west, notwithstanding their exotic language and obscure origins. Among these attractive cards is a certain Diego Maradona, and, for Fulham fans there is a dubious treat: a card of Felix Magath, the notable 2017 manager.

Ardath *Photocards*

Aral Petrol, 1966 Postcard

Arbeshi, 1972 Postcard

Arga 1953 and 1954 cards of Kubala

Ava Americana 1977 stickers

Americana's Italian version, 1977

Aral Petrol in West Germany did its bit in 1966. *Fussball WM* was a collection of trade cards in the format of postcards. A full series glued into the official album is often of less value than one or two unused, high quality cards of great players. The value of a complete album is quite low due to the quantity issued.

Arbeshi was an oddity of a series. Issued in 1972 these are caricature illustrations of footballers printed on elongated postcards. Single cards, free of glue or damage, are worth about £20 each. Unmarked checklist cards are worth more.

Ardath dates from the so-called golden age of cigarette cards, the inter-war years, yet what a dull name it is! While Embassy, St.Moritz and Gitanes respectively evoke stateliness, splendour and wild sensuality, Ardath's name seems dour (and may bring hard maths to mind). No surprise, then, that many of their cards were also colourless. Yet, in terms of numbers they are cardinal, and for local club interest they remain superlative. However, in 1934, Ardath issued cards in colour. *Famous Footballers* consists of 50 cigarette cards showing the *State Express 333* brand. Easily available, their values lie between £2 and £5 each. A sister series called *Sports Champions* included footballers and have similar values.

Ardath inaugurated 1936 in stark monotones. Its black and white *Photocards* were launched upon an unsuspecting world. Colourless they may be but they're also the best chance you'll have of finding your local league team on a tobacco card. The collection includes over 750 photographic cigarette cards of players and teams from Hulme Hall to Shilbottle; from Elm Park Rangers to Arthurlie. Valued at £2 to £20 each the cards can also be found with red overprints, and such red lettering results in premium prices! Most cards show teams but some feature single players.

Ardath's *Photocards* of Lancashire, Scottish, Midlands, Southern, North Eastern and Yorkshire teams include over 100 cards in each sub-series. If you are interested in football in the Midlands, for example, aside from bigger clubs like Aston Villa, Wolves, West Brom, Birmingham City, Coventry City and Walsall you can also find, from the Walsall area alone: Walsall Phoenix, Walsall Jolly, Walsall Wood, Pelsall Wood Swifts, Pelsall, Rushall Olympic and Darlaston. Alas, Rushall Olympic's nemesis is omitted, Rushall Crusaders are not included. This author's uncle managed that very team.

Arga took its brand name from a river that falls from the Pyrenees in northern Spain. In

the early 1950s Arga printed cards that have become highly sought-after today. The initial series, *Futbol*, in 1953, consisted of 176 stickers. Printed in sepia, most are valued below £10 each but premiums must be added to the prices for Gento, di Stefano and Kubala. A second series was issued, also in sepia, and the same players appear anew, with different photos. Values can exceed £100 for the greats.

Arga followed the two sepia *Futbol* series with *Campeones del Futbol*, in 1955. All 176 stickers were printed in black & white, not sepia. Values for these cards are similarly mostly below £10 each but higher premiums will be added to prices for cards of the all-time greats.

Ava Americana emerged from the wreckage of Americana München, the issuer dismissed in 1973 by Panini (Top Sellers), FKS and A&BC. In 1977 a comeback was on the cards – as was Mick Channon. The Southampton player was shown on all of the newly imprinted Ava Americana stickers (on the backs) and, as such, retains the world record for being the footballer printed on more stickers than any other player.

Alas, Ava Americana also chose unwisely with 1977. It was the year of Panini's new wave: *Euro Football* was on the shelves, and *Football 78*

Ave 1949 Italian comic cut-out cards

was due. There was also a Top Sellers collection in the air. Ava's *Football Special 1977-1978* attempted to slot betwixt the Panini collections and FKS's *Soccer Stars 1977-78*. Suffice to say it does better these days than it did back then. Today a complete album of all 386 stickers may cost you £200. Unused stickers, with frames, cost between £5 and £50 each! The frames are what make the unused stickers so valuable. The footballer stickers were not only peeled away from backing paper, they were removed from a colourful frame which remained attached to the Mick Channon backing paper, and was usually thrown away. This also makes Channon the footballer most disposed of throughout the history of football cards. Note: unused stickers from this collection are rare and the Johann Cruyff and George Best stickers, in particular, attract premium prices.

During 1977/78 a very similar collection was issued by Lampo, trading as Calcio Flash, in Italy. It was titled *Calcio Lampo 1977-1978*. The album would make a striking companion in contrast to the British Ava Americana edition, and the stickers are complimentary, being of the same design. Look out for the rookie of Paolo Rossi.

Ava Americana's second attempt to succeed in the British market came in 1978, with *Football Special'79*. Due to its relative success today a complete album is easily available. £50 is about the most you'll have to pay to get a superb example. Unused single stickers are ubiquitous and £1 apiece is the typical maximum value today.

AVE, Anonima Veritas Editrice, was a post-war Italian publisher. In 1949 it produced *Concorso Grandi Campioni*, a series of 241 comic paper package issues (cut-out stickers) to be collected

Ave 1958 Brazilian sticker

A Pelé sticker, unused, in very good condition regularly tops £1,000 and many sellers ask far more than that! Whether they sell at £5,000 and more is another matter.

in an album issued specially for the challenge. The stickers were cut from the back page of an Italian comic called *Il Vittorioso*. The comic had been founded by a church action group to *cultivate* youngsters. Issued weekly the sportsmen include British Isles football stars such as Charles Norman Adcock, an Aston Villa player in his youth; and Ireland's Bill Jordan of Juve (also of West Ham, Spurs, Sheffield Wednesday and Birmingham City!) Complete comics sell for up to £50 while most cut singles are valued at around £5. The aforementioned players are another matter. Expect to pay a lot more for Jordan and Adcock.

Ave of Brazil shared only the Catholic connection to the Ave of Italy. Ave in Brazil is

best known for its 1958 series of 300 stickers, *Colecao Titulares (Titulares means Headlines)*. It's an issue that has become notable for including two of the most valuable Pelé stickers in the world. High prices are paid for stickers that have not been glued down. Condition is all! A Pelé sticker, unused, in very good condition regularly tops £1,000 and many sellers ask far more than that! Whether they sell, at £5k and more, is another matter. One thing is for sure: there are more of these out there than meets the eye. In 1959 Brazil had a population bigger than that of Great Britain now. That means a lot of stickers were made. As Brazil mines more of these – and there are more to come – values may waver.

Aquarela album, 1958

JESUS ANGEL IRIBAR
Spanien - Torwart

FELICIANO RIVILLA
Spanien - Verteidiger

JESUS GLARIA 3
Spanien - Läufer

IGNACIO ZOCO ESPARZA
Spanien - Läufer 5

...NANDO OLIVELLA
...pien - Verteidiger

JOAQUIN PEIRO 20
Spanien - Stürmer

AMANCIO VARELA
Spanien - Stürmer

LUIS DEL SOL 4
Spanien - Stürmer

CARLOS LAPETRA
Spanien - Stürmer

FRANCISCO GENTO 11
Spanien - Stürmer

LUIS SUAREZ 10
Spanien - Stürmer

...MARTINEZ
...Stürme

BRASILI...

Wappen

(Gilmar dos J...)

C. ALBERTO - Verteidiger
(Carlos Alberto Torres)

RILDO - Verteidiger
(Rildo da Costa Menezes)

BRITO - Verteidiger
(Hercules Brito Ruas)

ORLANDO - Verteidiger
(O. Pesanha de Carvalho)

ZITO - Läufer
(José Ely Miranda)

DUDU - Läufer
(Olegario Tolot Oliveira)

JAIRZINHO - Stürmer
(Jair Ventura Filho)

LIMA - Stürmer
(Antonio Lima dos Santos)

GERSON - Stürmer
(Gerson de Oliveira Nunes)

SILVA - Stürmer
(Walter Machado Silva)

PELÉ - Stürmer 10
(E. Arantes do Nascimento)

GARRINCHA - Stürme...
(M. Francisco dos San...

Coupe du Monde
1966

NORDKOREA

...as Celeste

Al comenzar esta interesante Coleccion
Deportiva no podemos dejar de expre-
sar nuestro mas profundo agradecimiento
aquellos que tan gloriosamente nos repre-
sentaron en tierras de Colombes y
...sideraban luego en Montevideo y mas
...de en maracana estos dos ultimos
Campeonatos Mundiales que nos llenan
de glorias y de prestigio.
...todos ellos que vivan siempre en nuestro
recuerdo.

SUPARSA S.A.

...VIDEO (URUGUAY)

Uruguay Campeón del Mundo
1950

Campeones del Mundo 1950 - Maracuná Brasil

OBDULIO J. VARELA

Bold and Bright

BAB electronics books

Earlier incarnations of the Babani family brand, watches and perfumes

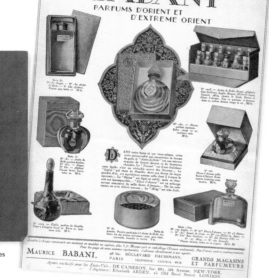

Bold and bright, BAB soccer stickers were born of a family of French olfactory sages. Bernard Babani, the founder of BAB, had turned his back on Paris and perfume for London and publishing. He'd forsaken the family boutique for a niche in books on wireless radio valves and football stickers! As is often the case in cards there is a distant connection between one issuer and another, and more than the odd coincidence. The Babani family's Abdulla perfume ostensibly had no connection to Abdulla cigarette cards yet truth be a strange thing. Who would have thought BAB soccer cards shared roots with the likes of Chanel No5?

Babani came to issue BAB soccer stickers through an eponymous publishing imprint. This author's grandfather's electrical goods repair shop was festooned with BAB books. Unbeknown to granddad the younger ones in the family were buying stickers made by the very same publisher who'd put radio valve reference books on the household bookshelves. Tracing BAB's trek from books about diodes and transistors all the way to sticky soccer cards requires a little creative joining of dots.

In 1966 Babani seized the soccer moment, and he wasn't alone in doing so. Other non-sports publishers were also moving into soccer. Manchester-based book importers, World Distributors Ltd, published a notable football sticker album in 1966, *World Cup Stars*. It followed a curious British tradition of pre-printed sticker albums (like those by Anglo American's Bellboy gum). As a pre-printed sticker collection it was a strange beast; bought ready and finished, with nothing to collect it was more of a book than a sticker album. Collectors ought to note there are three known variants of this album, two in English, and one in Spanish. £100 has been the price to pay, which is why an American seller recently issued home printed bootlegs, which are worth very little. The World Distributors album would morph into *Soccer Stars*, in 1967, the defining British soccer stickers of the 1970s. That's another story (see: FKS).

Babani's in-laws worked for a firm called Northern Trancessories, in Leeds, which had been hatching slick stickers from its Yorkshire presses since 1966. The stickers were made of PVC, not paper. Among its subjects were illustrations of football players, not only as stickers, but as tinplate

pin badges too. Babani was impressed. He took the idea and turned it into the marketable creation of football club colours on stickers, also in PVC. The Leeds firm's artwork came to be used on myriad BAB stickers and the two firms were eventually incorporated as one, in London.

Boldly designed in brilliant colours, the first series of BAB soccer stickers oozed on to the football scene during the flower power years. They flourished during the times of lengthy locks and wedge heels [and that was just men's fashion]. BAB's plastic, not to mention its psychedelic use of hue and tone, seemed born of another world. Was BAB's art director experimenting with more than just shades of colour? The firm's chronology perplexes contemporary collectors with questions that beguile: when, how many and by whom? Rival firms, like Somportex had cross-over collections that shared design features with BAB. Why? In particular, a certain rival, Monty Gum, issued an album in 1972 that featured BAB designs. Why? F.K. Gum also issued BAB stickers. Why?

Attempts to comprehensively date the collections made by BAB have resulted in vexation. Retrospectively tracing the number

BAB 1970 Football Badge stickers

BAB and Northern Trancessories stickers

BAB and Northern Trancessories stickers

of stickers issued for a single collection, of a seasonal release, or of particular variations of type has caused wailing and gnashing of teeth. Like that of Northern Trancessories, BAB's fare was issued without numbers, and often without series titles. The cards themselves are always unbranded. Precise dates of issue, number of stickers, and collection titles may be traced by scouring original wrappers, packaging and point of sale promotional wares. BAB *Soccer Dip* paper packets were sold for 3p each. The price dates the packet to 1973/74, a time when rival brands also sold packets of cards at 3p. The very same packet advertises the fact that 38 stickers were issued in the series. Further collecting and dating clues can be found on the peel-off papers. *Fas-Print* logos on the peel-off backing paper means the stickers were printed in Holland – the home of a certain rival: Monty Gum. More questions!

BAB's first issues consisted of several series of football club escutcheons, more commonly known as shields. The many and varied series of these stickers are easily confused with one another. The later shields, from 1969, can be identified by their straight edges. Earlier escutcheons show softer curves towards the

base of the shield. The earlier stickers date as far back as 1966/67. They were re-issued at least twice, by BAB, which explains the many colour varieties, and different backing papers found on these stickers. The inclusion of division III champions, promotion-winning Oxford United (1967/68) and Watford (1968/69); and cup-winning clubs, like Swindon Town, confirm the series spanned these years. Further, during 1967/68 Leyton Orient had become simply Orient, having dropped its London borough name. Leyton Orient's inclusion, with its fuller name, suggests its sticker dates from 1966/67. Carlisle's inclusion also hints at 1966. Preston North End are included due to being a certain in-law family favourite. The shield-shaped stickers generally sell for £5 to £20 each, but rarer types may fetch as much as £50!

During 1969/70 BAB updated its design of the football club escutcheons. Black borders remained the norm but the die-cut was straighter. Yellow field chiefs (the upper, inner part of the escutcheon) employed a division of two black lines. A parallel issue showed named players in club colours, including George Best. Design variations are also known, for example, a celebratory Brazil shield

sticker, released during summer 1970 exhibits stylistic peculiarities. An improved series of shields was launched with golden borders. It showed club nicknames on some stickers. The yellow field chiefs on the golden shields are divided by a solitary black line. Orient's inclusion in this set is due to honours as third tier divisional champions in May 1970.

In 1970 BAB also issued a completely different type of sticker in a series called *Football Badges*. These large, circular stickers were printed in matt tones. They were made to fit the oversize tinplate pin badges worn at the time. They show strained faces of domestic stars drawn in a curious *potato-head* pencil line. Their Breughelesque portraits also graced a series of shield-shaped stickers, the farewell collection by Northern Trancessories, in Leeds. The gnarled likenesses, twisted visions and hall-of-mirrors distortions must have seemed quite a *trip* in 1970. Notwithstanding the particular vision of the artist responsible, this series sold in sensational numbers. These days the player shields may cost £20 each though some will exceed £50, but the cartwheel stickers cost a lot less. Point of sale display units, card hangers with plastic window pouches for showing off the stickers, are worth around £150 each.

BAB 1970 World Cup badges   BAB 1971 circular stickers

BAB 1971 shield stickers   BAB 1972 Shooting Stars stickers

1970 was synonymous with *Mexico 70* and BAB made a collection of 40 *World Cup Badges* to celebrate. These stickers are very similar to the domestic *Football Badges* above. Most of the international stars can be had for less than £5 but you may pay a lot for images of Pelé. Stickers with variations are also known. Notably there are three printings of the Pelé sticker. The two rarer types of the Brazilian legend are excessively costly!

In 1971 BAB issued sheets of small stamps called the *Century Series of Sticker Stamps: Soccer Favourites*. A hundred stamps show club crests, team colours and footballers. These days an entire sheet may cost you £200! Not bad for a penny or two invested in 1971. Issued due to the British postal workers' strike of that year, these gaudy stamps were BAB's colourful contribution to the very topical debate that occupied British people then: making alternative postage stamps to get their mail through. Football clubs made postage stamps, football supporter groups did likewise, and so did just about every other organisation during the stamp printers' strike of 1971.

In 1971 BAB revisited the circular sticker design but reverted to PVC. The new issues were shinier affairs than the dull matt produce of 1970. The radiant cartwheels are bolder and glossier than before. They bear the same illustrations used in the *Century Series of Sticker Stamps series*. BAB also reprised shields in 1971 – and with quite a flourish. The new shield stickers were designed in a fancier style than the 1960s types. Many and varied, they show domestic British club crests and coats of arms. Some shields show national team liveries. A few, like Manchester City, Rangers and Sunderland have no armorial crests but show generic footballer figures. The Brazil sticker has the legend: *World Cup Winners*.

The various escutcheon designs are these:

i.   a flat chief escutcheon
     (a flat top line to the shield)
ii. a wedge chief escutcheon
     (a flat top line with 'clipped' top corners)
iii. a square-eared, nicked chief escutcheon
     (a little like an open book profile)
iv. an engrailed chief escutcheon (it looks like it
     has two scoops taken out of the top)

Between 1971 and 1973 BAB switched from coats of arms to *Shooting Stars* shield-shaped portraits of players. Most of these colourful stickers sported two five-pointed stars. They use the same artwork seen on the BAB 1971 Century Series stamps. See, for example, the sticker and stamp of Gordon Banks. It's clearly the same artwork on both items. At least two series of *Shooting Stars* are known. Values vary but these rarities can cost from £25 to £100 for unused examples.

The first series of *Shooting Stars* came out in 1971/72. The 30 stickers can be dated by the inclusion of Rodney Marsh sporting QPR hoops. A second series, issued for the 1972/73 season, has Rodney Marsh in Manchester City colours. The stickers are known on both light and dark paper backs.

In 1973 BAB issued *Soccer Dip*. It was a move away from the pick-and-choose displays to sealed packets. Packets were thought to sell more because there is no way of choosing which stickers are wanted. More must be bought to make sets or to get the required collectibles. So, 38 shaped stickers were issued. They came in the form of

During 1974 and 1975 BAB reverted to pick-and-choose collections, issuing football club rosette stickers in PVC. These were a great success, being reprinted season after season yet they were BAB's final whistle in soccer cards. About 30 different plastic sticker rosettes were produced.

Baggioli 1965 and Galbani 1965 Joe Baker

Baggioli 1965 Law and Greaves

Baggioli Goal Magicians, Gerry Hitchens

footballs, scarves, and other shapes. A dud, the series did not sell well, which is why there are fewer surviving examples today. Values range from £10 to £25 each.

During 1974 and 1975 BAB reverted to pick-and-choose collections, issuing football club rosette stickers in PVC. These were a great success, being reprinted season after season yet they were BAB's final whistle in soccer cards. About 30 different plastic sticker rosettes were produced. The inclusion of York City celebrates that club's first ever promotion to the second flight of English football, in 1974.

Baggioli (pronounced: *badge-JOH-lee*) is a brand of football ephemera named after one of Italy's noted sports journalists. During his retirement Vincenzo Baggioli revisited his boyhood passion of football cards by launching various 1960s and 1970s collections, often including British players amidst other world stars. Baggioli's *Maghi Del Gol (Magicians of the Goal)*, from 1964, includes Cardiff City and Aston Villa player Gerry Hitchens. Values range from £10 to £100.

Baggioli launched *Calcio Italia Campionato 1965-66*. It's available with printed (blue) and with plain backs, on thin card and on paper. The series includes England's goalie Ron Springett, Jimmy Greaves, Denis Law, Joe Baker, John Charles of Wales, Eusebio of Portugal, Lev Yashin of Russia and Pelé, amidst a host of Italians. The numbered paper stickers are very similar to an unnumbered issue, on card, by the Italian confectionery producer Galbani. The Pelé cards from both series, all three versions, have been seen to sell for about £150 each. Prices for other cards, including Law, Baker, Greaves, Yashin and Eusebio have also reached over £100!

Baggioli Goal Magicians packet

John Baines of Bradford

Sharpe's buttonhole team flower cards

1886, Arthur Wharton, the first black pro

Baines Walsall Town Swifts and Steve Bloomer

Baines Blades and Manchester United as Newton Heath cards

Baines, also known as John Baines of Bradford, claimed to have been the first football cards maker, the inventor of the soccer card, however, his application for a patent was never granted. Whether or not he invented the idea of football cards he certainly invented the packet of cards, which he successfully patented in the early 1890s. That's almost 70 years before Panini cheekily claimed the credit for the same!

The oldest known football cards are from around 1880. It remains uncertain by whom the very first card was made but the prime suspects include: Sharpe of Bradford, and Cooke, Briggs, Petty & Sons, and Richardsons, all of whom were based in Leeds.

Hundreds of thousands of different designs were drawn, coloured, etched and printed. It is claimed that more than 13 million cards were sold by the various Baines family firms between 1890–1920. The best sales results were in Scotland and northern England. Relatively few of these cards survive today. Generations of young Victorians and Edwardians played games with Baines cards, ensuring the decay and destruction of many millions. After a century of handling, humidity and sunlight, not to mention world wars and worse (like mothers cleaning out children's *junk*) it is surprising that any Baines cards survived. Duplicates are few. Most known cards are the uniquely surviving example of a certain design.

The first Baines cards were printed by a Leeds printer named Richardson but by the 1890s Baines was using a lithographer in Bradford, Berry Brothers. At the height of production Baines cards were printed on six presses. One of the six printing presses was visible to the street through the windows. Children would gaze agog through the glass as if watching miracles. Endless reams of paper were turned into thousands of printed cards, daily, week after week, year in, year out. A typical sheet of Baines cards would contain many rows of coloured cards of various teams, different sports and players. Rows of shields consisted of eight upright and seven inverted designs. Most of the cards were players, and these were printed singly, but some cards were printed in trios, notably those of national teams. The workers at Berry's were mostly women. They spent all day packing the die-cut cards into envelopes and were paid by the gross. A packer would earn a groat, or fuppence (4 old pennies, about 1p today) for every 144 packets. So, she could earn two shillings (24 old pennies) an hour by packing six gross – that's a lot of dainty finger work and over 5,000 cards every hour!

Baines cards were issued with a plethora of different backs. The earliest cards advertised little, if anything, and were left plain for retailers to add their own mark. By 1890 Baines was employing the backs of cards to tell his own story. Cards boasted of his industrial awards and his patents. Cards also advertised competitions and offered prizes.

These days collectors rarely find the same Baines card twice though English roses, Scottish pipers and Welsh mountain goats are a little more

Various 1880s-1920s cards by Baines and its competitors

common than cards showing individual sports stars. This writer once owned an entire sheet of Baines cards and published the layout of its contents in 1998, in his magazine, *Football Card Collector*.

In terms of values, Baines cards printed by Richardson typically cost £50 to £500 each. It is possible that Richardson was the earliest football cards printer in the world. Cards with the Richardson legend, from the 1880s, are known to advertise many and varied businesses in the north west of England, Baines being just one of them.

Later in the 1880s, up until 1909, shield-shaped and other fancy-shaped cards were issued by John Baines himself. Prices paid for cards from this period depend upon condition, club, the player featured, and the style of card. For example, shield shapes are the most common whereas fans, ovals, clovers, stars, diamonds and button-hole flower cards are much rarer. The value will often be over £100 each card for well known teams, up to £500 or more for excellent condition cards of famous players. The costliest cards feature legendary stars

like Billy Meredith from football and W.G. Grace, in cricket. Big teams, famous clubs and great players will always sell for premium prices. Famous clubs and famous players fetch many times the price of smaller clubs and smaller teams. Woolwich Arsenal and Manchester United (Newton Heath) will typically sell for more money than cards of Rochdale and Arbroath.

After the death of John Baines, in 1909, the business was split amongst heirs. One heir inherited the trading name of J.Baines and sold cards from Oak Lane, Bradford. Another heir created a private limited company in Baines's name. Trading as J.Baines Limited the second heir continued to sell cards from the Bradford address at North Parade. Later generations took the respective firms to addresses in Barnsley and in Gillingham. Cards from after the family schism, made during 1910–1918, whether by J.Baines in Oak Lane, or J.Baines Ltd. in North Parade, are presently worth between £50 and £500 each.

After World War One the Baines family firms moved briefly from shields to cards in the shapes of balls (rugby, golf, cricket and football). These are perhaps the least attractive cards from the entire range. They are valued from £30 to £300 each. Golf balls tend to be the most sought-after types, while rugby balls are the least valuable. During the 1920s, for a few years, Baines Ltd. returned to making shield-shaped cards. These can be found on both card and paper. They often feature noted players and sell for high prices of between £100 and £300. Issued from Gillingham in Kent, these quality items harked back to the heyday of Baines but production did not endure past 1926.

There is much more to write upon Baines, and myriad cards to show. A future book will shed more light on these rarities and on Sharpe's, Ormerod, Richardson, Brigg, Cooke, Schofield and other Baines copyists. A selection of Baines cards, in full colour, can be viewed at www.footballsoccercards.com

Balilla

Balilla 1930s Italian cards

Balilla, in Italian, is an heroic boy. It was also the name of Mussolini's military youth. In cards Balilla is best known for being one of the bigger Italian producers during the fascist years. Its 1936 black-bordered *Figurine Sportive* cards included many footballers. Values are around £10 but heavier prices must be paid for world greats like Meazza and Piola. Another series, showing players under the Italian flag, also included such legends and is priced similarly. During the war Balilla continued to issue cards. In 1941 the *Raccolta Nuove Figurine Squadre Calcio* included over 100 cards with 76 footballers and teams. Today values for these cards start at around £20 each for players of note.

Bailey's Agencies issued *Famous Football Internationals* in the late 1940s. There are two types: cards, issued in pairs, in two booklets of eight; and stickers, which were sold in sheets of 16. Note: each set comprises different players.

Today, a complete booklet of eight cards, in four pairs, may cost over £300. A sheet of stickers will fetch similar money. An uncut pair of cards is valued at around £80. Cut singles are worth about £30 each, whether card or sticker. The booklets are titled: *Cigarette Card Book Series A & B*. The cards and stickers themselves came without the *Cigarette Card Book Series* name. In pairs the cards will exhibit a stapled border at one side. The cards have italicised script whereas the stickers do not. See also: Sunnyvale

Bailey's Agencies also issued the *Cigarette Card Transfer Series*. This is a collection of water-slide transfers, or decals, which were sold in sheets of 16. Nowadays you may pay over £600 for a complete sheet! Like many decals most of these *were* cut and transferred, hence their great rarity today. Typically prices for single, cut decals are upwards of £40. The title of the series was only printed atop the complete sheet, so if you have only cut singles the way to identify

them is by the italicised script and backwards photos. They employ the same images as the booklet cards (see above). The earlier, similar looking stickers (see above) have regular script and are not printed backwards. For more decals (transfers) see also: Barratt, and Cadet Sweets.

Baker & Company issued a very rare series of tobacco cards in 1902. *Cricketers* have a value of £500 each! This set includes the legendary footballer Charles B. Fry, of Southampton, capped for England in 1891. See also: Faulkner, Charlesworth & Austin, and Rutter & Co., for similar issues.

Bancroft Tiddlers are not cards, per se, but they are often disingenuously sold as such. They are, in fact, cardstock pages pulled from miniature booklets, neatened by trimming, to make them look like cards, and sold to unsuspecting buyers. Sadly many booklets have been destroyed and much money has been spent on these little frauds. Stanley Matthews and Billy Wright are

Baileys decal of Morty and Sunnyvale card of Jones · Sunnyvale card of Macauley and Baileys sticker of Aston · Bancroft Tiddler page from a book, trimmed to look like a card

the footballers included in the booklets. Don't pay too much! Issued in 1967–1968 the booklets are called *Giants in Sport, I and Giants in Sport, II.*

Barker of Ireland, or John O. Barker, issued a series of *Footballers* in 1956. But for the issuer's imprint the cards are exactly the same as those issued by Mitchams Foods yet the values are much higher. These can sell for £40 each.

Barna, of Spain, issued a World Cup series called *Mexico 86*. It includes England & Scotland players, teams and emblems. Though modern these cards are hard to find. They include a stunner of Alex Ferguson, the Scotland manager of the day. Values are around £5 for famous internationals but up to £50 for Sir Alex – if the card is free of glue. Most of these cards were glued into an album issued for the series.

Barna Spanish cards

Today, a complete booklet of *Famous Football Internationals* from the late 1940s, which includes eight cards, in four pairs, may cost over £300. A sheet of stickers will fetch similar money. An uncut pair of cards is valued around £80.

Barratt.
The Best of Blighty

Various Barratt cards and related issues, 1923-1927

Barratt brings us more best of Blighty, this time from Wood Green, not that far from Tottenham Hotspur's *manor*, in north London. Barratt was the best known of all sweet cigarette manufacturers. It traded in junior *smokes* from World War One until 1974, the tragic year when A&BC Gum, BAB Products and Barratt all ceased to be.

The first series of football cards with a Barratt & Co. legend was issued in 1924 but this was not the first series of soccer cards available with Barratt confectionery. During 1922/23 a series of stunning photographic cards of footballers came into circulation. They were produced by a London printer, Hills & Lacy, to revive a mid-Victorian tradition whereby a printer would produce cards with blank backs for other firms to customise with their own branding. These cards, a series of unbranded footballers and cricketers, marked a sea change for confectionery trade cards. They can be found with makers' marks as diverse as Poppletons chocolates, VCC of London, and even a certain Watkins's Cough Mixture! The cards also found their way into Barratt's wares. The 1922/23 cards were such a success that Barratt instructed Hills & Lacy to print a series of sportsmen

exclusively for Barratt. These cards, first issued in 1924, became so successful that Barratt printed a new series yearly for decades to come.

Barratt made over 300 different sports cards between 1924 and 1927, and there are also rarer variations of some of these, making for a collection of well over 350 types, in all. Typically the backs of the cards show one of four different adverts for Barratt confectionery. All four types of cards were printed at the same time, as partial sheets of uncut cards have shown. The cards were printed tête-bêche, that is head-to-head, tail to tail. Yearly re-issues excluded certain players but included others, and team changes to cards were also made, so the same player can be found not only with different teams but with different backs too. The yearly re-setting of print matrices meant players' images were shuffled along, a place hither or thither, and long serving one-club players like York at Aston Villa, Cringan at Birmingham City and Rollo at Bolton Wanderers are known to each have at least three different backs. That's the result of three annual printings. Players with *Tarrab* backs in 1925 may have *Sherbet* backs in 1926, and even *Xmas Boxes* backs the following year. The span of football seasons covered by this mammoth series can be

illustrated by looking at different cards made for just one player. Jonah Wilcox appears on one card for Bristol Rovers, on another for QPR, and on a third for Gillingham. The Bristol Rovers card dates to 1925; the QPR to 1926, and the Gills card to 1927.

For 1924/25 Barratt issued 75 cards featuring footballers, rugby players and cricketers. The series also included a team card for Dick Kerr's Ladies. The women's team existed prior to 1925. Though it had been banned by The Football Association in 1921 the team found worldwide fame and recognition touring France and the United States of America. By 1926 it had reformed under a new name: Preston Ladies.

During the 1925/26 season Barratt released another 75 cards. This series includes a Manchester United team card. United had been newly promoted from Division Two in 1925. A similar series of 75 cards came out during 1926/27, which includes Derby County, newly promoted from Division Two in 1926. The last series was issued in late 1927. There are an unknown number of cards in this issue but Charlie Petrie, for Saints, dates this series. He played for Southampton some time after the 1927/28 season had already started. There is rumoured to be a card of Portsmouth FC in the 1927/28 series. This is not unlikely as previously unrecorded cards have been found as recently as 2016, when a Luton Town player came to auction and sold for £170! Having a Pompey team card would also be in step with Barratt's 1920s tradition of including a newly promoted team with each issue.

In 1927 Barratt also produced a very fine series of 50 cards titled *Leaders of Sport*. Starting values are around £25 each card but they rise to a staggering £2,000! Notwithstanding the dull tones these cards have a summery feel. Along with runners, walkers and cyclists, golfers and tennis players grace the issue. The inclusion of billiards players and hunt jockeys hint at an adult market. Such sports stars did not feature as typical favourites for children of the day. It seems these cards were included in a more expensive brand of confectionery. The design quality is upmarket. It is altogether of a higher class than the cards issued with junior sweet cigarettes. The *Leaders Of Sport* cards are refined with elegant

design, and unlike typical Barratt sports cards of the 1920s, they have potted biographies too.

Barratt & Company's 1928 series of 50 *Football Stars* consisted of humorous illustrations of great players. The cards are very rare and their values often start at £30 and may exceed £300! All the cards have black backgrounds, and most cards use only a single colour but some remain black and white. Once upon a time wrongly believed to be from 1930, this series is actually from the 1928/29 season. The inclusion of Jack Hill, for Burnley, dates the set to before 1929. Hill moved to Newcastle in November 1928. Further, Frank Barson played for Watford from springtime 1928 until April 1929. There are two *Football Stars* cards showing him at both Watford and at Hartlepool, so one will have been from this autumnal 1928 set, and the other from series two, issued in 1929. Series two consisted of a further 50 cards. Values for this series similarly start at £30 and go in one direction. The Jack Hill card in this set has team and colours amended appropriately to Newcastle United. Also, Billy

Blyth has moved from Arsenal to Birmingham and Frank Barson shows him in Hartlepool livery. David Jack also appears here, as an Arsenal player, a year after moving to Highbury in October 1928, which was a little too late for the first series of the *Football Stars* – an autumnal release – which had him with Bolton.

During 1930 Barratt issued *Football Greats*, a runt issue of 12 coloured cards. These cards were once thought to be from 1928. They were also once known as *Football Action Caricatures*. They are neither caricatures nor from 1928. The cards use real photographs of players' heads, much like the Barratt team cards of 1931. The photographic head appears upon a hand-drawn body, illustrated in colour on a painted background. There is no caricature per se. Moreover, the design on the rear of the cards uses a new matrix and the legend itself is clearly different from those of previous years. These cards fit 1930 very well yet a mere dozen makes this an atypical issue. They may have been issued with a special promotion or a new product. Values start around £30 but

 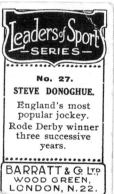    

Barratt 1927 Leaders Of Sport cards

Barratt Football Stars, 1928 and 1929

Barratt Football Greats 1930

In 1927 Barratt produced a very fine series of 50 cards titled Leaders of Sport. Starting values are around £25 each card but they rise to a staggering £2,000!

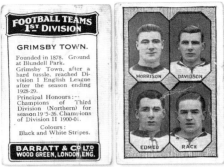
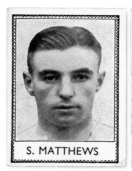

Barratt 1931 Football Teams 1st Division cards

Barratt 1936 Famous Footballers cards

Barratt 1935 F.A. Cup Winners cards

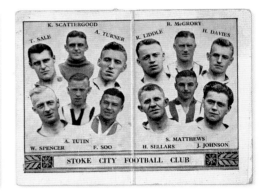

Barratt 1932-1934 football team folders

can rise above £100 for rarer cards and for hotly collected players. Everton's Dixie Dean tends to fetch a premium price and the Arsenal card is less often seen than the Bolton Wanderers card, so values vary considerably.

Barratt & Co. went back to fully photographic cards for the 1930/31 season. *Football Teams 1st Division* has 66 cards. Each shows four players and there are three different cards for each team in the set. Premiums tend to be paid for Arsenal, Liverpool and Manchester United. This series has been under-valued for decades. Values range from £20 to £80 each.

In autumn 1932 the first series of English League football team folders were launched. There would be two further series over following seasons. In the first issue 44 cards were made. Twentey-two of these folders are from the top flight. A further 22 come from the second division. Values for very good condition cards start at around £25 but rise above £50 for finer examples of popular teams. During 1932/33 a second series was issued. Values for these match the 1932 cards. The final series of football folders was issued for the 1934/35 season. It was not only wider reaching than the previous issues, it's a much rarer series altogether! It consists of 68 cards,

including Scottish and Irish clubs. Values start at £40 each and rise to £200 for the rarest of the 20 Scottish cards. The three Northern Irish team cards also command high prices. There is also one team from English Division Three, being the Welsh club Newport County. Amongst the cards in this series is to be found one of the first appearances of Stanley Matthews on a trade card. Though the earliest known Stanley Matthews rookie is the colourful 'red star' comic issue, a sticker printed during the 1933/34 season, the team folder card of Stoke City is, to all intents and purposes, the first card with Matthews.

Barratt's 1935 series, *F.A Cup Winners 1883 – 1935* shares design features with a set issued by John Players cigarettes but the Barratt cards are larger, more attractive and rarer. It boasts more teams too! It was released during the jubilee of King George V as a summer special. These cards are typically rarer than other Barratt cards from the 1930s. This is due to the short lifespan the series enjoyed, and its old fashioned presentation: yet more tiny pictures did not attract the buyers.

Famous Footballers, which came out for the 1935/36 season was something very different! One hundred cards, and one player per card. The series was numberless and printed in black. Values

start at around £25 each card and rise to £75. Stanley Matthews is one of the costlier items, as are the New Zealand rugby All Blacks. This series initiates one of the most complex genres of cards issued by Barratt. For five consecutive seasons this format would dominate. The same pictures came to be re-issued with different text and numbers. The similarity between the black cards of 1935/36 and the dark sepia cards of 1936/37 can be problematic for identification. Moreover, 80 years of daylight exposure changes hues and varnish tones.

The very similar *Famous Footballers* cards of 1936/37 consisted of 100 footballers but they were printed in dark sepia, not black. The cards are numberless and may be hard to distinguish from the 1935/36 issue. Values are between £20 and £50 each. In autumn 1937 the third issue of *Famous Footballers* was issued but this time the sepia cards were numbered. There were 110 cards in all. Most are valued between £20 and £50. Five of these cards, cards numbered 8, 9, 24, 99 and 109, appear, with the same numbers but with different biographical text, in the 1939/40 series. For reasons long since forgotten the *Famous Footballers* cards issued for 1938/39 consisted of a mere 20 different players. Values for these numbered cards range from £25 to £75. Card number 1 also appears in the following year's collection, albeit with different text on the rear.

The last of the pre-war *Famous Footballers* series was issued just as war broke out, in 1939. There were 112 sepia photos, with numbers. These cards are valued between £30 and £100 each. Two cards appear twice, with different numbers. Clue: Wolves and Derby County collectors will have high interest in this set. Furthermore, there are six cards from previous series that appear again, albeit with different biographical text. These are cards 1, 8, 9, 24, 99 and 109.

It would be almost seven years until Barratt issued its first post-war *Famous Footballers Series of 50* in 1947. However, it was anything but a series of 50 cards! Being reissued in 1948 and in 1949, with different stars, with differing letterpress, with new cardstock and other printing anomalies, the entire series consists of at least 93 different cards. Values for black and white cards start modestly, at around £10 each, but rise to over £100. Before the black and white cards were issued some very early cards were printed in sepia. Prices for the sepia tone cards are the costliest and have been seen to sell for over £150 each!

Cigarette card collectors of yore created an arcane technical reference number for this fascinating series. Its sterility resonates like a dystopian sci-fi film title: M-79.

A conservative estimate such as 79 barely begins to cover the myriad differences, variations, inks, varnishes, printing styles and finishes in this collection. Depending on your disposition it is either a fascinating or an infuriating series. The variations in players, team and name legends (inscriptions) and the differences of backs (being printed head-to-tail every other card has a back that's mirrored) mean there are now at least 93 basic types – but that's before considering the finer issues of hue, tone and photography. Most photos are reproduced in greys and blacks but not all. Early issues are sepia. The same player photo can be found with clear sky and partially cloudy skies – and even dark backgrounds. The player photos can be found printed sharply and clearly on some cards, yet fuzzily and dully on others. After World War Two paper was not in easy and free supply, hence the many types of cardstock used. Thick or thin card, smooth or rough card, grey, cream or white coloured card, and paper too! All types are known. Aside from

the different colours and varying tones, the most appealing varieties in these cards are the differences in legend to the fronts. Cards of A. Brown are known with both Burnley and Notts County legends; Horatio Carter is found on Derby and Hull cards; Len Shackleton is seen for Newcastle and for Sunderland; and Ted Hinton appears with Fulham and with Millwall. Some players have their international status added to some cards but not to others. Certain cards have team positions mentioned whilst other cards of the same player do not. There are mistake printings, players are known with the wrong team names... and on it goes. If you like a challenge this is probably the collection for you.

After World War Two decalcomania enjoyed a renaissance. Invented in the 1700s, in France, the process of transferring images from paper to objects had come and gone from vogue during Victorian times. Fashionable during the 1920s, Barratt had given that fad a miss but was on to the new craze. Joining forces with a decal manufacturer, WHC, Barratt produced a collection of water-slide transfers for Christmas 1948. They were called, simply, *Famous Footballers*. There were 20 decals issued per

Barratt 1936-1940 Matthews varieties

Barratt 1947 sepia card, and 1949 variety

sheet. A single sheet of 20 came in a pre-packed Christmas stocking. There were three different sheets of footballers, 60 transfers in all. The transfers are about typical cigarette card size. They show colour head and shoulders portraits of players. To identify and distinguish these transfers from similar decals issued a year later (by Napro & Barratt) these have a black name display box, with white text, inside the picture.

The dating of this series is based upon two players, Peter Doherty and Ted Hinton. Doherty played for Huddersfield Town until summer 1949. Hinton was a Fulham player until the same summer. By the time the 1949/50 season kicked off Doherty was at Doncaster Rovers and Hinton was at Millwall. In this series Hinton is still with Fulham, and Doherty is still with Huddersfield. A complete sheet of transfers is worth over £500. Few remain uncut as singles tend to fetch prices that make it worthwhile to cut.

Barratt reprised decals in 1949 with a firm called Napro. 20 *Full Colour Super Transfers* is how they were marketed. A complete sheet would be worth £500 but as single transfers make up to £60 each few sheets remain intact. In

1999, whilst publishing Football Card Collector Magazine, this writer discovered sheets of such decals being sold in a public auction. They remained packed for Christmas, just as they had been made, in 1949, in card-backed nylon mesh children's toy stockings. One sheet of footballers was given in each stocking, along with miniature toys and other small gifts. The stockings were inscribed "Barratt of Wood Green". For those who have the magazine, see issue 11. Unlike the earlier WHC issue, the Napro decals come in mixed sizes: the colour head and shoulders portraits are shorter, while action shots are taller. The Napro decals have the player's name and team printed outside the frame of the picture.

In 1949/50 Barratt celebrated the new half century with a fresh series of cards which it called *Famous Footballers New Series*. The cards have block lettering titles to the back which distinguishes the cards from a similar series issued in 1952 (with serif lettering). The basic set has 50 cards but there are far more than 50 different ones if you want all of the types of cardstock, shades of printing, and so on. A very similar series, also called *Famous Footballers New*

Barratt 1949 Napro decals

> **Barratt reprised decals in 1949 with a firm called Napro. 20 *Full Colour Super Transfers* is how they were marketed. A complete sheet would be worth £500 but as single transfers make up to £60 each few sheets remain intact.**

 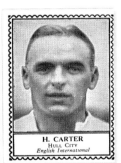

Barratt 1948-1949 cards

Barratt 1948 WHC decals

Barratt 1954-1956 cards

Barratt 1949-1952 cards

Series, was issued one year later, in 1950/51. Upon first glance the 1950/51 cards seem identical but many have small differences. One example is card 28, Joe Mercer of Arsenal. The first issue mentions '1946–47'. The second issue has '1949–50'. Values for cards from the two series range from £5, for most cards, up to more than £50 for the rarest variations.

By 1952 Barratt had changed the font matrix, so the third issue of *Famous Footballers New Series* had serif lettering. Values for the 51 known cards range from £3 to £25 each. The rarest card is one of two known number 39s (Derby County and Leicester City interest here). Incidentally, the Joe Mercer card in this series is numbered 26, not 28.

Famous Footballers series A1 was the first in a new genre of Barratt cards. There are 104 cards in all, due to varieties and errors – and two distinct printings! There is a set of 50 with the inscription: *Made In England*. There is also a set without this legend. There are three cards with distinctive varieties that make them essential acquisitions: cards 4, 7, and 9. Further, there is another version of card 9, with details on the back that do not match the player on the front. That's 104 different cards to find. Values range from £5 to over £50 for rarer types.

Famous Footballers series A2 followed, in 1954. Two of these cards have varieties: Ramsey

of Spurs is available with variations. Wayman of Middlesbrough is also available as a Preston North End player. The rarer varieties can make premium prices of up to £50 each. Otherwise cards from this series are valued around £2 to £5. In 1955, *Famous Footballers series A3* was to be the last set produced in large format. Future Barratt cards would revert to smaller sizes typical of the 1920s. Values for these cards range from £2 to £5.

In 1956 Barratt & Co. released *Famous Footballers series A4*. There were more cards in the set but they were smaller than earlier *A-series* cards. Values for the 62 cards range from a few pounds per card to £50 each for the two rarer varieties: John Charles and Jimmy Gauld, on cards 23 and 25, come in two versions. Barratt continued this type of card from 1957 to 1959. *Famous Footballers series A5*, *A6* and *A7* each consisted of 60 cards. Typical values are around £2 to £5 per card. Barratt finished the decade with a pan-sport set, *Giants in Sport*, with 48 black and white cards. Values for these have been known to hit £75 though most can be found for £5 each. There are four footballers in this set: Stanley Matthews, Billy Wright, Johnny Haynes and John Charles.

Colour dawned in 1960. Barratt & Co.'s *Famous Footballers series A8* has 50 colourful cards – and far more if you want all the colour varieties

and misprints too. The series includes two cards with the number 37 and there are endless colour variations. Some cards have plain backs, others show misprinted numbers, and so on. Values start at £5 and rise to well over £50 each for rarer types.

Barratt & Co. published *Famous Footballers series A9* in 1961. There are over 100 of these cards as an entire set was accidentally issued with the number A8 before the cards were replaced with A9! Due to type matrix errors some cards may show a deformed A9 letter and number. This series also includes a variety of card number 19 which lacks its penultimate line of text. Values range from £5 to £75 each. The 1962 issue, *Famous Footballers series A10*, was a more sober affair of 50 cards with no varieties. Values are a dull £2 to £5 each. Barratt's *Famous Footballers series A11* is an altogether more interesting prospect for hunters of rare cards. It has over 60 cards to seek including at least 10 cards with alternative titles, names and spacing. Peter Dobing, Alan A'Court, Jimmy Armfield, Gordon Banks and others have two different cards each. Values start at £2 but rise to £75 for rarer variations.

George Best made an appearance in *Famous Footballers series A12*, which was released in autumn 1964. His card fetches a very high price and breaks the set. Whereas 49 of the 50 cards sell for £2 to £5 each, Best can top £200! Rookie card collecting has devastated many sets thus. In 1965 *Famous Footballers series A13* featured a pair of variety cards, making it a series of 52. Look out for variations of the Burnside of Crystal Palace card, and the Thomas of Derby County card. Values range from £2 to £50 for the error cards. There are also colour variations, as in all Barratt early 1960s sets. The 1966 *Famous Footballers series A14* has 52 cards including varieties of Megson of Wednesday, and Ritchie of Stoke and Southampton. Generally cards from *A14* are worth £2 each but the varieties may make £50 each. In 1967 *Famous Footballers series A15* was the last of the A-series types. It has a different design to earlier sets. The cards are worth about £2 each.

After a break from football Barratt & Co. returned with two general sports series. *Famous Sportsmen* was first issued in 1970 and then again, quietly, with different faces, in 1971. Thus, there are at least 100 cards to find but you'll need over 150 if you want all the printing differences! *Made In England* legends appear in one release but not in another. There are error cards too. Look out for colour variations also.

Pelé and George Best were replaced in the second release, in 1971. Best was replaced by an athlete, John Davis; and Pele was replaced by Marilyn Neufville.

During the 1972/73 season Barratt returned to a series dedicated to football, with *Soccer Stars*. There are 56 cards including six known varieties: Mullery has two cards: one for Spurs and one for Fulham. Likewise, Marsh can be found as both a Manchester City player and as a QPR footballer. Rofe may be found at Orient and also as a Leicester City player. Ian Storey-Moore is on a card for Manchester United, and on another for Forest. Nicholl comes on a card for Luton and also on a card for Aston Villa. MacDougall appears for Bournemouth and for Manchester United. Davies is seen for both Manchester City and for Newcastle. Premium prices for these! Values for this series exceed typical values for 1960s Barratt cards. £5 is entry level, and £50 each is not uncommon for the variety cards.

In 1973/74 *Football Stars* was the last series of football cards issued by Barratt & Co.

Some of these cards are very rare. Excellent or near-mint examples of Manchester United's Lou Macari sell for over £20 each, while a near-mint Martin Chivers of Spurs card sell for way over £30. In 1974 Barratt was taken over by a firm called Bassett's.

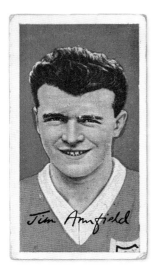

Barratt 1960s cards

Barratt 1960s cards

Football Stars

Series of 50

No.37

DAVID JONSTON
IPSWICH

Signed from Everton in October 1972 for Rod Belfitt plus £50,000. David soon made his presence felt with great goals. He scored in his first league game, his first F.A. Cup-tie and his first European Cup-tie. Packs a terrific shot. 5ft 11ins tall.

Issued by
Geo. Bassett & Co. Ltd.
(Barratt Division)   SHEFFIELD 6
PRINTED IN ENGLAND

Football Stars

Series of 50

No. 37

Malcolm Macdonald
Newcastle

Won Under 23 and three full England caps in 1972. He joined Fulham from Tonbridge as a fullback, with Palace also chasing him. He was converted into a centre-forward by Luton and was then sold to Newcastle for £190,000. He scored a hat-trick against the Wales Under 23's, and is determined to be an England striker for many years.

Issued by
BARRATT & CO. LTD
LONDON   -   -   ENGLAND
PRINTED IN ENGLAND

Soccer Stars

A Series of 50   No. 15

BOBBY CLARK
Aberdeen

Joined his present club from Rangers, where he had been playing as a full back. Was converted to a keeper and did so well that he earned Scottish caps, and until Bob Wilson qualified under the parents birth rule Bobby was first choice.

Issued by
BARRATT & CO. LTD
LONDON   -   -   ENGLAND
PRINTED IN ENGLAND

Barratt early 1970s cards, and Bassett card

After a break from football Barratt & Co. returned with two general sports series. *Famous Sportsmen* was first issued in 1970 and then again, quietly, with different faces, in 1971. Thus, there are at least 100 cards to find but you'll need over 150 if you want all the printing differences!

Geo. Bassett & Co.

Bassett, or Geo. Bassett & Co., as it was formerly known, took over Barratt in 1974 and continued to issue *Football Stars* – with a difference in logo. The same picture cards Barratt ended its days with were re-issued with the Geo. Bassett legend (and Barratt Division in parentheses). These cards are worth a lot less than those by Barratt. Values are around £2 each card. Bassett launched its first original series in 1974: *World Cup Stars*. The 50 cards were widely distributed and the set has a very low value today. Most cards can be had for less than £1 each. The Kenny Dalglish card may sell for a little more. Bassett's *Football Stars* 1975-6 [sic] is a more interesting series, and much rarer too – the 50 cards sell for £10 each. In 1977 Bassett created a series called *Football Action*. The action shots are from the 1976/77 season and should not be confused with very similar issues from 1977/78, issued in a new series a year later. To differentiate the two, note the lack of spacing between the series title, the number and the action titles on the backs. Values for both series range from £5 to £10 each card.

Bassett helpfully dated its next series. *Football 1978–79* has 50 cards. Likewise, *Football 1979–80* also has 50. These series can be found quite easily and the cards can be had for £1 each or less. Bassett produced football cards well into the 1990s. More on these in a future book.

Bassett cards 1974 to 1980

Bassett cards 1974 to 1980

Batger

Batger cards

Battock's 1923 cards believed by some to be by Baytch Bros

Batger cards

Battock's 1924 cards

Batger cards are of immense worth. Issued in 1900, *Well Known Football Clubs* cards sell for up to £1,000 each! These are extremely rare cards. In over 100 years of cartophilic endeavour the existence of these cards evaded the knowledge of collectors until recently. Less than 20 different cards have been recorded. In most cases it is believed there is only one of each card extant. Upon issue these cards were returned to Batger, to be redeemed for cash prizes and other rewards. Upon receipt by Batger the cards had their corners clipped, to prevent re-use, and were eventually destroyed. The few cards extant are usually found minus a corner or two.

Battock's issued various series of cards with football club colours. In 1923 the firm issued 108 cards made of both card and paper. Today their values start at around £30 for smaller or defunct clubs like New Brighton Tower, and rise to £250 for bigger names like Liverpool. The series represented all of the football teams from the four major English divisions and the top Scottish division during the 1923/24 season. The card fronts show coloured footballers on plain backgrounds and they come with various backs, which are known with these legends: *Snap*

Cards; Battocks Football And Jersey Cards; We Will Send You A Football Or Jersey; Save Battock's Cards; Cover Cards; Skimmer cards; and *Guessing Numbers*.

In 1924/25, Battock issued a new series of cards of football clubs to paint or colour in crayon or pastel. They were marketed as colouring competition cards. The idea was used by Battock to create a new series (see below) of fully coloured cards, in 1925. Customers sent in their coloured creations in the hope of winning prizes. Battock took the best designs and used them for future series. Values range from £100 to £250 each for this series of black and white cards.

Battock's issued more football and cricket clubs in 1925, 108 fully coloured cards to be precise. These show football action on colourful backgrounds. Values start around £100 and rise to £250. The 54 football teams included are from the top two English divisions and some from the Scottish leagues. Fifty-four cricket clubs complete the set. The backs of these cards advertise "Snap Cards...54 football clubs and 54 cricket clubs..."

Bauer, Josef not Jack, issued an Anglo Gum series out of West Germany in 1970: *Weltfussball 1970 / Football Mondial* are cards of European football teams, the same style as the waxy paper inserts issued by Anglo Confectionery. Value: £5 to £50 each.

Baytch Brothers were Scottish siblings in cards. According to generalist tobacco card guides from last century Baytch was a small producer with but one or two sets of cards to its name. Reference material in a Glasgow local history museum suggests otherwise! Abe Donaldson, the pre-eminent Scottish trade cards manufacturer of the day, saw the brothers Baytch as his main rivals. The brothers may well be responsible for the so-called *rogue* Donaldson cards, a series now attributed to Kiddy's favourites. Were Kiddy's and Baytch the very same outfit? This series includes some of the rarest post-war British footballer cards known, including Matthews of Stoke City, Mercer of Arsenal and McIlhatton of Everton. Baytch Brothers issued cards under their own names but they also used imprints such as S&B Products, amongst others. The many and varied series of cards known as *Torry Gillicks Internationals* were by Baytch yet the S&B cards bore no mention of the brothers. The first cards printed with the Baytch name was a set of 64 *Fighting*

Favourites (boxing cards). In a letter written by Abe Donaldson to his designer, John Barr, the boss laments, 'Baytch is now up to card 200 [and, also] a new firm has appeared with cards up to 120!' This letter dates from 1948. What were the 200 Baytch Brothers cards Abe Donaldson bemoaned?

Bazooka was typically associated with the American firm Topps. Bazooka Gum first appeared in the USA, in 1947, with miniature comics printed on the inside of candy wrappers. Thence came cards of sportsmen. In the British Isles the Bazooka brand of gum appeared early in the history of A&BC Gum. From 1962 it was given with *Footballer* gum cards in place of Oscar Janser's English gum which had been used prior to that. Gum cards issued by Bazooka came to dominate not only English-speaking markets. *Bazoka* [sic] was also issued in Spain (notably 1950s *Bazoka Futbol stamps*) and a firm called Xuereb issued similar issues in Malta. A gifts and souvenirs business, Xuereb was based in Valletta. It is known to have produced A&BC sticker stamps in 1966. Notably these bootlegs have been recorded on different stamps, probably issued by another, unknown party. See also: A&BC, Tip-top, Topps, Xuereb.

B.E.A. is an acronym for Buste Ed Affini. In English it means *Lucky Bags and alike*. This Italian issuer enjoyed success with cards and stickers throughout the 1950s but it issued sports cards during 1949–1951 only. Its *Stadio* football cards of 1948/49 have black borders with white roundels, and the letter B features in the angles. These cards

were issued in three types: with black numbers/ names in circles; with red numbers in circles; and with numbers without circles. There are 242 cards in all. Next came *Gool! Premio Sport*, issued halfway through the 1949/50 season. It boasted 620 cards. These cards have red borders. A third series called *Campionato di calcio* followed, during 1950/51. Its 264 cards have white lozenges on black borders. Values start at £5 each but values go much higher for cards of British Isles players Norman Adcock, Bill Jordan and Paddy Sloan.

The Beautiful Game – a firm using footy commentator Stuart Hall's historic phrase as its own name – issued *All Time Greats*, in 1999. As cards they are neither rare nor valuable so why are they mentioned here? Modern-day artisan cards like these have proliferated since the 1990s. The best are probably those made in the 1990s by Garth and John at Fosse Collectibles and JFSC; and by Harry Richards. Bill Priddy's cards are legends in their own right (see: Priddy). Alas, these days it seems everyone has clambered aboard the craft cards bandwagon and we have homemade cards coming out all over the place. If you do buy craft cards from internet sellers £1 or £2 a card is about the right value. However, older craft cards, made before the age of the internet, like those made by John Allen [RIP] in the 1980s (*London Legends*, etc.), are gaining in value. Some John Allen cards are listed on some collectors' wants lists for as much as £100 a card! (see: Allen, John).

Brits on 1948 and 1949 Bea cards from Italy

Bazoka 1950s Spanish wrapper and stickers

Bell Boy Bubble Gum

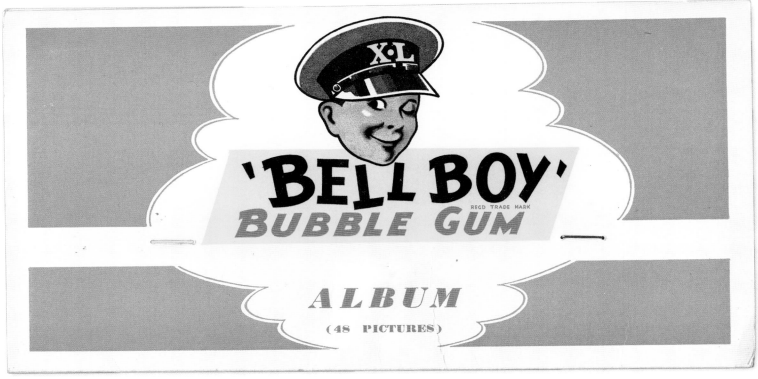

Bell Boy gum album

Bell Boy was a brand of gum made by Anglo American Chewing Gum of Halifax, in northern England (see also: Anglo Confectionery). It created the defining soccer stickers of the 1950s, notwithstanding the fact that Bell Boy stickers are not really stickers. They were made as redeemable gum inserts. They are very particular and they have become something of a cult collectible. Many and varied series and albums were issued between 1956 and 1965. Bell Boy stickers are sometimes wrongly referred to as wrappers. In fact they were distributed within

wrappers, as inserts, wrapped around a chunk of gum. This is why all of them have creases. However, so-called *proofs* (inserts without creases) are also known. These are premium collectibles which were redeemed from the issuer in exchange for a full set of creased inserts. Bell Boy's sports trend started with *Strange But True*, a general interest series, featuring subjects from the wide and wild world. The series of 48 includes one on football.

Bell Boy's next release, *Sports Gallery*, presented 48 gum inserts for sport lovers. Values for singles from this series depend on the theme but they start at around £5 each and rise to as

much as £100! Legendary golfers, world greats of the boxing ring and other sportsmen worthy of note command premium prices. As this series was issued in a World Cup year, 1958, there are various inserts with a football theme. Hall of Fame legends like Puskas and Wolves's captain, Billy Wright, are included. One insert shows four famous footballers: Hughie Gallagher, Dixie Dean, Alec James and Tommy Lawton. Needless to say this is one of the rarer items from the set and the number of collectors seeking it has driven its price skywards! There is also a sticker featuring the FA Cup Final of 1923, showing Bolton Wanderers and West Ham United.

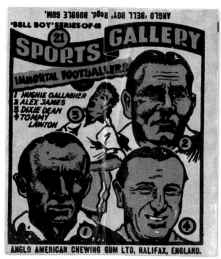

Bell Boy 1958 Sports Gallery gum inserts

Bell Boy 1960s gum inserts

Bell Boy moved with the flock in 1959. Comics like Adventure were issuing cards on training technique so Bell Boy followed suit, issuing *Soccer Hints*. The series lacked famous names so it's become a dud as a collectible. Its value remains very low. Bell Boy bounded back with *Sports Parade* in 1960 which includes worldwide sports greats from golfers to boxers. Stanley Matthews features amongst a cast of world legends. Values for these inserts start at £10 each and rise towards £150 each for unfolded *proofs*.

In 1961 Bell Boy launched what's become their most beloved series. *Famous Soccer Clubs*

included 130 different teams. Though many are almost impossible to find today, and some are believed to remain unissued, the myth of completion endures and collectors push on towards making a set. Values for these start at £5 each but may exceed £50 for rarer types. Printed albums were issued. Acquiring an album is the safest, and most economical bet if you want to see the lot. Bell Boy followed up with Noted Soccer Clubs, in 1962, a series of 72 which includes potted histories of lesser known British football clubs. These stickers show club crests and colours of teams like Rhyl and Pegasus FC! Albums of

printed wrappers were also issued. Values start at £5 and rise to £50 for rarer types!

Coaching Secrets was the success that *Soccer Hints*, in 1959, had failed to be. The 72 waxy paper inserts include the likes of Roger Hunt, of Liverpool, and Spurs's Jimmy Greaves. Values start at £10 but can top £150 for the likes of Pelé and Eusebio.

From Bell Boy to Bell

Bimbo 1967 - 1969 stickers

Bell 1902 Three Nuns cigarette card

Bergmann 1961, Spurs and Foxes on German cards

From Bell Boy to Bell. Three Nuns Tobacco [sic] was made by J&F Bell of Glasgow. Its 1902 series, *Three Bells*, included 22 footballers amongst 30 different sports cards. Values start at around £50 for a card in very good condition and rise above £200 for certain players. Rugby players also feature in this series.

Bergmann Verlag was to West Germany what A&BC and FKS were to Great Britain. There had been a pre-war incarnation of the firm but the best known Bergman cards were launched in the 1960s and 1970s. The earliest lack logos and issuer's names. They sported only a number and a team name (on the back) and are often mistaken for Monty Gum cards. This 1961 collection consisted of 40 international teams. Values can exceed £100 for certain hotly sought-after cards. This series includes fine examples of Leicester City (with Gordon Banks) and Tottenham Hotspur, not to mention a card of AC Milan showing Jimmy Greaves! Another noted Bergmann collection was the *Jules Rimet Cup England 1966*, which featured 38 large trade cards, in the style of postcards. Values for these rarities range from £20 to £100. This series has West German players and 20 World Cup action cards including Bobby

Moore, Franz Beckenbauer and Eusebio. In 1970 Bergmann issued *World Cup Mexico 70*. English stars feature widely in this series. Values start at £5 each card. There are many more Bergmann series, from the 1960s until the 1980s, and there will be much more on Bergmann's repertoire in a future edition of this book.

Bertcord of Brackley produced two boxed sets of game cards called *Big League*, in 1982. The portmanteau Bertcord remains as mysterious as the cards themselves remain curious cards of players without faces – other than moustaches – whereon you could draw a player's facial features. They created much mirth amidst gamesters. All in all there are about 200 cards to seek. Values for complete boxed games, of about 100 cards each, cost less than £50, which seems a bargain as individual cards may fetch £5.

Bimbo equates to child in Latin-based languages, so this is not the sexist vernacular employed by blokes in Britain during recent times. Between 1967–1969 Bimbo issued *Nuestro Mundos 1, 2* and *3*. These series of Spanish language stickers top £50 each for soccer legends like Bobby Charlton, Pelé and Eusebio. In 1974 Bimbo, a Bruguera imprint, launched a series called *Futbol en Accion*.

Included were decal transfers as much as cards. Values for intact, unused transfers start at £50 apiece! Bimbo revisited decals (water-slide transfers) in 1979 with *Historia del los Mundials Futbol*. The decals include national mascots and World Cup commemorative postage stamps, including 1966. Values are around £20 each for unused transfers with backing papers.

Bird's Eye, the British frozen foods producer, came up with a series of football cards called *England World Cup Trail*. The 12 cards show England players in the qualifying stages for Spain 82. Issued in pairs on large packs of fish fingers, and singly on smaller boxes, the values for these cut-out packet issues start at £10 for singles, and £30 for paired cards.

Birmingham Evening Gazette issued football ephemera as early as 1931. The *FA Cup Finalists 1930-1931* supplements of WBA and Birmingham City are worth £75 each. The same newspaper issued *FA Cup Finalists 1935* featuring Sheffield Wednesday and WBA. Values are also around £75 each. In 1945 it printed 100 numbered cards to be cut out, called *These Are Soccer Stars*. Values for such packet issues exceed £20 each. Designed to be cut out, *These Are Soccer Stars* are essentially cartophilic collectibles and not paper clippings.

Boys' Cinema and Bullseye cards, 1931

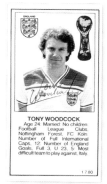

Bird's Eye 1982 card

Brum Evening Gazette 1940s shield card

Blue Cap cheese Burnley flixy

Brum Evening Gazette 1945 These Are Soccer Stars

Bovalone 1950s Italian cards

Boy's Friend 1922 cards

The newspaper followed with more *These Are Soccer Stars*. The *New Series* was issued in 1946, comprising 70 cut-outs. Values are similarly around £20 each. The *New Series* are numbered sequentially to follow on from the previous 100. The paper also issued shield-shaped cards to cut-out and stick, making two-sided escutcheons of footballers. These shield cards are extremely rare items and you may have to pay over £50 for one!

Blue Cap Cheese issued a series of bestial sports cards in 1953. The *Sports Series* consists of packet issues (to cut). Each was a paired card of an animal and a sport. Values for uncut pairs are around £20 each. There is one football item included. Blue Cap went on to issue another innovative series in 1958, called *Flixies*. The series consisted of 12 colour transparencies. Twelve football teams are included in this very large set of 140.

Bocnal Tobacco's 1938 series of *Luminous Silhouettes* may well have been as dangerous to health as were the cigarettes the cards were issued with. Low-level radioactive readings are emitted by the luminous substance found on the 25 glow-in-the-dark cards. If you are prepared to take the risk there is a mere single football scene included in this radioactive series. Values have plummeted

since the dangers of the set were discovered.

Bovalone Biscotti [sic] of Italy issued football cards in the 1950s. The easily distinguished yellow-frame cards have values around £5 each but that of Haas Jeppson, formerly of Charlton Athletic, often makes more.

Bowater Scott was a noted issuer of sanitary produce and paper handkerchiefs. In 1969 its brand *Scotties* tissue paper issued *Scotties Famous Football Teams*. There are nine large postcard-sized trade cards to collect. Values range from £10 to £25.

Boxing, Racing & Football Magazine issued *Personalities of British Sport*, in 1928. The 18 large, paper supplements include Dixie Dean and Charles Buchan, amidst other sporting greats. Values start at around £100 and may exceed £250 each!

Boys' Cinema magazine issued a series of 24 football teams in 1931. The monotone photos were issued on cards with plain backs. The same series of images was also issued with a sister magazine, The Bullseye, but while one series was printed in sepia, the other was black and white. Values start at £20 but rise to £50 for certain teams.

Boys' Friend, an Edwardian magazine, issued a series of supplements in 1908. The *Football!*

Teams 1908-9 supplements are valued between £100 and £250 each! Aston Villa, Chelsea, Wolves, Liverpool, Manchester United and Newcastle United await the intrepid collector.

In 1911 Boys' Friend issued *Picture Gallery*. These were strips of four cards. Each uncut strip of cards contained a flag, a boxer, a footballer and a military regiment. A strip may cost over £100 today but a single *Famous Footballer* can be had for a mere £20, or less. After a hiatus Boys' Friend returned to football cards in 1922, issuing five coloured cards. Each featured a pair of players. Uncut pairs may make £50 but cut cards are worth very little. Cut singles can be identified by the dating on the rear. There will be mention of either November or December 1922. Boys' Friend continued to issue footballers in spring 1923, with the so-called Special Photo footballers. When launched, Boys' Friend magazine announced these cards as *Hand-Coloured Real Glossy Photos*, though this title does not appear anywhere on the cards. Values are around £5 each.

Boys' Magazine

Boys' Magazine 1923 trios

Boys' Magazine 1924 quads

Boys' Magazine was the quintessential lads' comic of the 1920s. Though newer, trendier titles, the likes of Wizard and Adventure, offered stiff competition, Boys' Magazine fought its way through until the 1930s. Incorporating Pals comic on the way, it finally threw in the towel, bested by Champion, a rival comic, with which it became one, in 1934.

In its time, Boys' Magazine gave us some of the most notable football cards. The first of which were four large sepia photos of soccer teams on paper. Values range from £50 to £75 for these 1922 issues. Aston Villa, Chelsea, Manchester City and Tottenham Hotspur team groups are included. Each is inscribed, *Presented With The "Boys' Magazine"* [sic]. Note: the inclusion of *The* before *Boys' Magazine* differentiates this issue from later series. Later in 1922 Boys' Magazine issued two more teams: Huddersfield Town AFC and Preston North End FC. They are inscribed, *Presented With "Boys' Magazine"* [sic].

In the same year Boys' Magazine also released a series called *Art Photos of Famous Footballers*. The set consisted of ten supplements, each being a sheet of paper showing three players. Similar sepia prints of four players would come to be issued in 1923. The way to recognise

and differentiate these issues, if they are cut to singles, is to note the letter *B* in *Boys*. The 1922 players show a fatter lower band in the letter *B* whereas the 1923 letter *B* has two bands of equal size.

Boys' Magazine continued its 1922 gift output with the so-called *Football Series cards*. Ten small, black and white teams were co-issued with a sister publication called Pals. The front covers of Boys' Magazine announced the cards as *real glossy photos* but the cards themselves sport different titles. Most cards have the legend, *Football Teams* but some are titled *Football Series* (notably those of England and Sunderland). The latter title was concurrently used by Pals, on its cards. Pals went on to issue other complementary sets of cards and supplements in tandem with Boys' Magazine. Note: the West Ham card announced in the magazine, and also mentioned on card number 3, never materialised. It was replaced by an Edinburgh Hibs card. Values for the cards range from £5 to £20 each.

In 1922/1923 Boys' Magazine issued *Coloured Studies of Famous Internationals*, just as Pals comic issued a synchronous issue: *Famous Footballers Fine Art Supplements* (also known as *Natural Colour Studies*). These beautiful cards are

not difficult to acquire and are valued at less than £5 each.

Boys' Magazine's next issue was a series of football quartets called *Famous Footballer Photos*. Also known as *Splendid Sepia Photo Cards* (or, at least that's how these were advertised in the comic itself) the cards are without such an inscription. This 1923 set included 16 sheets, of four players each. Intact these are worth £50 to £100 each but single, cut cards are valued at less than £10.

Boys' Magazine's *Football Series 1923-'24* comprised six postcard-size cards. Inscribed, *Presented With Boys' Magazine*, they were issued one per magazine for six issues. Values range from £25 to £75 depending on the team and its condition.

Note: six similar team cards were issued simultaneously with Pals comic.

During 1925/26 Boys' Magazine issued 18 large paper supplements of teams. Inscribed in capitals, *PRESENTED FREE WITH BOYS' MAGAZINE* [sic], these teams are mostly dated, but three teams remain without dates: Spurs, Man City and Cardiff City. The values of the 18 cards range from £30 to £100 each. An extra paper supplement was given in 1926: *The Cup-Final Teams* (1925-26) [sic]. This large paper supplement of Manchester City and Bolton Wanderers is valued at £75.

Boys' Magazine issued its first decals in 1926. *Transfers of Big Heroes* came in sheets of six. These *fine coloured transfers of popular heroes of sport & screen* (so boasted the editorial) are waterslide transfers on small sheets, with six transfers each sheet. They are inscribed, *presented by Boys' Magazine*. Silent movie idol Charlie Chaplin shares a sheet with football great Charles Buchan, and the legendary boxer, Jack Dempsey. Values for such are over £500 for an uncut sheet. The magazine continued 1926 with more unorthodox gifts, issuing 12 coloured metal badges (discs with fold-over tabs). Values for these start at £50 each.

Later in 1926 Boys' Magazine issued *Famous Footer Clubs*, a set of 24 coloured, shaped cards, often in the form of escutcheons, resonant of cards once issued by Baines. Values for these beauties start at £50 and can top £150 each! During 1927/1928 Boys' Magazine issued a wonderful series of decals called *Transfer Photos of Famous Footballers*. Sheets of four, coloured footballers fetch up to £250 per sheet! Single, cut transfers may sell for £20 each. Boys' Magazine

had also issued more team photos on large paper supplements in this period. The date 1926/27 is printed below the teams and the supplements are inscribed: *Presented free with Boys Magazine*. Values can reach £100 each. Boys' Magazine continued to issue more, large sepia team photos in 1928. Inscribed *presented free with Boys Magazine* these are easily identifiable, being dated 1928.

The Famous Footballers series, by Boys' Magazine, in 1929, comprised 12 black and white photographic cards of players. Their value is around £5 each. It followed this series with an issue of nine coloured *Football Teams*. Smaller than the earlier sepia supplements, these diminutive paper cards are valued at £10 each. A larger supplement followed: *The FA Cup Finalists 1929* showed Bolton Wanderers & Portsmouth. Its value is around £50. Starting the new decade by launching pairs of football teams, Boys' Magazine looked back in homage to earlier times, and to a 1922 co-issue with Pals. The ten undated paper supplements which were launched in 1930 are worth around £50 to £75 – for uncut pairs. A year later the full-colour *Gallery of Famous Footballers* offered readers ten sheets of brightly daubed footballers, in quads. These pretty items are worth

at least £50 each, if uncut, rising to £150 for quads that include certain legendary players.

So-called *Dazzling Five-Colour Real Transfers* (also known as *Magic Transfers*) followed, later in 1931. These rarities were titled on a weekly basis, with fancy names like *Daredevils of Adventure, Stars of Sport and Speed, Famous Cricketers With Badges And Crests*, etc. There are eight known sheets of decals, each with five transfers. Values start at £100 a sheet, rising sharply for uncut sheets with All Time Greats. The magazine followed the exotic gifts of transfers and coloured cards with yet more monotone team line-ups, once again issued in pairs, dated 1931. These 12 paper supplements comprise 24 teams. Values range from £50 to £75 each pair.

In 1932 Boys' Magazine celebrated its history and its end by launching one of the world's first sticker collections! *Famous Footballers In Action* consisted of 36 stickers issued in sheets of six each, one sheet given weekly, and an album. Values for uncut sheets start at £150 each. Cut stickers are worth £15 and a full album, which is one of the first soccer sticker albums ever made, is worth well over £100.

Boys' Magazine 1927 Transfer photos

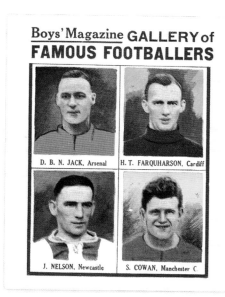

Boys' Magazine 1931 Gallery of Famous Footballers

Boys' Magazine 1926 Famous Footer Clubs

FREE INSIDE

4 COLOURED PORTRAITS OF FAMOUS FOOTBALLERS

BOND COLLECTING NOW

DAZZLING ALL-STAR FOOTBALL THRILL NUMBER

LOOK! 2 COLOURED FOOTBALL CARDS

2D

BOYS' MAGAZINE

EVERY SATURDAY

CHELSEA F.C.

PLAY UP

WELL PLAYED SUNDERLAND

CARDIFF CITY

The Boys' Own Paper

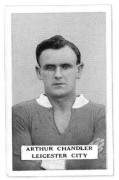 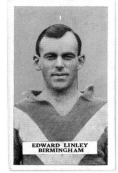    

BAT cards 1923 to 1925

British Automatic cards, with variations

Between 1879 and 1967 the BOP, as the Boys' Own Paper was known, often issued colourful gift supplements, including football supplements of great beauty. Sadly, these days, the magazines and surviving supplements are all too often found cut, for individual pictures of players, ruining their worth. Uncut soccer supplements can fetch £50 to £150 each so check any old issues of The Boys' Own Paper.

Boy's Own [sic] by Fry & Son of Bristol was a make of chocolate cigarettes. Issued in the 1910s their packets contained cards in mockery of real cigarettes. A packet, showing a young sailor, an officer cadet, sold for over £100 in 2018. A Fry's trade card from the same series will probably reach a similar price when it eventually comes to market.

The Boys' Realm comic issued a series of Famous Football Grounds before World War One, but its best known cards are those from 1920, notably the so-called Famous Footballers Big Art Plates. Four, large paper supplements include 80 footballers in all! Nowadays the

A Boy's Own cigarette packet, issued in 1910 and showing a young sailor sold for over £100 in 2018.

sheets are often found cut for pictures of single players, ruining the worth of the supplements themselves. Uncut supplements can command prices between £100 and £150 each. In 1922 The Boys' Realm followed Famous Footballers Big Art Plates with nine photographic cards also titled Famous Footballers. Values are around £5 each. A year later the comic issued a stunning series of Football Trophies in metal! There were four in all, each being flat metal badges, with flaps to fold out to make them stand freely. Values for these rarities start at £50 each. A few years later four similar metal cards were issued by the comic: F.A. Cup winners medals. Like the trophies of 1923 these were flat metal badges, inscribed to the rear, and dated 1927. Values start at £50 each.

Brigham & Company was a tobacco issuer from Reading. In 1912 it issued Pictures of The Reading Football Players. There are 16 cards in all and values start at £500 rising to £1,000 each!

British & American Tobacco (BAT) was one of the earliest giant conglomerates. BAT foreshadowed the world of today, a globe dominated and run by multinationals, for multinationals. In 1923 British & American Tobacco issued Famous Footballers, a set of 50 cigarette cards, and the first of three series issued by the firm between 1923 and 1925. Without a brand name this particular series can be identified by the dark, sooty backgrounds in the photos. The second and third issues of Famous Footballers were lighter. That from 1924 had 50

Presented with the BOYS' REALM, October 2nd, 1920.

FAMOUS FULL-BACKS.

B. HOBSON
Sunderland

F. E. BULLOCK
Huddersfield

J. BLAIR
Sheffield Wednesday

S. BLACKHAM
Bradford

E. LONGWORTH
Liverpool

J. PENNINGTON
West Bromwich

T. CLAY
Tottenham H.

J. HARROW
Chelsea

J. SHAW
Arsenal

R. DOWNS
Everton

A. McNAIR
Celtic

H. BAVERSTOCK
Bolton Wanderers

F. DUCKWORTH
Blackburn Rovers

F. WOMACK
Birmingham

T. WESTON
Aston Villa

A. STURGESS
Sheffield United

J. R. ELVEY
Bolton W.

A. E. KNIGHT
Portsmouth

W. McCRACKEN
Newcastle United

J. WALKER
Middlesbrough

(Photographs by A. Wilkes, West Bromwich.)

ABDULLA
NUMBER SEVEN
7
"Virginia"
A BLEND OF VIRGINIA AND OTHER CHOICE TOBACCOS

"TURF"
CIGARETTES
CARRERAS LTD. LONDON
(ESTD. 1788)

cards. It can be identified by the text box to the front, wherein the names of player and team have no space between. In the third series, a similar set of 50 cards, issued in 1925, there is a space betwixt the player and team names. Values for all of these cards is around £5 each. A year later BAT issued *Who's Who in Sport 1926*. The set's 50 cigarette cards include two soccer items: the teams of Bolton Wanderers and Huddersfield Town. See also: Lambert & Butler. The latter issuer printed very similar cards. Values for the BAT pair are around £10 each card.

British Automatic was a weight-telling company. It made weighing machines for apothecary and general stores. They'd often be seen on pavements outside shops. For a small fee people could have their weight measured. A card would be dispensed, showing the weight on one side and a colourful image to the other. In 1954 British Automatic issued a set called *Sportsman Series Of 24*. The cards include six footballers but there are, in fact, double that number to collect because John Charles, Denis Compton, George Young, Tom Finney, Stanley Matthews and Billy Wright were all printed in two types, with different colours. Some have plain backs, others printed. Thus, there are 12 cards to collect. Values for cards with printed backs rise from £5 to £15 each. Plain back types with different colouring can sell for over £100.

British Chewing Sweets (aka Oh Boy Gum) issued the second series of British gum cards in history. The series was called *Photos of Footballers of the Principal Teams*.

Sixty glazed photographic cards were issued in exchange for Oh Boy Gum confectionery wrappers, so there are not many wrappers out there! Curiously, in the same year, 1933, across the Atlantic the American gum giant Goudey issued sports cards with the same brand name: Oh Boy Gum. The cards are surely related: same idea, same year, same product, same name (see also: Goudey Gum). Note: the glaze on the British Oh Boy Gum cards is often found cracked or otherwise damaged. Premium prices may be asked for cards with a perfect finish. There are rookies aplenty to find in this series due to the inclusion of smaller teams, yet there is no Stanley Matthews amongst the Stoke City cards. In 1933 the legendary player was only starting out. Fame and fortune were still a few months away. As well as Stoke City, this series includes four cards from each of these teams: Aston Villa, Birmingham, Chesterfield, Coventry, Derby, Leicester, Mansfield Town, Northampton Town, Nottingham Forest, Notts County, Port Vale, Walsall, West Brom, and Wolves. Values range from £75 to £200. Issuing wrappers, in which the cards came, are extremely rare and they are worth over £500. Only one is known!

Brooke Bond PG Tips printed a series of packet issues on boxes of tea and tea bags, in 1972. Packet issues are cards printed on wrappers, boxes, cartons, or within periodicals, to be cut-out and collected. The series was called *Place The Face Bingo* and there are 15 different cards known. One of these is a footballer, Jack Charlton of England and Leeds United. He was issued both as a single card, and in a combination with other famous people (Star Trek's Leonard Nimoy and actress Elizabeth Taylor are typical of others in the series). Values rise from £25, for a single of Jackie, to £50 for a trio. Note: Packet issues cut with plentiful borders are worth more than packet issues cut very closely or badly.

British Chewing Sweets, Oh Boy Gum wrapper and cards

Bruguera

Bruguera stickers, 1950s

Bruguera's earliest series were creative. Opening football card wrappers in the 1940s revealed stand-up cards, an Iberian first!

ruguera, or El Gato Negro (The Black Cat), was one of the most important 20th century names in soccer cards. Bruguera issued stickers, cards and albums, in Spain, from 1939 until 1968. World Greats and hall of fame players aplenty grace its collections. Whilst Britain was at war, without cards and with shortages of food, there were 18 different football collections issued in Spain in 1942! Bruguera was foremost, making many collections each year. Its energy was put to creating stylish and colourful stickers. The sheer scale of its output ensured they became Spanish sticker kings and retained the sceptre for some decades.

Bruguera's earliest series were creative. Opening football card wrappers in 1944 revealed stand-up cards, a continental first! Britain's Rover comic had issued similar stand-up players in 1926 but, much like soccer stickers (a British invention from 1914) others did things bigger and better. By the end of World War Two, Bruguera, in relatively peaceful Spain, was creating other cutting-edge cards, including forerunners of pogs. Bruguera's outlandish designs of the time used abstract and pop-art themes, and they remain some of the most creative and attractive stickers ever made. The *Campeones 1957* collection and the psychedelic *Ben-Day dots* issues of the 1950s included stars such as Alfredo di Stefano, Kubala, Gento and Luisito Suarez, players cherished by collectors nowadays. There will be more on Bruguera and its collections in a future issue.

Bryant and May

Bunsen cards 1920s

Bryant and May was a household name in the British Isles. In the 1970s the match makers issued a series of packet-issue cards called *Great British Achievements*. The cards were to be cut from illustrated match boxes. One of the series included a colourful card of Bobby Moore as England captain in 1966. Values for cut cards depend on content but Bobby Moore can cost £20. An entire, uncut matchbox may cost more than that!

Bucktrout Tobacco issued a 1927 series of cards called *Football Teams of The Bailiwick*. These cigarette cards deal with footballers from the Channel Islands. They are not expensive to collect and can be found for as little as £1 each. Bucktrout's 1928 series, *Football Teams*, featured 50 cigarette cards and has a wider appeal. These attractive and colourful cards feature mostly well-known teams. Like the 1927 issue the prices remain very reasonable and most can be found for £5 each. The company returned to local soccer in 1937, issuing about 80 *Guernsey Footballers*, each of whom comes on one of four different backs. Quite a collection of Guernsey players then! These are similar in design to the Taddy tobacco cards, *Prominent Footballers*.

Bulgaria cigarettes were made in Germany in the Weimar epoch. *Sport-Photos* consisted of 272 cards. Values are around £5 each but premium prices are paid for football greats and other sporting legends – if the cards are in top condition. In 1935 Bulgaria issued 283 sports pictures on paper called *Deutscher Sport Vorschau auf 1936*. Its values are similar to the earlier series. This is a very brief mention of one of the major cigarette cards issuers in pre-war Germany. More in a future issue of this book. For images see: www.footballsoccercards.com

Bunsen Confectionery cards are gems. Issued between 1922 and 1925, the *Famous Figures Series* contains over 500 cards. Values start at around £100 a card and rise to well over £1,000 each! In the 1990s this author published Football Card Collector, a bi-monthly magazine devoted to researching historical soccer cards. Therein was found the first ever checklist for Bunsen cards. In the last 25 years more information has come to light about this fascinating and exceedingly rare series. Cards numbering towards 1,000 are now known, though whether all of the numbers were printed is not known. Bunsen cards feature cricketers, tennis players, royalty, boxers, horse racing jockeys, athletes, etc. The series offers

a rare chance for Northfleet FC and Guildford United fans to get their hands on a football card showing their team. Otherwise, most of the footballers are from the London area, from clubs like Arsenal, Brentford, Chelsea, Fulham, Millwall, Orient, West Ham and Spurs. Few other teams make it though one Leicester City card is known. Tennis cards featuring Tilden and Lenglen, the Jimmy Connors and Chris Evert of their day, have been seen to sell for £300 each. World champion golfers on Bunsen cards will take prices over £1,000 for one card! In time soccer cards will catch up. There are more collectors, after all; the market is potentially massive for football cards of great rarity like these.

Buster & Jet was a comic of the 1970s. *My Favourite Soccer Stars* was a series of cards issued by the comic in 1970. The 32 cards (with blue backs) were collected weekly. They were issued in four sheets of eight, one sheet per comic. Sheets of cards in this expansive series were also issued by Scorcher & Score, The Tiger, Lion & Thunder, Valiant and also by TV21 comic. It's complex and costly to collect the lot! A similar series of cards with red backs was issued the following year. Values for uncut sheets start at around £25 and may rise to £50. Single cards are worth around £2 each.

M. Peters *(Spurs)*

R. Pointer *(Portsmouth)*

J. Winfield *(Nott'm Forest)*

T. Cooper *(Leeds)*

D. Nish *(Leicester)*

T. Paine *(Southampton)*

W. Carr *(Coventry)*

T. Hazell *(Q.P.R.)*

Presented free with BUSTER and JET, Oct. 23rd issue

Buster & Jet was a comic of the 1970s. *My Favourite Soccer Stars* **was a series of cards issued by the comic in 1970. The 32 cards (with blue backs) were collected weekly. They were issued in four sheets of eight, one sheet per comic.**

Cadbury's Milk Chocolate

     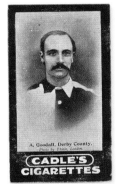

Keegan and McGrain by Cadbury's

Cadet sweets decals of John Charles

Cadle Cigarettes 1904 Derby County player

Cadbury's Milk Chocolate, *a glass and a half in every pound*, and *a finger of fudge to give your kids a treat*, so said the advertising by-lines. Occasionally real treats were actually given! In 1973 Cadbury's issued five footballer stickers called *Fantastic Football Badges*. Less like badges, more like stickers, the glossy paper footy stars were issued in exchange for eight wrappers from the dentist's friend, also known as *fudge*. The designs reflected the over-sized tinplate badges of the time and were meant to cover unfashionable, older badges bringing them up to date. Cadbury also issued 20 *World Cup 1974 Badges* of Scottish footballers. Values range from £10 to £50. The Scottish stickers are rarer than the English.

Cadet Sweets of Slough issued water-slide decals called *Footballers*, in 1954. The 48 transfers are very rare and values start at £25 each, rising sharply! In 1957 Cadet reprised transfers in a new series called *All-Sports*. The 48 sportsmen included are much rarer than those from 1954. Prices paid for some of the golfers, boxers and tennis stars have exceeded £300 each! In 1958 Cadet Sweets issued a set of *Footballers* cards. Including varieties there are

200 cards known, so it's handy that their values are low, starting at just £1 each.

Cadle cigarettes issued 20 Footballers in 1904. They remain affordable for such antiquities. Values range from £50 to £100.

Caramelos Carsel, a Portuguese confectioner, issued *Desfile Dos Famosos Futebolistas Mundiais* in 1966. These stickers are very similar to the World Cup cards of 1962 issued by Lampo in Italy, and to the stickers issued by Vecchi, in Brazil. The 1966 series uses many of the same images. Distinguishable by the red lettering and numbering the issue contains British players and world greats galore!

Caramelo Futbol cards were issued in Spain after World War One. They were given freely by confectioners. Very few of these colourful, yet fragile paper cards survive. The handful that do are now worth thousands of pounds each. Ricardo Zamora, Josep Samitier and Paolino Alcántara are known but only one extant example of each is known!

Carreras was an issuer of very attractive soccer cigarette cards. Like many inter-war tobacco cards they are not rare, and prices remain very affordable. In 1934 Carreras launched *Footballers*, a series of 75 cards, one per packet of

cigarettes. There are two versions of this series, one with larger lettering, and another with smaller typeface. Most of these can be found easily and inexpensively. It followed up with *Famous Footballers*, a series of 48 cards. Half of this series would be redrawn and printed as a new set of cards, later in the year. Values for both types are low and cards can be found and afforded easily. In 1936 the firm issued *Popular Footballers*, a set of 36 similarly attractive cards. After the war Carreras returned to soccer cards. In 1948 it produced footballers on its cigarette boxes, on the card sliders. More and more post-war packets were being made of card, not paper, and there was less need for card stiffeners – that's how cigarette cards came to be. Players were printed on the cigarettes slider, and could be cut out and collected. Uncut slides are worth upwards of £10 each but cut cards

Ricardo Zamora by Caramelo Futbol c.1919

can be found for £1 each. In 1951 yet more cards on sliders were issued. The series called *Famous Footballers* are known in pairs (from bigger boxes of cigarettes) and as single slides. Uncut doubles sell for more than £20 each.

Casera issued fizzy drinks, in sunny Spain. Its *Campeonao Mundial de Fùtbol* stickers fetch up to £100! The stickers were licensed by Fher, then over-printed with the brand name, Casera. They are similar to the 1966 stickers issued by Cibeles chocolates, and also those by Fher. Notably, the Casera sticker of Lev Yashin is markedly different to his stickers in the other collections. Pelé, Eusebio, Beckenbauer and the English players all command premium prices, as does Yashin.

Casket issued football fixture cards with tobacco during 1905–1908. Values for these exceed £750 each! They were designed to be redeemed for free pouches of tobacco, and most were probably traded in. Few have survived. Only English clubs from the midlands and the north of England are known.

Casket and Critic Cigarettes, by Pattreiouex Tobacco, issued *Famous Footballers & Football Teams* in 1922. Numbered F1 to F241, most cards are of a smaller size (numbered up to F191) but the team and cup cards are larger (numbered to F241). The larger cards were issued in higher-priced boxes of cigarettes. The smaller cards came with economy paper packets. Titled, *high class photos*, a complete sub-set of 50 team cards, including both versions of the Manchester City card – there are two – has only been recorded twice! For many years it was believed that only 49 larger cards were issued. Due to the number of rookies in the team line-ups, and the fact that the large cards are needed to complete the F1 collection (F1 to F241) the larger, rarer cards often command very high prices. Proof cards with plain backs are also known to exist. Values for small cards up to F191 are around £20 each. For larger cards prices start at £50 but exceed £500 for certain teams. Casket and Trawler Cigarettes also issued three series of smaller, *Famous Footballers* cards, in 1923. The *FA series*, the *FB series* and the *FC series* included 96 cards each. Values are around £15 for these highly attractive and rare photographic cards. See also: Pattreiouex.

Castello of Italy issued *Lo Sport* in 1961. The series includes Joe Baker, Denis Law, John Charles and Jimmy Greaves. You'll have to pay up to £100 each for these exceedingly rare stickers of British players – if you can find them!

Castoldi cards were issued, in 1948, in sheets to be cut. A single sheet featured 12 cards. British Isles players feature amongst Italians, including Paddy Sloan, for AC Milan; and William Jordan in Juve colours. For identification, the cards have film strip edges, a circled black number, and a club badge. The issue is very similar to Nannina cards from the time. Values for uncut sheets are around £250 for some teams. Cut single cards can be had for £5 each but the above-named Arsenal and Spurs players will exceed this figure. See also: Nannina.

Cedip, of Italy, issued *Campionato di Calcio* in 1961. Its 198 exotic cards include Joe Baker, Denis Law, John Charles and Jimmy Greaves. Values exceed £50 each for these British players. See also: Nuzzi.

CET issued *Forza Goal Figurine Discoidale* in 1967. The collection consisted of early plastic pogs. This Italian issuer's wares are very rare so expect high prices.

> Casket issued football fixture cards with tobacco during 1905-1908. Values for these exceed £750 each!

Caramelos Carsel Charlton (right) with a smaller, Spanish Casera Charlton (left)

Castoldi cards cut from bigger sheets

A cut Carreras Turf slider of Stan Mortensen

Casket cards, smaller and larger types including Dick Kerr's Ladies

Champion Sportsmen of the World cards from an uncut strip of four

Champion

The Champion Album of Famous Footballers

Champion was a 1920s British comic. Like its rivals, Adventure and Boys' Magazine, it issued trade cards to attract readers. *Sporting Champions*, of 1922, included 34 monochrome cards. Alternative footballers were issued for the readership in Scotland – and they are worth the most (up to £50 each), far more than typical prices paid for English cards (less than £5 each). Champion followed this series with *Famous Football Captains*. Comprising 28 cards, these often paired players. Values for such pairs are higher if they remain uncut. Cut doubles are worth very little indeed. In 1923 *Famous Footballers* and *Famous British Record Breakers* added eight more cards to Champion's oeuvre. Values for many 1922–1923 cards are around £3 each. However, a seller can expect to multiply this price by a very large factor if a card is sold with an original comic, the particular issue with which it was given. Prices over £100 have been seen for such rare combinations, partly because of the cross-over to the comics market.

In 1925 Champion allied with a sister comic to issue its 22 *English League (Div.1) Footer Captains*. Of these, 11 were issued with The Champion, and 11 with The Triumph. The venture

was a success and encouraged young readers to cross over to the other comic. In 1926 *Famous Footer* Internationals reprised the scheme. Twenty-four cards were issued, half with The Champion, and half with The Triumph. Values for both series range from £5 to £30 each card.

During the 1920s and 30s Champion issued mini-magazines of English and Scottish teams. These *League Photo Albums* were not meant for clipping yet the blue-tinted team pictures within are often found cut and sold singly. Cutting pages ruins the value of otherwise attractive, rare and valuable booklets. Uncut they sell for upwards of £30 each whereas cut pages – single teams – may struggle to make even £1 each.

Glossy photos of Famous Footballers were some of the world's earliest soccer stickers. In 1930 Champion issued one of the earliest sticker album collections in the world: *The Champion Album Of Famous Footballers*. The 1930 *glossy photos* (the stickers were so advertised) came out weekly, in sheets of eight stickers. They are circular, square and of other geometric forms, and all are monochrome. An album was given, in which to glue the stickers. Uncut sheets sell for £150 each, and a complete album is worth about the same. Individual,

cut stickers sell for prices up to £20. Such was the success of the series that Champion's gifts returned again and again to the sticker and album format. *Record Breakers* included 64 stickers of sportsmen, including Dixie Dean and Hughie Gallacher. Some of these stamps have been seen to sell for almost £100! Such high prices resulted in a lot of albums being destroyed, cut for single stickers, so the price for a complete album has risen and it's now worth about £200.

A third album, *Sportsmen of the World*, was issued in 1934. Its 32 sportsmen cards were given weekly, in strips of four. An uncut quad of cards is worth between £50 and £100, depending on the players included though individual cut cards sell for less than £5 each. The complete album is not rare, as most cards were cut, stuck down and kept. It can be found for less than £50.

Soccer's Wily Wizards was one of eight Champion sports folders issued in 1935. Designed to be collected into a *Portfolio Of Sport* booklet, the miniature card folder contains a concertina of seven soccer images. Other folders in the series included boxers, racers, cricketers, etc. This particular soccer folder includes Dixie Dean and Alec James and will cost

Champion Record Breakers, Dixie Dean

The value for uncut football folders is £75 each.

Champion Autographs album

Champion Portfolio of Sport

over £100 if it's free from glue damage – most were glued into the portfolio. The *Portfolio Of Sport* was so successful that Champion issued a second, similar collection. Its folders, which included *Football's Finest Goal-Getters* and *Wizards of the Football Field*, were to be collected into *The Champion Sports Wallet*. The value for uncut football folders is £75 each.

The 1930s was fast becoming a decade of sticker albums. Champion issued more of the same starting with *Autographs*, in 1935. It's the earliest of a trio of similar autograph sticker collections. It had spaces for 120 autograph stickers, to be set alongside the art deco printed images within the album. To distinguish it from later issues this album has a cover in red and white, and it shows ten blue sporting vignettes. In 1936, *Famous Footballers Autographs & Photographs* became the second of the trio of albums. This is the only one that is devoted to football autographs. The final album is, once again, titled *Autographs* but the series is also known as *100 Autographs Of Famous Sportsmen*. To identify this album, to distinguish it from the others, the cover shows a cricketer, a jockey, boxers and a speedway rider upon quartered colours. Unusually this collection also includes train drivers' autographs! As kings of speed they too were stars in their day. Uncut sheets of autograph stickers are worth £75 each. Single, cut autographs have nominal values. Full sets in albums are worth £50 to £100 each.

In 1936, Champion's sister magazine, The Pilot, issued a

similar collection to *Sportsmen of the World*. The set consisted of an album and cards. The cards, issued in eight strips of four, were to be cut and inserted into the album. The cards are inscribed simply, *Football Fame Series*, and are often confused with Champion issues, hence their inclusion at this point in the book. The collection can be acquired inexpensively but uncut strips of cards are very rare and prices paid often exceed £50.

The last pre-war Champion issue was *Prominent Football Teams* in 1938. Sheets of three cards were issued, to be cut. Values for uncut trios are over £50 each whereas cut single teams can be found easily at around £3 each. After the war, in 1950, Champion issued *Stars of the Sports World*.

Champion Prominent Football Teams strip of three

Like Adventure comic's cut-out footballers, these were to be cut and collected. The 64 stickers are rare, especially uncut. Also known as *The Champions Weekly Picture Gallery*, uncut pages have sold for £25 each and a full album has been seen to sell for over £200. It took some years until the next free soccer gift, 17 years to be exact! In 1967 Champion issued *The Lion and Champion Album of Soccer Stars*. It included 110 stickers, issued in sheets of 25s and 15s. The collection of red-framed tiny photos boasted, '*specially picked by Carson's Cubs*'. Well, yippee ki-yay! Uncut sheets fluctuate in value, from £25 to £40, depending upon the players included, though cut singles barely manage to make even £1.

Charles Buchan Football Monthly

Charles Buchan Collectors Club postcard and Charles Buchan World Stars

Charles Buchan Football Monthly was *the* soccer magazine of the mid-century modern era. Named after a legend in the game, Charles Buchan was also a founding member of the Football Writers' Association. The magazine created a collectors club, in the 1960s, which allowed readers to send away for photographic postcards, and suchlike. These have become valuable, and prices can exceed £25 for certain teams and stars. The postcards can be identified by the copyright number. Some have blank backs, others come with postcard-style backs. See also: Longacre Press.

In 1969 the magazine issued its own sticker and album collection: *World Stars*. Eighty small stickers were issued in sheets of 20, to cut. Today, uncut sheets of stickers have values from £50 to £100 each though a full album is only worth around £25 as most sheets were cut and single stickers were stuck down. Cut singles have nominal values, though Pelé will always top £10. The sheets with Pelé, George Best and Eusebio fetch the highest prices.

Charlesworth & Austin was a very elegant brand of cigarettes. In 1902 it issued 20 *Cricketers*. It includes a card of a legendary footballer, one Charles Burgess Fry. The value for this card is around £750.

It's Chinese to me! Casca and idioms aside, cigarette cards with abstruse Chinese lettering and pictorial hints on football were issued by British & American Tobacco, but you won't find that name on the cards. The Chinese script will be illegible to most western collectors but a set of 50 may bring a seller £30. Copied from cards issued by Players cigarettes, these were issued in Hong Kong.

Chix issued football gum cards during the 1950s. The English and Welsh issue, *Famous Footballers*, consisted of 48 coloured cards in six different, numbered issues: three series are numbered 1–48, while three series came in halves, numbered 1–24 and 25–48. Further, the various series are known to contain errors, picture varieties and other printing anomalies. Values remain low for most of these cards. Complete albums can be found for less than £50 and though values do rise for rarer variations most singles fetch just £1 or £2 each. The Scottish Chix cards are a different matter! A 1953 series issued only north of the border, *Famous Scottish Footballers*, comprised 24 black and white photographic cards whose rarity and value factor

Chinese language cards from Hong Kong

Chix cards: a pair of similar cards from different issues

Chix Scottish cards from 1953

Chix's Charles Buchan
Magazine card

is extremely high. Such cards are worth £50 to £100 each! Chix also issued 24 unbranded Scottish stars in 1959: *Famous Footballers SFBL1*. Typical values for these cards range from £10 to £25 each – look out for a certain Liverpool goalie.

Chix mimicked Bell Boy's style with its 1960 series, *Facts & Feats*, a collection of 50 gum inserts made of waxy paper, of which the sports-related issues are highly sought after. Later in 1960 Chix returned to gum cards with a series showing footballers in action and in portraiture. These twin-image cards are known in three types: cards with black and pink caricature backs (the rarest type, worth £40 each); cards with monotone caricature backs (the commonest type, worth £2 each); and cards with backs that display advertising but no image (these are worth £20 each). In 1961 Chix joined forces with Charles Buchan Football Monthly, issuing *Famous Footballers*, a set of 50 cards inscribed *Buchan Publications*. The widely distributed cards remain low in value and easily obtainable, at about £2 each.

Chocolate Juncosa was a Spanish issuer of splendid soccer cards during the 1920s.

A sample series, for there is too much to list in this volume, is *Campeonato de España 1927-28*, an issue comprising 21 cards of football teams. Values range from £20 to £50 each, depending on the team. Many all-time world greats and soccer legends feature on Juncosa cards and some sell for well over £100 each. In a future book there will be much more on this fascinating firm, and its rivals.

Churchman is a name beloved of cigarette card sellers. No matter the volume of cards made, nor their relative commonness, their beauty and scarcity assures perpetual sales. In 1907 Churchman started out with soccer by issuing *50 Football Club Colours*. The pictures are of unnamed footballers, for example, the Derby County card shows Steve Bloomer, and Alexander Tait is the player seen on the Spurs card. It's quite a challenge to name them all! Values start at around £10 for less popular cards but may rise considerably for Bloomer and other notable players. There are actually 51 cards in the series no matter that the cards themselves state 50. The series is very similar to that issued by Ogden's in 1906 and is quite easy to come by.

Churchman's rarest series of soccer cards is a dull issue of 50 cards, in sepia, called simply *Footballers*. Released in 1914, the sombre series seems like a memoriam to the grim state of world affairs to come. Many footballers would perish in battle. Such cards often sell for £40 or more. Easier to find are the coloured Churchman

Juncosa card of Josep Samitier

Churchman 1914

Cibeles Gordon Banks
from 1966 and 1970

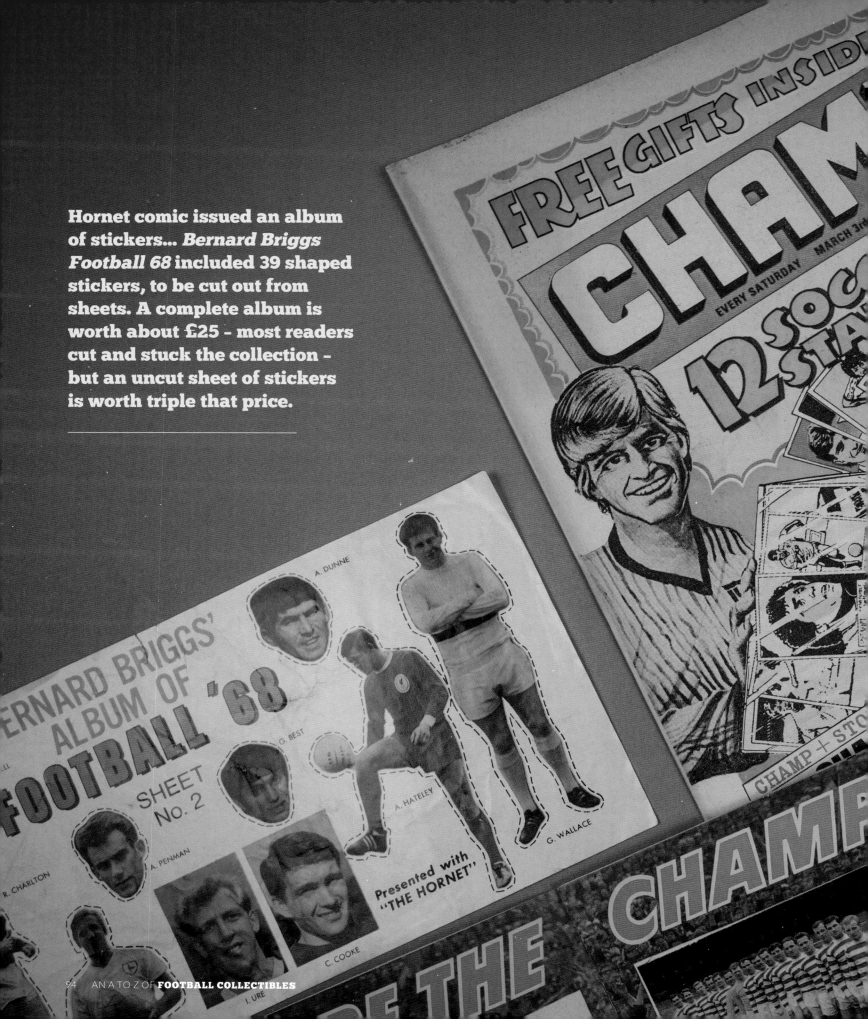

Hornet comic issued an album of stickers... *Bernard Briggs Football 68* included 39 shaped stickers, to be cut out from sheets. A complete album is worth about £25 – most readers cut and stuck the collection – but an uncut sheet of stickers is worth triple that price.

Footballers cards with action scenes and oval portraits. These colourful cards sell singly for about £20. Churchman issued more soccer cards in 1931, as part of a pan-sport series, *Sporting Celebrities*. In 1938 the firm released *Association Footballers*, followed by *Association Footballers, 2nd series*. These cards are readily available and cost a mere £1 or £2 each.

Cibeles stickers came with chocolates. Issued in 1966, in Spain, *Campeonato Mundial de Fùtbol* was licensed by Fher, whose stickers are overprinted with the Cibeles logo, making for some unusual variations to regular stickers. Similar to the issue by Casera, the series includes rare stickers of Pelé, Yashin, Eusebio, Beckenbauer and the English World Cup winning stars. Values for suchlike start around £25 each and rise to £100. Cibeles issued *Campeones y Estrellas* in 1967. A mixed collection of sportsmen and TV personalities, it includes stickers of Bobby Moore, Bobby Charlton and Jimmy Greaves. These can be easily identified by the offer, on the back, of a free ticket in a raffle to win a Seat car. Values for these English greats start at £35 each.

In 1970 Cibeles were back with more rebranded Fher stickers. Cibeles's *Mexico 70* includes unusual and attractive variations of otherwise familiar stickers. Pelé and the English players attract prices upwards of £25 each.

Cicogna means stork, in Italian. A year after the end of World War Two, footballers on diminutive trade cards started to reappear in the impoverished, war-torn peninsula. Some of them were made by the brand named after the bird. Cicogna (pronounced chick-ON-yah) issued cards until the 1960s but a mere sample of their wares is covered here. There will be more in a future book and more can be seen on the footballsoccercards.com website. In late 1945 Cicogna issued *Sportsmen*, a series of small, cellulose cards with Italian flags to either flank. Values for such rarities exceed £50 each. Similar, coloured designs made of card followed. The flags were replaced, in 1946, by black and white borders (on all four sides) for a series of 100 footballers in action, set into both landscape and portrait format cards. Many, though not all, have circular insets of a player's face. A bigger series, of 200 cards, was released in 1947. These have black and white borders (on just two sides) which resemble the sprockets of movie projection film stock. They also feature a giant, golden ball behind the players. In 1948 Cicogna issued *Tuttocalcio Serie A & B*, comprising 400 cards. These can be identified by the black and white chevron frames, a small, golden ball and shield-shaped club colours. Names and numbers are in rectangles and squares. *Omnia Sports* followed in 1949. It was a pan-sport series of 100 sportsmen. These cards have tri-colour chevron borders and include Paddy Sloan, the Irishman who managed both Irish international teams. Sloan was also a Brentford, Arsenal, and Sheffield United player, not to mention AC Milan. His card will fetch over £50 but most others from the series can be had for much less. Cicogna returned to football with *Tuttocalcio* in 1949/50, issuing 200 cards identifiable by 5 Olympic rings which appear on every card.

Cicogna opted for a starkly different design to mark the half-century. In 1949/50 footballers in strips of 4 were issued. Separated to singles the cards can be identified by the perforations (like those of stamps) and the 3 yellow & white horizontal bands in the background. Values start at £10 each but prices paid for complete strips of 4 can exceed £100. In 1950 Cicogna pressed on with different designs, issuing a series of two footballers on single cards: one face shows a monotone caricature while the other shows a different player set against a giant football. Values for star players exceed £10 each. Expect to pay more still for Piola! For more types of cards by Cicogna, including 1950s and 1960s designs, some of which feature British stars, go to footballsoccercards.com website.

Cigarillos Londres silk cigarette cards came from Buenos Aires. Made by a firm called Danckleman & Schrader the beautiful satiny football teams may cost you more than £50 each – if you can find them! The Similar sounding Cigarillos Plus Ultra was another Argentine brand from the golden age of Tango. Its 1920s cigarette cards of footballers & teams command values of up to £200 for stars like Andrade. There will be more on such South American rarities in a future book.

City Bakeries was a Scottish firm. To commemorate the first post-war World Cup it launched 24 *Soccards* in 1950. *Soccards* [sic] is the collection name displayed on the front of each shield-shaped card. Each features a generic design showing two footballers shaking hands. The *Soccard* set includes Australia and New Zealand. Though neither country played in the 1950 World Cup the Anzac nations were highly favoured friends and allies, and very much in the public eye due to their independence movements. The inclusion of Austria but neither West nor East German teams speaks volumes about public feeling at the time. The value of cards from this rare release is over £50 each. During the early 1950s City Bakeries issued an enormous series of cards of British football clubs. 300 monotone shield-shaped cards nowadays fetch prices of between £25 and £100. The

Cicogna, 4 cards from 1950.

Cicogna 1950 strip of cards with Faas Wilkes

Clark's Toffee cards of 1925 remain some of the rarest and most valuable footballer trade cards ever printed. The 78 cards issued are inscribed, Presented With Clark's Toffee. Their values exceed £400 per card!

City Bakeries card from 1978

City Bakeries shields, 1950-1954

Clark's Toffee cards from 1925

series spanned four years of issue and there are up to four cards for each club. Generic designs of football action, and illustrations of footballers, come with differing text styles, contrasting letterpress and various generic graphics. The cards are made of different grades of cardstock and paper. They usually have plain backs. Up to ten different types of letterpress on the card fronts are known. In 1954 the firm added individual footballers to the collection. Twenty-four players are known. Their values range from £75 to £150. The footballers are mostly Scottish, like Torry Gillick and Willie Woodburn, but from England there's Stanley Matthews of Blackpool.

Whether the firm called City Bakeries, of 1978, is the same as the 1950s baker remains a mystery but for in that year City Bakeries issued 24 *World Cup All-Time Greats*. Values for these cards exceed £40 each.

Clark's Toffee cards of 1925 remain some of the rarest and most valuable footballer trade cards ever printed. The 78 cards issued are inscribed, *Presented With Clark's Toffee*. Their values exceed £400 per card!

Clarke, Nicholls & Coombs, also known as Clarnico, issued a wide range of footballer cards without title, in 1922. The 96 known cards are sized similarly to cigarette cards. They are usually found in monotone black and white, but are also

known in sepia. Both types can be found with rubber stamp impressions from other firms, for example, Poppleton of York has been seen on the backs of some cards. It seems the cards may have been produced by an independent printer and used by two or more firms independently of each other. This was once a common practice. The cards are worth £50 to £250 each, the highest prices being paid for notable players.

Clarke's 1902 *Football Series* cigarette cards are valued at about £30 each card, with exceptional prices being paid for certain world greats. See also Wills Cinderella cards, a sister series from 1902, which used the same images.

Clevedon Confectionery issued very attractive cards of footballers and even *Football Club Managers* with their sweets, in the 1950s. The rarest are the managers. They were issued in two versions, with violet and with light blue backgrounds. The set includes Johnny Carey and Matt Busby. Such cards have been known to sell for over £100 each! Other series, like *Famous Football Clubs*, and *International Sporting Stars* are worth around £3 each card but certain notable sportsmen and women may fetch much more.

The Clifford Series of cards was issued in 1950. A so-called *First Edition* was all that was produced. Fifty cards were issued stapled together in booklets of nine. Values depend upon

Clarnico card of legendary sportsman Max Woosnam

Clifford card of Bill Shankley

Cloetta card from Sweden

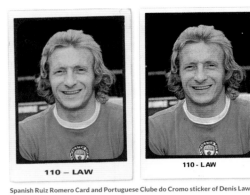

Spanish Ruiz Romero Card and Portuguese Clube do Cromo sticker of Denis Law

Cohen and Weenen cigarette cards

trim and condition, and the particular player. These cards were issued as trading cards rather than as trade cards. Closely trimmed cards – people tried to cut away the staple holes – are common and their values are lower. Values for un-trimmed cards start around £40 yet can exceed £100 for the most sought-after players. A booklet of nine cards would fetch £250 or more.

Cloetta, of Sweden, issued cards of sportsmen in 1934. The series of about 190 cards includes mostly native Swedes but there are some notable exceptions, like the boxers Jack Dempsey and Gene Tunney; and tennis players like Fred Perry. Also included is David Jack for Arsenal. There are officially 168 cards in this collection but there are over 20 variations to collect too, so look out for cards of the same number bearing different images. Most cards can be had for less than £5 but you may have to pay £100 or more for the notable international sportsmen. See also: Alifabolaget

Clube do Cromo issued stickers in 1974 in Portugal. *Futebol Campeonato Mundial Munique 74* included hundreds of soccer cards commemorating World Cup 74. These cards include many Scottish players. They are similar to those issued the same year in Spain but include notable differences in print matrices, names and

the paper used. The Scotland-related footballers have been seen to sell for up to £30 each.

Coffer was ubiquitous in the London of 1970. It was a commercial firm that made footballer postcards. hundreds of different cards were made. Values range from £5 to £30 each card. Coffer wares were sold by tourism stores in central London and by vendors outside football grounds across Great Britain. Values start at £5 a card.

Cohen & Weenen was a cigarette producer of Victorian times. In 1897 it issued *Heroes of Sport* cards. The set includes 44 footballers. The cards are marked with the brand name *Circus Girl*. Most cards are worth between £100 and £200 each but exceptions are known to have smashed the higher figure. In 1900 the firm issued 250 *Celebrities*, with Sweetcrop cigarettes. Values for these cards range from £25 to £100 each, with even higher prices paid for legendary sportsmen. There are seven footballer cards in the *Celebrities* series but you'll need 14 if you want all of the known variations in lettering. The set includes C.B. Fry and G.O. Smith and their cards have been seen to sell for sums exceeding three figures.

Cohen & Weenen included footballers in its 1905 series, *Actresses, Footballers and Jockeys*. It comprised 40 photographic cards whose

values may exceed £100 for footballers. In 1906 *Owners, Jockeys, Footballers, Cricketers, series* two was issued. Its 52 cigarette cards included nine footballers. A year later, *Owners, Jockeys, Footballers, Cricketers, series 3* included but eight footballers. Values for cards from both series are around £20 each. In 1908 a series dedicated solely to soccer, *Football Captains 1907-8*, included 60 footballers. They are worth around £25 each.

Colgate Palmolive, the scent of 1960s bathrooms, issued sanitary goods with football cards to celebrate the 1970 World Cup. Very rare *Mexico 70* packet issue footballers are known. To help identify these unbranded cards, the backs are plain, and the fronts sport a red, top corner, in which lies a number. The series includes some of the England stars of 1966. Values start at £25 each card.

Colinville was a British gum issuer of the 1950s. Around 1958/59 the firm issued tiny, black and white cards known as *International Footer Photos*. The 48 cards, if free of gum residue, are valued between £25 and £200 each! The series title, as shown on the waxy paper wrappers, reads *FOOTER bubble gum FOTO* [sic]. It differs to that on the album which calls the series *Football Supporters*

Colinville wrapper

Colinville album page with Jimmy Greaves and a similar card by Soiree Cigarettes

Pocket Album: British International Footer-fotos. The cards display player names but not team names, and the backs are blank. The team names for the cards are only found in the album, where there are one or two errors. The Don Revie card has a Manchester City spot in the album but he's seen in the stripes of the Black Cats – he was at Sunderland, and had long since parted company with City. Another design error has Trevor Ford appearing alongside a Cardiff City legend. He'd been long gone from Ninian Park – for two years – when this series was launched. The series was not issued before the 1958/59 season as some sellers have disingenuously claimed. Cliff Jones is here, for Spurs, a club he had not played for until spring 1958, and there is a celebratory feeling about the collection, with Irish, Scottish and Welsh World Cup 1958 players making appearances. However, the dating could be later due to the inclusion of a lesser known Harry Haddock, of Clyde. Haddock did not play in the World Cup but he did win the 1958/59 *Scottish Footballer Of The Year* prize, the so-called Rex Kingsley Award, which was given in 1959. If he's included because of that award then

this is a 1959 collection and both the Bobby Charlton card and the Jimmy Greaves rookie cards are 1959 issues, not 1958 as some sellers have claimed. Colinville's gum cards were printed by Gordon & Company but many of the photos used were also used for the extremely rare, coloured tobacco cards issued by Soirée Cigarettes, in autumn 1958. Sadly there's no Brian Clough, nor Nat Lofthouse, in the Colinville series, though they both appear on Soirée cards. Rookie card collectors take note: the Jimmy Greaves and Bobby Charlton cards, though early, are not as early as the Soirée cards. The Soirée cards are far rarer, and much prettier too.

Comet Sweets (C.S. Ltd) issued a 1963 series of trade cards called *Footballers and club colours.* The 50 cards are easily available and values remain below £2 each.

Comic Life of 1922 issued four paired cards of sportsmen known as *Sports Champions.*

Values for uncut pairs are between £20 and £40 each. The series includes three footballers and the legendary boxer Jack Dempsey. See also: Lot-o-Fun for a similar set of four paired cards issued in that publication.

Compton's Gravy Salts issued *Football Clubs Series A, Series B, Series C, and Series D* trade cards with their meaty stock. The earliest cards are in colour and came out between 1923 and 1926. They have printed backs and their values range from £30 to over £100 for the rarest types. In 1927 the firm cheapened its ephemera with a series of 22 black and white cards, *Football Clubs*

A, which were issued with plain backs. A similar monotone series appeared later in the year but *Football Clubs B* is known in two types, with and without the legend *'see other side'.* Values for these cards range from £20 to £80 each. The rarest type of Compton's Gravy Salts football card is a variant of *Football Clubs B* and it appears with a blue ink, rubber-stamped back.

The Co-op (Co-operative Society) was once a very successful British general store. In 1982 it ventured into football cards with *España 82.* The Co-op was a store lost in time, a little out of touch with the ugly, modern world, and quaintly refreshing because of it. There was barbershop hair cutting off the menswear department, where you could be measured up for a bespoke suit by a dandy chap asking about your inside leg. It sold food, hosiery, ironmongery, flooring, toys, vinyl records, curtains, glassware – and World Cup 1982 cards! The challenge of tackling this huge collection reflects the frailties of its behemoth issuer. Some cards were issued in sheets, others not. Some cards are known with three different types of back. Some cards were produced for an album whilst others were made for a poster – but which one? There were two posters to collect. One was Scottish, the other one English. Today, uncut sheets of cards may sell for decent prices but shortly after 1982 masses of unsold, excess stock was burned! A full set of all the varieties, albums and posters would be quite a sight and cost a fair amount too. Uncut sheets are worth over £20 each but singles have only nominal value.

Copcards! During the 1980s Kent, Northumbria and other local police forces got together with local businesses – and the England Football Team – to produce police soccer cards! Such cards usually carry advertising for local businesses and products, thereby confusing collectors as to the issuer, so we now use the generic term Copcards, for clarity. In a vain but well meant attempt to encourage children away from train lines, and on to soccer pitches; to steer wayward youth from illicit drugs, towards mown grass and *astroturf*, police officers gave out the cards as little lessons in life. Children of the time were often cynical of such ploys. Unimpressed by the cards some used them to set fire to things,

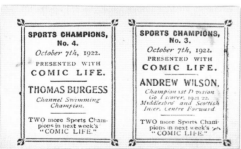

Comic Life cards

Compton's Gravy Salts cards

Copcards

Cope Cigarette cards

Courage England World Cup 82 beer mat

while others found the firmness of the card was stout enough to slide into door fissures and prise open weakly latched locks. Arson and burglary went up, just as football came down in a depressing wave of hooliganism and tragedy. Copcards can be found for as little as £5 each though rarer types now top £20 each.

Cope Brothers issued cigarettes. In 1908 Cope released a series of footballer cards with their Solace brand tobacco. *Noted Footballers* included 195 cards, all numbered, with plain backs. These delicate photo cards are often found with cracked glazing due to aging. Values start at around £25 but soar to £250 for rarer, sought-after players. In 1909 Copes launched a fresh series of *Noted Footballers* with their Clips brand of cigarettes. The 120 cards are numbered and have printed backs. Values range from £15 to £50 each. The following year Copes issued 282 more *Noted Footballers* with Clips Cigarettes, for which values are higher, at £20 to £100 each card. In 1911 a third series of *Noted Footballers* included 501 cards! Most are numbered but one unnumbered card proves exceptional. Values start at £25 and may exceed £200 for the rarest.

Corriere dei Piccoli was a 1960s Italian magazine for kids. In 1966 the England team was given half of a full-page. Printed to be cut out, a selection of players was given stand-up status.

Similar self-standing players from Manchester United, Celtic and other British teams also came to be published.

Counterfeit cards. Illicit copies of some rare cards are known. When the rarest cards sell for thousands (some American cards have sold for millions!) it's not surprising that some cards get copied. Entire collections, like those issued by 1960s sticker firms Edis and Imperia, have also been copied. Peruvian printers have been known to reproduce rare sticker albums including the first FKS issue, originally issued by World Distributors. Cards purporting to be Edis originals of George Best, or pretending to be 1958 Brazilian stickers of Pelé are known. Forgeries of rare 1960s Panini cards and packets have also been spotted. Football caricature cards of 1967 from Argentina, purportedly original Crack cards – but not – have also been seen. Though there are differences between the originals and the fakes, notably the paper or cardstock used, not to mention the printing quality – aroma is hard to fake! Old cards do not smell like new print and virgin paper. Be careful! Copyists are out there, and fake stuff sometimes surfaces on the internet. Collectors are advised to buy from reputable sellers, like those mentioned in this book. Trade with knowledgeable suppliers you trust and maintain a vigil with others. If cards

seem too clean, they probably are. Too mint to be true? Caveat Emptor.

Take Courage! The brewer, John Courage, launched various series of soccer cards in the early 1980s. *Know Your Team, Sporting Heroes* and *World Cup* 82 are examples of their beer mat football series. Collecting public house breweriana overlaps with cartophily. Football beer mats are fascinating additions to any card collection. They also offer a reminder of how bad the England team was, back then. If only Brian Clough and Peter Taylor had been national manager and coach in 1982. [This entry is dedicated to one of this writer's favourite scribes, baron of barstool banter, the one and only Jeffrey Bernard, RIP.]

Crack has been a River Plate issuer since the 1960s. It produced spectacular football cards and stickers in Argentina and Uruguay, some of which have become highly sought-after, like the various Pelé cards issued either side of the Rio De La Plata estuary. Of extraordinary note is a 1978 issue. The *Crack Argentina 78* series mirrored various sticker series in Europe (Fher, FKS, AGEducatifs, etc.) but with a crucial difference – it included a sticker of The Hand Of God! In fact, it included more than one of Diego Maradona. The Crack Maradonas will cost you up to £200 each!

Credit cards. Bank credit cards from the 1990s boom sometimes came with football club

Counterfeit and genuine Pelé cards

Cropan stickers of Wolves and Dundee United

Cresent later issues, two types

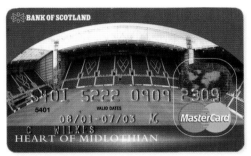

Credit card Hearts football team card

Cropan Johan Cruyff Goool!

Cresent earlier issues, two types

affiliated deals. Such cards featured football clubs. Teams, stadia and emblems appeared on Visa and Mastercards. Values start at £100 each. Rarely seen for sale, most credit cards are destroyed after their validity has expired. Few remain for the collector. Much like phonecards these are an integral part of cartophily.

Cropan issued a set of Johan Cruyff stickers and cards in 1974. *Asi Juego al futbol! Johan Cruyff* values start at around £10 each. In 1975 Cropan went on to issue a series of very attractive world football club emblems on glossy and colourful stickers. This series of club crests and team badges includes many British clubs. Values start at £30 each.

In 1976 Cropan issued *Goool!* The series comprised colourful stickers set within frames, much like the 1977 Ava Americana peel-out stickers. These days few remain unused, fewer still remain in mint condition with frames intact. Top prices have been paid for the original unused sticker of Cruyff – of £200! Values for others in the series are around £30.

Crescent Confectionery was a British sweet cigarettes producer from 1923–25. *The Great Novelty House*, as it was known, issued 100 cards with greenish-grey backs. These rare cards display the firm's address: *37 Crescent, Salford*. There are 100 different cards known but they were issued in

two series of 50 cards each. One issue is slightly smaller than the other. The earliest cards were issued in 1923. The second series dates from 1925. Values for the cards start at £100 each. Some have been seen to sell for more than £500! The demise of the first Crescent firm, sometime before 1926, led to the company being re-founded by different owners.

Crescent Confectionery (1926) Limited [sic] was the later incarnation of Crescent Confectionery Limited. In 1927 the newly registered Crescent firm launched a general series of trade cards. The cards have plain backs and were issued in 10 sub-sets of 10 cards each. A decem featured players of one sport, or pictures on one theme, including military, royalty, views, ships, etc. The eighth decem consisted of 10 footballers. Values for these start at £100 but may exceed £500! The Crescent Confectionery of 1926 issued more sports cards in 1930. Its series of *Sportsmen* included 100 footballers, cricketers and golfers, etc. The cards are numbered to the front, below the titles. They have plain backs. A certain golfer card from this series has been seen to sell for over £1,000. Most cards are valued between £100 and £500.

Crosse & Blackwell, the food firm, issued a series of footballers in 1970. *World Cup Action* included 16 cut-out, stand-up footballer cards.

Values of uncut cards start at £50 each!

Cypal International issued a set of Liverpool and Manchester United player cards in 1977. Values start at £30 each and may exceed £100 for the most sought-after stars!

Daily Citizen

Daily Citizen supplement of Cardiff City

The daily newspapers did their bit for football cards collecting. Daily Citizen, an Edwardian newspaper, gave free soccer gifts on the eve of World War One. It issued 70 different supplements showing football teams. The 1913/14 rarities are valued at £100!

Daily Dispatch issued *Scott's Football Stars* [sic] in 1946. They are typical of post-war soccer collectibles. In a time of limited pleasures – and no football cards – newspapers printed what they believed to be the next best thing. There were 200 of these football caricatures, issued one daily. Though they were not intended to be football stickers, they became so by habit, as many readers cut them out to keep.

Daily Express's *Famous Footballers* were designed to be cut out, folded and glued by readers. The design was very much in the style of a typical cigarette card. A very similar idea had been employed by the 1920s children's magazine, The Popular (see: Popular). The Express cards are worth £35 each. Its next football cartophilic fare was issued during 1955 and 1958. Daily Express's *Full Report: Kick-off To Final Whistle* are postcard-size trade cards. All 50 show

football teams and advertise match reports. In 1958 the newspaper also launched *Always On The Ball Sports Coverage*, a series of eight fold-out football-shaped cards. During 1965 and 1966 the same paper issued 20 *Top Soccer News And Pictures* [sic] of football teams. Values for the various Express cards are around £50 each.

Daily Graphic, formerly known as The Golden Penny, produced some very notable Edwardian football specials which were often cut up, and devalued to the point of worthlessness, by readers clipping out individual team pictures. However, even the cut-out team pictures can be quite valuable. They are not cartophilic, per se, but they are of great interest to football card collectors. Values start around £250 for an uncut magazine. More than a generation later, in 1948, the Daily Graphic returned to soccer with 70 *Football Stars* and *Goalkeeper Stars*. Values are around £10 each. Daily Graphic's final football cards, from around 1950, were the miniature *Star Pictures Of Players*. The small cut-out cards were issued daily, a full team every fortnight. Values for these diminutive cards start at £10 each.

Daily Herald is a name known to football collectors. During 1951–1953 it issued various series of small black and white photo cards, in

paper folders, called *Sports Stars* (*Sportfotos*). Issued in sets numbering 32 cards each, the cards are known in three designs. Cards inscribed *Daily Herald Copyright SPORTFOTO*, and cards inscribed *Daily Herald Copyright* use the same player photos. The third type, inscribed simply *Sportfoto*, is the rarest, and it sports different photos to the other series. The three series include varieties and error cards, and a redemption card with a star. An album titled *Sports Stars* was issued for the cards. Very rare, large unbranded Daily Herald (*Sportfoto*) cards are also known to exist. They are some of the rarest mid-century modern cards known! Values start at £100 each! The smaller cards can be found for £5, for easier types, up to £40 for rarer varieties. Daily Herald's final soccer cards series was issued in 1958: *Pencil Pics* comprised 20 newspaper cut-outs of single, and some paired, player portraits.

Daily Graphic miniature star pictures, from 1945

Daily Express 1947 Famous Footballer card

Daily Express 1955 Cardiff Everton report card

Daily Herald, small and large
Ted Ditchburn cards

Daily Mail issued soccer supplements as far back as 1934. *Football teams 1934-5* are large, pictorial free gifts whose values exceed £100 each. In 1955 Daily Mail released an actual series of footballer cards called *Sports Parade*. Its 22 caricature cards of footballers were drawn by Eric Thompson. Most cards are very rare and are valued at over £100 each!

In 1970 Daily Mail issued a free souvenir gift set: *England's World Cup Footballers*. A year later the newspaper issued *Follow The...* [sic] stickers. The entire series of 22 was issued on one sheet. Values for uncut sheets of Daily Mail stickers start at £50.

Daily Mirror, not to be outdone by its conservative tabloid rival, issued *Mirrorcards Stars Soccer Sides*. The 1970 series consisted of 100 cards. Values are low, around £1 or £2 each. However, the redemption collection associated with *Mirrorcards*, called *My Club*, included 96 postcard-sized team cards. They were available from the newspaper for a small amount of cash and a series of tokens collected from the newspaper. Values for *My Club* cards are £10 to £50 each.

The Daily News Football Annual of 1924-27 issued very fine *Football Supplements* in the form of fold-outs showing many teams and players on one.

These have been seen to sell for over £200 each! Each featured a melange of stars and clubs. For example, the 1925 issue showed England, Scotland, Arsenal, Leicester City, Sheffield United, Cardiff City, Huddersfield Town, WBA, Chelsea, Spurs, Blackpool and Plymouth.

Daily Sketch issued 28 *World Cup Transfer* decals in 1970. Readers could send away for two different sheets of 14 decals each. Uncut sheets are worth £100. Cut singles are easier to find and are valued at only £5 each. The same newspaper also issued so-called *World Cup Souvenirs*, 40 cards, in strips of five cards each. Today uncut strips of five may sell for as much as £50 each – if Pelé is one of the cards.

Daily Star, the British comic tabloid newspaper, joined the cards carousel with *Top British Teams*, a collection of 412 stickers issued as pairs, or in quads. Uncut pairs and quads hold some value but these 1980s stickers are very common and have only a nominal value.

Damm beer gave away stickers called *Xibeca Sport* for World Cup 74. The 260 stickers included Johan Cruyff (valued at £50) and a selection of 20 world teams, including Scotland (valued around £20). The stickers were all issued with a fold.

Dandy Gum of Denmark issued a *Football Club Series* of 200 cards of club colours in 1970. Dandy was probably best known to British children in the 1970s for its *Kinky Dan* stickers. *Dan* was a bubblegum cartoon creature with a triangular body and a ... bubble for a head. He graced many school exercise books, bicycle frames and bedroom doors. The 1970 *Football Clubs Series* was only available in continental Europe but it featured some British football colours – like you've never seen them before. Club strips were modelled by Danish men who looked a little ill at ease standing in a far flung, desolate spot that looks like the Danish equivalent of Beachy Head. Dandy Gum would issue copious cards in various football card series during the 1970s and 80s. More on Dandy in a future issue.

Danone was behind the *Daddies Football Greats* in 1982. The 30 cards are scarce and nowadays fetch more than £10 each.

Davit was a chocolate manufacturer in Italy. In the 1930s it issued a series of footballers and teams. Values start at £20 each and rise skywards, with very high premiums for World Cup stars.

De Beukelaer biscuits gave free *All Sports* trade cards in 1932. The set of 100 small, monotone photographic soccer stars can be found today for about £5. Values for single cards are about £5 each but Gallacher [sic] and Dean fetch higher prices.

Daily Mirror My Club redemption card of Rochdale

Damm folding card of the Scotland World Cup squad from 1974

Daily Sketch football transfers from 1970

Daily Sketch strip of five football cards from 1970

De Haas & Van Brero of the Netherlands issued football stickers between 1949–51. *Goal Voetbal Campioenen, 1 & 2* included over 230 stickers each collection. The stickers are inscribed with the name *Leo Pagano*. British club stickers are worth a lot!

Davit and De Beukelaer cards from 1932

Daddies Sauce card of Gordon
Strachan from 1982

De Haas sticker of Leicester City and
Wolves, and a typical back

Di Stefano on a card by De Jonge

De Haas & Van Brero of the Netherlands issued football stickers between 1949–51.

Goal Voetbal Campioenen, 1 & 2 included over 230 stickers each collection. The stickers are inscribed with the name *Leo Pagano*. British club stickers are worth a lot!

De Jonge of West Germany issued cards in 1959. This series of very rare cards numbered *70 Sportbilder*. The cards show mostly West German subjects but there are 12 cards featuring football involving foreign clubs, notably three with Nottingham Forest, and three of Real Madrid, one of which is Alfredo Di Stefano. Generally the foreign cards are the most valuable issues, widely sought, with hefty premium prices being paid. Most cards sell for around £20 each but £120 is closer to the price for international players of note.

Devlin of Ireland produced soccer trade cards under licence from Barratt of London. Its 1950s cards followed the British pattern and are, more or less, the same as the Barratt cards but for the Devlin logo and legend. However, unlike the wider British packets that were made to fit the cards printed by Barratt, some types of Devlin packaging were tighter resulting in some cards having to be trimmed to fit! So, cards for packets of *5's* (sweet cigarettes) had their flanks removed. Uncut cards were sold in wider, more expensive packets of sweet cigarettes, and trimmed card in smaller confections.

Devlin's 1952 issue, *Famous Footballers New Series*, is the rarest of all its collections. The 50 cards are valued around £75 each for uncut cards, while trimmed cards are more affordable at only £10 each. During 1953–1955 Devlin issued three Barratt series: *Famous Footballers A1*, *Famous Footballers A2*, and *Famous Footballers A3*. Each collection had 50 cards. While uncut cards are worth £50 each, trimmed cards are £10.

Dickson Orde, a British foods issuer, jumped on the cards bandwagon in 1960 with *Footballers*. The 50 cards are easily available and can be had for £10 a set.

Di Dasco stickers originated in Italy. Issued twice in 1950/51 the *Albosport* collection comprised hundreds of perforated stickers. It's a multisport series with boxers, cyclists, tennis players, etc. Most of the soccer stars are from

Italian teams but the England national team is generously represented and the series includes many British greats, including Raich Carter of Hull City, Tom Finney of Preston, etc. Values for British players are around £75 to £100 each.

Dipul was a Portuguese issuer. In 1971 it issued a series of stickers called *Campeóes Europeus de Futebol 1970/71*. The 320 stickers include Arsenal and Glasgow Celtic players. Values start at £20 each, for unused stickers. See also: Palirex.

Doctor Storm's Winter Drops. What a wonderful title for football cards! The 1920s cards feature only Bolton Wanderers players. Only 12 different cards are known. Values start at £100 each.

Dolcificio Lombardo was an Italian legend. The Perfetti brothers were a decade ahead of Panini. They made Italy's first post-war gum cards. Dolcificio Lombardo gum was sold everywhere, initially with cards of film stars, and then, by the 1950s, with photographic cards of footballers. The early black and white photo cards are sought after by Italian *cognoscenti*. By the 1960s the brothers Ambrogio & Egidio Perfetti had put their own surname on the cards: Perfetti – with a languorous letter *f*.

The various footballer picture cards from this issuer are worth £10 to £100 each.

A sheet of stickers by Di Dasco

The Perfetti brothers issued a 1967 series of sports cards that included 20 footballers. In days of yore some collectors thought this to be a series by a Dutch firm called Monty. It is not! They also once thought the cards were from 1965. They are not. The wide range of Lombardy football stars in the collection, in particular from the two big Milanese clubs, says Italy – not Holland. As well as 10 *Serie A* footballers the set also features Denis Law and Jimmy Greaves – both were former *Serie A* players. There are also cards of Bobby Moore, Bobby Charlton, Pelé, Eusebio and Franz Beckenbauer. The key to assuaging doubts about the date of this series is the kit worn by the Inter players. It's the yellow star strip first worn in 1966/67. The single yellow star was added to the blue and black stripes as testimony to Inter's tenth championship win, in summer 1966. This is important as sellers have often demanded high prices for the Beckenbauer and Eusebio cards, claiming wrongly that 1965 was the year of issue. It's assuredly a 1966/67 series.

Domus was an Italian issuer of the 1930s. Domus cards show caricatures drawn by *Carlin & Unica*. The cards were issued with chocolates. Values exceed £50 each.

Donald, named after the Disney duck, was the name given to an album of football stickers issued in 1966, in Uruguay. *Donald Campeonato Mundial 1966* is as bizarre a collection as it is rare. Fulham's George Cohen, sticker 166, has extra colouring, and George Eastham, sticker 171, wears his Arsenal kit. Jimmy Greaves and others from the England team are pictured with Disney gnomes, dwarves and other imaginings of Walt's whimsies. Also included in this rare collection are stickers of English football league grounds, notably the clubs involved with the hosting of the 1966 World Cup, for example, Ayresome Park, in Middlesbrough. There are also stickers of former World Cup champions, including Pelé. Values for the England players and stadia are worth over £150 each. Such world legends have sold for more than £250 each. In 2016 a partially complete collection sold for £2,000 on a Spanish collectibles site.

Dipul Celtic stickers from Portugal

A sticker of George Cohen, by Donald, in Uruguay

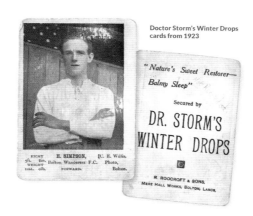

Doctor Storm's Winter Drops cards from 1923

Typical Dolcificio Lombardo cards, front and back

Donaldson

Donaldson big head cards, front and back

Donaldson small head cards, front and back

Donaldson Golden Series cards, front and back

Donaldson made some of the most beloved post-war football cards including various series of *Sports Favourites*. The firm's cards birthed many imitations, so-called rogue issues, and stiff competition from rivals like Kiddy's Favourites, Junior Pastimes and Baytch Brothers, to name but three. In 1946, due to shortages caused by the war, card stock was varied and printers used what they could get. The styles of letterpress, print settings and biographical details on the earliest cards came in many and varied forms. There are error cards, corrected cards, different coloured backs, and cards with other tweaks in their design. The first set of Donaldson *Sports Favourites* included 90 different caricatures – plus varieties. Four printings of this series are known to exist. That's almost 400 cards to collect! The earliest cards had no manufacturer's name, nor address. The address (Ingram Street, Glasgow) was added to later issues from 1947 onwards. Some cards use one or more types of fancy letterpress, whilst others have only

plainer lettering, often in different fonts. Some cards have *COPYRIGHT* [sic] in block capitals, others not. There are cards with team changes and differing biographies for the same player, and there are rookies galore!

Values for the early Donaldson cards, of footballers with very large heads, range from £5 to £100 each!

During 1948 and 1949 Donaldson issued over 500 *Sports Favourites*! The later *Sportsmen* show footballers with smaller heads than those issued in 1946/47. Though some remain distinctly out of proportion, a little over-sized, none are as grandly inflated as the potato-head men of earlier years. Due to immense popularity this series of over 500 different cards was re-printed time after time. Issued in miniature booklets, the cards came stapled together. As with the earlier cards, this series has many varieties. There are different types of letterpress, different fonts, different coloured inks; and some cards (re-issues) noted a player's transfers. There are some cards without numbers, notably a sub-

series of Oldham Athletic players. See also: Muat; John Barr; Donaldson-Rogues; LaPorta-Sartori, Kiddy's Favourites, etc.

In 1949 Donaldson issued eight *Sports Favourites Postcards*. There is some speculation that these may have been redemption issues, available in exchange for many smaller cards but it's not certain. Their values are £50 each.

For the Festival of Britain, in 1950, Donaldson issued *Sports Favourites – Golden Series*. The 64 cards (there were two series of 32 cards each) are much rarer than most of the earlier *Sports Favourites*. The higher numbers, particularly, are the most valuable. They have been seen to sell at over £100 each. Values for cards numbered 1–32 range from £30 to £80; those over number 32 exceed £100 each.

In 1954/55 a series of attractive cards was issued to celebrate the 1954 World Cup and the inaugural European Cup of 1955. The *Gold Cup* (Football Team) set comprises 160 die-cut, cup-shaped cards. They were issued in packets, much like cards of today.

Donaldson Gold Cup cards for World Cup 54 and European Cup 55

Dunkin issued bubblegum inserts in Spain as far back as the 1960s. Forty-eight waxy papers showed sports caricatures in a 1969 series called *¿Cual es su nombre?* (what's his name?)

So-called rogue Donaldson cards are probably by Kiddy's Favourites

SPORTS FAVOURITES
No. 34
McILHATTON
(Outside Right)
Everton

Transferred to Everton from Albion Rovers at a large fee, this go-ahead winger, noted for his dribbling ability, has been a valuable acquisition to his new club. Has settled down well at Goodison Park, and he should have a successful career in English football.

Spanish Dunkin wax paper gum inserts from 1969 and 1973

An album was also issued for the cards. Manchester United and Celtic figure highly amidst the rarities in this series. Values range from £20 to £150 each.

A word on the so-called Donaldson Rogue cards. They were issued in 1947. For some years they were believed to be bootleg issues of *Sports Favourites*. However, it is probable that the cards were the first series by rival Glaswegian firm, Kiddy's Favourites. Kiddy's used similar red lettering, and the numbering of the cards also fits with Kiddy's. One thing is certain: these cards are exceedingly rare, far rarer than most Donaldson cards, and much more valuable. A handful of English team players are known (Arsenal, Everton, Stoke City, etc.) but most show Scottish subjects. The 52 cards are valued between £75 and £150 each.

Following Celtic's European Cup win, in 1967, Donaldson cards reappeared briefly. A series called *Celtic European Cup Winners*, consisting of 16 plastic cards, signed by John Barr, is now valued at £250 for an uncut sheet! Cut singles are worth around £15. Donaldson cards seemed to reappear as

recently as the 1980s but the series of 12 black and white cards was a private issue by a certain R.T. Muat of Penicuik. The cards state *not for sale* but they've certainly done well for the printer! Prices paid are around £20 each.

Dubreq is a name synonymous with 1970s games. In 1977 Top Trumps, a card game of the time, unveiled a soccer game: 32 *British Soccer Stars*. Similar trumps games followed: *British Strikers*, *International Greats*, *World Cup 78* and *British Stars*, *sets 1* and *2*. Collecting Top Trumps is a passion in itself. The aforementioned games (sets of cards) tend to be among the easier to find Top Trumps and they can sell for about £25. The rarest football Top Trumps games are the so-called team sets. Sets of 16 cards (and one tin badge) have been snapped up by club collectors, leaving a hole in the Top Trumps market, and higher prices for the few that remain. Boxed sets of 1970s team trumps may cost you £75. In 1980 the team sets were all re-issued, with updated player information. These tend to be the hardest to find.

Dunkin issued bubblegum inserts in Spain as far back as the 1960s. Forty-eight waxy papers showed sports caricatures in a 1969 series called *¿Cual es su nombre?* (what's his name?) As well as football greats, like Alfredo Di Stefano, Kubala and Pelé, the series includes inserts of Muhammad Ali and The Beatles. Values range from £50 to £100 each.

Dunkin returned to waxy gum inserts of footballers in 1973. A Spanish series called, *Kubala Te Enseña A Jugar* (Kubala shows you how to play) included 144 football-related inserts. It was an attractive series but was issued creased due to being wrapped around gum. It includes Pelé, Bobby Moore, Bobby Charlton, Johan Cruyff, Eusebio, etc. Values start at over £50 each for these players.

Dura of Spain issued *Deportes*, a sticker and album collection. The 1968 series of pan-sport stickers included a certain Bobby Charlton, of Manchester United. Values for Sir Bobby and other top sportsmen of the day can exceed £50 a sticker!

Barathy, v. d. Budapester Hungaria, ist ein Fußball-Innenstürmer v.großerKlasse. Unser Bild zeigt ihn ungewöhnlich hoch nach einem Balle springend.

Markworth, Magdeburg, gehört zu den erfolgreichsten Handballrepräsentativen Mitteldeutschlands. Unser Bild zeigt ihn bei einem seiner kraftvollen Schüsse.

Eagles & Swifts

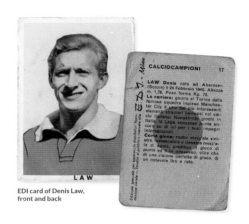

EDI card of Denis Law,
front and back

Eagle Swift cards, as issued, in strips

EAGLE SWIFT
SOCCER STARS
BOBBY TAMBLING
(Chelsea and England)
You cannot tell Chelsea fans now that they miss Jimmy Greaves. And that is the greatest tribute possible to Bobby, his successor. He began as a winger—England remembered that last November when he was hurriedly called in at the last moment against Wales for his first cap—but he has been a revelation at inside-forward. Last season he was Chelsea's leading scorer with 20 League goals. He had already galloped past that mark with less than half this season gone. Joined Chelsea in 1958, made his League debut in 1959, and has a tremendous future.

EAGLE SWIFT
SOCCER STARS
BOBBY CHARLTON
(Manchester United and England)
A dynamic, dangerous raider who wins matches in one explosive burst. Out of the game for the first half of this season after an operation, he missed the chance of raising his total of England caps to 40. Bobby was rated by experts the only England forward in Chile as being world-class. One of the most lethal shots in the game, he has also operated with distinction at centre-forward and inside-left. Comes from Ashington, is related to the famous North-east family of Milburns — Jackie is an uncle . . . and brother John is Leeds' centre-half.

EAGLE SWIFT
SOCCER STARS
DEREK KEVAN
(West Bromwich Albion and England)
The big, bustling, blond 'hammer' of the Albion attack and their most prolific scorer over the past few seasons, his best being the 33 League goals of last season. Holder of 14 England caps, he has played at inside-left and centre-forward. Was in the World Cup party of 1958, where his continued selection raised a storm from critics who wanted a more subtle player. But Kevan, who was born in Ripon and went to the Hawthorns in 1953, has gone on getting goals in typical, big-hearted fashion.

EAGLE SWIFT
SOCCER STARS
DAVE MACKAY
(Spurs and Scotland)
Soccer's "iron man", he has been a wonderful bargain for Spurs, even at £30,000. This was the figure which brought him from Hearts where he was an established international, capped for Scotland more than a dozen times. A fierce tackling wing-half, he never knows when he is beaten and he has also scored many important goals for his club. Has been prominent in Spurs' wonderful run of success over the past few seasons. A craggy, colourful character, he is never happy unless right in the heat of the battle.

Eagles & Swifts rule Swallows & Amazons. Eagle was a post-war newcomer that revolutionised the world of British comics. In 1950 it sold almost a million copies of its first issue! Eagle found a post-war audience eager for a change. The 1930s adventure stories told in plain text were old hat. Swallows & Amazons had their day. Kids who had lived through the Blitz wanted fewer words and more pictures. Dan Dare's rocket ships seen in glorious graphic design were just the thing. Eagle's sci-fi swashbuckler and features on technology and science were a great success. Combining with another comic, Swift, Eagle attempted to bring the footy contingent on board. In 1963 it launched a maiden series of football trade cards. Though the first release was named simply *Swift Soccer Stars*, by the following week the Eagle landed. The cards, now branded Eagle Swift, were issued in strips of four. These days they are often found cut to singles, making intact strips quite valuable. All in all there were 16 single cards and a plastic wallet for keeping them safe. Values for uncut strips of four cards may exceed £40 each but cut singles barely make £2.

EDI or EDJ? Think of a Leeds United 1970s winger, of whom it was said, he never left footprints in snow, and you are getting warmer. It looks like EDJ on some of the cards but EDI, or Edizione Divulgative Illustrate, is the initialism. EDI was a publisher born under a Milanese star in late 1961. Surprisingly the firm was gone without a trace by 1963 yet it was responsible for some of the mythic football cards of the 1960s, and arguably some of the most beautiful – and for the wee red balls. The Italian cards producer EDI died an early death due to sheer over-ambition. In 18 months it produced more series of cards than some producers make in many years. EDI made large, attractive gum cards that became known as the red ball cards, due to a small red circle that appears on the front of every card. A red ball occasionally pops up on the backs of the cards too. EDI made four different series of *Calciocampioni* (football champions). That's about 800 cards in just over one year! Pelé appeared in most EDI series, and there are plenty of other world stars to share the company of hundreds of Italian players. EDI cards are known with a variety of backs. Pelé appears with a plain back, with a back that has a large red spot over a biography; with a spot-less biography, and on cards with different numbers to boot! There are also cards with red overprinted numbers (as well as the original black numbers). The red ball cards of EDI have garnered enormous interest from collectors and have been seen to sell for stratospheric prices. All of the various designs, even cards with plain backs, are valuable. Internationals start at £20 each. British players, like Denis Law, have sold for prices over £100. A Jimmy Greaves card in top condition may sell for £200.

What about Pelé? Well, don't believe people who want the card but tell you the top price paid is £300! You can triple that.

Edições 7 Cores (Portuguese for winning the World Cup 7 times?) Winning in Bavaria would have been the fourth time

Edições 7 Cores album page and
a reproduction of Vava, with
original Vava on left

Brazil had taken the World Cup home. Seven Colours Editions (Edições 7-Cores) decided it was a good idea to re-print previous Brazilian sticker collections to set the mood for 1974. The firm never imagined how its new editions would come to cause gnashing of teeth and agonised wailing amongst card collectors of the future. Edições 7 Cores printed four collections of stickers, which came perforated and in sheets, together with an album. These reprinted collections were made to be enjoyed easily. There was no desperate collecting needed. The collection came as one lot, in one go. Stickers were detached and stuck into the albums. Simple. In five minutes you were done. Over time these issues became all too easily forgotten. Some decades later new collectors found them and presumed they were originals, or pretended they were! The stickers are easy to confuse with originals as, sometimes, the only way to tell originals from reprints is the colour of the number on the back. 1974 issues have black numbering and roughly cut perforations. Older stickers have blue numbers and the perforations are more like those on most postage stamps. Most stickers, whatever the collection, were stuck down. Finding unused stickers, after 50 years, is almost as unlikely as finding a winning lottery number. If a sticker seems unused it's probably been carefully removed from a page with steam, water or acetone. These reprints are almost as rare as the originals – they may be rarer. More

blue numbers from 1958 are seen than black from 1974. Whereas an unused, complete sticker sheet from 1974 may make £500, a single 1974 Pelé sticker, removed from the album, ought to be no more than £250 though one has been seen to sell for £800! The originals, with blue numbers, are another matter. Originals in good condition start at quadruple that price!

Ediguia, of Portugal, issued *Munique 74* for the Bavarian World Cup. There are over 300 FKS-style stickers of players and flags, including Scottish stars. Denis Law will often fetch over £30, while King Kenny tops £100!

Ediraf, not to be left behind, also produced a stunning series of large cards and silk stickers for the Munich World Cup. The series, *Calcio 74*, was issued solely in Italy but it was internationally inclusive and contained Scotland footballers aplenty, mostly shown in their English and Scottish league club colours. The silk stickers of national emblems are rarer than the hardest to find *Calcio 74* cards. The silk stickers, which include Manchester United, Celtic and Scotland emblems, were issued one per packet. Most got stuck to something back in 1974. Few remain unused. The cards fared better and we can still acquire Pelé and Cruyff though they may cost premium prices of up to £100 each. Note: Ediraf had printed one Top Sellers series, *Football 73*. See: Top Sellers

Edis, in Italy, issued *Calciatori 1969/70 - Mexico 70* [sic]. The highest priced stickers are those of

international stars, like Eusebio and George Best. Caveat emptor: there are forgeries of Eusebio and Best doing the rounds! Finding an unused original sticker from a small issuer, like EDIS, from 1969, is almost impossible. If you want a genuine example you'll have to buy an album, to be sure, and even partly finished albums from this issue cost thousands!

Edito Service was the Wikipedia of 1978. It issued large, coloured cards designed for use in reference libraries, schools and other institutes. Every subject was covered, including football. Issued in various languages there are many variations to collect, from French to Serbo-Croat. Values range from £2 for British cards, £20 for French cards, and £30 for Serbo-Croat cards.

Elah, an Italian desserts and sweets producer, gave away free coins (metallic card discs with the look of money) of sports favourites, during the 1930s. Its first solely football release came after the war. *Calciatori Foot Ball Mou* was issued in 1955. The series can be distinguished from later Elah issues by the single swift on the back of the card, and a single brand name. This rare series of cards includes Lennart Skoglund and other foreigners of note playing in the Italian league in the mid-1950s. Values for the 1930s coins are £50 each but the 1955 cards start at just £5 each, but rise sharply, depending on the player featured. Elah's second series of cards was called *Calciatori 1956-57*. Values range from £5 to £30

Ediguia sticker of Billy Bremner, left, with Spanish Eher sticker, right

151. BOBBY MOORE   203. GEORGE GRAHAM

Eridaf, various cards from Italy, Sweden and the British Isles

FOOTBALL 73
CARD NO. 194
WILLIE DONACHIE. Glasgow-born half-back who forced his way into first team a couple of years ago and is now regarded as a regular member of the top squad. Compactly-built but very strong in the tackle.

TOP SELLERS. LTD.
Printed in Italy by Ediraf S.p.A.

Elah coins

Elah, an Italian desserts and sweets producer, gave away free coins (metallic card discs with the look of money) of sports favourites, during the 1930s.

for certain players. The cards are recognisable by the two swifts and two brand names on the back.

Epoca magazine was issued in Italy. It gave free football supplements in 1966. A pull-out and cut-out series of stickers called *Coppa del Mondo 1966* may sell singly for as much as £100 each for all-time greats like Yashin and Beckenbauer. Most stickers sell from £5 to £25 each. Uncut sheets of stickers make more. English stars feature. Most stickers have no brand, just a player's name and a team, though some show an AGFA logo.

Esso, the tiger of football collectibles. *Esso Action Station* cards, issued in 1969, came with facsimile autographs of players. They are the rarest and most valuable of all the cards issued by the petrol tiger in Britain. Esso also issued colour posters of British teams in 1969, though they are a little outside the scope of this book. Cartophilic issues by Esso since 1970 have little monetary worth though they are unusual and highly attractive knickknacks with which to colour a collection. Esso had put its name to continental football memorabilia long before its wares appeared in the British Isles. It had been issuing soccer goodies in Holland since the 1950s, where it produced a deluxe series of Dutch teams on large colourful cards. Twenty years later its British football memorabilia would come to include a set of 1970 England World Cup coins; a 1971 series of football club stickers; FA Cup centenary medals, in 1972; and so-called Soccer Superstars, a collection of colourful metal discs which rust badly with time. A rust-free set of such pretty progenitors to pogs is worth having yet nothing by Esso is worth very much, not even 50 years later. The sheer amount of stuff produced and collected by motorists in the 1970s ensures contemporary prices remain flat.

Este was one of Spain's biggest issuers of football cards. Though many of its collections are domestic there have been notable exceptions, for example, the *Liga 80-81* collection, with its various puzzle sets of Trevor Francis (for Nottingham Forest), Graham Rix (for Arsenal) and Diego Maradona. Values for such sub-sets of puzzle cards are climbing rapidly. For more on Este see footballsoccercards.com

Estratto Este was an Italian food producer of the 1930s. *Campioni dello Sport serie 1°* cards originated as pages in a miniature booklet given with Este foods. Cut to single pages is how most of the booklets ended up. If you have them, and never knew what they were, these words will show on the backs of the cards [pages]: '*il purissimo... estratto... lievito....concentrate... vitamine*'. The pages were not meant to be cut

but they have since become valuable items and have been seen to sell for £25 each.

Evening All! The evening newspaper was a tradition this writer remembers well. Growing up in the Midlands of the 1970s his best friend delivered newspapers from a bicycle and his uncles would buy evening papers on their way to working the turnstiles at floodlit midweek matches, at Villa Park, St Andrews, Fellows Park and The Hawthorns football grounds. Myriad news vendors outside these grounds called out sales of The Argus, Evening Mail, and the Evening Post. The newspapers often had football supplements either printed or tucked away inside, as free gifts. Local papers from Brum to Glasgow promoted players and teams from their cities. Notable cartophilic rarities came with the Manchester Evening Chronicle in 1947. It gifted readers what it modestly called *Souvenir Pictures*. These small paper posters of Manchester United and Manchester City have become very valuable. Few have survived the ravages of time that are often dealt to paper supplements. If you have an Evening Chronicle team from 1947 it's worth £100.

As was done in Manchester they did in Glasgow, Edinburgh and Birmingham. In Glasgow the Evening Citizen launched an attractive promotion called the *Evening Citizen Autograph Club*. Readers would send away tokens for postcard-size monotone footballer cards bearing a facsimile autograph and photo of a well-known player. Nowadays these are valued from £30 each

Esso Action Station cards, issued in 1969, came with facsimile autographs of players. They are the rarest and most valuable of all the cards issued by the petrol tiger in Britain.

Epoca stickers, Nobby Stiles, front and back

Esso 1970s match cards

Este, Laurie Cunningham

Evening Telegraph of Grimsby, a Grimsby Town card

AN EVENING MAIL-SPORTS ARGUS
SOUVENIR SERIES 1969-70   No. 3

WALSALL F.C.

Popular with the Fellows Park crowd

TWO
IN
GEAR

Stan Jones

Nick Atthey

Evening Mail Sports Argus, Two in Gear, Walsall

Evening Citizen
Autograph Club card
of Jimmy Mason

Evening Dispatch Football Star
Series, Bobby Parker

(for smaller clubs) to over £50 each for stars from bigger clubs. Meanwhile, the Evening Dispatch in Edinburgh. not to be outdone, issued a rival series of 75 different *Sports Pics* (some were stamped on the back: *Football Star Series*). The cards came with a facsimile autograph, in white. These days this colour difference helps identify the Edinburgh series of picture cards from those with black names, issued in Glasgow. Later, in 1960, the Glaswegian Evening Citizen issued a series of football gifts called *Starpix*. These colour supplements of players are valued at around £25 each.

In 1962 *The Evening Despatch*, of Birmingham. launched an unusual collection. Its brewery advertisers co-sponsored the newspaper's freebies: footballer beer mats. As if drinkers in Birmingham needed a reason to spend more time at the pub. Expelled from happy homes, the boozy blokes of Brum slung their proverbial hooks and found John Sleewienhoek at the bottom of their pints. Northern Ireland's Derek Dougan is also found in

this series of inn table glass comforters.

The Evening Mail & Sports Argus, in Birmingham, issued an unusual collection of football cards in 1969: *Two In Gear Souvenir Series* pairs of soccer stars. Values are around £25 for uncut cards. Note: the Newham Recorder, in East London, issued very similar pairs, with West Ham United players. At around the same time, in

Greater London, The Evening News issued black and white photo cards of players. *Stars in Action* feature players from all of the bigger London clubs. Values are around £25 each card.

The Evening Mail & Sports Argus, in Birmingham, issued an unusual collection of football cards in 1969: Two In Gear Souvenir Series pairs of soccer stars. Values are around £25 for uncut cards.

BURNLEY

Founded: 1881. Ground: Turf Moor. Ma-
ager: Jimmy Adamson. League Champions
1921, 1960. F.A. Cup: 1914.

CALDERWOOD

Faulkner

Cards issued by FCCM in the 1990s

F aulkner furnished fairly humourous examples of the *double entendre* with football cards of 1900. Its Grenadier fags came with frivolous sketches of muddied oafs. The 24 fin de siècle *Football Terms* raised smoky sniggers in Victorian salons. The cards came to light anew when Clarke tobacco reissued them in 1902, bringing levity to Edwardian parlours. The Clarke's cards may tickle your fancy, if soccer silliness is your relish, but at prices of £100 each wallet moths may slumber. Faulkner cards cost less but the collector seeking the most affordable printings will find similar cards by Wills Tobacco (Capstan and Vice Regal brands) to be the most economical. The Clarke *Football Terms* form part of a much larger series, *Sporting Terms*, consisting of 50 cards. In 1902 Faulkner also broadened its sporting field with a series of *Cricketers*. A notable footballer is included in this costly set: Charles Burgess Fry, of Southampton, Pompey and Corinthians. If you find Fry on a Clarke's card you have something that's worth £1,000!

FCCM is Football Card Collector Magazine. This writer created it, launching the first issue in 1997. Before FCCM there was nothing on soccer card collecting. No other publication in the world had dealt specifically with football cards.

In the 1980s and 90s there was no internet, so finding, buying and selling cards was a challenge. It was done, as best it could be, at ephemera fairs – rare gatherings of dealers in old paper – and at antiques markets; through classified adverts in newspapers, at postcard fairs, and so on. Before FCCM this writer used to advertise for soccer cards in Record Collector magazine, in Angling Times and in The Erotic Revue. The latter, especially, was rather rewarding. In the early 1990s collectors researched and collected cards in solitude, or amongst pals at a local football club. For football cards there was no market, no research, and no specific catalogue. Cards were considered marginal by most football memorabilia and programme dealers, and there was but the occasional seller for whom cards were an income, notably *Matchday* in Lincolnshire. FCCM changed the scene in 1997. By 2001 the magazine had thousands of readers. The growing internet expanded the interest. Before long anyone could find, buy and sell cards – to everyone! During the 1990s FCCM issued various laminated promotional cards that were only available to subscribers. If you have such a card by FCCM – and if you have original FCCM magazines – you have a piece of football cards history.

Fedora tobacco cards from Spain, 1966

Fedora football cigarette cards were issued from the Spanish Canary Islands in 1966. A very rare series of cards, it comprises images of World Cup footballers including Lev Yashin, Eusebio and Pelé. The England players from the team of 66 are also included. The cards came in boxes of Fedora cigarettes but the images were licensed by Fher, the handlers of FKS. Typically the England stars will cost up to £150 each.

Felsinea was one of myriad chocolatiers, in 1920s Italy, by whom photographic cards were given with candy confections. Cards had been seen to encourage customers to return, to buy more chocolate. Felsinea produced its own cards, and classy they were! All-time greats and football legends are known amidst such wares. Though starting modestly at around £20 each prices may top £150 for players like Piola and Meazza.

Ferrero is a name to make mouths water, if not teeth to tremble. Beloved of private practice dentists, the Italian sweets and praline giant has been churning out goopy chocolates and nutty spreads since 1946. The firm bestowed quite a legacy to sports cards collectors. Ferrero created some very unusual wares. Its metal pogs, and card roundels, are almost unique to Ferrero. Though pre-war celluloid and metal discs are known, Ferrero made them its own. Its signature wares included boxers, motorcyclists and footballers. Nowadays the discs command prices into the hundreds!

In the United Kingdom Ferrero opted for less costly gifts. Humble cardboard was deemed suitable for British stars. However, the discs issued in 1962 are no less valuable than the 1950s Italian metal roundels. Thirty small, circular and very colourful cards of British footballers include the Charlton brothers and Welsh wizard Mel Charles. Cricketer cards are also known and one of them doubled as an Arsenal footballer: Arthur Milton. Typically the Ferrero cards of British players are so rare they are unavailable, at any price. However, if you do see one expect to pay at least £100.

Ferrero made the most of the World Cup in 1966, issuing *Coppa del Mondo 1966*, a series of 100 international footballers. The diminutive series of stickers came with an album, which meant most stickers ended up with a sticky fate. Eusebio and Pelé typically steal the show with the highest prices paid but Roger Hunt, Jimmy Greaves, Bobby Charlton and Lev Yashin are not far behind. Prices may exceed £100 each for the choicest players on stickers in the finest form.

Felsinea italian cards

Ferrero 1955 metal disc of Charlton Athletic's Jeppson

Ferrero card discs of Ron Flowers and Wilbur Cush, Great Britain, 1962

Ferrero, 1966 World Cup stickers

Ferrero made the most of the World Cup in 1966, issuing Coppa del Mondo 1966, a series of 100 international footballers. The diminutive series of stickers came with an album, which meant most stickers ended up with a sticky fate.

Fuentes Hermanos

Fher, early 1940s sticker

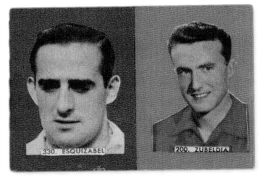

Fher, 1950s stickers

Fuentes Hermanos probably won't mean much to most readers, but what about FKS? FKS made British *Soccer Stars* albums and stickers from 1967 until 1982. Most houses in the British Isles probably had an FKS sticker floating around at some stage. FKS was the British agency licensed by the Spanish firm Fher for the divulgation of its product in Great Britain. Fher was also known as Fuentes Hermanos (the brothers Fuentes) and as Disgra.

Fher was founded in 1937, in Bilbao, by Germán and José Fuentes Lizaur. Peaceful 1940s Spain was replete with fine publishers of top quality soccer cards. No one needed more. Enter Fher. The difference with Fher was that it ventured beyond Spain, and its international exploits left competitors outmanoeuvred. *Fotos Deportivas* (Sports Photos) was Fher's first football series. The series includes Ricardo Zamora, as manager at Atletico Madrid. You'll pay £20 upwards for some of the rarities from

this collection, and complete albums sell for many thousands! By 1953 the fledgling Fher had formed an axis with the Italian founders of Lampo, a brand of stickers. Together they published a quality sports sticker album which was sold in both countries. *Sport Magico* was a revolutionary concept. It included 3-D stickers! The album came equipped with 3-D spectacles to bring to life the otherwise abstract and nonsensical sticker designs. Keen to experiment, in the same year Fher made an unusual collection called *Escenas Deportiva* (Sports Scenes). It consisted of an album, stickers and miniature booklets. The tiny publications were glued to dedicated spots in the album, just like stickers. Sticker-booklet cards without glue-damaged back covers are very rare. The costliest, nowadays, feature footballers, racing car drivers, boxers – including Joe Louis – and American baseball. Whereas stickers from this collection may fetch £20 each, the miniature booklets can better £100. By the 1960s, after many annual

collections of football stickers, Fher allied itself with a firm named Pirata, in Portugal. Together they produced a stunning World Cup album in 1962. Thenceforth the brothers ventured to Uruguay, and made an accord with Crack Novelties in Montevideo, where Fher enjoyed enormous success. Its Chile World Cup 1962 football collection, titled *Campeonato Mundial de Futbol 1962*, sold well across Latin America. England stickers from such series sell for between £30 and £100 each, while Pelé and Yashin have been known to fetch more than £200. By 1966 Fher struck a deal in England. The Pemberton Brothers, who ran FKS's predecessor, World Distributors, agreed to produce the first Fher album, *World Cup Stars*. Fher also banded together with Swedish, French, Dutch and West German publishers and various foreign firms (Semic, AGEducatifs, Vanderhout and Sicker-Verlag) came to issue Fher stickers across Europe.

Astonishing all and sundry, not to mention arch-rival Panini, Fher's far-reaching 1960s

Fher, 1962 World Cup stickers, and a wrapper

Fher, a typical Argentina 78 sticker, like FKS in Britain

Fher, World Cup 70 stickers, Spanish and Brazilian types

Fher, World Cup 74 Scotland stickers

successes were surpassed in 1970, with *Ases del IX Mundial del Futbol*. It became the defining international sticker collection for the 1970 World Cup, no matter what's become trendier since. Notwithstanding its recent renaissance, Panini's rival collection was not as widely successful, in its day. For every one Panini *Mexico 70* collection completed in Britain, there were 100 FKS albums also finished. This is one of the reasons, nowadays, why the Panini album is worth more – but that's another story. The value of England players from the afore-mentioned Fher collection, if unused, is about £25 each. They are much more attractive than the simpler FKS issues due to the inclusion of biographies, albeit in Spanish.

It had been a matter of when, not if, the fraternal empires clashed. During the dog days of 1970 the mighty Spanish, of Fher, met the implacable Italians, of Panini. The world that summer was all eyes on Mexico yet after the World Cup was over the war betwixt card

giants went on. The struggle distracted Fher and come 1974 things were amiss in Bilbao. Fher's inferior World Cup 1974 collections blighted Europe. For a start, a very strange Spanish album called *Munich "74"* [sic] sported a cover featuring West Ham United! British collectors would have recognised it as the cover from FKS's *Soccer Stars 1973/74*! Further, the stickers featured four players each, in miniature. Cheap! Fher withdrew the pusillanimous (West Ham) paper collection of miniature pictures, replacing it with the fuller *Ases del X Campeonato Mundial de Futbol 74*. It was altogether more polished, and there was no need to use a magnifying glass! Unused cards from this collection, including Scottish players, can be found for as little as £10 each.

The generic *Argentina 78* series is known to most collectors worldwide and, apart from some West Germany stickers, and those made in Portugal, it is generally the very same issue, one country after another. Portuguese

stickers had different text to the front, and some German issues came with advertising on the plain backs. The most exotic edition of the album was that made in Argentina, which included Diego Maradona! He's not to be found in other editions. The stickers of Maradona, for there were two, often fetch many hundreds of pounds, no matter what the condition is!

In its 40 years of life Fher produced over 60 series of stickers. Some of the most fascinating series were those made in collaboration with producers of other products, like Cibeles Chocolates, Casera fizzy drinks and Fedora tobacco. Such collaborative stickers tend to be the rarest, and worth a lot of money. Note: the name Disgra is often seen printed on Fher packaging and albums. Disgra was the administrative wing of the Fher business. For more related to Fher and Disgra see: FKS, Lampo, Crack, Semic, Vanderhout, Ageducatifs, Sicker-Verlag, etc.

Fabbrica Italiana Dolciumi ed Affini Serravalle Scrivia

Fidass, 1946 Grande Concorso Caramelle Sport cards

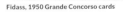

Fidass, 1950 Grande Concorso cards

idass? Well, it's a lot easier to say than Fabbrica Italiana Dolciumi Ed Affini Serravalle Scrivia. Founded in 1926, Fidass, the Italian Confectionery & Allied Products Factory, emerged from World War Two unscathed and immediately returned to its pre-war product: cards. Its earliest football cards are stunners, and rare at that! From 1946/47, *Grande Concorso Caramelle Sport* hit the mark. Its success led Fidass to launch an even bigger series in 1948: *Figurine dei Millioni*. Well, it seemed like millions. Twenty-five player cards for each Italian team were made. Goalies and strikers were very hard to come by – so says an historical commentary made during the bankruptcy hearings for Fidass, in 1981. Fidass followed the collection of *millions* with a slightly more modest series, the *Grande Concorso 1950*. It went on producing football cards until the 1960s. Look out for some colourful bubblegum wrappers with football teams from the Psychedelic years. More on Fidass, and its rare cards, in a future book.

Field Favourites. Find one of these cigarette cards and you will have found your fortune! The semi-mythical tobacco cards from the 1890s are sought high and low. Only one has ever been seen! Its value to cigarette card collectors has been said to be around £5,000 but to Liverpool collectors it's priceless. When it finally comes to market expect the price to exceed £50,000! American sports cards dealers are already eyeing this card for their richest clients.

Filshill leading the way to a lost horizon of Lotus Toffees may evoke a 1920s wireless adventure but this isn't a Sexton Blake story. It's the sticky tale of a Glaswegian man, by the name of John Filshill, and the temptations that led him to stray from innocent cards of birds – the feathered variety – unto the hurly burly of sports, and the subsequent end of his business. Colourful trade cards had been the Filshill way of things yet a slide from delicate nature sketches to soccer stars brought his Scottish confections of toffee to an inglorious end. Inscribed Lotus Toffees Lead The Way, the toffee was soon lost to the world. Its

foggy end came shortly after the series of 1924 footballer cards was issued. The 25 cards can be found with Lotus Toffee backs but also with plain backs. Original Lotus Toffee cards in fine order ought to secure at least £30 each but famous names will push prices over £50.

Filshill Lotus Toffee cards

301 - SENTIMENTI PRIMO
anni 24, nato a Bomporto, ala
destra della LAZIO

302 - GONZALVO MARIANO
anni 28, nato in Spagna,
il più grande mediano
nazionale spagnolo

303 - ONORATO ELIO
anni 26, nato a Salerno, ala
destra del TORINO

306 - PIOLA SILVIO
anni 37, nato a Robbio Lomel-
lina, centro avanti del NOVARA

307 - HOVE JACK
anni 31, nato in Inghilterra,
capitano del Derby County

308 - TESSARI LUCIANO
anni 23, n. a S. Martino Buon-
albergo, portiere della ROMA

311 - PIAN FRANCO
anni 28, nato a Gradisca di
Isonzo, terzino sinistro della
LEGNANO

312 - GRILLON ANDREA
anni 28, nato in Francia, terzino destro della Naz. Francese

313 - SKOGLUND LENNART
anni 21, nato in Svezia, interno
sinistro dell'INTER

Di Dasco Italian stickers, 1951

TOTTENHAM HOTSPUR

Founded: 1882
Ground: White Hart Lane
Attendance record: 75,038
Manager: Bill Nicholson
League Champions: 1951, 1961
F.A. Cup Winners: 1901, 1921,
1961, 1962, 1967

PHILIP BEAL
MARTIN CHIVERS
PETER COLLINS

MIKE ENGLAND
RAY EVANS
ALAN GILZEAN
PAT JENNINGS

CYRIL KNOWLES
ROGER MORGAN
ALAN MULLERY
JIMMY PEARCE

STEVE PERRYMAN
MARTIN PETERS
JOHN PRATT
TONY WANT

26

JEFF ASTLE
TONY BROWN

DOUG FRASER
ASA HARTFORD
BOBBY HO

JOHN KAYE
GRAHAM LOVETT
JO

COLIN SUGGETT
JOHN TALBUT

Mexiko 70
9. Fußball-
Weltmeisterschaft

3 3c Achte

Quartett 0218
Bielefelder Spielkarten

Fotos
Sven Simon

griffs, Sch
(UdSSR).

Uruguay

Ils sont en 1975 à VALENCIENN

le nouveau livre à illustrer avec les vignettes-images

FOOTBALL
1974/75

3,00f.

Préface de Philippe Piat
président de l'Union Nationale
des Footballeurs Professionnels

Partie à coller

265

Un pur Valenciennois formé
au club où il a gravi tous
les échelons. Cet arrière
gauche de 20 ans est
surtout un battant. Il joue
avec toute la fougue de sa
jeunesse. Un "dur au mal"
qui ne craint pas les chocs.

Christian COPIN

FKS

So, what does FKS stand for? Sydney, John and Alfred may have known but you'll need a Ouija board to ask the three Pemberton Brothers. It's a question that's driven collectors crazy. What does the initialism FKS stand for? We've all had their stickers and albums. Since 1967 we've spent a fortune on *Soccer Stars* but most of us still don't know what FKS stood for. Here's a clue. It's not just an initialism, it's an acronym. So, say it as a word, not as letters. Being based in London's erstwhile red light district, Soho, might suggest the theme to more imaginative readers. FKS, like Top Sellers, was a merchant of smut, as the conservative bigot Mary Whitehouse once

put it. Frank Norman, the Soho commentator of the 60s, and Jeffrey Bernard [*just the one*] noted the furtive, kinky and smutty picture book dealers scuttling about the alleys off Wardour Street. Pretty youth in paltry amounts of clothing, sexual activity and strip shows were the core of Soho business. At the centre of Soho sat FKS. Can you guess what the acronym FKS stands for now? Coach & Horses drinkers of the 1970s recalled the firm well, as they also remember Top Sellers: filthy magazines and kids' stuff.

The Pemberton brothers, better known as World Distributors of Manchester, siblings Sydney, John and Alfred, published the prototype FKS album in summer 1966, under licence from

Fher, in Spain. *World Cup Stars* can be found in both Spanish and English editions. Collectors paying less than £100 for one of the trio of finished versions (the stickers were already printed in the album; it was printed in three distinct variations) are doing well, but they should look out for contemporary reprints made in Peru. In its day, collectors abroad had been able to enjoy the series as it had been designed to be enjoyed: as stickers. Moreover, adult collectors in Spain had been able to collect the stickers as cigarette cards. Fedora tobacco had done a superb job with the smokers' version of the collection. Further afield, in Italy, there were two versions of the series available: as cards and as stickers. Both were issued by

Various proto-FKS stickers from West Germany and Italy, 1966/67

FKS stickers of Sheffield United players, from 1967/68

FKS packet from 1968/69

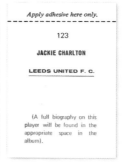

FKS stickers of Albert Johanneson, from 1968/69

FKS sticker backs, Charlton 1969/70 and Hibbitt 1970/71

FKS 1970 World Cup wrapper

Verbania, an offshoot of Lampo publishing, itself licensed from Fher. Similarly, in Portugal, Uruguay, Brazil, Argentina and West Germany stickers of these images were issued and collected, yet in the United Kingdom, where there had been a tradition of stickers since World War One, there was nothing but a finished collection, an already complete album.

The FKS name first appeared in 1967 with *The Wonderful World of Soccer Stars, England First Division 1967-1968*. This collection marked the start of something really big. Its 330 modest paper stickers now sell for between £15 and £50 each, if unused, and a complete album is worth around £1,000. Initially touted as a swapping and collecting game, neither the stickers nor the packets bore the date. Only the album cover shows *1967-68*. It is very similar to the series that followed, in 1968, but the earlier stickers are easily identifiable by their backs, which show just the name of the player and the team. In the 1967 series you'll find stickers of Fulham and Sheffield United players. They were gone in 1968. The 1967 packet is very similar to that of 1968 but identifiable because it contained eight stickers. There would be one less in 1968.

The very similar collection from 1968 included two newly promoted teams: Ipswich Town and QPR. All of the *1968-69* series stickers have biographies putting them among the most

appealing stickers made by FKS. Most can be found for less than £5 each, and complete albums are easy to come by. At less than a tenth of the value of the 1967 collection they cost relatively little for mostly the same material.

The Wonderful World of Soccer Stars 1969-1970 forsook portraits of players for 330 action shots. To distinguish them from the similar stickers from in the *1972-73* album, note that the earlier examples have numbers above the player names. The names are printed in taller, tighter fonts, themselves set above the team names, which are in flatter, smaller fonts. The later, *1972-73* issues have more or less equally sized letterpress matrices. The *1969-70* wrapper features Wolves and Arsenal. The album cover features George Best. Prices paid for unused stickers are up to £5 each. A complete album may cost as little as £50 – it was a popular series, and many were completed.

World Cup year heralded the *Mexico 70 World Cup Soccer Stars* collection. It had 272 stickers which are quite easily available today, at £1 or less. A full album can be found for around £50.

The Wonderful World of Soccer Stars 1970/71 Gala Collection [sic] is perhaps the hardest of all the FKS series to complete because it not only consisted of 420 paper stickers, there were also paper sheets of 22 second division teams, including the likes of Birmingham City, Orient and Sheffield Wednesday. Most collectors failed to

send away for a Division 2 team sheet so, whereas unused player stickers can be had for less than £5 each, team sheets – in any condition – may cost a small fortune! An album with a team sheet and all the stickers is worth around £200, whereas an otherwise complete album without a team sheet is worth less than £50. The single stickers are easy to identify. The lack of underlined names on the rear, and the instruction *'glue here only'* make these stickers readily identifiable as *1970/71* items. The packet shows England and Wales match action.

Due to the rarity of the second division team sheets a completed collection of all 22 is unknown. Were one to come up for sale it should make £4,000! Images of the team sheets of QPR, Sheffield Wednesday, Orient, Middlesbrough, Sunderland and others will be printed in a future book.

The autumn of 1971 saw the release of *The Wonderful World of Soccer Stars 1971/72*, with 352 stickers, including self adhesive team emblems. These days unused club emblem stickers with backing papers would set you back a small fortune! Ordinary, unused stickers of players, which cost below £5 each, are very easy to identify. The backs show a black and white photo of the same image used on the fronts. The packet features Manchester City and West Bromwich Albion match action. A full album may cost around £75.

FKS 1971/72, Mick Jones sticker, front and back

FKS 1972/73, Crystal Palace stickers, fornt and back

The 1972 series was similarly titled, *The Wonderful World of Soccer Stars 1972/73*. It had 355 stickers, 25 of which were circular and were designed to be glued to a poster, which was available from FKS. The remaining 330 rectangular stickers are similar in format, and in text design, to the *1969-1970* collection but these have similar sized letterpress matrices for both team and player names. The packet for this series shows Derby County match action.

In autumn 1973 FKS launched *The Wonderful World of Soccer Stars 1973/74*. It had 304 stickers, most of which were different to earlier designs and, therefore, quite easy to identify. Each sticker uses quadruple images: a player action picture, a player portrait, the player's name in a coloured text box, and a team colours flag. A celebratory sub-series of Sunderland stickers includes the FA Cup and the club's victorious players and staff. There are also four commemorative stickers of brothers Bobby and Jackie Charlton. Both sub-sets of extra stickers are easily identifiable by the letters on the backs, and not numbers.

Domestic football collecting was given a jolt in spring 1974 with the FKS *World Cup 1974* collection. Stunning stickers of Zaire and Haiti players opened young eyes. The 270 stickers may still be had for as little as £1 each but the album is rarer than that from 1970. The series was issued

around the world by Fher agencies, for example, Vanderhout in The Netherlands. See also: Fher.

Autumn 1974 felt a little strange as Manchester United were missing from the best FKS collection yet [it was this writer's favourite]. *Wonderful World of Soccer Stars 1974/75* stickers were made of card, not paper, and the photos were glossy. Gone were the matt stickers. The new cards felt like they were worth something though they made school trouser pockets bulge. Bundles of spares were thrice as thick as earlier paper stickers. Today most of the 320 cards may be had for about £2 each, if unused. A complete album costs around £100. The packets show Pat Jennings of Spurs.

Paper stickers were back for *Soccer Stars '75'76* [sic], which included stars of Scotland, Ireland, Wales and European teams too. The stickers were smaller than previous issues but included some stunners, notably Garry Pendrey sporting the *Belgian flag* Birmingham City away kit, possibly the best alternative club colours of the era. The packets show Leeds United and Manchester United. A complete album, in top condition, would be worth about £100.

In Autumn 1973 FKS launched *The Wonderful World of Soccer Stars 1973/74.* It had 304 stickers, most of which were different to earlier designs and, therefore, quite easy to identify.

FKS 1973/74 and a similar Fher sticker from Spain

FKS World Cup 74 and a similar, larger sticker from Holland

FKS 75/76 packet

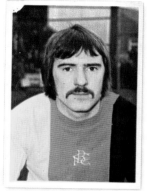

FKS 1974/75 Leeds United card and 75/76 Birmingham City sticker

FKS finished 1975 with a series of postcards, the Euro-Soccer series. The 55 cards includes 22 British teams. Values range from £3 to £10 each for unused cards but a complete album might set you back £150 if it's in very good order.

FKS finished 1975 with a series of postcards, the *Euro-Soccer* series. The 55 cards includes 22 British teams. Values range from £3 to £10 each for unused cards but a complete album might set you back £150 if it's in very good order. Note: used postcards bearing 1975 commemorative post office cancels and postage stamps, sent at the time, especially with mention of football matches played, would raise the values of these cards considerably! The packets show Derby County and Bayern München. Similar postcards were issued in other lands, including Spain and Benelux, and some of the British team cards were issued abroad too – but with different backs.

Soccer Stars '76'77 [sic] was released with 360 paper stickers, most of which are in landscape format, each sticker showing two photos: an action shot and a portrait, or a flag. Included in this collection are two sticker-puzzles made up of lots of stickers each of Kevin Keegan and Pat Jennings. There are also team managers and football action shot stickers. Blue packets show Liverpool in action.

Euro Soccer Stars '77 [sic] revisited the continental theme started in 1975. Of the modest collection (there are only 135 stickers) Cruyff fetches the premium price.

Queen Elizabeth II's Silver Jubilee saw innovation in gaming cards, if not elsewhere in British society. Top Trumps games had become very fashionable and FKS launched their own version, *Soccer Stars*. The boxed game consisted of 32 footy cards in the format of playing cards. The first of three similar series caught imaginations and emptied pockets across the playgrounds of the land. To identify cards from this series, from later types, note the backs of the cards have a football on a blue field. The second series was confusingly titled *Series One*. The card backs show a football player in red. The game cover shows Everton and Coventry City. *Series Two*, which was actually the third series, included 32 football teams, not players. The cover card shows England, a team that was about to fail to qualify for Argentina 78. FKS was as distracted as the nation was glued to World Cup qualification –

FKS 1975 postcard

FKS 1976/77 Bobby Robson and Coventry City sticker

FKS Euro Soccer Stars 1977, Cruyff

Allan Clarke, FKS 1977/78, and an Argentina 78 Portuguese Dalglish

150 RAY HANKIN
LEEDS UNITED

Made his name as a 17-year old youth international for England. Striker given his League debut by Burnley as substitute v. Luton in April 1973. Fourth season with Leeds. Under-23 cap.

FKS Golden Series and Soccer 81 stickers

FKS Top Trumps

or not. FKS was stretched. It had fingers in cards, in games and in coins. It lost focus.

Soccer Stars 1977-78 [sic] was a collection of 400 cheap stickers. It was the worst thing FKS could have produced in 1977, the year of Panini's new wave. Panini had three collections for sale: *Football 77* (by Top Sellers), *Euro-Football* and, later in the year, *Football 78*. The cheapness of the FKS collection, the plain backs, and the repetition – swaps – did FKS no good at all. This writer remembers opening packets to find nothing but the same sticker, over and over: half a dozen Leicester City Frank Worthingtons in one packet! It was a low value collection but it's since picked up in price. These days a full album would cost £100.

The *Argentina 78* collection of stickers was almost as weak as the 1977 domestic issue but the fault lay with Fher as much as FKS. The 300 stickers were the product of little imagination, small photos of players and plain backs to boot. The saving grace was the inclusion of home nations teams notwithstanding the fact that only one of them made it to Argentina. £1 is about the top price to pay for these, even for unused stickers, because so many of them were made. The

same stickers were for sale in many other lands. Though most versions were printed in exactly the same format, those from Portugal and the River Plate estuary are worth having. Portuguese stickers show different letterpress and the Argentine collection included a sticker or two of Diego Maradona!

Feeling the heat from Panini, and seeing sales fall drastically during 1977 and 1978, FKS went all in with *Soccer Stars 78 79*. The series was advertised as a *Golden Collection*. Its 448 golden foil stickers were quite something! Even today they hold higher than usual values for FKS ephemera, selling upwards of £5 each, if unused. The packet for this collection shows Coventry City match action. Alas, the golden stickers failed to do the trick. FKS failed to close the gap and lagged behind Panini. Something special was needed. Money!

The *Football League 1st Division 1978-79* was a collection of coins! There were 23 coins to collect. The bronze token collection was a late attempt to buy back the gaze of youngsters awestruck by Italian wares. The coins proved too costly for youngsters living off pocket money, and

the series flopped. Regret is a funny thing. Is it better to regret something you did buy than something you didn't? In this case it's the latter. The coins are now worth over £50 each! A complete set, in near mint condition, with the folder issued, would sell for over £1,000! The 23 coins consisted of 22 teams and one coin celebrating the Football League itself.

FKS's 1979 new wave collection, *Soccer Stars 80*, failed to give FKS the makeover it needed. *Soccer Stars 80* had 450 stickers which included player biographies on the reverse – of some issues – the first appearance of such in 20 years. Due to previous financial losses, *Soccer Stars 80* and its successor, *Soccer 81*, were cheap collections of self-adhesives

FKS coin

whose glue has long since failed. The later series included an attractive selection of British stars from American Major League Soccer. These days most of the 1980 to 1982 stickers fall out of the FKS albums due to an adhesive that did not stick. Loose, unused stickers often meet the same fate. Backing papers fall away from stickers making a mint set somewhat less than perfect.

World Cup Special, which was issued in 1982, was anything but special. It seemed more like a desperate exercise in balancing the accounts. The kids of the time were unimpressed and went to Panini. These days the 307 stickers have become sought after though finding them with backing papers that don't fall away is quite a challenge. The adhesive has often dried and unused stickers are doomed. *Soccer 82* was FKS's last big domestic launch, comprising 400 stickers.

The *Spain 82 World Cup* collection, the second in a year, bemused children and angered parents. The end of FKS was assured. Collectors take note: the Spanish release, by Fher, was made of card, not paper. The cards fared better than the English stickers.

FKS ceased trading, due to huge losses, in 1983. Staff briefly battled on, against the all-conquering legions of Panini stickers, with a short-lived new firm, called Quadriga. It made two collections: *Laws Of Soccer* and *Soccer Stars 83-84* [sic]. These have become the most sought-after FKS-related stickers since those made for the initial collection in 1967. A complete album of either Quadriga series would sell for over £500.

Unused stickers are worth £10 to £25 each. The name, Quadriga, was chosen to evoke the fighting spirit of Boadicea, riding her chariot into battle against The Romans. It proved an unfortunate choice of trope. Had no one told the die-hard Brits at FKS that Boadicea lost? Besides, the brothers Panini were not Romans. Panini hailed from Emilia Romagna. The British chariot went over Beachy Head.

A complete album of either Quadriga series would sell for over £500. Unused stickers are worth £10 to £25 each.

FKS Soccer Stars 1980

FKS Soccer Stars 81 American MLS sticker

FKS Soccer 82 stickers

FKS Spain 82

FKS Quadriga stickers

Flash

Fol-Bo shiny sticker from Mexico 70

lash is a trading name used by Lampo, one of Italy's foremost sticker producers. Under the Flash imprint Lampo issued collections during the late 1970s, notably *Calcio Lampo 1977-1978*, and *Mondiali Argentina 78*, and also *Calcio Internazionale 79*. The two firms were tied to Americana München, in West Germany and Ava Americana in Britain, France and elsewhere. A very similar 1978 collection by EAM/KPA is often wrongly credited to Flash. It's actually by Americana München and Keystone. If you know the earliest cards by the West German issuer Heinerle, from 1960, you'll also see the Keystone imprint on those cards. The domestic 1970s Flash albums look very similar to the British editions by Ava Americana. During the

1980s Flash continued to issue football stickers in Italy, and British and Irish players abound in such series. Mint Flash stickers of British players from 1978 and 1979 are valued around £30 each; and unused British Isles players in Flash collections from the 1980s are worth £20 each, though Paolo Rossi's rookie garners a higher price.

Fleetway is responsible for two series of well known but unbranded football team cards, dated *1958/59* and *1959/60*. The black and white postcard-size cards came in sheets of two cards and four cards, with Tiger comic and also with Lion comic. Children had to buy both comics to get all of the cards. See Lion and Tiger listings for values and more details on these. Fleetway is less well known for issuing postcards. In 1925 it produced FA Cup Final postcards featuring West Ham United and

Bolton Wanderers. Postcards such as these are widely collected and valuable. Expect to pay well over £50 each.

FM Brand Foods was the trading name of a Welsh grocer, Fred Morgan. In 1926 he issued a series of cards. *Welsh Sportsmen* consists of 40 sepia-tinted cards of rugby and football players. Fred's cards are worth around £80 each.

Folgore was an Italian printer. Based in Bologna it's also known as Fol-Bo. In the 1960s it issued many series of stickers including *Calcio serie A 1964-65*, and *L'ABC del Calcio*, some of which were metallised and reissued for the collection, *Mexico 70 - Sempre Forza Italia*. Values for unused metallic stickers of Bobby Charlton and other famous world stars may exceed £100 each.

Flash stickers from Italy, 1977 to 1986

FM Brand Foods was the trading name of a Welsh grocer, Fred Morgan. In 1926 he issued a series of cards. Welsh Sportsmen consists of 40 sepia-tinted cards of rugby and football players. Fred's cards are worth around £80 each.

Brazilian albums by 7 Cores

FORT, Millwall.

Football & Sports Favourite

Presented with FOOTBALL SPECIAL, September 23rd, 1922.

OUR FOOTBALL BOYS—No. 2

TOM CLAY (Spurs' right-back). Five feet ten high, eleven stone ten in weight, and every bit of him brilliant. Has several caps but still has room for more.

Max Woosnam, the larger type Photo Stamp

Our Football Boys postcard

ootball & Sports Favourite, a 1920s magazine, had incorporated Sports Fun in 1922. Its claim to fame, in cartophily, is a 1922 collection of sports stickers. The *Photo Stamp* collection was issued in part by Sports Fun, then by Football & Sports Favourite. It was the second album and sticker ever issued! It comprised 200 perforate (printed perforations) and imperforate stickers in sepia. They were issued in sheets of three large stamps, and in sheets of 12 smaller stamps. Given weekly with Sports Fun and then with Football & Sports Favourite, the exact number of stamps remains a mystery. The number of known stamps exceeds the 144 spaces available in the album, with spaces for 96 small stamps and 48 larger stamps, as 200 stamps are known. This may be due to the disruption to printing that occurred when Sports Fun was taken over by Football & Sports Favourite. The collection has rookies galore, and includes a very early sticker of the boxer Jack Dempsey, which predates his other 1922 rookies by some weeks. It has been seen to sell for £500! Most of the stickers are worth around £50 each though legendary sportsman Max Woosnam will fetch a higher price. Values for uncut sheets are in the hundreds!

Football & Sports Favourite also issued various paper supplements featuring a host of players. Supplements are often rarer than cards due to their fragile nature, and their size. In the 1920s, supplements were not easily collectible, not without gluing them down into scrapbooks, which in turn caused damage, if not ruination. Few remain. Fewer still remain in un-glued, top condition. In 1924 the same magazine issued *Football Moves & Transfers*, and in 1927 a series called *Straight From The Stars*. Values for examples of each are worth over £100. As far back as 1910 Football Favourite, as it was known then, had been issuing soccer supplements. *Players in Their Club Colours* (52 art plates of coloured caricatures) are now worth around £100 each. Note: these supplements have often been wrongly identified as being by Liverpool Weekly Courier. This was all due to an advert for that newspaper that once appeared in Football Favourite.

In 1922 Football Favourite & Football Special issued 12 colour postcards called *Our Football Boys*. They are valued around £50 each. These colourful caricatures are more widely known than some trade cards from this era. Postcard collecting was a well established adult hobby in the 1920s and most families had someone at home who collected postcards. Thus, these particular cards were saved when other issues by the same magazines were played with, destroyed and discarded by younger collectors, which is one of the reasons why so many early trade cards are so rare. Most trade cards didn't make it to the safe harbour of an adult's collection.

In the 1950s a magazine called Football Favourites – no connection to the earlier publication – issued a series of cards, to cut out, called *Art Plates Grand Pictures, Your Favourite Soccer Stars*. The values for such sheets, uncut, are £75 each. Cut singles sell for around £20.

Football Pictorial magazine and Football Supporter magazine issued *Super Strikers*, *Pennants*, and *Team Set* football cards between 1969 and 1974. Back covers and pages within the magazines featured cards and team pennants. There are almost 400 cards to collect! Further, there are also over 100 known cut-out paper pennants.

The Football Post, in Scotland, issued *Our Series of Popular Footballers* supplements in 1904. Values exceed £200 each.

Football Snaps date to 1948. *Football Snaps* are paper stickers. They were issued in two series. Values for series one, numbered 1-24 are around £25 each. Series two stickers, numbered

T. REYNOLDS (Sunderland)

An Art Plate from Football Favourites

Football Star All-Britain Team

LIDDELL

DITCHBURN

MATTHEWS

Frame cards, issued in Scotland, 1948-1951.

No. 20 Chilton
Manchester U.

Football Snap sticker

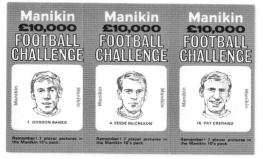

Freeman Football Challenge trio

25-48, are worth £40 each. Packets came without a maker's mark but were inscribed 'registered at Stationers Hall...copyright #14765'. The packet advertised an album, for free, on presentation of all 48 stickers.

Football Star issued the *All-Britain Team* of stand-ups in 1973. The series consisted of 12 cards, issued in sheets of six. Each player came with a name card which was designed to assist with stability of the standing players. If loose, the cards can be identified by the backs. They are without brands and logos but show '*height, wage, age,* and *first cap*'. An uncut sheet with the original magazine, with which it was issued, has been seen to sell for over £100. Single cards of players – with name cards – fetch £10 a pair. Football Star also issued *Super Strikers*, in 1973, comprising 18 hexagonal cut-out stickers, now worth £20 each. A poster was issued for the collection.

Football Supporter magazine issued *Portraits by Rex Benlow*, in 1969, a series of eight large cards with monotone illustrations of players. Their worth is around £20 each.

Formaggino Mio by Locatelli issued cheesy footballers in 1965. The *Serie Campioni di Calcio 1965-66* consisted of 18 3-D lenticular photo cards, each with two players.

Values are around £20 each.

Foto Calcio issued a series of *Calciatori 1965-1966*. The series includes a British footballer,

Gerry Hitchens. Most of the cards are valued at only £5 each but Gerry will cost you more.

Fotopropaganda, an Italian firm, issued *Rotalfoto* in 1950. Such black and white photographic football cards are worth £25 each.

Frame was a Scottish issuer. In 1948 M M Frame issued *Sport Stars*. The 48 cards of players were sold in miniature booklets. In 1950 Frame followed *Sport Stars* with *Sport Aces*, which included 40 cards, also issued in booklets. Values for cards from either series are around £100. For a complete booklet insurance of £500 is advised. In 1951 Frame issued *Smashers Sport Photos*. The 96 cards, also issued in booklets, are more widely recognised than the earlier types. The cards are worth around £20 each, but some fetch a lot more – it depends on the player. These cards were re-issued, in 1952, with a slightly different text matrix on the back.

Franklyn & Davey cigarette cards of 1906, *Loadstone Football Club Colours*, feature the same images used by Ogden, and by Churchman, in that year. Though the artwork is available for a lot less by buying the 51 Ogden cards, values for some of the Franklyn & Davey cards exceed £100 each, notably for Steve Bloomer.

Freeman made Manikin Cigars. In 1969 boxes of such cigars included a *£10,000 Football Challenge* card, which featured a triplet of players, from a collection of 33 illustrated stars. Uncut

trios are worth around £60. Singles fetch £10 apiece. Note: there are three versions of each card.

Fullers, the brewers, celebrated 1974 with *Scottish World Cup Squad Munich 1974*. The 16 water-slide transfer decals are now very scarce and command prices of £50 each, for unused examples.

Fun Products issued a series of *England's World Cup Squad* stickers in 1982.

The 24 stickers are unbranded and without logos but can be identified by a bronze plaque design, a nameplate afoot each sticker. Values are around £10 each.

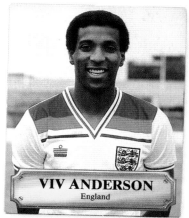

Fun Products, Viv Anderson

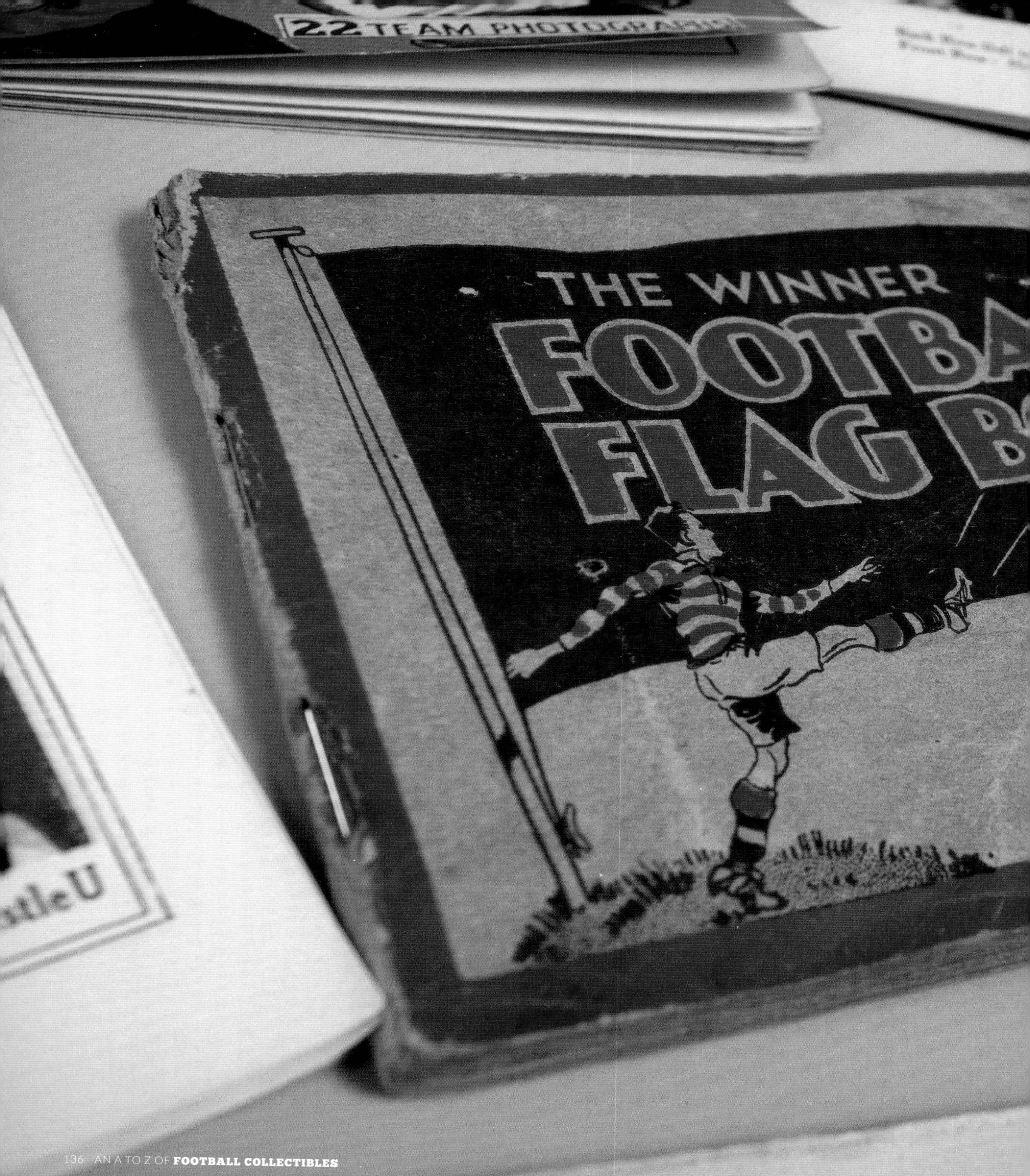
22 TEAM PHOTOGRAPHS
THE WINNER
FOOTBA
FLAG BO
stleU

PRESENTED WITH
"THE SKIPPER"
THE FAMOUS BOYS'
STORY PAPER

Goalkeeper. Born in

joined Preston North

junior side in 19

Gabardine

Galbani Stella, 1962 Kurt Hamrin

Galbani 1965 Yashin, with a numbered Baggioli Yashin

Gabardina 1950 World Cup card, front and back

abardine raincoats from Spain, and cartoon football cards? To advertise his wet-weather wear, a Spanish tailor, trading under the name of Detrás De La Universidad (Behind The University), issued *Mundial 50*, a set of 12 cartoon football teams, based on the World Cup competitor nations. The cards are postcard-size but they are assuredly trade cards. Each card advertised gabardine trench coats for inclement climes. Well, the rain in Spain falls… seldom, if at all, so that's probably why these cards are so rare. Values for such scarce 1950 World Cup ephemera may exceed £100 each card for USA, England and Brazil. Other teams start at £50.

Gabriel was a British tobacconist. In 1902 the firm issued *Cricketers*. One footballer of legendary fame features in this series: C.B. Fry. The value of the card is around £750!

Gaceta del Norte (Northern Gazette) issued a World Cup series in 1974. *Mundiales 74* consisted of 16 large, colour stickers of international teams, including Scotland. The value for these Spanish rarities is about £25 each.

Galbani, in Italy, allied with cards issuers to promote its products. In 1962 it publicised its products on cards by Stella, and, in 1965 it

chose cards made by Baggioli. The latter alliance resulted in a series called *Gli Eroi Della Domenica*, in 1965. The Sunday Heroes (the name of the series) include Jimmy Greaves, Denis Law, Joe Baker, Pele, Eusebio and Lev Yashin. The cards are very similar to the 1965 Baggioli paper issues. However, whereas the Baggioli stickers were numbered, the Galbani collection is numberless, and it's made of card. Most of the cards are worth £5 each, but you'll see British internationals sell for £75, or more. £150 is paid for Pele.

Gallaher, of Belfast and Dublin, was once the biggest cigarette producer in the British Isles. Its first collection of footy cards consisted of 100 *Association Football Club Colours*. The 1910 issue showed generic footballers in team liveries. Within two years a second series of 100 cards followed. The 1912 *Sports Series* includes few football subjects but it's an affordable set, and the cards are highly attractive. Values for most soccer cards by Gallaher, of this period, range in value from £10 to £15 each, with certain exceptions for more popular clubs, and sports.

In 1924 Gallaher launched *British Champions of 1923*, a series of 75 cards, two of which feature football teams: London Caledonians and Bolton Wanderers. These tend to be the most sought-after cards from the series. Values are around

Galbani 1965 Wrapper

Gallaher and Teasdale cards

£10 for each team. Gallaher reverted to just football in 1925. *Famous Footballers* (cards with green backs) was a hugely successful collection of 100 players. The idea would be repeated twice in coming years, firstly with *Famous Footballers* (brown backs), a series of 50 cigarette cards; and secondly, with *Footballers* (cards with red backs that also feature match action on half the series) in 1928. A fourth series included just scenes from matches: *Footballers In Action* (blue backs). Values for all Gallaher cards from this period are around £5 each. Around the same time as Gallaher was producing such fare, a sweet cigarettes issuer, Teasdale, used scenes from some of Gallaher's *Action* cards on its paper, black and white inserts. Ironically the monotone paper children's issues are now worth far more than the colourful cards collected by adults. See also: Teasdale.

During the 1930s Gallaher failed to issue football series. However, they did release *Park*

Drive Champions. The 48 card pan-sport series from 1934 includes two footballers: Everton's Dixie Dean and Alec James of Arsenal. Both cards are known in two varieties: with and without names to the front. Prices paid have exceeded £30 for a pair. Gallaher issued a second pan-sport series in 1936. *Sporting Personalities* is lowly valued due to its availability – like so many 1930s cigarette cards many millions were made. It includes seven footballers, which tend to be the most sought-after cards from the set, including Arsenal, Everton, Birmingham City and Sheffield Wednesday players. Prices for single footballer cards may exceed £5.

Gallina Blanca (White Hen) was a fowl of Iberian pedigree. It issued two general collections of stickers in the late 1940s, both of which included Spanish football subjects. The *1° Album Gallina Blanca* included 10 Spanish league teams,

and the *2° Album Gallina Blanca 1949/50* [sic] included players and teams. The players were issued in pairs. Uncut pairs and teams may sell for over £20 each.

Garbaty was a German tobacco issuer. In 1931 Garbaty's Kurmark Cigarettes came with *Sportwappen – Fussball (Sports Coats of Arms – Football)*. The stunning series of cards consisted of 645 club colours and emblems. A set of unused cards would be worth well over £600 but in an

Three Gallaher cards

Gallaher's Park Drive Champions, two types

Four Gallher backs

Gallina Blanca, 1947

Sport Gazette 1934 postcard of Giovanni Ferrari

ARDILES   MACARI

Sport Gazette cut-out stickers of Ardiles and Macari

Gem Library
card, 1992

Presented Free with
"THE GEM" LIBRARY
July 1st, 1922.

No. 13.
Special Action Photo
of
TOM HAMILTON
Preston North End's famous
Full-back.

TWO splendid Real Photos of
Famous Footballers will be
given Free with next Wednesday's "Gem."

Order your copy TO-DAY.

The Gem Library Picture Album, 1933, with
Dixie Dean, Bill Woodfull & Jack Crawford

album, a complete set, glued down, will cost a lot less. Gartman, another German issuer of the 1930s, issued *Sportbilder, sportserien 1-15*, a series of 90 cards, in which there are many notable football subjects. Garbaty, Gartman and other pre-war German cards cover a vast territory and need a book just for themselves. More on them, their series, the cards, and their values in a future edition of this book.

Gazette of Sports, or Gazzetta dello Sport, as it's called in Italy, is a sport lover's newspaper. Since the 1930s it's been giving away football cards. In 1934 it issued redemption trade cards, available for tokens and cash, in the format of postcards. The cards featured the stars of the victorious Italian national team of 1934, World Champions. Up until more recently the newspaper has continued to issue cards. In 1978 it included free sheets of soccer stars, called *Argentina 78 Copa Mundial*. The cards, to cut out, came in two sizes, and an album was available for them. These days an uncut sheet of cards is worth £50. Single, cut cards fetch about £10 - with premiums for famous names like Cruyff, Ossie Ardiles and Ricky Villa. Each of the 15 Scottish stars have been seen to sell for £15 to £20 each.

The Gem Library was a British publication for school children. In 1922 it gave free *Special Action*

Photos and also *Footballers*, in pairs. All in all there were 22 players on eight large cards and seven smaller cards. The series includes a card of Max Woosnam, the sporting legend, and it commands a higher value than the other cards. Values for uncut pairs start at £20 but cut single cards can be found for £2 each. The Gem issued two follow-up series later in 1922: *Autographed Real Action Photo Series* (six cards, worth £5 to £10 each) and *Autographed Action Series* (four cards, again worth around £5 to £10 each). In 1926 The Gem issued something decidedly different: The *Footer Puzzle*. The puzzle was a supplement and a game, in one. The idea was to fold, and refold the supplement, to reveal hidden footballers. It featured 16 pictures of stars of the day. Due to very few of these surviving the ravages of time, not to mention scissors, values exceed £100 for undamaged games.

The Gem Library issued its first sticker album in late 1933, which included a page dedicated to *The Year's Sport*. Sheets of sports stickers were issued to cut and glue into the album. The sticker of Everton's captain, Dixie Dean, as imagined by an artist, receiving Everton's second FA Cup, is worth as much as the entire collection, around £125! There are also cricket and tennis stickers of some worth in this early sticker and album issue.

Gente (People) was an Italian glossy magazine. In 1970 it issued stickers in sheets, to cut out and glue into an album. The *Mexico 70* stickers are worth £20 each for single English lions. Uncut sheets fetch premium prices.

Gezelle Cigars issued various series of cigar bands involving football. Cigar band collecting, like cards, is a passionate hobby, with a history. A hundred years ago four out of five men in the west smoked cigars! Billions of bands were made yearly. Images of football world greats appearing around a cigar were designed to mark the comfortable smoke-to point, a stain protecting holder, and for advertising. Vintage cigar bands showing great sportsmen are much sought after. Values depend on subjects but a price of £25 for a cigar band of a famous player from the 1960s is typical.

Gilda of Benelux issued *World Championship 1978* stickers with Mintina sweets. The 20 stickers include players from the Dutch team. Values peak with Johan Cruyff, at around £30.

Gines Hellin Abelian of Spain issued *Album Chicote* in 1946. Its 308

Gente cut-out
sticker, 1970

football stickers are worth around £10 each but Gainza will fetch many times that figure!

Giornalino, the little daily journal, was a 1980s Italian news magazine for children. International players were occasionally given as free cards, in sheets of eight or ten. Various 1970s and 80s issues of Giornalino include British and Irish stars from the World Cup and European Championship tournaments of the time. Values for these cards and stickers range from £10 to £30 for cut singles, and uncut sheets of cards command premium prices.

Glasgow Weekly Mail issued *Series of Famous Footballers*, in 1913. The set consisted of 11 coloured sheets, each featuring nine players. Sadly most seem to have been cut up for singles as few intact sheets remain. An entire sheet of nine players would be worth £300. Cut singles make about £25 each. Glasgow Weekly Mail also issued 14 large colour supplements of single footballers. Their value is over £100 each.

Globo Gum, from France, issued *Les As du Football (Football Aces)* in 1937. The collection looks similar to the *Val Footer Gum* cards by Klene Confectionery. It comprised 64 cards, in black and white. Values are around £25 each card. Globo Gum also published *Champions Tous Sports* in 1938. Its 64 gum cards include the legendary boxer, Joe Louis. The value of this card is around £1,000! In

1939 Globo Gum printed a third series of trade cards: *Footballers*. The cards were in postcard format, in black and white. Values are around £30 each card. After the war Globo returned to sports cards in 1951 with *Equipes Et Scenes Du Foot*, a series of action and teams; and *Footballers* in 1952. Values for the post-war cards are around £20 each.

Goal Crisps gave away *Steve Heighway All Star Series* in 1971, a series of 22 game cards. The firm also issued a series of Steve Heighway autograph cards. They were double-sided, with puzzles on one side, and action shots to the other.

Goal Magazine gave away *Goal Gallery of World Stars* stickers in 1969. A series of 20, it consisted mostly of British players, and Pele. Values are around £20 each.

Golden Wonder crisps issued a trio of football & sports cards series in the 1970s: *Soccer World Cup All Stars*, *Soccer All Stars* and *Sporting All Stars*. The cards are worth £1 each but if they are still contained within a protective plastic wrapper, as issued, values rise enormously.

Goodies sweet cigarettes issued a commemorative football series of 25 cards to mark the 1974 World Cup. Values for such cards are around £5 each.

Green Shield footballers are so called because of their format and colour. The unbranded cards are by an unknown issuer. Abe Blight, of Barnsley,

Goodies sweet cigarettes World Cup 74 cards

and his 31 goals scored during 1933/34 – and his team's promotion from Division 3 North – assured this card a place in the series, and dates it accordingly. The shield-shaped series comprises 16 cards, some with stars to the rear, others without. Other great players in this highly attractive and sought after series include Birmingham City's Harry Hibs, Sam Cowan of Manchester City, Hugh Gallacher of Chelsea, and William Cook of Bolton Wanderers. Values range from £100 to £250 each.

Giornalino cut-out sticker, 1982

Gladgow Weekly Mail cut-out sticker, 1913

Globo gum, 1937

Goodies sweet cigarettes issued a commemorative football series of 25 cards to mark the 1974 World Cup. Values for such cards are around £5 each.

Green shield footballers, 1933

Greiling, 1930s German cards and stickers, with Fulham v. Preston

Groothoff Dutch card of Liverpool v. Arsenal, 1933

Greiling backs

Greiling's tobacco issues could fill a book of their own. This is just a sample listing of Germany's massive cigarette producer of the Weimar democracy. In 1926 *Fussballsport* included 934 cards of players and teams. It was followed by *Fussball – Moment*, a series of 451 cards. The same year Greiling issued *Fussballsport*, a collection of 902 cards! It wasn't done with 1926. *Fussballsport, series 1-14* (270 cards) and *Fussballmoment, series 1-26* (810 cards) followed. That's about 3,500 different cards in just one year! Greiling included many non-German teams and players in its issues so they have become sought-after outside Germany as well as within. Values for Greiling cards showing British teams and players start at £25 each. Much more on Greiling cards in a future book.

Grimsby's Evening Telegraph issued *Town Stars* in 1952. The 25 cards have values from £25 to £75 each. One-club sets of cards by local issuers are not going to be covered in depth in this book, but much like the Huddersfield Town cards of the 1920s, these cards are classics. See also: Evening Telegraph.

Groothoff, a Dutch tobacconist, gave *Voetbal Techniek en Tactiek* cards with cigarettes in 1933. This colourful series of tobacco cards from Holland featured a host of British stars and teams in action, including cards of players from Arsenal, Bristol Rovers, West Ham, Newcastle, Liverpool, Chelsea, Everton, Sheffield United, etc.

Values start at £25 each, and rise significantly for cards featuring all-time greats.

Guardian Journal, in Nottingham, issued *Two In Gear*, pairs of footballers, in 1969. Many local newspapers issued similar twin cards at the time. Like most print media outlets today, many papers can be owned by one very rich person in Monaco, or by a faceless multinational. In 1969, EMAP, the East Midlands Publishing group, owned papers up and down the land. Hence, papers from as far afield as London, like Newham Recorder, which issued pairs of West Ham players in 1969; to Sports Argus in Birmingham, which issued twinned Villains the same year, were being directed by a hidden hand. Values start at £25 each paired card.

Guara roundels from Brazil, 1958

Guara is one of the legendary issuers of early Pelé cards. The Brazilian issuer of the 1950s made *Cartela Campeoes Mundiais Futebol*. The 24 packet-issue cards are circular, a little like pogs, but roughly cut. Refrigerante Guara encouraged its clientele to collect the diminutive roundels and stick them to a chart (a small, fold-over paper pamphlet) which, once complete, was to be sent to the firm to redeem prizes. It's no wonder there are not many left in circulation. Most were destroyed by the issuer to ensure used, redeemed cards could not be reused. Values range from hundreds of pounds for players like Garrincha, to thousands for bigger names like Pelé. The 1958 World Cup winning team issue is one of the later Guara series. Similar discs and charts had been produced by Refrigerante Guara throughout the 1950s, mostly featuring Brazilian domestic soccer players. The 1958 World Cup chart was of a pinkish-orange hue. Blue and white coloured roundels, seen singly, may have pinkish-orange paper glued to their backs. Until now the only known examples are either stuck to, or cut from the charts. No original packets with intact cards have been seen. To see Pelé from this series go to footballsoccercards.com

Chix Gum cards album, 1950s

Heinerle

Heinerle cards from 1960

Heinerle cards from 1961

Heinerle cards from 1962

einerle is a name to make rookie card collectors cringe. Heinerle cards of Pelé were once believed, by wishful thinkers, to be from 1958 – Pelé's first year on football cards. They were wrong. Heinerle football cards were not issued in 1958. Then they hoped it was 1959. Well, one of the earliest Heinerle football cards shows the date, on a card showing the end of the West German football championships that year, but the series was not issued in 1959 either. The earliest Heinerle soccer cards were issued after the 1950s were over. The West German firm included its first football cards in its general, mixed sports issue of 1960: *Die Kleine Regelecke*. Specialist reference books on cards, issued in Germany, categorically date the first Heinerle football cards issue to this time. These include an excellent book by Päsler, and a comprehensive tome written by Koberich. Heinerle had made its first cards in 1959 but they were not soccer cards. The 1959 series contained only movie stars and singers. The *Die Kleine Regelecke* of 1960, with the football cards, was issued in *Wundertuten* (sealed packets, a little like *lucky bags*). There are 252 cards, of which 142 relate to soccer. The inclusion of Ernie Taylor, of Manchester United, has confused many collectors. He played at Old Trafford for half a

year, betwixt equinoxes, in 1958. In the light of his inclusion some collectors had erroneously presumed the entire series was made in the late 1950s. By the time the cards were distributed, in 1960, Taylor had long since left Old Trafford. He'd been included in the series in homage to the rebuilt Manchester United team. A card featuring the team was also included, as were cards of retiring Wolves captain Billy Wright, for England; the evergreen Stanley Matthews, and FA Cup winners, Bolton Wanderers, in 1958; and Nottingham Forest, in 1959. The re-dating of Heinerle's earliest soccer cards to 1960 will have a striking effect upon values of the Pelé cards. However, the Pelé action card (jumping for a header) will still fetch £200, even as a 1960 card. The Brazil team card (with Pelé) is worth around £100. British players and teams from the series are valued at about £50 each.

During 1960 Heinerle went into production overdrive, printing many series of cards. The winter Olympics were on so they featured on Heinerle cards. Other series included TV stars (120 cards), transport (144 cards) and there were two more sports collections. In 1961, *Fussball* consisted of 183 soccer cards. This series includes Danny Blanchflower, of Spurs. Other soccer legends featured include Alfredo di Stefano, Pelé and Raymond Kopa. There

are British and Irish players to be found in the series, for example, Dennis Stevens of Bolton Wanderers, a goal scorer in the 1958 FA Cup final; and Manchester United's Harry Gregg. Prices paid for British stars from this series have reached £100 each. A similar series was issued by a rival firm, Schütt, during the same 1960/61 season. The Schütt cards can be distinguished from those issued by Heinerle due to the back, which shows four sporting figures, one of whom wears a ponytail and seems to be escaping from a more masculine image of a ball player. A notable Pelé card from Müller & Son's *Schütt* series is worth £200. (See also Schütt).

In 1962 Heinerle issued a further 144 footballer cards. They can be differentiated from earlier issues due to the frameless fronts and featureless backs with no sporty graphics (earlier cards had shown suchlike). The backs of the cards are crammed full with information and statistics. Amidst the many players in this series are stars from Barcelona, Inter Milan, Torino, etc. Luisito Suarez, Denis Law and other British players feature. There is Everton, Aston Villa and Burnley interest, to name but three British Isles teams included. There are also cards showing Northern Ireland international action. Cards with British Isles players and teams sell for £30 to £50 each.

INGHILTERRA 🇬🇧

SPRINGETT — J. CHARLTON — VENABLES — HUNTER — PEACOCK — BOBBY CHARLTON

Helvetia

Helvetia was an Italian chocolatier from Reggio Emilia, in central Italy. In the 1920s it issued 90 cards in a collection called *Album Cioccolato Sport-Regalo* [sic]. The collection includes various sportsmen, with 15 footballers. Values for these cards are around £50 each.

...presenta l'album con la collezione... di queste 90 figurine diamo... L. 26 in denaro. Dopo... la collezione viene... e resta in proprietà del collezionista. Spedire raccomandato a "HELVETIA„ Fabbrica Cioccolato-Reggio E.

Zaccagna

An Italian Helvetia chocolates card from the 1920s

MOORE — CONNELLY — WILSON — THOMPSON — GREAVES — COHEN

Italian 1966 England stand-up cards

Palirex 1968 album from Portugal

Hignett Brothers

ignett Brothers released a series of 50 *A.F.C. Nicknames* [sic] cigarette cards, in 1933. It followed these, in 1935, with *Football Caricatures*, a further series of 50. Hignett's third series, *Football Club Captains* was out in 1936. Most Hignett soccer cards are worth between £5 and £10 but you can get the same images for a lot less by buying Ogden or Players cigarette cards of the same series, for just £1 or £2 each.

Hill Tobacco issued what's become a very rare series of football cards, in 1906: *Football Captains Series* included 20 cigarette cards that are rarely seen nowadays. Values for the cards exceed £100 each. Hill printed a similar series in 1912. The cards were given with its Nyasa brand of cigarettes: *Famous Footballers*. This series contains a stunning and costly, rare card of Manchester United's Billy Meredith.

The grim look of Hill's Edwardian cards cheered up, with lighter hues, after the Great War. The 1920s sepia-toned *Sunripe Famous Footballers*, whose values are around £8 each, were followed by decidedly colourful cards in the 1930s. Various pan-sports and soccer series were issued: *Sports* (50 cards including a couple of soccer stars); *Popular Footballers* (issued with Gold Flake Honeydew, and Navy Cut brands); *Famous Footballers* and *Celebrities of Sport*, all of which are valued at around £5 each card.

Hitschler, a West German firm, issued 91 cards, including 14 England stars, in a series called *Mexico 70*. England cards are worth £30 each.

Holy Head Football Rock was a 1920s firm. It issued 60 trade cards from its base in Birmingham. The *Football Teams* have values exceeding £100 each. As redemption issues (they were returned to the supplier for rewards) few have survived.

Holmar of West Germany issued a series of Sportsmen and other images in the 1950s. The various small but colourful paper cards may exceed £25 each.

Hunter Tobacco was a Scottish cigarette maker based in Airdrie – so sayeth the cards. A baker's dozen football cards by Hunter are known. They were printed around 1900.

These cards have fetched thousands of pounds each, on the rare occasions when they have come to the market. So, if you collect north-eastern teams like Boro, Toon and Sunderland; or Scottish teams like Rangers and Celtic, save your pennies!

Hignett cigarette cards from the 1930s

Hill cards of Crystal Palace and Man Utd players from 1906 and 1912

Hill cards from the 1920s and 30s

Hurricane

A Hurricane 1964 sticker

1. GORDON BANKS
(LEICESTER C.)

Presented free with
HURRICANE
More pictures next week

JACK MILBURN *Newcastle United*

A decal transfer by Hobbies Limited of Dereham

urricane was a comic of the 1960s. A collection called *Footballers of 1964* (40 different) was issued in sheets of 10 stickers. Values for intact sheets with the comic of issue exceed £100. Sheets are otherwise worth around £50 each, and single stickers sell for around £5 – more for those with an attached advert sticker.

Hobbies Limited, of Dereham in Suffolk, was a printer of books on pastimes. In 1956 it published a book that contained a sheet of transfers. The so-called *Hobbies & Handicrafts Sportsmen* decals included eight stars of sport which the publisher advised be cut and stuck to blocks of fret-sawed wood, as game pieces. Uncut sheets of decals have been seen to sell for over £200. Single transfers can make £50 each.

In 1964 Hornet comic gave away a series of 16 football cards, called *International Cup Teams*, which were issued in sheets of four. These are often found cut to single cards. Not many quads survive intact. A plastic wallet was issued to keep cut cards together. An uncut sheet of four cards is worth £50. Cut singles are easier to afford at just £2 each. The following year Hornet launched *Top Players* and *Teams of Today and Yesterday*, a series

Hornet International Cup Teams

Publicity flyer for Hornet's sister comic Wizard which also issued a sports stickers ring

Hotspur

of colour supplements, which included 48 images, published on fold-over sheets – most of which are typically found cut to single teams and quartets of players. Not many sheets survive intact. Likewise, with Hornet's 1966 series, *Top Cup Teams*, a series of 12 cards, not many are to be found as they were issued, in sheets of four. The *Gallery Of Sport*, from 1967, was more of the same: a series of folding supplements of footballers and teams. Uncut supplements may fetch £50 but cut singles are worth very little.

Hornet comic issued an album of stickers in 1968. *Bernard Briggs Football 68* included 39 shaped stickers, to be cut out from sheets given with the comic. A complete album is worth about £25 – most readers cut and stuck the collection – but an uncut sheet of stickers is worth triple that price. Cut, single stickers are worth £1 each. It's an unusual collection of players' heads, torsos, bodies, with a few team pictures to boot. Hornet joined forces with sister publication, Hotspur comic, in 1970, to issue *World Cup Stars*, each comic giving 36 cards, in sheets of eight or ten.

In 1972 Hornet treated its readers to one of the most unusual comic free gifts of the time. *The All-Star Ring* comprised a plastic finger ring and a sheet of small stickers of sportsmen. The reader would peel off the sticker of the player she/he preferred and wear the chosen sports star on a finger. A complete sheet, uncut, with the ring would sell for well over £100! Single stickers are worth £10 each. A similar ring and *20 super photos of stars to stick* [sic] was given away, in March 1973, by Wizard comic

Hotspur comic issued fare similar to Hornet. In 1965 it gave away *Stand-up footballers*, in sheets of five each, with name cards. Uncut sheets, with five players and their name cards, are worth over £75.

In 1975 Hotspur revived the idea with a new collection called *Super Stand-up Stoppers and Strikers*. Two sheets of 12 players were issued, each being worth £100. See: Victor comic for images.

Hotspur comic stand-up football cards, as issued

BEST
A. HATELEY
G. WALLACE
Presented with
"THE HORNET"
BERNARD BRIGGS' ALBUM
OF FOOTBALL '68
Presented with "THE HORNET"
Stars
giv
in we
REME

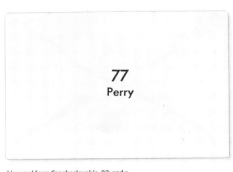

Lisa card from Czechoslovakia, 83; and a modern forgery, numbered 77

Ideas Magazine

Ideas magazine was an Edwardian periodical. Between 1908 and 1910 it gave away various football free gifts. Such gratuities include a pair of English Cup Finalist postcards, of Wolves and Newcastle; and a score of Irish and Scottish teams, as frameable supplements. Values for such ephemera start at £100 apiece.

Ilsa, the name, may bring exploitation movies to mind, yet, in the pre-war land of Czechoslovakia it connoted candy and cards, not wicked wardens. Ilsa issued sports cards with its *Milk Mocca* and other sweets. A collection known as *Album Sportovcù* was issued in 1933/34. Included in its cards is one of Everton's Dixie Dean. Caveat Emptor: modern copies of these simple monotone cards exist and are even known to be graded as genuine by supposed experts. Ways to spot fake Ilsa cards: the numbers on the back of the cards were cursive, not block lettering. There was no name. Cards with names, and squarer numbers are fakes. Values for originals start at £50 each.

In the 1890s Imeson's Boots issued *The Boot People Of The North* football cards. Football shield-shaped cards, like those by Baines of Bradford, were all the rage and Imeson indulged itself in the sporty Victorian trend. It's escutcheon ephemera includes teams like Accrington Stanley and Leek FC. Values start at £150 each.

Imperia publishing, of Milan, printed many series of football cards and stickers in the 1960s, starting with *Calcio 1963-64*, which consisted of 294 footballers. The stickers were reprinted more than once, to cope with demand, and are known on various materials from thin paper to card. Having plain backs, the coloured stickers are easily misidentified. There are two distinct designs in the same collection: world stars, and Italian league players. Caveat Emptor: modern reprints (primitive copies) are in circulation but you can spot them quite easily. Original paper will have tiny small blotches of foxing (acidic residue in the paper that is coloured brown) and its paper content will be rich. The originals, whether card or paper, have an uneven, broken varnished sheen that shows up as a shiny, uneven film when a card is angled to the light. Values start at £15 for most Italian players and rise to over £500 for Pele.

Indiana-Sport gum cards were issued in France, in the 1930s. The beautiful series of sports cards includes football, rugby and a host of other sports. The cards are rare and valuable. Some of them have sold for more than £100 each.

Industria Argentina: two words that have confounded collectors – and so-called experts! The words translate, simply, as Made In Argentina. Cards or albums with this legend often relate to Crack, a firm from Buenos Aires. It issued various pogs, cards and stickers but *Album de Figuritas El Libro De Los Mundiales Supercoleccion* is about as unrefined as Crack football cards got. It was more 1958 than 1978. Some of its stickers resemble clippings from advertising newspapers. As useful to grease monkeys, for wiping oil, as it is attractive to collectors. The paper series includes 200 stickers, many in primitive monotones, of emblems, stadia and players. The few copies that survived being cast unto the dingy reaches of garage pits, and the darker recesses of the world, have accrued values starting at £20 each sticker – with much higher prices paid for big-name stars! Crack would issue finer fare for the 1978/79 season. *Super Futbol* includes many appearances by Maradona, on stickers, both action and caricature; and on a card pog.

Imperia cards of Vava from 1963, two distinct printing

Indiana-Sport gum card from France, 1930s

Crack, a pog of Maradona from 1978/79

Crack, a card of Maradona from 1978/79

Lion transfers, 1979, Nottingham Forest versus France!

Éditions du Lion s.à.r.l.

Jackdaw Publishing

Jackdaw, 1970

Jardinière Chicory 1930s card from France

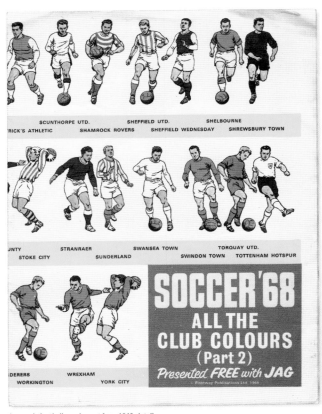

Jag comic football supplement from 1968, detail

ackdaw Publishing, in Great Britain, issued cards as part of a weekly encyclopædia. Buying the publication from the eve of 1970, onwards, ephemera collectors were no doubt exhausted by issue 104, in 1971, which included the 12 black and white cards of Billy Meredith, Alex James, Ricardo Zamora, etc. Edited by Doug Gardner, the portfolio of collectibles – it was issued as a collection of ephemera, papers, cards, a game and some reproduction football programmes – has increased in value in recent times. Individual cards may sell for more than £10 each but a complete portfolio, as issued, is worth significantly more!

Jag was a short-lived comic. In 1968, the first issues came with *Soccer'68 All The Club Colours* [sic]. The free gift consisted of two paper fold-outs of team strips. An uncut fold-out supplement is worth around £40. Rarer are the 1968/69 footballers packet-issue cards that were meant to be cut from front covers of Jag comic. Uncut comics with football cards covers are worth about £50, while cut singles are £5 each.

Jardinière Chicory was a pre-war French issuer of coffee-like drinks. During the 1930s it gave away free sports cards with its chicory produce. The unnamed series includes footballers, drivers, cyclists, tennis players, and so on. These rare cards of notable sportsmen have been seen to sell for more than £100 each.

JAS are Spanish cards from recent times. This is an exceptional inclusion, for this book, and the JAS cards are mentioned albeit briefly by way of an example of rarities that can be found by trawling Spanish collectibles websites, like TodoColeccion (www.todocoleccion.net). In 2012 the series of tear-apart JAS cards were given as free gifts with an Iberian magazine, much as cards and stickers come with Match magazine, in the United Kingdom. Such fare would remain unknown to collectors in the British Isles were it not for websites such as TodoColeccion. Buying from sellers in Spain will give you the edge over British and American dealers, and it will save you money. It's easier than you think. TodoColeccion's website has an English language option (click from *ES* to *EN*, at the top of the page). Register and buy – it's that simple! However,

searching in Spanish works best. Click back to *ES* and use these terms: *cromo* and *Inglaterra*, *Escocia*, *Gales* and *Irlanda* for home nations football cards. That's just the start of the adventure. Try the word *tarjeta*, for a postcard; and *pegatina* for a sticker. It's so simple! It's similar to Ebay but TodoColeccion has long been considered a secret treasure trove by British and American card dealers. Now you know too. The only issue with TodoColeccion is you have to check whether sellers accept internet payments, as some Spanish sellers insist on bank transfers (costly for Brits with exchange penalties from pounds to Euros but safe enough if you use certified or insured postage). The JAS freebies of 2012, which included an early Gareth Bale Welsh card, were scarce upon issue and have escalated in value in the UK. While prices on the British market are £20, in Spain you'll get the same modern card by JAS for less than £5! For reasons of copyright JAS cards, like most recent cards, won't be shown in this book. In its place is a much more valuable card, by Jarab Climent, of Spanish soccer legend Alcantara. This card was found on the Spanish collectibles website mentioned above.

Jay Dees Newsagents once issued matchbox football labels. They all bear the legend, *The Cornish Match Company*. Issued between 1979 and 1983, the footballer matchbox labels caught the public imagination at a time when soccer stickers were in the ascendancy. Though they were, by no means, the first, they are probably some of the best known of their type. Matchboxes and match booklets with soccer labels and covers go back over 100 years. When it comes to collecting, matchbox labels and boxes are in a field of their own. They are a little outside the scope of this tome but there will be more on footy phillumeny (matchbox collecting) in a future book. Values for Jay Dees labels are £1 each but antique boxes featuring great players and teams can sell for over £100!

Jean's Fussball was a West Germany imprint that issued denim-like stickers in the 1970s. Made by a firm called Ali Erzeugnisse, Jean's Fussball issued three series of *Wappen* (*Emblems*) between 1976 and 1978. British collectors will be pleased to know that Ali had a soft spot

for home nations footy. Clubs like Arsenal, Newcastle, Leeds and Liverpool can be had in a raft of variations. Values start around £15 each for the easier to find 1978 issue, rising to £50 for earlier rarities. The 1978 series is easily differentiated by the weave of the denim pattern – and the 1978 club emblems had enjoyed an upgrade too. The earlier series are very similar to one another.

Job cigarette papers is a firm that has come to be pronounced like the Biblical prophet but the firm's name is actually Papier J◆B. The French business was created by Jean Bardou. He marked his produce with initials and a diamond shape. His wares were issued across Europe, including Italy, where, in 1934, card stiffeners for packets of cigarette papers featured footballers in colour. The cards have become almost mythical, as collector's items, due to their rarity. The international collectability of Job ephemera ensures prices stay high. The various slim, colour cigarette cards may fetch over £100 each, if they come to market.

Job cigarette papers, three cards from Italy, 1930s

Spanish card from TodoColeccion, of Alcantara

A typical football matchbox from the 1970s, more elegant than those by Jay Dees

Jean's Fussball three types of denim sticker

Junior Pastimes, 1950s cards from Scotland

C. MILLIGAN

JOCK McNEE

Junior Pastimes issued quirky cards. They were sold in Scotland, in small booklets, in which the cards were stapled together, in small selections of five or seven. The series, *Popular English Players*, issued in 1950, and *Popular Players*, from 1951, consisted of 52 cards each. Values start at below £5 a card but rise significantly for rarer types. Note: the cards can also be found stamped with the mark of a rival brand: Kiddy's. Perhaps Junior Pastimes came to be taken over by its rival. See: Kiddy's Favourites.

Jugoslavija, or Yugoslavia, was formed after the fall of the Austro-Hungarian Empire, following World War One. During the 1920s the Kingdom of the Southern Slavs (Jugoslavija means just that) enjoyed football card collecting just as much as countries in the British Isles. Across the former Balkans kingdom cards were issued throughout the 1930s and 1950s, often featuring foreign footballers. Some of the rarest known British

players on football cards were issued in Belgrade and Zagreb. You can find such rare gems for sale by sellers in former Jugoslavija – which is the way you will need to spell the name, as a search term – on international collectors' auction and fixed sales sites, like Delcampe (www.delcampe.net), however, even in Serbia, Croatia, Bosnia and the other, former Yugoslavian lands such cards are very rare. Patience is a virtue but if you cannot wait you can see a selection on www.footballsoccercards.com

Juwo-Vereinigung, a publisher from tri-lingual Switzerland, issued *Fussball–Football –1962* [sic], a collection of over 100 stickers, to mark the World Cup in Chile. The series is partly coloured, and in part black and white. It was printed in a trio of different sizes: large, medium and small stickers. World greats like Pele, Fontaine, and Di Stefano are included in the series. Values range from £25 to £100 for unused stickers.

Jugoslavia cards of Welsh stars Burgess and Daniel, and England's Tom Finney

Jugoslavia cards of John Charles; and Fulham & Newcastle United stars

Junior Pastimes issued quirky cards. They were sold in Scotland, in small booklets, in which the cards were stapled together in small selections of five or seven. The series, Popular English Players, issued in 1950, and Popular Players, from 1951, consisted of 52 cards each. Values start at below £5 a card but rise significantly for rarer types.

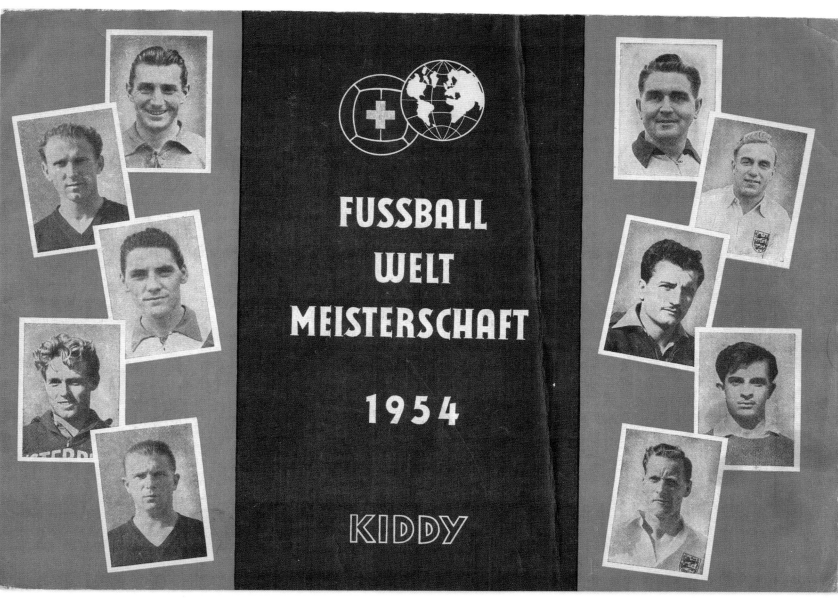

FUSSBALL
WELT
MEISTERSCHAFT
1954
KIDDY

Kiddy, German issue,
1954 World Cup album with
Wright, Finney and Puskas

Kauvit World Cup sticker from 1954, with Puskas

Kane Products

Kane Products issued candy, of which *Roy Rogers Sweet Cigarettes* and *Red & White Confectionery Cigarettes* are examples. The series of cards, *Football Clubs and Colours*, was issued with such candy sticks, during 1956. Though the 25 trade cards are quite easily available, there are two types of cards. They are available printed with and without the Kane brand logo. No matter which type, their worth is around £2.

Kauvit was a German chewing gum. In 1954 it issued *Deutsche Nationalfussball & WM'54* [sic]. The collection shows international footballers in action. The 71 stickers feature the legend, *Kau'Mit Mit Kauvit, Kaugummi* [sic]. The firm also produced various national football collections from 1951 to 1954 but they are mostly outside the scope of this tome, however, Kauvit's *Die Deutsche Weltmeisterschafts-Elf 1954*, a collection of 11 large cards, deserves mention for its exceptional design. There will be more on Kauvit and other West German issuers, in the future. Values for the 1954 stickers start at £5 and exceed £50 for certain world stars, like Puskas.

Keisa of Spain made some very attractive cards in the early 1970s, including *Campeones Del Deporte Mundial*. The cards, which have plain backs and no logos, include footballers, tennis players, boxers, etc. Values start at £5 but stars like Chris Evert, Ali and Johan Cruyff sell for premium prices.

Kellogg's cereals first issued soccer cards in 1961. The classic *International Soccer Stars* consisted of 12 footballers in a cigarette card format. A folder was issued in which to collect the cards. Like most cereal issues – every household had them – these cards are quite easy to find, as singles, but a completed folder, with all 12 cards, is becoming quite scarce. Values start around £3 each for single cards but Bobby Charlton may sell for more. Kellogg's equally commonplace *International Soccer Tips* (eight cards) from 1973, look like someone took a felt tip pen to colour in the backgrounds. They are worth £3 each.

Kenner were the Corinthian toy and cards issuers of their day – and they were a little before their time, too. In 1989 Kenner started to issue *Sportstars*. They were small plastic figurines of footballers, sold in blister packets, with cards, much like Corinthian figurines and cards, for

which Kenner paved the plastic way. Kenner cards are rare – rarer than Corinthian cards. Starting at £20 each they may exceed £50 per card, and are probably the 1980s cards with the most potential for huge reward. The figures and cards, which were packaged in bulky blister card display boxes, were different country by country. In West Germany there were about 40 different players from the Bundesliga. In France, Netherlands, Italia, and Great Britain scores more were issued, including Scotland's Mo Johnston, England's Chris Waddle, Liverpool's Peter Beardsley, and Manchester United's Bryan Robson. Cards issued with toy figurines are always undervalued, and often rarer than imagined. Most cards were thrown away, stuck down into a scrapbook, or otherwise lost. While Kenner and Corinthian loose figurines remain numerous, the cards become dispersed and often more valuable than the plastic effigies of the players themselves.

The *Kentalong Football Card Game* [sic] was launched in 1978. It was clearly a cashing-in, copycat deck of cards, issued to rival Top Trumps. A black and clear plastic case, which is all too often found with broken fastenings, included 38

Kane CBT card, issued with sweet cigarettes, England, 1956

Keisa card of Barcelona's Rexach

Kellogg's 1973 Jackie Charlton card

Kenner card of Jean-Pierre Papin

cards of English club crests, a goalie card and a penalty card. The game, complete, is worth £50. Individual cards sell for about £3 each.

Kiddy's Favourites are post-war classics. The firm issued various series of caricatures between 1947 and 1952. The first Kiddy's cards may well be the series known as the *Rogue Donaldson* cards. These have the legend *Sports Favourites* (just like Donaldson cards) but they are unbranded. They are numbered up to 52. The cards are exceedingly rare and sell for £75 to £150 each. Kiddy's are known to have issued an unbranded series, *Footballer Stars*, during the 1947/48 season. Reflecting the stellar title of the series the cards are decorated with little black stars. Including varieties there are 140 cards to collect, each of which is worth £35 to £100. Cards are known with straight edges and in fancier, die-cut formats. The unbranded *Football Stars* cards are numbered not from 1, but from 53 through to 120, thus, they follow on from the numbering of the aforementioned 52 unbranded cards. During 1947/48 Kiddy's launched a parallel series of *Football Stars* (around 140 cards are available, in all, with red stars). Values for all *Football Stars* cards, red or black, range from £25 to £150. The higher prices are paid for players of note and for the rarer varieties, of which there are many.

Kiddy's Favourites launched *Popular Footballers*, a branded series, of 52 cards with shamrocks, in 1948. Most of the cards are easily available but card number 44 is exceptionally rare and commands a price of about £50. In 1949 the firm launched a new series, *Popular Players*, showing footballers with red hearts. The 80 die-cut cards are worth £10 to £50 each. A similar-looking series of 48 cards was issued in miniature, but there is no mention of Kiddy's on them. There is no logo nor maker's mark, and no biographies either. They bear only a card number, the player's name, his team and his position on the field of play, and they are very rare! Note: during the 1950/51 season, Junior Pastimes, a former rival to Kiddy's Favourites, produced two sets of cards, the earlier cards being found with both Kiddy's Favourites and Junior Pastimes brands.

KHA initials have been seen, as a spurious brand, on very small cards, supposedly issued around 1955. The rubber stamp branding has been applied since the time of issue. These cards originally came with blank backs as a part of much bigger cards featuring many footballers. Someone cut them to singles, then applied a homemade legend: *free with K.H.A.*[sic]. Cards like these have been seen to sell for £30 each.

Caveat Emptor!

King Chewing Gum was made in France. During the 1950s and 60s it issued gum cards. A 1955 set of 50 footballers was issued with and without the brand name, King. These sell for about £10 each, with premiums for all-time greats. In 1957 King issued larger cards showing football teams whose values exceed £25. The firm returned to single players, in the 1960s, with 25 postcard-size colour photo cards, values for which exceed £15 each.

Knorr made little brown cubes of food stock [or something!] that fed a billion school children during the 20th century. The German firm issued a series called *Siege Rekorde Sensationen*, in 1954, which consisted of 64 sportsmen, including many British soccer players. The card of boxing legend Joe Louis fetches the highest price, though there are highly desirable cards of Blackpool, Arsenal, Tottenham Hotspur, Chelsea, Bolton Wanderers and Cardiff City, which have been seen to sell for up to £50 each. A decade later, in 1966, Knorr was one of many issuers to produce a series of World Cup cards, one of which features Franz Beckenbauer – one of his rookies.

Kunold, also of West Germany, issued *FussballWM 1966*. The 16 monotone postcards include England players, Pelé and Lev Yashin, which are worth £50 each.

Kiddy's Favourites backs and fronts of unbranded cards

Kiddy's Favourites cards, various types

King Chewing Gum card, from France

Knorr sticker from 1954 showing Arsenal and WBA action

Lacey's Chewing Wax

Lacey's Chewing Wax gum cards, 1926

Ladbroke Spot-Ball, 1975

acey's Chewing Wax issued the first soccer gum cards issued in the British Isles. The untitled 1925/26 series includes at least 100 different cards, in sepia. Fifty famous footballers from the time appear on the obverse, while two types of card are known for each (the cards came with different legends on the backs, advertising either chewing wax or chewing wax and gum) and there are many cards with varieties. Syd Puddefoot can be found on cards for both Falkirk and Blackburn Rovers; Chas Buchan has been seen on cards for Arsenal and for Sunderland; while Jack Swann appears on cards for both Watford and Leeds United.

Ladbroke issued football cards with Panama cigars, in 1975. The series was called *Spot-Ball*. It consisted of six folding cards, each with two parts, to be separated along a dividing line. Values for complete cards, in pairs, are over £20 each.

Lambert & Butler tobacco made *Who's Who in Sport (1926)* [sic], a series of 50 pan-sport cards that feature two cards showing soccer teams: Bolton Wanderers and Huddersfield Town. The

value of most cards in the collection is £5 but the football cards are worth more. Prices rise substantially for cards paired with very similar, twin issues from an unbranded series by British & American Tobacco, from the same year. Lambert & Butler issued a collection of cigarette cards, devoted solely to soccer, in 1931. *Footballers 1930-1* [sic] includes 52 footballer cards whose look is very similar to the Carreras *Footballers* series of 1934. Most of the Lambert & Butler cards are valued at around £5 each but popular teams and rarer varieties of cards – look out for cards amended with team transfers – fetch much more.

Lamberts of Norwich is known to have a set of the 1958 Amalgamated Tobacco cards of *Football Clubs and Badges* printed in its name. The series of cards is shared with brands like Mills Tobacco, Johnny Bunny, etc. The cards are worth £2 each.

Lampo, the Italian stickers and cards giant, was Panini's greatest rival, and an international competitor with Fher from Spain. Lampo started making stickers in the early 1950s, when it was known as Casa Editrice Vecchi. Working with

Fher, in Spain, Lampo produced collections like *Sport Magico*, a 3-D series that needed 3-D glasses for viewing the stickers! Amazingly such multi-dimensional madness was a success. Lampo syndicated other issues, under its own Vecchi imprint, as far afield as Brazil. Throughout the 1960s Lampo issued stickers and cards under other guises too. In 1966 it used the name Verbania; and, in 1970 it issued cards as Moderna. During the 1970s it was involved in issuing the international Ava Americana collections, and throughout the 1980s it traded as Lampo and Flash. See also: Vecchi, Moderna, Ava, Verbania, EAM, Flash.

The 1958 Lampo footballer sticker album, *Calciatori*, included 272 numbered, colour stickers. Having plain backs, with no branding, many collectors have struggled to identify them correctly. The series includes British stars Tony Marchi from Spurs, for Torino; and erstwhile Leeds United star, John Charles, in the black & white stripes of Juventus. Charles was to be featured in a host of other Lampo collections through until 1963. Typical values for such

Lambert & Butler and similar British & American Tobacco cards

Lampo sticker of ex-Spurs player Tony Marchi

Lampo sticker of John Charles from 1960

Lampo 1961 sticker of Jimmy McIlroy

Lampo 1961 sticker of Pelé

Lampo and Vecchi card and sticker of England's goalie, Springett

stickers range from £5 to £30, with more money being paid for Charles and Marchi – and for Pelé, for whom prices have been seen to exceed £500 for a single paper sticker from the 1961 Lampo issue, *Calcio Campionato*. The collection consisted of 285 colour stickers, and includes a fine selection of world stars alongside Pelé. Note: the album title differs markedly to that shown on the stickers. The stickers have this legend: *Albo Figurine del Campionato di Calcio*. The world stars include Alfredo di Stefano, Puskas, Kubala, and Just Fontaine; Jimmy McIlroy, John Charles, and Denis Law; Roy Bentley of Chelsea, Arsenal's Joe Baker, for Torino; and Jimmy Greaves, in Milan colours. Values for such British Isles stars can top £50 each, for unused stickers.

For the World Cup, in Chile, in 1962, Lampo issued *Calcio Mondiale 1962*, a collection that consisted of cards – 262 of them. They are very similar to the 1962 paper stickers issued by Vecchi, in Brazil (Vecchi was an imprint owned by Lampo). Unlike their Brazilian cousins, the Lampo cards came unbranded, with blank backs. The collection includes 244 players, with six team

cards, and 12 extra Brazil cards, which were issued some months after the collection was launched, to celebrate their win. Values: £150 is the worth of a clean Pelé card (for Pelé by Vecchi, you can triple that figure) and British stars may fetch up to £30 each for similarly very good condition cards (while Brits on unused Vecchi paper stickers have been seen to sell for up to £100 each). Lampo issued stickers as Verbania, in 1965. As such it produced 425 perforated stamps of players and emblems. Some of these are valued at over £100 each. In 1966, Verbania also produced a series of 256 cards inscribed, *Coppa Rimet 1966*. Values range from £10 to £100 each card. Note: a small selection of players from this series, including Jimmy Greaves, was issued on paper stickers, also by Verbania. For the 1970 World Cup, Lampo now trading as Moderna, issued *Mexicorama*. The collection consists of 256 cards, whose values often exceed £50 each. There will be more on Lampo and its many editions in a future edition of this book.

La Pie Qui Chante (The Magpie That Sings) was a French brand of sweets. La Pie Qui

Chante was founded in 1921, in Marseilles. By the 1930s it was issuing cards of internationals like Fred Kennedy (Middlesbrough, Everton and Manchester United) and Raoul Diagne. Kennedy is the most sought after card from this series, and his price is high – £150 to £200 – due to his relationship with three teams of note. The 1930s series containing the Kennedy card is called *Hollywood Sports*, whereas that called *KikLac Football* is the later edition, from the 1950s. It has mostly French stars and teams.

Laughing Cow Cheese, or La Vache Qui Rit, has been making cheese in France since the 1930s. In that time the cow that laughs has produced far more than just cheese. The French processed cheese manufacturer may not be the top cheesewright in France but it is popular, and it has certainly produced some valuable and rare sports cards since its first issue, back in 1931. During Euro 96, and throughout various World Cups, its stickers of Cantona, Henry, Petit and Deschamps were in every food shop across the British Isles. La Vache Qui Rit's first collection was issued in 1931. *Sports Vedettes* are rare, and valuable, but

Lampo 1965 stamp of Gerry Hitchens

Lampo Verbania 1966 card and sticker of Jimmy Greaves

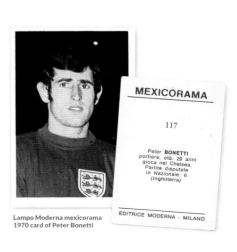

Lampo Moderna mexicorama 1970 card of Peter Bonetti

Calcio Lampo packet from 1977

La Pie Qui Chante cards from 1960

La Vache Qui Rit cards

the series contains no international soccer stars. *Sports Vedettes* are valued from £25 to £50 each, for unused cards. The firm's later fare, like the 1982 series, *Nouvelle Collection Football World Cup*, is worth £15 each, for intact triple cards. The 1983 collection, *3rd National 7-a-Side*, includes a rare Maradona sticker that's worth over £50, if unused.

Leaf, from the Republic of Ireland, made gum and cards. From 1961, a series called *Soccer Internationals*, consists of 30 black and white photo portraits of players, and 20 illustrated caricatures paired with photos. The 50 cards have plain backs, and are without a brand name or logo. Quite easily available, they cost below £5 each.

Lees Tobacco is responsible for a 1912 series of *Northampton Town Football Club* cigarette cards. The 21 cards are worth around £80 each, though some far exceed this figure, notably the card of Walter Tull, a British infantry officer of Afro-Caribbean descent, who died in action whilst leading men of the Middlesex Regiment during the final stages of World War One. Walter Tull's card may fetch £500.

Letraset issued *Kevin Keegan's Action Replay* in 1981. The eight Action Transfers are worth about £30 each, if unused. The individual sets feature Nottingham Forest, Liverpool, Leeds United, Newcastle United and Leicester City, as well as home internationals.

Lewis's Hollywood Scales were weighing machines. In the 1930s the machines issued weight tickets. These came with various designs, including soccer stars. Prices paid for such footballers have exceeded £125 each card.

Liebig soups issued a World Cup series of half a dozen cards, in 1966. The inclusion of Pelé makes *Campeonato Mondiali di Calcio* sought after; however, as a set it's quite easily available and can often be found for around £30.

Lincolnshire Boot Stores made football cards as early as 1900. It issued shield-shaped cards of local clubs (Grimsby and Lincoln are known on its fare). Prices exceed £150.

Lion was a British comic that was well known in the 1950s and 1960s. One of Lion's earliest football free gifts, *Sports Stars In Action*, is all too often found piecemeal, cut up for individual images. Taking scissors to comic free gifts, like this, to clip out single images, ruins otherwise attractive and quite valuable publications. Such cuttings are not cartophilic, so do not pay too much for clipped, single images from this or from similar butchered publications. In 1959 Lion announced its first proper football cards: *Famous Football Teams* – but this title does not feature on the cards themselves. The cards, which were also issued with Tiger comic, a sister publication, show football squads in black and white, dated

Leaf gum cards

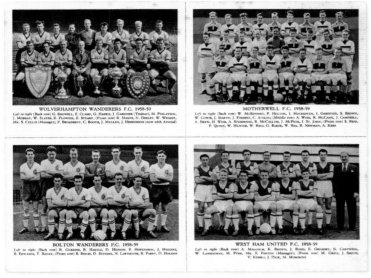

Lion, a sheet of four cards from 1959

Lion, a sheet of red-back cards from 1971

1958–59, after the team name. The series consists of 14 sheets of teams, issued in quads and pairs. The 28 teams are found, mostly, cut to singles. A follow-up series of more teams was issued in late 1959, and through early 1960. The subsequent set shows teams names with the date: 1959–60. Values for uncut sheets of four teams exceed £50. Uncut sheets of two teams are worth about £20, and cut singles can be had for around £2 each.

In 1961 Lion issued a very attractive series of cards called *Famous Football Trophies*. The collection of 26 was issued in sheets. They are shaped, with tabs, to allow the cups to be slotted into a display card which was also given freely with The Lion.

The value of a complete collection of trophies, and winning team name tabs, in uncut sheets, would be around £75. Lion issued its own album and sticker collection in 1967: *The Lion Album of Soccer Stars* includes 110 red-framed stickers that were given in sheets, to cut. Uncut sheets are valued at £25 to £50 each but cut singles are worth little, around £1 each.

In 1970 Lion joined Thunder comic in an expansive series of *My Favourite Soccer Stars*. The series of cards was issued between many different comics allied to Lion. Issued in sheets of eight cards, the 32 cards are part of a shared issue comprising 132 cards, with blue backs.

Other cards in this expansive series were issued by Buster & Jet, Scorcher & Score, by The Tiger, and also by Valiant & TV21 comics. A very similar collection was issued in 1971, with red backs. Values for sheets of eight cards, from either series, are worth £25 to £50. Some issues were rarer than others, notably TV21 sheets. Single cards are worth around £2 each.

Lipton Tea made soccer cards for the American market in 1979. *New England Tea-men* consisted of 22 tea bags cards, and included Noel Cantwell and Dennis Viollet. Values are over £20 for each card. In 1982 Lipton issued English and Arabic language World Cup footballer cards. The series of 60, mostly British Isles players, is worth about £5, each card, though the Arabic cards are rarer and may cost more. Pairs of cards, the same player on English and on Arabic cards, have premium values.

The Liverpool Daily Post issued *Goals That Led To Wembley* in 1974. The series included four large cards, each with black and white illustrations. Values exceed £30 each

London Daily Chronicle issued circular cards of teams and players, in 1904. A year later, the same newspaper issued rectangular football team cards, which are dated 1904-5 [sic]. Values for any surviving London Daily Chronicle soccer cards start at £150 and may exceed £250.

Lion, Famous Football Trophies cards

Lipton tea cards, English and Arabic varieties

London Evening News card

Lovell's cards from 1909

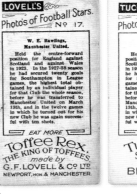

Lovell's and two similar cards from 1927

Lot-O-Fun, a paired card

Luratti cards, with Eric Brook of Manchester City

London Evening News joined the 1960s trend of evening papers issuing football cards. For the 1967/68 season it launched a set of large cards, *Stars In Action*. Consisting of 36 monotone cards of, mostly, London club players, it includes stars from Spurs, Chelsea, Arsenal, West Ham, and QPR. The set also includes Manchester United players, which were, no doubt, included for cockney red devils. The cards are worth about £25 each.

Lord Neilson [sic] was an ice cream merchant. In 1971 Neilson's ice creams gave away *1st Div. League Club Badges* [sic], a series of 24 hexagonal cards. The cards have long been under-valued, and are often confused with the less valuable ice cream cards by Mister Softee, and by Tonibell, but they are rarer and more costly. Expect to pay over £20 for one.

Lovell's *Football Series* of 1909 is one of the rarest in the world. Its 36 trade cards show quaint, colour illustrations of footballers. Values start at £100 each, and often exceed £250! The images on the cards bear a certain similarity to the illustrations by an illustrator called L.C. Bennett, whose work was employed in early issues of Football Favourites magazine. Almost 20 years later Lovell's issued *Photos of Football Stars*, with

Toffee Rex, in 1927. Once again there were 36 trade cards. Values are around £40 per card. Look out for similar issues by Pattreiouex and Tuckett. A triplet of three cards, the same player by each of these issuers, has a premium value.

Lot-O-Fun issued *Sports Champions* in 1922. The four cards in the series consist of pairs of sportsmen, mostly footballers. A mirror set of four cards (eight more sportsmen) was issued by sister publication, Comic Life. Values for uncut pairs start at £25 and exceed £75. Cut single cards are worth very little. Cards with legendary sportsmen, like Billy Meredith, sell at premium prices.

Luratti, in Italy, issued cards in the 1920s and 30s. The firm included sporting photographic cards, including many hundreds of football cards, with its chocolates and other produce. Values start at £25 and may exceed £100 for certain all-time greats, like Meazza.

Lutter, of West Germany, issued *Schütt* during 1961/62. *Schütt* cards showed sporting greats and teams, and most that remain on the market today are firmly glued into albums – which diminishes their value. The 72 cards, which can be identified by the weight-lifting figures on the back, sell from £10 upwards – to huge amounts for world stars like Gento, Di Stefano, Suarez, etc., and for popular

Lutter, Manchester United card, 1961

teams (Manchester United is included in the series). See also: Heinerle.

Lyons Maid ice cream issued *Soccer Stars*, in 1971, and *International Footballers* in 1972. Each included 40 trade cards with token tabs attached to each. The cards are worth less without the tabs. Values range from £5 to £30 for intact cards.

Album issued in Chile, 1962

Mabilgrafica

Mabilgrafica, Northern Ireland's Tommy Cassidy, 1982

Mabilgrafica, Glenn Hoddle, 1986

Maga comic cover sticker

abilgrafica is one of many strange names entwined with football stickers. A Mabilgrafica series of *Caricaturas e Fotos Mundial de Futebol Espanha-82*, borrows a design from Fidass cards, squeezing well known footballers into small, circular photos alongside larger, farcical renditions of the same. The series includes 11 players from the British Isles home nations involved in the 1982 World Cup. There's Martin O'Neill for Northern Ireland, Alan Rough for Scotland and Paul Mariner for England, etc. The next World Cup collection by Mabilgrafica, in 1986, substituted caricatures and small mugshots for classic photographs. The various cards and stickers of footballers from the British Isles, issued in both 1982 and 1986, tend to sell for around £25 each. Being Portuguese neither series is easy to obtain. This is because football cards in Portugal were made in smaller numbers than elsewhere. Spain, Italy, Britain, Germany, France, Brazil, Argentina and, of course, the countries of North America, have

many tens and hundreds of millions of people. Smaller populations mean smaller numbers of cards. Portuguese ephemera ought to be top of your list of wants, along with Greek, Scandinavian and Balkans issues, to name but a handful.

MacDonald cigarettes are responsible for some of the rarest sports cards – ever! Its tobacco card series of football and cricket teams was issued in 1900. Four football teams are known: Bury, Glossop, Everton and Liverpool. Values range from £2,500 to £5,000 each. This may seem a lot of money, yet, these cards are far rarer than the American card of Honus Wagner, a noted baseball player. There are over 50 examples of the Wagner card in circulation. One example has sold for millions of dollars! Rare soccer cards have long been undervalued – and many of them are far rarer then most people realise. MacDonald cards ought to be priced in the tens of thousands. There's a fascinating book about the Honus Wagner million dollar cigarette card. See the section on slabbers, in this book, for more.

Maclure & MacDonald (no relation to the previous entry) issued football postcards during

the later years of Edward VII's reign. There are 28 known, all being Scottish. Values exceed £100 each card.

Maga is the Spanish publisher that issued *Olimán* comic. The fortnightly rag came with a cut-out sticker on the back cover. International footballers, as well as domestic Spanish players, were issued this way during the build up to the World Cup, in 1962. Values for cut stickers are around £10 but an uncut page would fetch £30 for a well known player, and an entire comic, uncut, with someone like Di Stefano or Suarez could exceed £50. Maga also issued collections of soccer stickers, like the 1975 issue of *Futbol (cromos troquelados)*. Values for the shaped stickers, intact, with undamaged frames and unused peel-off paper may exceed £25 for stars like Cruyff, of whom there are two stickers in this collection.

The Magnet Library was a comic of the 1920s. During summertime 1922 The Magnet issued 15 cards which it announced as *Real Photos of Famous Footballers* though the cards do not show this title. It's a mixed set. Some cards have pairs of footballers, and others show single players.

Manil stickers from Portugal

Magnet Library, 1922 cards of single and paired players

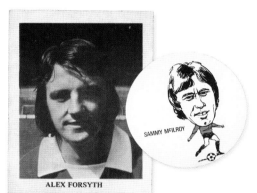

Manchester Evening News stickers, two types, 1970s

1970s Manchester Evening News Pink Final cards

Between 1922–1923 the publication issued its second series of free football photographic cards, this time showing football teams. There are 10 to collect. Cut paired cards are almost worthless. Undamaged team cards and single players are valued at around £5 each, and uncut pairs are between £10 and £20 each.

Major Drapkin included a couple of Arsenal and Man City players amidst its *Sporting Celebrities in Action*, a series of cards from 1930. The set of *actual photographs* followed an issue of *Sporting Snap*, which was anything but actual, being a colourful offering of sporty cartoons derived from the *Happy Families* and *Quartets* chest of card games. The value for Drapkin footballers is around £10 per card. Don't pay too much for other cards from this issue. Cards have been seen for sale at exaggerated prices. Low, single figures are closer to the mark for most other cards in this series.

Manchester Evening News issued caricatures of footballers in 1973. The 30 circular stickers (with *Fasprint* backs) feature lampoons of Manchester stars from both blue and red halves of the city. The same newspaper also issued a series

of large photo stickers. The value of suchlike is around £30. A few years later came cards: a score and ten, in sheets of half a dozen. They featured colour illustrations of players, and sported the Pink Final legend. Values are around £5 for cut, single cards, and £50 for uncut sheets.

Manil will provide collectors with a challenge. There are British players galore, from World Cups as early as 1982, through the Euros of the 1980s and 1990s to USA 94. The problem is they are Portuguese stickers. This means attractive fare but rare wares. Relatively few were made and far fewer remain unused. Diverse collections by Manil include metallic stickers for *Mundial Mexico 86* (Souness, and many other players from the British Isles were included), calendar cards for *Italia 90*, and a 1993 build-up issue to the World Cup in 1994. Ian Rush, for Liverpool, Gazza in a Lazio tone of England blue, and many other British stars decorate this colourful collection. The stickers are worth working hard to get, maybe on your next holiday to Porto, or Lisbon. Values paid outside Portugal may reward the trip. Single, unused Manil stickers from the 1980s have sold for over £25 each.

Marcus Cigarette cards are rare beauties! Marcus issued a series of football club colours and footballers in the 1890s. The 25 cards feature 12 teams, two cards for each, and a single card of an Aston Villa player. The cards may be found rubber stamped, in purple, both with, and without the name *Kinnear*. Values for Marcus cards range from £100, for lesser known clubs, like Suffolk, to over £500 for rarer types, like the card of Aston Villa's Jack Davey.

Maple Leaf was a Germanic gum that brought the taste of North America to post-war youngsters in Benelux, West Germany and Italy. The earliest Maple Leaf trade cards date to the late 1940s. A collection of 160 black and white photo cards, with a Maple Leaf album, was

Marcus cigarette cards, 1890s

issued in Italy, by Genescambi of Rome, in 1951. The series, *Voetbal 1ste Klasse 1951-1952*, is a more typical Maple Leaf issue, being made and distributed in the Benelux region. Later, German Maple Leaf cards, issued in Wesel, are better known to international collectors. The Amsterdam firm pressed on with Dutch issues until the series of Dutch sportsmen playing cards, issued in the late 1950s. [Like many rare issues of yesteryear, it seems that as soon as a collector's attention is brought to bear, the cards soon disappear from the market, becoming rarer than ever. These cards are all but impossible to find, today, yet just 30 years ago they seemed common]. The playing cards, which were issued in at least two, different series (see the backs in the photo) have come to be worth around £200 for the set. Aside from playing cards, of which Maple Leaf made many different series (mostly film stars) the firm is best known, amongst soccer card collectors, for its Wesel issues of cards like the yellow-framed series of *International Football Teams*, from the 1960/61 season. The 56 cards include various British teams, many other European teams, and some internationals, like

Brazil and England. The British team cards typically sell for around £20 each. The Brazil national team card features Pelé and typically sells for a higher price. There will be more on Maple Leaf cards in a future edition of this book and more images can be seen on www.footballsoccercards.com

Marshall Cavendish, a book publisher, issued an album and sticker collection in 1971. Its *Book of Football Top Teams* included 320 stickers of British footballers, which were issued in sheets of 16 – and that's where the value lies, not in the cut-to-single stickers. A sheet of uncut stickers may sell for over £25.

Mas issued *Ases Mundial Espanha 82* to celebrate the Naranjito World Cup, in 1982. Francisco Mas was a Portuguese publisher. Its circular stickers have become a hit with collectors, partly due to their contrast with a similar, larger Spanish language issue by Reyauca. Values for the smaller Mas stickers start at £10 each but premium prices are paid for Maradona and Dalglish, amongst other international greats.

Masters Winners Matches included a series of packet-issue sports cards as part of the

packaging on boxes, in 1980. *Winners Against The Odds* include Stanley Matthews, Billy Wright and Puskas, and also the 1973 Sunderland team. The cards were designed to be cut out and collected but the 12 uncut boxes are worth a lot more than the 12 cut-out cards. In 1981, Masters Winners matches were issued with a second series of cards: *Footballing Winners*. The cards, with footballers of yesterday and a Concorde flight offer to see the New York Cosmos, are worth around £20 each, but an entire matchbox may sell for a lot more.

Master Vending was a British gum ball and card issuer of the 1950s. *Cardmaster Football Tips* were issued in 1958. They were first printed without an address and such cards are rarer and worth more than later, addressed cards. A variety of different cardstocks were used in various printings, so if you want all the known types of these cards you'll have some collecting to do. Likewise, there are 50 cards – and more varieties – in the 1959 series, *Did You Know?* Typical values for most Master Vending Company cards are around £2 to £5 each. Perhaps the most attractive, yet, most difficult to find cards by Master Vending

Maple Leaf, Arsenal team card, 1961

Maple Leaf, playing cards, 1958

Mas and Revauca stickers, 1982

Master Vending cards, same player, different variations

Master Vending Italian card of John Charles

Maynards, 1933 Celtic

May Gum, Dundee

Mateu Spanish stand-up, 1954

come from Italy. In 1959 the firm's Rome office launched *Cardmaster – Sport*, a series of 58 gum cards. Values for these rarities start at £25 for domestic Italian stars of the day but you'll pay over £100 for soccer legends like John Charles and over £1,000 for Pelé!

Match Magazine first gave free football stickers with its maiden issue, in 1979. Cards soon followed. Notable freebies include *Goals & Goalscorers* [sic], from 1984, a series of 70 cards that are now worth £5 each – and more, if the cards remain in uncut sheets, as issued. Match Magazine's soccer cards output since 1979 has been extraordinary but recently its circulation has fallen, so newer issues are printed in smaller numbers than ever. The lower print runs mean one thing: potential for future rarity. It would be possible to fill many pages on the 40 years of Match's myriad football free gifts, and this is but a brief introduction. By way of a final word on Match, for now, look out for Match magazine rookies of David Beckham from 1996, and beware Raven cards – Raven S.A. is the brand name – which were millennium issues of Fergie's Fledglings. The Raven cards have been wrongly dated too early by seven years, due to an eager but ignorant American slabber. Raven made pretty cards of Beckham

and pals some years after their European Cup Champions League success in 1999. The Raven cards are distinctive in their 2000s print and design styling. None of the cards are rookies. No matter how badly certain sellers want their woefully graded and slabbed cards to be 1995, they are not 1990s cards! Cards consultancies abroad, that charge cash for telling you what you already know, don't make the best British soccer cards experts. A word of advice: do not take slabbed cards dates for granted. A gallery of slab errors, which are as permanent as plastic pollution in the oceans, can be found on this writer's Facebook page. For more on the multinational business known as soccer card grading [otherwise called card death by suffocation in a polypropylene pouch, smothered in polymers, badly graded with wrongful descriptions, and sealed in a plastic coffin – and all for a price] see the section: Slabbers.

Mateu, of Spain, issued sheets of cut-out, stand-up footballers during 1954. There are some valuable rookies in this series, not least Alfredo di Stefano for Real Madrid. Values of such sheets start at £150 each. Cut, single stand-ups are worth £10 to £15.

May chewing gum, from Portugal, issued waxy paper inserts, which were given with sticks of gum,

in 1970. *Emblems, Equipamentos e Bandeiras* (club badges, strips and colours) included British teams amongst 200 known inserts. They were issued folded so they all have creases. Values exceed £100 for examples of certain British clubs. Some of the figures of players shown are obviously based upon real footballers. For example, though he is not named, on the West Ham insert it's Bobby Moore, for sure.

Maynard's Quality Brand Confectionery distributed beautiful football cards with its fine chocolates, in 1933. Club colours and potted histories are shown on the 20 different trade cards. Values range from £50 to over £100 each.

McVitie's *Know Your Superstars* were partly perforated cards, issued in sheets, in the early 1980s. There were 10 sports stars including a duo of Arsenal and QPR footballers, amidst boxers, cricketers and other athletes. Single footballers are worth £15 each but sell for much more intact, in a large sheet of cards.

Melrose Tea cards are something that most tea cards are not: valuable. Melrose celebrated the World Cup of 1986 with *World Cup Promotions*, a series of Scottish soccer star cards. The 28 cards in the series include an early card of Alex Ferguson, as Scotland manager, and one of Jock Stein, the man he replaced. Card values start at £25 each. Some have sold for more than £40.

Mera & Longhi, from Varese, issued beautiful sports cards in 1936. *Concorso Assi dello Sport* is a collection of footballers and other athletes (cyclists, boxers, etc.) whose value exceeds £50 each. Football greats from the 1934 World Cup feature, and the set includes footballers in club colours too. Allemandi in Roma colours is worth £100. Foni of Juventus, Andreolo of Bologna and Meazza of Inter are also included, and these cards may also fetch triple figures each.

Merlin is a name known beyond the kingdom of Pendragon largely thanks to a group of former Panini sticker marketing men. They rebranded the 1990s as the decade of the wizard. This writer appeared in the 2017 ITV television documentary, *Stuck On You*, by Fosse Films. The show was based on the fine book of the same name, by Greg Lansdowne. Merlin is a little beyond the boundaries of this edition, a book which is focussed on rarer cards and scarcer stickers, however, a future edition will look more closely at Merlin and its wares. Of worthy note, and worth mentioning right now, is Merlin's 1996 *UEFA Euro 96* collection of stickers. Few collectors know that there were two collections to be had! Buyers should look out for stickers from the earlier, withdrawn – and supposedly destroyed – series of first editions. The withdrawn stickers featured England, Scotland and other national players in full international kits. The series of full-length shots caused the problem. The edition became the victim of a legal action brought by a certain rival. It was replaced by stickers showing just head-and-shoulders shots of players. A complete collection would be worth a considerable sum, and individual stickers will fetch prices that dwarf those of the regular issue.

Mercurycard issued a series of cards showing football teams and football club emblems, in 1990. Such plastic cards were used in payphones during the era before mobile phones came to eradiate the groin with electromagnetic fields from hip or backside pockets. Unopened presentation packets are worth over £100 each, and single, used cards sell for £20. Overprinted cards are worth a little more (£25). Mercurycards are a lot rarer than many collectors realise. They are a cross-over collectible, with phonecard collectors vying with football collectors for the rarest issues. Phonecards have been strangely undervalued by cards collectors in the same way trade cards used to be undervalued by cigarette card aficionados.

Midjy was an example of British post-war creativity. Unemployed war office boffins turned their attentions from cracking codes and designing bouncing bombs, to these, miniature self-developing photo cards of footballers. Issued in a kit which contained a negative, a packet of sensitised photo paper, chemicals for fixing the image, a folder, instructions and a metal clasp for securing the chemical reaction in place, the 1948 innovations must have been all the rage, so it's surprising that any remain intact. Those that do are rare and costly! Complete kits are almost impossible to find, hence their value. The *Midjy Photo Outfit* would be banned today, not least due to the chemicals included, yet once upon a time it was possible to buy and collect 25 of these self-printing footballer cards, and cricketers too! Most kits were used, most photo papers were at least partly developed, and many of the home-made photo cards were discarded once developed. Few remain, in any state. An intact kit may sell for £150. Developed, single Scottish player cards are worth over £50 each; and rarer English stars sell

Stan Bowles – Football
Born in Manchester, and plays for Queen's Park Rangers. A brilliant striker with great skills, who has helped Q.P.R. to a big share of success over the past few years. Recently recalled to the England Squad.

McVities card

14 GRAEME SOUNESS

Melrose Tea card

FREE
Collect your own Scottish World Cup Squad. In each packet of Melroses' Tea is a free photo-graph. Write for your World Cup Folder by sending a Stamped Addressed Envelope (minimum 32 × 23 mm) with 3 World Cup wrappers to: Melroses World Cup Promotions, Couper Street, Leith, EDINBURGH EH6 6HQ.

COMPETITION FREE
On completing your collection you will be entitled to enter our World Cup Competitions. Competition Entry Forms and Rules will be included with your Folder.

Mera & Longhi card

Mercurycard

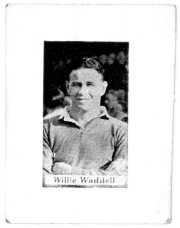

Midjy, a developed card

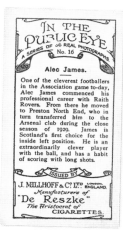

Millhoff De Reszke, Arsenal card

for more. The English series, and the cricketers, were less well distributed, hence premium prices are paid for the few that are known, today.

Millhoff De Reszke Cigarettes issued cards called *In The Public Eye*, in 1933. The series of 36 cards includes four football subjects. Values for these are: Dixie Dean £25, Alex James £10, Joseph Bradford £5 and Patsy Hendren, at £10. Other cards from the series are worth £2.

Mira, of Italy, became one of Panini's competitors during the 1960s. Its maiden collection was *Mondiali di Calcio 1962*, a series of about 300 cards, with an album. It was issued in the hinterland of Piacenza. In the 1960s Italian card distribution on a national scale was controlled by a few special interest groups (no further comment needed). Mira took time to break into the national scene and this collection is its rarest. It includes very rare varieties of the regular cards. Values start at £25 for most cards in the collection, and rise to over £1,000! This is, actually, one of the rarest football card collections in the world. Officially it was meant to be a series of 272 cards, though far more cards were made, and over 300 different cards exist. In the album there are 17 spaces for each team, but there are well over 20 cards known for some, including England. Similar over-production for other teams seems likely. Player cards for Spain and Russia are rarely seen at all (and a poor Yashin card was seen to sell for many £100s on its market debut), whereas the Italian, Swiss and German players come to market more often. The cards are known in two types, with and without series titles. Most cards are very rare and command high prices. Pelé will top £2,000 the next time his card - either version - appears on the market. The better known England players, those from bigger teams, like Jimmy Greaves and Roger Hunt, have been seen to sell

for up to £200 each, and their prices are expected to rise. There are a finite number of these cards out there. The production run was small. Those available on the market are going ever upwards in value. The day will come, shortly, when most of these cards become unavailable, at any price.

Mira's position strengthened and in 1967 it was able to offer stiffer competition to Panini. It issued yearly card sets that included self-adhesive stickers, in collections called, *Tutti I Calciatori (All The Footballers)*. Values for such cards start at £10, and the metallic stickers sell for more than £25, if unused, and often top £100 each! The British teams and players in this set may attract premiums to such prices. In 1968 Mira joined forces with Italy's second biggest sports newspaper, Tuttosport, which allowed for better nationwide distribution. The publishing alliance resulted in a set of 750 cards called *I Campionissimi (The Greatest Champions)* that reached all corners of the peninsula. Certain *Campionissimi* cards fetch prices over £75, though most can be had for less than £10. The generic *Tutti I Calciatori* collection was launched anew, in 1969. The British teams and players attract premium prices. Some of the metallic foil stickers, with backing papers intact, sell for over £100.

Miroir-Sprint was a French sports newspaper. During 1958–1960 it issued football stars on monotone postcards with deckled edges. Pelé is known on two of these cards, as a portrait, and also as the subject of an action photo. Both cards are very rare and fetch over £500, while other players in the series sell for £25. During 1960 Miroir-Sprint issued, as a series of 132 cards with Sport Gum. They feature teams, crests and players. Values start at £20 and rise markedly for cards with famous world greats.

Mira, 1962, a pair of varieties

Later in 1960 the publication issued playing cards of footballers and teams. The 54 cards are known in various sizes and styles. Cards of Pelé sell for £100 each.

Miroir-Sprint returned to larger cards in 1961, issuing colour cards of internationals like di Stefano, Puskas and Gento, amidst a legion of domestic stars.

Missing cards? Missing from this issue, but not forgotten, are cards in preparation for the next edition. Look out for news of future projects on the author's internet channels and on his website. Many cards not contained in this book are viewable on www.footballsoccercards.com so, please, do have a look. It's not possible to put all the brands, all of the photos into just one book. A following tome will be coming. It's in preparation now. Myriad more brands, like Donat (French all-sports cards); Guillen (metal cards from 1950s Spain); Dolomiti (chocolates cards from 1930s Italy); Fleece Hotel shields (1880s sports cards in the style of Baines); Galli (cards of British stars of the 1960s, from Italy); Joly (1950s gum cards from West Germany); Kemmel (French sports stars gum cards); Llorent (Spanish trade cards from the 1960s); and Bartola (Maltese cards of British players); and football cards issued by Gunsberg, Jubalcain, Knapper, Baramundi, Brahm Brot, Karpatenland and a thousand more brands are also being readied for inclusion in the next issue, so sign up for news updates, and be assured of not missing anything. Add your name and address to this author's contact list for all future projects. Send your email address to cards@rarecards.co.uk

Mister Softee's tinkle alerted households to the imminent possibility of choc-ices, lollies and plastic tubs of *screwball* ice cream (and their collectible lids). Vanilla twists sold from street

vendors may bring Assault On Precinct 13 to mind, but the British chug-along, ding-dong vans of the 1970s, driven by blokes on busmen's holidays, offered British kids nothing more dangerous than a whipped *99* cone and a raspberry ripple down the front of your t-shirt. During 1972 Mister Softee distributed *1st Division Football League Badges* cards. The 24 hexagonal cards can easily be found for as little as £1 each. Very similar cards by fellow ice cream issuers, Lord Neilson and Tonibel, are much rarer.

Mitcham Foods are one of the commoner types of football card. Over-production of a 1956 series lead to excess stock, which was sold to a cards dealer in the 1980s. Values for *Footballers* are very low and complete sets of 25 cards are easy to acquire, for a few pounds.

Mitchell, the tobacconist, issued a series of cards called *Scottish Footballers*, in 1934. Another series, *Gallery of 1934*, was issued a year later than it's dated, and contained but a solitary Arsenal footballer. *Scottish Football Snaps* came out in 1935, and *Gallery of 1935* followed in '36, with 50 cards, including one Celtic footballer. Values for such cigarette cards are around £3 to £5 each. Most tobacco cards from the 1930s were produced in vast numbers, hence the modest prices paid for such cards today.

Mobil Oil issued 30 silky stickers called *Football Club Badges*, in 1983. They were very popular and can still be found quite easily. Values are around £3 each.

Modern cards. Buyers should be wary of the possibility of managed, stashed stocks of contemporary cards held by certain individuals. Since the 1990s some people, with connections to producers, printers and distributors, have withheld supposedly rare cards for future cashing-

Mira, a mistake card

Mira, Celtic metallic sticker, 1967/68 series

in on the collectors' market. This is no slight against cards issuers, nor against distributors and other commercial parties involved in the multi-billion industry, none whatsoever. It's a gentle reminder to collectors. In general, cards from before 1990 are a safer bet. Cards since the 1990s have been managed by big buyers and enjoyed by big sellers. Collectors paying a lot for

Mira cards, two series from 1968/69

Miroir-Sprint, a large card of Alfredo di Stefano

Miroir-Sprint, small card of Just Fontaine

Miroir-Sprint, playing card, Kopa 1962

More to come in a future issue, rare stickers of Brits

More coming in a future edition, exotic Brits

Mitcham foods trade card

FOOTBALLERS
(A Series of 25)
No. 20
Tom Finney
Preston & England
(Cols.: White)
The only man who could rival Stanley Matthews in the England side, Tom is almost as great a ball artist as Stan and a more dangerous goalscorer. First capped in 1946. A Preston local, he joined the Club at inside left and played outside left for England. Height 5ft 7½in, Weight 10st 7lb.

MITCHAM FOODS
LIMITED
MITCHAM IN SURREY, ENGLAND

Moncar, a sealed packet of Spanish stickers

26 - SCHNELLINGER

Monello comic, cut-out stickers

25 - SANI

supposedly rare, limited editions in recent years may be playing roulette on a wheel with 0, 00 and even a 000. The dealer with the garage full of cartons of cards from 1999 to 2019 wins. There is less risk in putting a money into cards from before the 1990s, and cards from before 1980 are even safer bets.

Mohr of West Germany made *Fussball, Das Spiel Der Welt (Football, The World's game)*, in 1952. The 120 paper monotone stickers are worth around £10 each.

Moncar of Spain issued unusual British soccer fare in 1975. Its football team emblems of Liverpool, Rangers, etc. were printed on silk stickers, issued two per packet. Values for sealed packets are around £30. Singles stickers sell for £10 each.

Monello is a brat, in Italian. In 1972 brat magazine, Monello, issued *I Divi Della Domenica (The Divas Of Sunday)* to be cut out from the back page of the publication and collected in an album. Jimmy Greaves, Denis Law and other all-time greats feature in the collection. Values for uncut magazines with such packet issue cards start at £50, and single cut-out footballer stickers of great names sell for £20 each.

Monopol of Germany was a producer of tobacco cards during the Weimar years. In 1932 Monopol issued *Sportphoto, serie A und B*, consisting of 1,080 cigarette cards! The two series contain cards with British teams and players, like Pym of Bolton Wanderers, and Goodall of Huddersfield Town but most were glued into albums. Values range from £5 to £50 for unused cards. This is but a cursory mention of the firm and its massive range of cards. There will be more on Monopol in a future edition of this book.

Monty mastication makes rookie card collectors mad! Originating in the Low Countries, Monty Gum issued football cards as early as the 1950s, but most of its internationally known cards, whether in playing card format, or as Happy Families, a form of the game that's also known as Quartets, were issued after 1960. Monty game cards from 1960–

12 - JULINHO

9 - GREAVES

20 - NETZER

1961 seem to come in all shapes and sizes, with different backs (cards are known with red, green and blue triangle and circle designs) but they are all versions of the same, or at least, a very similar game, and they were issued around the same time: 1960–1961. The game cards have either playing card fronts (mostly for the British market) or they come in the style of Quartets (Happy Families) which were more popular games in Benelux and West Germany. Values for domestic and international players on such cards start around £20 each, and rise, and rise... but may soon fall back again. This is because some sellers have wrongly dated the series as 1958, which inflates the price of cards with Pelé. In fact the cards are from 1960 and buyers have been carried away by wishful thinking, hoping they are acquiring a 1958 Pelé, when, in fact, they are not. The international cards were

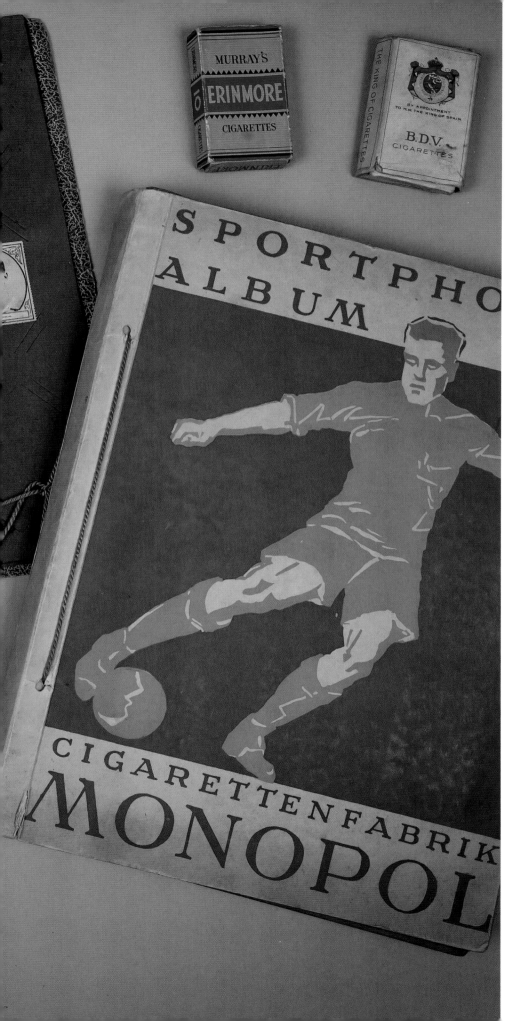

issued in the run up to the first European football tournament, in summer 1960. Brazil was included because of its World Champions status, Sweden due to its close call. West Germany and England stars and legends were also included, due as much to the need to market the cards in England and the BRD, as to the various players' legacies. England did not enter the Euros in 1960. Teams that did, that were outside Monty's market, like Turkey, Bulgaria and Romania were not recognised, and no player cards were issued for those countries. Similar Monty Gum playing cards were issued for a domestic, British market, during the 1960/61 season. See the card of Alex Elder, below.

Monty Gum cards have also confounded wishful thinkers regarding a series from 1967. Confusion has been sown by men on the make, about a series of Perfetti cards. They have been wrongly attributed to Monty, and wrongly dated to 1965. The Perfetti series, which includes many Italian Serie A clubs and players, as well as cards of Pelé, Denis Law & Jimmy Greaves (both of whom are former Serie A players) also includes a card of Franz Beckenbauer. Greedy rookie card sellers have

Monty Gum, Inter-national playing card and Quartets card

Monty Real Madrid, 1964

VENABLES, Engeland

Monty Sheffield United, 1968

Monty QPR, 1969

Monty World Cup 1966, Terry Venables

Monty Midlands trainers in Holland, 1971

Monty World Cup 1975 Hearts Donald Ford

Monty, 1960/61 British footballers card game

claimed 1965 as the year of issue – to make more money on Beckenbauer sales – and Monty as the issuer – for profits by smoke and mirrors, perhaps. Well, it's not Monty, it's Perfetti, of Milan. The 1967 date is also certain. See the Inter players in the series. They wear the 1966/67 jersey, the first strip to bear the yellow star awarded to Inter after the 1965/66 season win. For more, see: Perfetti.

During the 1960s Monty Gum made at least three series of *Football Teams*. The best known cards are a series of 60 monotone pictures of squads with orange borders, and a series of 72 colour cards, with a Benfica football team puzzle on the backs. The least known series shows teams in black and white, with white frames. Whereas values for the 1968 and 1969 cards range from £15 to £25 (for British teams such as Crystal Palace, Bristol City, Stoke City, Wolves, Villa, etc.) the much rarer, earlier, white-framed cards may fetch over £50 each.

In 1972 Monty Gum issued *Fussball Football Voetbal Club Stickers*, a series which included pennant-shaped stickers of players and clubs once thought exclusive to BAB, in Great Britain. Values

for such stickers, if unused, garner £25 for British stars. An album was issued, and some of the very same stickers once believed to be BAB, and only by BAB, are pictured within, in black and white. The BAB images included in this collection are specifically those from the 1971/72 *Football Stars* collection.

Monty celebrated the World Cup of 1974 with a collection of 200 stickers. They look a little like the FKS stickers of 1973: landscape format with graphics and flags. The packets showed the series title, *World Cup '74* [sic] but this was not displayed on the unbranded stickers. Values start at £10 each but Scottish players often sell for over £25. Cruyff is usually the highest priced sticker from the collection.

Monty Gum saw out Elvis, The Beatles and Beach Boys, The Rolling Stones, Progressive Rock, and Glam Rock too. Though Monty cards lost something special, and became cheapened during the disco years, its later, blander cards are much easier to acquire than the 1960s rarities, and they cost a lot less too. A 1976 series, *Football*, consists of 193 cards with plain backs. They are easily

identifiable by the footballs at the top and bottom corners. This writer remembers having the cards and being disenchanted with Monty due to the nastiness of the product, its rough cardboard stock and the glaring mistakes in the careless misnaming of players. Buyers can find most of these cards for £1 each, or less, for a quantity, unless rarer variations are needed. Some cards come with the legend *Football* printed in various colours, and sell for more. In 1978 Monty made *Hannah's World Cup*. Who was Hannah? The 224 Monty *Hannah* cards look similar to the Monty 1982 *World Cup Football* cards. The way to differentiate the two is this: 1978 cards are larger and have the legend *world-cup*, whereas the 1982 cards are smaller, and are inscribed *world-cup football*. Thankfully *Mexico 86* cards were easier to identify, having the dated legend, if not the firm's name, printed on the cards. Monty issued various cards for the Euros, in 1980, 1984 and 1988, inscribed *Euro Cup*, and, latterly *Euro Cup 88*. Perhaps the most attractive Monty collection from the end of the third age of cards (the early 1980s) was *Football Parade*. The attractive cards are of European teams, and the series includes about 30 England and Scottish teams from the top divisions in 1980. Values for most Monty cards from the late 1970s and 1980s are generally low but the *Football Parade* series is

exceptionally rare and the cards of British teams can sell for more than £30 each!

Motta made some of the best and rarest 1970s cards of internationals. The Italian ice cream manufacturer teamed up with a football cards issuer, Edis, to launch two series of cards in 1974–1975, the most interesting of which is *Monaco'74 Coppa dei Campioni* [sic]. It included 111 circular cards that doubled as ice cream tub lids. Values for Scottish players are £75 to £100 each. World greats sell for similarly high prices. On the 1974 lids (cards) the names of players are printed in a format that follows the curve of the circular design, whereas the later series, from 1975, shows player names set into a rectangle. The later series is called *Coppa dei Campioni*, and includes Italian domestic league players, for example, Dino Zoff. Prices for the 136 lids of Serie A stars kick off at £25 each.

Muratti Cigarettes from Germany made *Brennpunkte des Deutschen Sports* in 1936. The 720

cards of footballers and sports stars are worth £20 each.

Murray's was a British brand of tobacco that issued cards during the first years of the House of Windsor. In earlier, Edwardian times it was less well known so its 1908 Maple brand of cigarettes cards, *Football Colours*, 30 flag-shaped cigarette cards, are extremely rare. Values start at £250 each card. Murray's *Football Rules* cards are also rare but they do come up for sale and they are affordable. The 25 cigarette cards may cost below £20 for a type card in less than perfect condition but, typically, you will pay £30 or more for better quality cards. In 1912–1913 Murray's issued *Footballers*, *series H* and *Footballers*, *series J*. The 32 footballers from *series H* and the 120 players in *series J* are worth £50 and £90 each, respectively. Cards with perfect black borders are worth more still but this has encouraged some unscrupulous sellers to use a black marker pen to *improve* the cards! Look at the borders for added black.

Murray, Series H card, Everton, 1912

Murray, Series J card, Middlesbrough, 1913

Motta, 1974 Ice cream cup lids

Monty, 1976 and 1986 cards

£.50

EDIZIONI **PANINI** MODENA
VIALE EMILIO PO, 380 - 41100 MODENA - TEL. 28.224 (3 linee automatiche)

DIE WELTMEISTERSCHAFT

Colecção
de 140 AUTOCOLANTES
ASES MUNDIAL
ESPANHA-82
5$00
AMADORA
Francisco Mas, Lda.

SOBRE SORPRESA
ASES
DEL
FUTBOL
1953 25 CTS.
4 FOTOS ESMALTADAS A TODO COLOR

FUTBOL 76/77
2,50 Pts. 4 CROMOS
AUTOADHESIVOS
EDICIONES VULCANO, S. A. - BILBAO

FUTBOL
ampeonato
acional
978

TOP 100

"DDY&Co's"

"MYRTLE GROVE"
CIGARETTES.

SÉRIE "AVIATION"
1er prix BAPTÈME de L'AIR

SÉRIE
"G. MEN"
AVEC
PRIMES

Participez
à nos
Concours

GLOBO

PORTvedettes

4

ADHESIVE
TURES

STKLEBE -
ILDER

nettes
LANTES

PARTICIPEZ A NOTRE GRAND CONCOURS
DES GEANTS DE LA ROUTE
PREMIER PRIX UN VELO MOTEUR 125
3 BICYCLETTES A MOTEUR · 10 BICYCLETTES ET DE NOMBREUX LOTS
DEMANDEZ A VOTRE FOURNISSEUR UNE PARTICIPATION AU CONCOURS
POUR 10 FEUILLES D'ENVELOPPAGE

TOUR de FRANCE

CYCLISTE

GOMME À MÂCHER

GONFLABLE

Le Globo

Nabisco

Shredded Wheat 1960s cards, with and without tokens

Nabisco is a name that brings back memories of hurried breakfasts before suffering the quotidian pain known as secondary school. That pit of despair that stifled creativity and kindled dreams less sweet. Psychics aside, most people knew not what Nabisco stood for. There was no internet encyclopædia to check such trivia in the TV-free mornings of the 1970s. Nabisco's breakfast boxes displayed a logo with an antenna design. It resonated with the radio receiver near the dining table, and resembled the Lorraine cross of Free France, but there was little of French culinary tradition in the dry crunch of Shredded Wheat. Nevertheless, the produce was considered a healthy munch. These days Nabisco is nowhere to be seen. Shredded Wheat is owned by faceless, food multinationals, the ones that seem to own most processed foods.

Back in the 1960s Shredded Wheat issued *Champions of Sport*, a series of 10 large cards, with tokens – they are worth more if they still have the token attached. The brand turned its attention to the gum cards craze in 1970. Nabisco issued a series of 24 cards, which resembles the Anglo Confectionery bubblegum issues of 1969. The cards are creatively titled *Footballers*. Varieties of the cards are known, including blank backs, errors in the biographies, and there are also different versions of the brand name to be found. Look out for the cards of Peter Bonetti and Ron Davies – whose erroneous versions have Leicester City and Spurs doppelgängers at heart! A basic card's worth is around £2 but this rises substantially for certain star players, especially for error cards and other, rarer varieties. Nabisco also issued 24 large photo cards, presented in folders, redeemable by sending packet tokens and a little money to Nabisco. The redemption cards bear the same images as the smaller cards. The value for these is about £40 each.

From cards to stickers went Nabisco in 1971. An attractive and scarce collection called *Cup Winners Badges* included 18 home nations national squad emblems, and domestic club badges, in pairs. Values today reflect the scarcity

Nabisco 1970s cards

Nabisco Cup Winners Badges

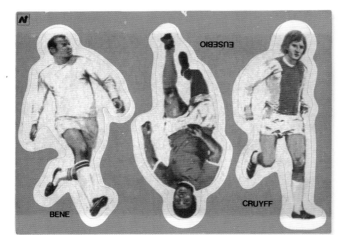

Nabisco Champions of Europe

Nabisco Football leage Ladders

LEIGHTON JAMES

ALLAN CLARKE

Nabisco football transfers

COACHED BY JOHAN CRUYFF

Cut around dotted line

Coached By Johann Cruyff

Johan Cruyff Demonstrates

Johan Cruyff Demonstrates The Volley

"Good shooting means scoring goals. It requires a combination of power, accuracy and timing. The volley - demonstrated here - is a perfect example. The eyes must be kept on the ball, the body behind it and fully co-ordinated with the foot to give maximum power and direction. Timing is crucial since the most difficult part of the volley is to hit the moving ball cleanly and accurately with the instep of your foot. It is a very difficult skill but if you master it, you will score many exciting goals for your team".

COLLECT ALL THE CARDS IN THIS SERIES WITH SHREDDED WHEAT

© Austin-Toppan Promotions London.

Keegan Quiz Cards by Nabisco

Remember there are 12 different scratch card games available for collection covering Football, Rugby, Cricket, Tennis, Basketball and Table Tennis.

Keegan Scratchcards by Nabisco

'CHAMPIONS OF SPORT'
BRYAN ROBSON

Bryan Robson was born in Chester-le-Street, County Durham on January 11th, 1957. He became the costliest player in Britain when, after eight years with 'the Baggies' - West Bromwich Albion, he was transferred to the mighty Manchester United. Bryan's proudest moment came when he was given the England captaincy by Bobby Robson, the England Manager. His tremendous work rate in midfield for both club and country has made him one of Britain's outstanding players. Bryan holds the record for the fastest goal in World Cup history — he scored in 27 seconds against France in 1982.

Henry Cooper's Bryan Robson sticker

of intact pairs, which are worth around £20, whereas a cut, single sticker is worth only £2. Breakfast blues were postponed in 1972 as Nabisco launched its own league tables. Moving sticky team names up and down the back of cereal boxes, upon which league table ladders were to be found, diverted attention from required attendance at church – it was usually Sunday morning when tables were changed, back in 1972. There are 44 team name stickers in this unusual collection. Values for clean, unused league table stickers with all 11 stickers intact, are around £20. Nabisco glided into 1973 with ghostly images that graced iron-on transfers. The latest freebies could be transferred to any surface using a hot iron. Hospital burns units saw a rise in visitors as kids did all sorts of clever stuff with scalding electrical equipment. This writer ironed Allan

Clarke on to the soft fabric tummy of a teddy bear. Bears are tough!

During 1973 Nabisco issued triplets of football star stickers. *Champions of Europe* consisted of four sheets of stickers, including 12 players, like demigod Johan Cruyff, Billy McNeill of Celtic, Eusebio, Beckenbauer, etc. Values for mint triplets exceed £50. They are valuable because very few remain unused. Trade stickers, given with produce, especially those showing famous names and teams, were quickly stuck to something. Such stickers, usually issued without albums, fared less well than sturdier cards or commercial stickers which get stuck into albums. Premium prices will be paid for uncut trios that include Cruyff. The Ajax legend became a favourite for Nabisco after his move to Barcelona. His recognisable features were adjudged just right for marketing dry fare to depressed youngsters. He featured on the cereal boxes, and on many fine free gifts inside the packets, including *Coached By Johan Cruyff*, a series of six large, oval stickers showing the star in his Barcelona colours. Values for uncut and unused stickers are around £25 each. Cruyff also featured on a series of Nabisco lenticular (*3-D*)

cards called *Johan Cruyff Demonstrates*. Nabisco free gifts were often inscribed with the Shredded Wheat brand but not always. Many gifts came with other produce, hence this listing. See the section on Shredded Wheat, for more.

During 1976 Nabisco's favours came to focus on the legendary Kevin Keegan. Boxes of cereals showed him emblazoned in glorious red but a series of six cards called *Kevin Keegan's Play'n'Score* failed to generate the enthusiasm that Cruyff had roused. The cards were awful. Not only did they feature games that looked like tests from a remedial maths class, Keegan sported no club colours, not even an England shirt! Another series showed him as an England star but the road pizza colouring on the *English Soccer Star Tactics* cards upset expectations. Someone at this writer's junior school was sick after looking at them. The overly excited nature of the colouring of these cards makes the series one for studying in cold sobriety, with an empty stomach. Keegan's perm followed. With straight hair he'd been a hero to many but the perm, and the move to Hamburg, shocked the nation. Moreover, why were there no Nabisco photographic cards of Keegan, like the Cruyff photo cards? The fall in popularity of England's wayward striker, not to mention the cycling incident on TVs Superstars show, foreshadowed a man whose cereal packet days were on the wane. Neither *Keegan's Skill Scratchcards* nor the garish *Superstar Ace* sticker of Keegan redeemed matters. *Quiz Cards*, in 1980, finally showed a coloured snap of the great man but it was too late. Nabisco turned to a British boxer, Henry Cooper, to market its brand.

North of the border Nabisco embraced the 1978 World Cup. *Scotland World Cup Argentina 1978* was a series of 21 stickers which heralded the British bravehearts on their quest for glory. The stickers are perforated, like stamps. Values for unused stickers start at £20 each. A complete album is worth seeking out. Be prepared to pay. It's a rare one.

Nannina, Nannina, *Nan-neena*. With a certain intonation it sounds like a mantra chanted by Homer Simpson. Mandalas of doughnuts aside, Nannina, from Milan, is a name to remember. The firm was unintentionally responsible for the creation of the biggest sticker producer in the world: Panini. Not only did Nannina birth Panini (millions of Nannina's unsold, over-produced football cards were bought cheaply, in 1961, by two brothers from Modena) it also produced one of the most valuable rookie cards in the world: a 1947 portrait of Puskas, the Hungarian legend. The card has been seen to sell at prices of over £2,000 – and that's for a cut-out card! It was issued in a sheet of Hungarian player cards, to cut out. The Magyarország squad was issued as part of a four-leaf card folder, with other soccer teams and subjects. Imagine what the price would be for the entire, uncut issue. Many thousands of pounds!

Nannina first published colourful folders of cut-out cards in 1947. *Figurine Tecni-Color* [sic] included teams of footballers and other sports stars, actors, actresses and miscellaneous comic cards. As intended, most cards were scissored to singles, which is why the one or two intact sheets that remain are valued in the thousands of pounds. There were four seasons of such issues, from 1946/47 until 1949/50. The first and last of the four issues have names to the fronts. For identification purposes, note that the issues from the two seasons betwixt show legends and inscriptions only on the backs of the cards. When cut, the 1948/49 cards look similar to Nannina's 1951 collection, both using film reel sprocket designs on the sides of the cards. To differentiate the two: the *Tecni-Color* 1948/49 cards have no names to the fronts, whereas the 1951 cards do. Both series are similar to issues by Castoldi and Cicogna, which also used the film reel sprockets design. Note: Castoldi cards are often mistakenly called Nannina cards by sellers both abroad and in native Italy. Few know what's what. There will be more information, more images and more values, another time, in a future issue of this book. In the meantime Nannina cards can be seen on www.footballsoccercards.com

Nannina's *Calciotavolo (Table Football)* was a folded card with cut-out football parts, issued in 1949. It came with two teams of 11 cards, to cut out and play. They are recognisable, when

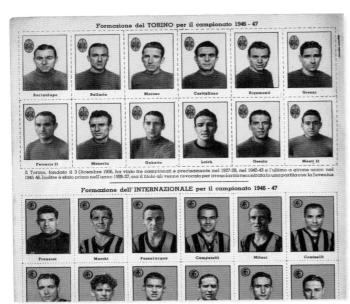

Nannina 1946, sheet

Nannina 1948, sheet

Nannina 1947, cards

Nannina 1948 British players

Nannina 1949, Wamar

Nannina early 1950s, 3 types

Nannina Gol cards,
large and small varieties

Nannina, 1961 cards of Denis Law & Torino

Nannina, 1961 different team card of Torino

cut, by the four fold lines; a pair at either side, and a paper tab for gluing the matchbox-like hull together. Red numbers and lettering to the rear also helps identify these unbranded cards. The squads were issued in pairs, for example, Sampdoria came in the same game as Bologna. Uncut, these games are worth many hundreds. Cut teams of 11 players sell for over £100 each.

Following on from four seasons of *Tecni-Color* [sic] folders, with its cut-out cards (and sought-after British Isles players Paddy Sloan, Norman Adcock and Bill Jordan; Frank Swift, Laurie Scott and Stan Mortensen) Nannina started the new decade by allying with rival biscuits manufacturers Wamar and Bovolone, issuing two series with the former and one with the latter. During 1951/52 Nannina also issued a series called *Calciovaluta* (that second series with film strip sprocket edges). Nannina switched to black and white cards in 1952 before producing colourful matchboxes with cut-out cards, two per box. Both series include Haase Jeppson, the Charlton Athletic player. Starting in 1954 Nannina released *Calciatori 100 Magnifiche*

Figurine Campeonato 1954-55. The series of 100 cards would be re-issued yearly with differently coloured borders, yellow, green, red and blue. The cards were not sold in packets. They were distributed in sheets of 100, then sold by shopkeepers in strips of 10. John Charles (the Welsh wizard, the former Leeds United player) was featured in some of these series. Nannina's first World Cup collection, *Campionato del Mondo 1958*, was issued after the tournament. This autumnal series included the two finalists, Sweden and Brazil. The value for a certain Brazilian from this series is in the thousands of pounds!

In 1959 Nannina created the first of two beautiful series of football cards known as *Gol 1959-1960* [sic]. For some reason it seemed a clever idea to re-launch the entire collection in a larger format, thus, *Gol 1959-1960 Gigante* came to be. What may have been successful in 1959 was anything but in 1960. A new series, *Gol 1960-1961*, and its inflated cash cow cousin, *Gol 1960-1961 Gigante*, failed to sell. Nannina was left burdened with millions of unsold cards.

Enter the Panini brothers! The first Panini series was made up of repackaged Nannina cards from the *Gol 1960-1961* collection, which Beppe and Benito Panini re-issued in small black, red and white envelopes during early 1961. They sold 3 million packets! Nowadays it's not possible to tell which cards were sold by Panini and which were sold by Nannina but Panini packets from this reissued *1960-1961* series are exceedingly rare, and forgeries abound. Although Nannina had inadvertently helped to create a dangerous competitor, in its parturition of Panini, it continued in the cards market for a decade, until the neophyte prodigy from Modena occluded the Milanese magus.

During the 1960s Nannina issued collections of cards without albums, as well as sticker and album sets. These are very rare. Both Dennis Law and John Charles can be found on single portraits, and in team line-up cards for Torino and Juventus, respectively. *Cile Mondial 62*, a series of 66 cards for the 1962 World Cup included Jimmy Armfield, Ron Flowers and Bobby Charlton, of England. Values for such Brits exceed £50 each

Nannina 1963 postcard

Nelson Lee was a Victorian detective hero from 1890s comics. By 1915 he was given a weekly in his own name. During 1921 the Nelson Lee Library issued *Photo Plates of Noted Players*. The 20 paper cards known consist of 10 English players, issued in England; and 10 Scottish stars, only issued in Scotland.

FLOWERS   Inghilterra

ARMFIELD   Inghilterra

Nannina World Cup 62 cards

Geoff Hurst
Presented with the compliments of the
Newham Recorder
© South Essex Recorders Ltd., 1968

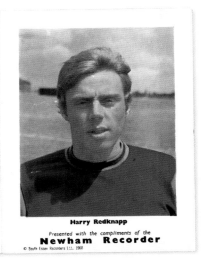

Harry Redknapp
Presented with the compliments of the
Newham Recorder
© South Essex Recorders Ltd., 1968

Newham Recorder

but that's dwarfed by what collectors have paid for Pelé – there are two, different cards of Pelé in this series. Around £350 is the typical price, for either card, if buying on a European auction site. The cards tend to get bought and inflated by the buyers who flip them (re-sell) into the thousands. The very same card will have cost the seller a fraction of this price just a year earlier. Internet auctions on Italian Ebay and on Delcampe.net, not to mention TodoColeccion.net, will reward buyers who are patient in their endeavours. Of others in this series, £150 has been paid for cards of Lev Yashin, the legendary Russian goalie; and up to £50 each for Didi and Garrincha.

Nannina's market was shrinking. Its recent cards had seemed distinctly old fashioned. It battled on, bravely making two radical collections of which myths have been spun. Due to its sheer rarity, a scarcity created, no doubt, by the paucity of stickers printed, and maybe also by poor distribution, the *Calciatori in Azione* stickers of 1963 are some of the rarest Nannina issues known. There is an unknown number of these rare, glossy, colourful stickers. An album has

never been seen and only a handful of the stickers have been seen. Pelé and Jimmy Armfield are known amongst those recorded by collectors. Caveat emptor: colour copies of the Pelé sticker have recently entered circulation. 1963 also saw Nannina's series of 64 postcard-size cards, with 38 smaller cards, issued together, of which Pelé's card garners most attention, and most money. It's rarer than collectors realise, being issued in a series produced in relatively low numbers. The packets bore different titles to the album. Each *Campioni Del Goal* wrapper included one postcard, and one metal disc with a club emblem. However, the album was confusingly called *Squadre E Campioni 1963/64 (Teams And Champions of 1963/64)*. Nannina stumbled on with soccer until the 1968/69 season but 1965 was the last year of real interest for international collectors.

The National Spastics Society joined in the craze for football cards, in 1959, with a series of 24 *Famous Footballers*. The cards are quite easily available and are worth around £2 each.

Nelson Lee was a Victorian detective hero from 1890s comics. By 1915 he was given a

weekly in his own name. During 1921 the Nelson Lee Library issued *Photo Plates of Noted Players*. The 20 paper cards known consist of 10 English players, issued in England; and 10 Scottish stars, only issued in Scotland. Values for English players range from £30 to £50 each; while Scottish start at £50 and exceed £100! Billy Meredith and Charles Buchan are but two of the English talent in this collection and they tend to add premiums to the prices paid. In 1922 the Nelson Lee Library chose to issue so-called real photographic cards. The series *Photographs of Famous Footballers* consists of 15 cards, each showing a pair of players. Values for uncut pairs start at £20, whereas cut cards are worth £2.

Newham Recorder, of London, issued supplements of footballers in pairs. In 1968 West Ham players made for colourful fish'n'chips. Values start at £30 for uncut pairs.

News Chronicle's oldest cards go back to 1922/23 but few collectors are aware of this. In the early 1920s a firm called Hulton, of Manchester, ran a newspaper called the Daily Dispatch, the very same paper that merged,

Daily Dispatch card, 1920s

News Chronicle card, 1950s

Northern Trancessories artist at large

Nuzzi colour card and shield sticker

Nuzzi Gerry Hitchens

in 1955; to form the News Chronicle. Many collectors think its sports cards were first issued in 1955, however, the publishers had issued soccer stars cards more than 30 years earlier! It's not known how many but at least five different cards are known, mostly Everton and Manchester United players.

News Chronicle's *Famous Soccer Teams*, issued in 1955, was a prototype to the better known *Pocket Portrait* cards of the late 1950s. Values for the *Famous Soccer Teams* cards start at £50 each. The better known *Pocket Portraits* cards offered local teams to local readers, so, for example, the north Staffordshire issue of News Chronicle & Daily Dispatch would offer Port Vale and Stoke City cards to its readership. A series of over 800 cards is known, in all, covering many different teams. Values vary wildly in this series because some teams are much rarer than others, for example, Liverpool and Manchester United are much rarer than Everton and Manchester City cards. Some players are more sought after. Stars like Duncan Edwards, and other members of the team involved in the Munich tragedy, are highly sought after, doubling the desirability of the Red Devils cards. Equally difficult to find are cards of Huddersfield, Hearts, Leicester City and Hibs, to name but four. In a future issue of this guide there will be full listings of all the teams, of the many card varieties, with prices for all and sundry.

News Chronicle issued one more series before the decade was out. In 1959 the *FA Cup Final* cards of Nottingham Forest players (11 cards) now fetch £50 to £100 each.

Nimbus was Switzerland's FKS. During the 1970s bilingual collections like *Vedettes du Football / Fussball Spieler in Aktion 72/73* [sic] were licensed from Fher, and printed in Spain, just like Semic, Sicker, AGEducatifs, and FKS, etc. Unused Nimbus stickers are very rare. Complete albums are worth around £200 each.

No maker's name? No year? No title? No brand? No logo? [No Logo. Naomi Klein – recommended reading!] If your card or sticker bears no identification marks, see the unknown section, in this guide. Unsure about a card's origins? The card is seemingly not listed elsewhere? Known manufacturers, like Galli and Crack, often issued cards with no logos. Other, unbranded cards remain mysterious to this day. See: unknown.

Not included in this book are many cards that will be prepared for a future edition. There's a limit to what can go into one book, so a future tome will include hundreds more pictures of cards not shown here; and many more descriptions, histories and values, too. That's something to look forward to! It's now in preparation. For news on the next edition make sure you follow this writer's social media for updates. If you don't have suchlike then

send a letter – see the address at the back of this book – and you'll receive notice, when the book is ready. Also see the website: footballsoccercards.com

Northern Trancessories has been covered in the section on BAB. The firm was responsible for some of the strangest looking soccer cards. Based in Leeds, in England, Northern Trancessories was the manufacturer of rather bizarre self-adhesives, which it released upon the world at the wilder end of the 1960s. Stickers were sold from clear plastic holders, hanging high in newspaper shops, way above little children's heads. Kids would point up at the psychedelic, warped images of soccer legends and demand, 'I want that one!' Such stickers now fetch £20 to £50.

Nuzzi was the Italian issuer that took over the cards maker known as Cedip (see also: Cedip). During the early 1960s it issued cards of British stars like John Charles and Gerry Hitchens, whose values now exceed £50. A 1962 series, called *Giocatori di Serie A Campionato 1962/63*, included a highly unusual selection of monotone coloured cards in red, green or orange! Nuzzi's shield-shaped club emblems of 1954 are some of the most attractive stickers, and some of the most valuable. Gerry Hitchens's card of the same collection shows a similar shield. This is how to differentiate these cards from the similar Panini issues of the same time.

MATTHEWS

Stanley Matthews
252   England

F.C. BARCELONA

BOBBY MOORE

8   LAW   TORINO

Bradford Champion

5 SANSON - INGL.

Levratto - Calcio

BRASIL   PELE

CAMPEON

442   INGLATERRA

JACKIE
CHARLTON

53

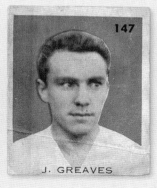

J. GREAVES

A. Ramsey   Engeland

COUPES D'EUROPE 1980

262

DUNDEE UNITED (Ecosse)

FOOTBALL BENJAMIN

Odhams Press

Odhams Press card

Ogden's cards
1896-1900

Ogden's cards
1900

Odhams Press was a newspaper and magazine publisher. In the early 1950s its various periodicals carried advertising for a series of trade cards of sporting heroes. The cards were issued weekly, to be redeemed by readers over the course of a year. Printed in the format of postcards, the illustrations lacked the modernity that was cherished in post-war Britain, which may explain their rarity, these days. Postcards, generally, are a different kind of collectible to trade postcards. Commercial postcards were typically bought from post offices, carousels in newspaper shops, or from street vendors. Trade postcards, by contrast, were issued with products, specifically to market said wares. Trade postcards are often much rarer than commercial postcards. The Odhams sports cards are a case in point. The 52 numbered cards include a score of soccer stars. The 20 footballers are worth between £75 and £100 each.

Ogden's so-called *Sporting Girls* tobacco cards date from the middle years of the 1890s. The cards feature demure, unmuddied ladies at play. The known cards show womenfolk as footballers and rugby players, and womankind in cricket whites – whereon a mistress of the wicket is seen akimbo, stumping the bails! The images appear on various cards by different brands of tobacco, including Silver Veil, Fruit & Honey and Navy Cut, to name but three. The cards were also issued in the USA with American makes such as Gloria, Buchner. etc. Values are high, and rarer types command sums in the hundreds.

Ogden's initial offering of sportsmen, in 1896, numbered one square dozen and six cards. The cards bear the legend, *Guinea Gold*. The 150 rugby and round ball footballers include subtle variations in print matrices and photos. The series includes plenty of soccer players from Sheffield Wednesday, Aston Villa and Sunderland; with one

or two from Bury, Everton, Nottingham Forest, Corinthians, Small Heath, Woolwich Arsenal, Leeds City, Bradford, Liverpool, Millwall Stoke, Rochdale and WBA. They are valued from £50 to more than £1,000 each. Note: images from this series were used by Cohen & Weenen on its *Heroes of Sport* cards. One score and a baker's dozen more *Guinea Gold sportsmen* were issued in 1899. The 33 cards of footballers and cyclists include a full team of Sheffield United players.

The first of Ogden's *General Interest* cards, and the first of many similar general series to come, emerged in 1900. The unnumbered series of 196 cigarette cards includes 56 cards showing footballers. The cards all have plain backs, and show the Ogden's Cigarettes legend with the wafting, smoky tail from the second letter g, but no longer carry the *Guinea Gold* inscription, as seen on earlier cards. Values start at £30 and rise to well over £200 for certain types. Varieties of the same card are known. Dow, for Middlesbrough, in this series, happens to be the same player described as Gow, for Sunderland, in the 1896 Guinea Gold issue. Billy Meredith is included in this series, as is Steve Bloomer for Derby County. A slabbed Meredith card has been seen, in recent times, at an asking price of over $1,000! The seller bought the card in a British auction, circa 2015, for less than £100. Such is the way of flipping football cards. Flipping is something that is done by some sellers. They hunt for cards in the wilds (European auction houses), and buy rare cards at almost any cost – the point being to get the card, to better the competition, and to set a new price for it; making a profit and a name for themselves in the process. The captured card is bound and sent home, where it is looked at for about 20 seconds by the buyer who then sends it off to a person who's breathed far too much plastic dust, and made far too much plastic pollution. The plastic slab treatment is meted out and money is

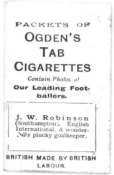

Ogden's cards 1901-1902

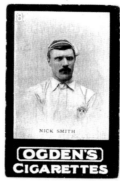
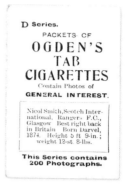

Ogden's cards 1902

Ogden's buttonhole cards

paid. The slabber puts the card in a soft plastic sleeve then seals that within a rigid plastic box, sometimes with erroneous information added for good measure. Then the plastic entombed card is offered for sale, anew, at a price that's many times higher than was paid just a few weeks earlier. This writer does not disagree with the practice of finding the right price for a card but the plastic boxes are another matter. Imagine having a collection of 10,000 cards. Whereas loose cards may be collected in a handful of albums, philatelic stock books, or on philatelic display cards, etc., pollution plastic slabs covering 10,000 cards would fill a house full! See the section on slabbers, for more.

Ogden's helpfully titled one of its many Edwardian issues. The *Our Leading Footballers* series was issued with Tabs cigarettes. It has 17 cigarette cards, with players from Glasgow Rangers, Aston Villa, Liverpool, etc. Values range from £25 to £75 each. Two unnumbered series, of 100 and 300 cards, were issued around the same time; as was a numbered series of 420 cards (which comes in many variations). Gone altogether is the fancy lettering of the 1890s and 1900. The newer logo is suitably Edwardian. Its cartouche oval enthrones the manufacturer's name. Descriptive text, titles and brand names to the rear of the 100 cards makes them easily identifiable. The series includes a trio of scenes from the 1902 FA Cup final. Alas, the following series, of 300 cards, reverted to plain backs, no titles, no numbers, and no descriptive identification at all! It includes 25 footballers, with Gilbert Oswald Smith, of Corinthians, appearing for a third time on an Ogden's card.

The cards in the series of 420 come with and without numbers, and there are three types of backs known, which makes for some collecting!

From 1901 onwards, Ogden's Tabs cards issued various *General Interest* series that were initialled, making the various series easier to identify. *General Interest A* Series cards include 150 images, of which Spurs players abound! Such footballers command values from £20 to over £75 each. The *General Interest B Series*, from 1902, includes a certain Charles Burgess Fry, for Saints. Fry will sell for over £100. He also appears in *General Interest C Series*, numbered 255, as a cricketer; accompanied by G.O. Smith, of Corinthians, on card number 252, making his fourth appearance for Ogden's. Players from Hearts and QPR are also to be found in *General Interest C Series*. Values for such footballers range from £30 to over £100 each. Ogden's *General Interest D Series*, also from 1902, includes 13 footballers (Hibs, Rangers, Celtic, and Newcastle United players) in the set of 200 cards. Values for these players range from £20 to £50 each. *General Interest F Series* (there had been no footballers included in *General Interest E Series*) contained 320 cigarette cards of which almost 50 show either football action or portraits of footballers. Smith, of Corinthians, makes his fifth showing for Ogden's, and Fry is included on two cards, in whites and in soccer colours. There are Sheffield United and Southampton players galore, Walsall, Rangers, Hearts, Derby County, etc. Values range from £20 to over £200.

Ogden's went with colour in 1906. *Football Club Colours* are very attractive cards. Amongst the cards Steve Bloomer is perhaps the most

costly player. Not that he's named. None of the players are named. It's quite a game identifying them all! Values start at as little as £2 but exceed £20 for famous faces like Bloomer and Meredith. Note: these are the same images used by Churchman cigarettes, and also by Franklyn and Davey cigarettes, in their *Football Club Colours* series, also of 1906. The Ogden's tobacco cards cost the least. Ogden's next series, *Famous Footballers*, of 1908, is equally attractive. The cards were produced in some numbers, so most can be acquired for a lot less than £5 each, and, if you are willing to accept cards that are far from perfect, you would end up with a set for less than £50.

In 1910 Ogden's issued *Club Colours Badges*. This very unusual series of cards of team colours was designed to be worn in lapel buttonholes, or in hat bands, which explains why few survive. The tradition had been started by Sharpe's, Baines and similar Victorian issuers, with buttonhole football flower cards. Ogden's issued a series of four dozen cards – an unusual number, for a set of cards, and one which Ogden repeated in other issues of the time. Values start at £20 each but rise significantly for more popular cards. The simpler colours, red, white, and blue, which represent more teams than combined colours cards, tend to be sought after, yet, it's a card featuring Reading that has not

Ogden's card, 1920s

Ogden's card, 1930s

Ogden's Nickname cards, 1930s

been seen for decades! Aston Villa enjoy similar exclusivity, being the only club listed on the claret and blue striped card (West Ham and Crystal Palace are on a claret and blue banded card). Clubs such as Fulham, Clyde and Carlisle United share their simpler colours with as many as 15 other teams. Scarcity often follows such demand.

Ogden's first set of soccer cards after the Great War was *Captains of Association Football Clubs & Colours*, in 1926. The four dozen cigarette cards are quite easy to obtain. Values are around £3 for singles but full sets of 44 often come up for sale at just £50 – about £1 a card. Ogden's *AFC Nicknames*, from 1933, are wonderful cards! The 50 mascots, emblems, club badges, and cartoons are a must-have for every football home. Values start at about £5 for single cards, but sets can be had for as little as £50. Ogden's issued *Football Caricatures*, in 1935; and *Football Club Captains*, in 1936, both of which contain 50 cigarette cards (values are similar to *AFC Nicknames*) while *Champions of 1936* contained but a pair: Sunderland and Arsenal team cards, which can be found for as little as £5 each.

Oh Boy Gum branded a series of cards, in 1933, called *Footballers of the Principal Teams*. Its 60 glossy photographic Midlands players were actually issued by a firm called British Chewing Sweets but they did so under the auspices of the American gum giant, Goudey, famed for Oh Boy Gum. Values for single cards start at £75 and can exceed £200. An Oh Boy Gum packet from this series is worth far more than the cards. Only one surviving wrapper is known. It's rarer than most gum card wrappers because such envelopes were only issued to store owners, and were not sold with the cards themselves. The packet contained a selection of cards, enough to give one each to customers presenting tokens, collected from confectionery packaging. Thus, there were maybe one or two envelopes issued to a shop, whereas later gum cards came with hundreds or thousands of wrappers, per shop. For more information on the series, see: British Chewing Sweets.

Olympiad gum issued Gallic football cards during the 1950s. The French issuer included international stars and teams with its confections. Whereas the earliest cards known are in

monotones, colourful postcard-size trade cards of teams were issued for the 1954 World Cup. A series titled, *Collection Chewing-Gum Olympiad* [sic], was printed in black and white, during its first series, then full colour after the World Cup. Values start at £20 each, for teams, and £10 for players, with certain stars hitting triple figures. Olympiad gum also issued playing cards showing footballers in action. The same photos were used on the regular gum cards, of which there are 160 known, including new signing from Nice, Just Fontaine. Values for them start at £10 and exceed £50 for world greats like the aforementioned, Moroccan born, Spanish–French star.

Onze means eleven, in French. It's also a magazine that issues football cards. As Onze, then latterly as Onze Mondial, the most famous French footy magazine of modern times, has issued free soccer cards, and similar gifts, since inception, in the 1980s. Formed of a merger between two publications, Mondial and Onze, the journal is to French football fans what FourFourTwo is to readers outside France. Onze has released stickers, albums and cards too. Its wares tend to includes plenty of British Isles footballers as well as stars and teams from around the world. A 1979 Onze album and sticker collection, called *Les 100 Ecussons des Plus Grands Clubs du Monde*, includes large, colourful emblem stickers of Aston Villa, Arsenal, Liverpool, Celtic, Rangers, Everton, Hibs, Leeds, Manchester City and Manchester United, and the extraordinary Nottingham Forest, the then current champions of England, for the first time. Onze cards are typically serrated, issued in sheets, to tear apart. Many hundreds, maybe even thousands, of different cards have been issued, including certain rookies! Prices for Onze cards are surprisingly high for modern cartophilic ephemera and the special ones are not easy to find.

Opera Mundi, of Italy, made football self adhesives of a certain ilk. Its 1967/68 football

Olympiad Gum cards

Onze stickers

Opera Mundi

mascots – stickers and postcards – show female football frolics in fanciful and fantastical situations. The Genoa CFC sticker shows a vestal virgin in the oldest of Italian club's colours, innocently skipping over the phallic lighthouse in the port of Genova. With backing papers intact, such stickers are worth £20. Postcards are £10.

Ormerod Brothers of Rochdale were one of the earliest football cards issuers in the world. During the 1890s Ormerod printed thousands of shaped football cards, whose design is often similar to cards by Baines. Though ovals became beloved of Ormerod, probably due to the amount of rugby clubs featured on its cards, other shapes are also known. Values start at £100 for lesser known teams and players but prices paid may exceed £500 for bigger names.

Or.ve.do [sic], in Alessandria, south of Turin, was the successor to VAV of Verona. It issued four series of soccer cards during 1962–1966. The various issues of *Campionato Nazionale di*

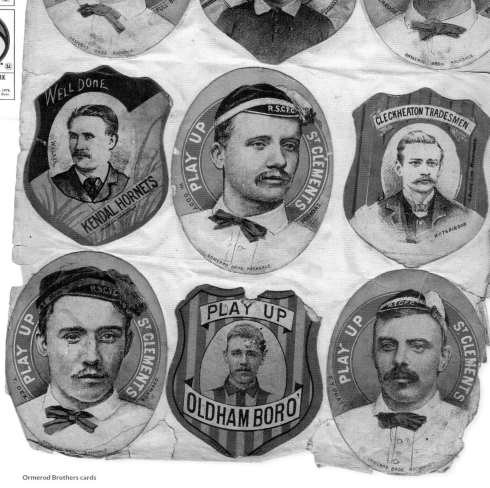

Ormerod Brothers cards

Calcio include various cards of John Charles and Gerry Hitchens. Or.ve.do also issued footballers on *playmoney*. Look out for children's currency with famous players – and be prepared to pay! Prices for such toy bank notes are rising, just as the value of fiat money in your pocket is diminishing in value [thanks to all that cost-free printing the central banks did for themselves]. The first Orvedo cards of Gerry Hitchens come in two types: unadulterated Aston Villa claret and blue; and colour tinted red, for his first Italian club, Torino.

HITCHENS - Torino   HITCHENS - Torino

Orvedo cards

H.J. Packer

Packer's cards

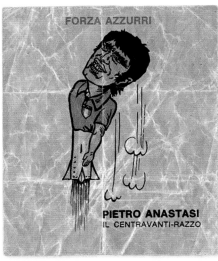

Pagliarini gum insert

Packer's, or H.J. Packer, to give the firm its formal name, was a Bristol-based manufacturer of chocolate. It was established by a former employee of Fry's, another well-known Bristol confectioner. Packer had seen a gap in the market and formed his own chocolate factory. Charlie was his name. Well, not really, but it sounds better than Edward. By 1908 Edward Packer's chocolate mill had grown into a well known business that was worth almost a million in Sterling – that's about a billion today! Alas, it's a pity, then, that Edward had let go of his entire shareholding during a market slump in the 1880s. Henry John Burrows – he of Packer's H and J initials – had taken over. During the 1909/10 football season Packer's added footballer cards to their chocolates. The cards are typically found with glue marks to the backs. This is due to being adhered within Packer's packaging. The cards are known in monotone and also in colour. They are to be found only with considerable difficulty. The rare series of 30 includes 17 different English teams, including Manchester United, Bristol City, Chelsea, Notts County, QPR, Fulham, West Ham, Spurs, Everton, Liverpool, Sunderland, Newcastle, Middlesbrough, Blackburn Rovers, Barnsley, Aston Villa and WBA. Prices for cards, be they colour or monotone black and white, poor or good, range from £100 to £250 each.

Packets. It may be hard to accept but the wrappers, packets and small envelopes we threw in the bin, after taking out the cards, the gum and the sweet cigarettes, may be worth more than the cards we kept, as children. Wrappers from A&BC gum cards of the 1950s sell for as much as £300 each and the earliest Panini wrappers can top £1,000. Some FKS packets sell for more than £100 and pre-war gum wrappers are as rare as the scarcest cigarette packet from over 100 years ago. Cigarette box and confectionery wrapper collecting is in a field of its own but there is a cross over to cards, as many card collectors want the wrapper, or the box that the cards were issued in. Wrappings of yesteryear are ever up in price! There will be much more on packets, wrappers and cigarette boxes in a future book. In the meantime readers will find many more displayed at www.footballsoccercards.com

Pagliarini (pronounced *Pal-yee-a-ree-nee*) made a great series of waxy paper gum inserts for Italy's quest to win the World Cup, in 1974. *Forza Italia* consisted of 12 great Italian footballers of the day, including Luigi Riva, Gianni Rivera, and Dino Zoff. Values for the dozen delicate papers are upwards of £25 each, with premium prices paid for the aforementioned legends.

Palirex of Portugal made *Campeoeos Europeus de Futebol* in the late 1960s. The collection consists of hundreds of stickers, including premium value team adhesives that had to be redeemed from the issuer. The series includes legendary players like Johan Cruyff, Billy McNeill and George Best, as well as players and team line-ups of Celtic, Manchester United, Manchester City, and Glentoran, among many other European Cup sides of the time. Prices paid for single stickers from this collection have exceeded £100! Expect to pay £20 for a single sticker of a player, and much more than that for team stickers of the above, and for Milan, Inter, etc.

Palirex was to the Portuguese what FKS was to British collectors. In 1970 the firm issued *Ases do IX Mundial de Futebol*. The generic Mexico 1970 collection is familiar to collectors across Europe but each country's version was slightly different, and Portugal's was one of the best! The hundreds of stickers include England stars, as per the FKS collection, but with different backs. Values for the

Palirex stickers

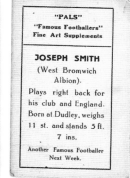

Pals 1922 cards

ZARRA   BEN BAREK

Palmera razor blade cards

Palmin cards

England team start at £20 each sticker.

Palitoy produced *Top Team* games, in 1978. It made a selection of different games dedicated to Aston Villa, Nottingham Forest, Everton, Manchester City, Liverpool, Everton, Arsenal, and Manchester United. Each game included 11 cards of players. The cards came in miniature attaché cases. Values for complete games range from £25 to £50, but single cards may sell for up to £5 each.

Palmera made razor blades. They also made some really fine football cards, many of which are worth a small fortune. In 1945 the Spanish razor blades manufacturer issued cards called *Los Clubs de 1° Division de la Liga* with razors. It was to be the first of three series, each with 154 different cards! To distinguish the first series of cards from later issues, note the lettering: it is white, on blue. Values start at around £10 but prices paid have been seen to exceed £150 for legends like Gainza. In 1948 Palmera issued its second *Los Clubs de 1° Division de la Liga* collection. The cards can be identified by their light blue lettering. Values are similar to prices paid for cards of the first series but a card of Telmo Zarra has been seen to sell for some hundreds! The last of three series of such cards was issued in 1949. The

third series of *Los Clubs de 1° Division de la Liga* includes cards with white lettering on red. Values range from £10 for most cards to over £100 for legends like Ben Barek.

Palmin-werke of Germany has issued coconut oil since the 1880s, and soccer cards since the 1900s. The palm oil flows on but the cards came to an end with Hitler. *Moderne Sport* and other Palmin series, like *Palmin Post*, were published from Edwardian times until the Weimar years of the early 1930s. If you like naturalism in art, and styles like New Objectivity, you might appreciate the later, painterly images of soccer action. If you prefer the look of Art Nouveau then the earlier, Edwardian series have something for you. Palmin cards come to the market every now and then, and prices are often low, less than £10 per card.

Pals was a comic. In 1922 it issued cards in tandem with Boys' Magazine. Together they awarded free gifts with their weeklies. In the midst of the 1922/23 season a series of coloured football cards was given away, one card per week. The eight cards show colourful head and shoulders portraits whose value is about £5 each. Known as *Natural Colour Studies of footballers* (so says an advert in a 1922 comic), the cards are

actually inscribed: *Famous Footballers Fine Art Supplements*. Great players abound, including Arthur Grimsdell of Spurs and Frank Moss of Aston Villa. This series was launched in unison with a simultaneous release by Boys' Magazine, of a further eight cards, called *Coloured Studies of Famous Internationals*.

Pals also gave away a dozen football team cards, inscribed *Football Series* (though one of the cards bears a slightly different legend: *Footballer Series*) which includes Burnley, WBA, Liverpool, Stoke, etc. Values for these are around £5 each. This series mirrored a similar issue by Boys' Magazine, which came out at the same time. The Boys' Magazine cards have the legend *Football Series*, or *Football Teams*.

Pals celebrated the season of 1923/24 with a series of half a dozen postcard-size pictures of footy teams. Prices paid for these rare, sepia-toned cards of Crystal Palace, Bury, Rangers, Bristol City, Third Lanark and Nelson diverge wildly due to team popularity. Prices have been recorded at £25 for Nelson, to £40 for Bristol City, to over £75 each for Crystal Palace and Rangers. This series was issued at the same time as Boys' Magazine released a similar half dozen cards, entitled *Football Series 1923-'24* [sic], which include Spurs, Liverpool, West Ham, Sunderland, Huddersfield Town and Man City. Values are similar to the Pals cards. See also: Boys' Magazine.

Pals issued its *New Football Series* later in 1923. The collection consists of 15 cards, each bearing a pair of postcard-size pictures, 24 of which are soccer teams. Others include rugby clubs and race horses. Values for uncut doubles range from £50 to £100. Single cut cards are worth much less.

Panini, the publisher from Modena, in Italy, has become the most famous name associated with soccer stickers, however, the Italians were by no means the first to produce such football ephemera. In fact, soccer cards and stickers were produced in Great Britain before anywhere else in the world. The first adhesive paper portraits of players were made in Scotland, before World War One. The first football cards go back even further, dating back almost 150 years! During the early 1880s cards emerged in Leeds, Rochdale, Bradford, Oldham, Blackpool, Shipton, St.Helens, Carlisle and other towns in northern England. That's eight decades before the brothers Panini

arrived, in 1961. Of course, since then, the Italian firm has made soccer stickers its own thing, thanks in part to its fine public relations gurus, not to mention the hacks in MSM (mainstream media, i.e., state and multinational corporate press and TV) by whom it's often erroneously claimed that Panini let the light in: *fiat stickers*. So, the Panini family name has become synonymous with football cards as much as with the country of Italy itself; the land of great wines, quality food, warm weather, friendly people, pizza, a passion for life, and Panini stickers!

Since the time of the rebel poet, D'Annunzio, and the dawn of fascism and Mussolini, in the early 1920s, Italian sports cards have been given with chocolates, cheese and ice cream. Glossy, photographic issues were packaged with just about all types of confectionery until World War Two. The cards featured football stars, teams and scenes of match action. Italian creativity, and the Italian adoration of futurism in design, bequeathed unusual ephemera such as metallic tokens with impressions of great players in action; card discs wrapped in silver foil, as if they were coins, then stamped with the impression of a sports star's profile; and celluloid roundels, a little

Pals 1923 double cards

Pals and Boys' Magazine
1922 pictures

Italian cards from before Panini

Nannina cards

Panini's first cards, those made by Nannina, in 1960, were remaindered stock from a series called *Gol Gigante 1960-61* [sic]. The cards are enlarged versions of a smaller collection, also by Nannina, titled simply *Gol 1960-61*.

like church communion hosts, with sacred images of footballers wearing radiant halos. Amen. Such atypical tokens were issued throughout the Era Fascista. They were not meant to last the best part of a century. That they have done is testament to their innate beauty, and their social history value, if not their innate quality – card discs wrapped in silver foil take some care to get them through 90 years of handling. As pointers to how we lived, consumed and collected, such tokens of yesteryear they are invaluable. Wreathed in fabulous designs, or wrought of materials previously unimagined for such use, creatively designed cards, coins and paper tokens were the keepsake of generations long before the brothers Panini emerged from boyhood. Yet, it is by Panini that the modern history of soccer stickers is still being written. Viva Panini!

The first Panini cards were actually produced by a rival, Nannina, a Milanese firm which had been printing football cards, yearly, since World War Two. In 1960 two of the four Panini brothers bought unsold, remaindered cards from Nannina. The cards were repackaged and distributed from the Panini family news stand, in Modena. They were sold in white envelopes, a pair of cards per packet. The brothers were more than pleased to sell 3 million packets in 1961! Such rapid sales convinced the Panini family to print its own brand of cards for the next season.

Panini's first cards, those made by Nannina, in 1960, were remaindered stock from a series called *Gol Gigante 1960-61* [sic]. The cards are enlarged versions of a smaller collection, also by Nannina, titled simply *Gol 1960-61*. The smaller issues had plain backs and were made of paper. The larger cards had potted biographies and were made of card, so it's quite easy to tell them apart and, therefore, to find the first Panini cards ever issued. However, buyers are advised to distinguish the cards from an earlier series, *Gol Gigante 1959-60*, which is also of large format, and which includes many of the same players, for example, John Charles of Juventus. The two series used different pictures. Knowing which is which comes of experience. Some of the larger cards of the second, larger, Nannina series are found with an overprint, in red, displaying the word VALIDA. Do not expect to find them with ease. Young collectors sent them back to the publisher for prizes. Few survive. Values start at £20 and often exceed £250 for the rarest and most sought-after cards. The

wrapper, an envelope, has been reproduced but there are easy ways to spot the fake, which is now quite valuable in itself. The flap of the fake is sealed with a zig-zag crimp. The original was made before crimp-style seals were used. It simply tucked into itself, and was not glued. The original envelopes were made of very thin paper, almost palimpsest. Copies are typically of heavier stock. If you see an original for sale expect to see a price of £1,000. The design shows pink hatching at the edges, a thin, black frame line, and a goalie, in green, with a pair of outfield players, one in green and black, the other with pink and black stripes.

Panini's first in-house series of cards, made, mixed (in a butter churner) and marketed by the family itself, was called, *Grande Raccolta Figurine Calciatore, Campionato Italiano di Calcio Serie A* – in English that's *footballers*, in a word. The collection was issued during 1961/62 and comprised 288 stickers. In those days stickers were generally all made of card, and the collector had to apply a glue to stick them into the dedicated album. The unbranded cards feature teams, emblems and player portraits. Later series came without branding, and without recognisable years of issue, so, to identify the cards from this

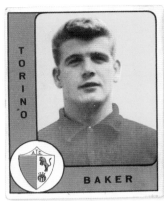

Panini's first cards

Panini's second series

Panini's collection of *Calciatori* from 1962/63 consists of 379 cards and stickers. Most of the cards were issued with plain backs so identification of the series is done by noticing the particularities of the player photos, which have sharp corners; and the club emblems are set within shield designs with straight edges.

series, note the soft corners to the photos, and the inset, circular club emblems. The cards have mostly plain backs, though some, very rare cards are known with red and blue 'valida' offers for a leather football, which could be redeemed by sending in 100 such cards. The album had three different printings during the months of 1961 and 1962, and a fourth edition was issued a few years later. Wrappers are made of delicate, thin lucid paper, with light green borders, showing a red goalie and red goal, and two outfield players in red and blue. An original wrapper is worth about £750 but, be careful, there are fake wrappers in circulation. Cards from this series sell from £20 to over £200 each. The collection includes British stars like John Charles, of Wales, Cardiff City, Leeds United, Swansea Town, Hereford United and Merthyr Tydfil; Denis Law, of Scotland, Huddersfield Town, Manchester City and United; and England's Joe Baker, of Hibernian, Sunderland, Arsenal, Nottingham Forest and Raith Rovers.

Panini's collection of *Calciatori* from 1962/63 consists of 379 cards and stickers. Most of the cards were issued with plain backs so identification of the series is done by noticing

the particularities of the player photos, which have sharp corners; and the club emblems are set within shield designs with straight edges. The shields themselves are free of circular or square frames. The team photos also have sharp, square corners, whereas those of 1961 are rounded. Some cards are known with *Premio* prize offers on the backs, and they are worth more. This and later collections, until 1965, have very similar team picture cards, and one series is hard to distinguish from another. This collection includes Panini's first self-adhesives (stickers with peel-away papers) of club emblems. The stickers are shaped like shields. The wrappers are made of paper, with wide blue polka dotted borders, and a pair of outfield players in yellow and magenta. Values for the various wrappers (three varieties are known) are around £500 each. Caveat emptor: there are fake wrappers in circulation. Values for cards are mostly around £10 each though prices may exceed £100 for rarer varieties. Stickers with original backing papers are worth £200, and used stickers, recuperated from an album, may still fetch £50 each!

Note: many Italian sellers use the term REC to mean recuperated from an album. This means

a card will have glue damage to the back, and a sticker will be without its backing paper. This is not good news for many collectors. Recuperated stickers and cards are only good for sticking into an album with gaps.

Panini produced a third set of cards with mostly plain backs for the 1963/64 season. The player cards can be identified by the escutcheon used for the club emblems: its shield shape has soft curves and is wholly set within a square. *Calciatori 1963-64* had 421 cards and stickers, of which a sub-series of 10 cards relate to international cup competitions. Other cards feature Alfredo di Stefano, Puskas and Real Madrid; Mario Coluna, Eusebio and Benfica, and Maldini, Altafini and Milan. There is also a trio of self-adhesive stickers, one for each of these teams. There are colour differences known among these cards. Tip: look out for Eusebio. The Benfica and Portuguese legend has been snapped up by rookie card dealers and prices for his cards exceed others in the collection. Though the market may seem flooded with blue variants the yellow Eusebio is scarcer. Many sellers scour partly complete albums, remove the valuable cards and sell them as 'recuperated'.

Values for most cards in this series start around £5 but unused stickers can fetch as much as £200. Cards with rarer colour variations may exceed that figure! Some cards are known with prize 'valida' backs and they are worth more. Recognising the team cards from this collection can be difficult. Other than Benfica, Milan (for whom there are two team cards) and Real Madrid, the team picture cards are very similar to those issued in 1962. The wrappers are made of paper, with wide pink polka dotted borders, and show a diving goalie, in a yellow shirt.

Panini first branded its cards in 1964. From this point onwards Panini's footballers, and sports stars, would be identifiable by a logo, or a brand, if not yet by a date. The 1964/65 season's collection of *Calciatori* included 421 cards and stickers, mostly with plain backs, mostly of Italian Serie A and B players, with some foreign stars in the *Tutte Le Coppe* (*All The Cups*) section. The cards are easily identifiable by the triple hexagons, with the initials EPM, and a lance, to the front of the card. Some cards have prize offers on the backs which show Panini's address. Team cards are hard to distinguish from earlier collections. Barring a

small selection of cup-winning teams, which have the lance and hexagon logos, most team cards have no identifying marks that place them in this collection. Club emblem stickers are printed in landscape format. As with all early Panini series a variety of different wrappers are known, all being made of paper, showing a pair of players, a goalie, and penalty box action. Wrappers show the initials EMP in triple hexagons. They are worth about £200. Unused emblem stickers may sell for over £100. Player cards are valued between £5 and £50 each but foreign stars like former Aston Villa player, Gerry Hitchens, and Pelé, have been seen to sell for much more.

In 1965 Panini added identifiable logos, text and biographies of stars, and histories of teams, to the backs of cards. The *Calciatori* collection for 1965/66 includes 480 cards and stickers. The cards have red and black backs. They are undated but easily identifiable by the black oval and two triplets of hexagons on the backs. Prize 'valida' cards are known. Unused cards from the series may sell for as much as £100 each for rarer types. However, the typical value is £5. Pelé collectors have much to chase herein, for there is a card of the great man himself, and three teams

in which he is to be found: Santos and two Brazil line ups. The club emblem stickers are shaped like gonfalon flags. If they remain unused, with original backing papers, they may sell for over £100 each.

Two sports collections in 1966 confirmed Panini's ongoing success story in stickers. *Campioni dello Sport* (*Champions of Sport*) was the family's first pan-sports series. It includes 447 cards, whose values are around £5 to £10 each, with notable exceptions, of which 27 are self-adhesives, showing sports emblems for tennis, golf, boxing, etc. The most valuable card in the series is that of a certain boxing legend, the one and only Cassius Clay, a card which has been seen to sell for over £200! Some sellers slab commoner cards from the series and inflate prices up to levels that are quite ridiculous for such a relatively easy to find collection. Muhammad Ali is one of the exceptions. So too are the cards of Pelé, Puskas, and Eusebio; racing drivers, Bruce McLaren, Jackie Stewart and Graham Hill; and boxers, like Sonny Liston. Perhaps the other rarest card is that of Bobby Moore. It shows Moore in a blue top. Its number is 161, and it is unusually hard to find. It's one of

Panini's third series

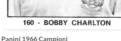

Panini 1965 cards

Panini 1966 Campioni

Panini 1966 football cards

Panini 1967 football cards

the rarest cards from the series, and when it comes up for sale it usually sells for more than £50.

Panini's 1966 football collection was the first to show seasonal dates. The *Calciatori 1966-67* series included 498 cards and stickers whose values range from £3, for basic, unused cards, to £25 for highly sought-after players and teams. The cards, which are easily identifiable by their yellow coloured frames, include England's Nobby Stiles, Roger Hunt, Bobby Charlton and Bobby Moore; a pair of cards for victorious England and one for Manchester United. The club emblems, on foil stickers also include England. They sell for up to £50 each.

Panini's second Sports Champions series, *Campioni dello Sport 1967-68* [sic] consisted of 564 cards, including 30 metallic stickers. The cards have green borders. Amidst boxers, rugby, baseball and basketball stars this series also contains about 80 football cards. Values range from £5, for unused cards, to over £50 for the boxer, Cassius Clay. Metallic stickers with backing paper are rare and valuable. Caveat emptor: certain unscrupulous sellers outside Italy claim some of these cards are 'rookies', including that of Fangio. It is untrue

(Fangio rookies go back to 1950, to the Albosport stickers by Didasco). Do not necessarily believe what you see boasted by internet sellers. Most 'rookie' cards on Ebay are not actually rookies, just as most 'mega-rare' sales are not rare at all. Do your own research. Try foreign sites, like ebay. ie or ebay.it and save a fortune. Instead of buying slabbed cards on ebay.com buy the same, raw material on ebay.de or ebay.es

Panini's football series of 1967, *Calciatori 1967-68*, comprised 619 cards, including 84 stickers, 30 of which are in pairs. Values range from £5 to £150. The stickers of international teams, Celtic, Liverpool, Manchester United, Santos, Real Madrid, etc. are in gold foil. Domestic club emblem stickers are silver. There are also team cards for Celtic, Manchester United, Liverpool, Santos, etc. Player and team cards have magenta borders, and green and black backs. George Best makes a tidy price of £50 or more – but be careful, recent forgeries abound. Also at premium value are cards of Roger Hunt of Liverpool, Billy McNeill of Celtic, Pelé, Beckenbauer, Eusebio, etc.

In 1967 Panini issued a general series which includes some cards with sports interest, and one

Panini 1967 Best & Pele

footballer. *Uomini Illustri*, which means illustrious men, includes the world speed record breaker, Sir Donald Campbell; Everest conqueror, Sir Edmund Hillary; famous painters, astronauts, inventors, and so on. Note: do not confuse this collection with a later series of the same name, from 1980, which includes Pelé. The earlier cards have red and black backs with the firm's initials, EPM, in triple hexagonals. Values for unused cards start at £5 each, and may exceed £75 for cards of specific interest, for example, Stanley Matthews, the only footballer in the set.

Panini's third *Campioni dello Sport 1968-69* series included 561 cards of which 50 are stickers. The cards have purple and red backs. Emblems come in three types with green, blue and red borders. Two types of backing paper are known on the metallic stickers. Some have the legend *stemma autoadesivo*, and others have *scudetto autoadesivo*. Values for the cards and stickers in this series range from £5 up to £40, for unused emblems.

Panini's *Calciatori 1968-69* included 519 cards of which 133 are either stickers or decal transfers. The cards have green and yellow fronts, and magenta and black backs. Some

transfer decals show British clubs, and one has the England national emblem. Look out for Tottenham Hotspur, Celtic, Manchester United, Leeds United, West Ham, etc. The decals are especially rare because of their nature. As waterslide transfers they were all too often transferred. To find unused decals, with backing papers, is not easy. English players and teams feature across the collection. There are three cards of Manchester United, three for Spurs, two for Leeds United, Celtic and West Ham United, and one for England. Values start at about £5 for unused cards and may exceed £100 for unused decal transfers. Buyers beware: some vendors sell used transfers that are cut out from album pages. Original, unused transfers come with a protective backing paper, like the A&BC transfers of 1970.

Panini's fourth pan-sports collection, *Campioni dello Sport 1969-70*, included 460 cards and 24 self adhesive stickers. The cards have blue and red backs, and there are 'valida' prize offer cards, as with every Panini collection of this era. Promotional cards, so-called *buono* or *buoni* cards, with a coupon and two cards attached to each other, are very rare and their values range from £5 to £100 each. *Buono* double cards and

Panini's fourth pan-sports collection, *Campioni dello Sport 1969-70*, included 460 cards and 24 self adhesive stickers.

Panini decals

Illustrious Men 1967 Matthews

Illustrious Men 1980

Panini cards 1968

coupons are worth from £20 to £500! Caveat emptor: some sellers slab certain cards from this series and ask enormous prices. Buyers do not need to pay huge costs. Just go to ebay.it and, sooner or later, you will find the same cards for much less. The only really valuable cards, that are almost impossible to find, are the promotional *buono* coupons.

Panini's *Calciatori 1969-70* consists of 475 cards and 76 stickers. The cards have mustard yellow borders to the fronts, and red & black backs. Many of the self-adhesive stickers come in pairs, one of which shows an England emblem (value for an uncut pair is £25). Single, cut emblem stickers are all but worthless. Cards values are mostly below £5 each.

In 1970 Panini issued its first World Cup collection. *Mexico 70* has become mythic, not least, because of the amount of money spent on it by collectors around the world. It's also special due to the three known varieties of cards. Yes, there are three types, not just the two well known issues. The album was printed in Italian and in

international versions. So were the 270 cards and various, self-adhesive stickers. The cards are known with Italian green backs and with international black and red backs. There are also cards with backs coloured blue and red, with Italian language. The blue and red cards were issued early on, at the initial launch of the series. They were issued as cut-out cards, attached to promotional coupons. Most of them were cut and pasted into the earliest albums, to get collections started. Uncut cards are extremely rare and have premium values. Cut blue and red cards retain worth also, due to their rarity. The collection includes various, self-adhesive stickers, some of which came as two-in-one stickers, others as singles. The green back cards were the regular Italian release. Cards with red and black backs, printed in different languages, were available in many lands, from Belgium to the British Isles, West Germany to France, and beyond. Values of unused cards (green, and red & black types) range from £5 to over £100. Values of unused stickers, and unused pairs of stickers, with backing papers, sell for up to £200. There are also

stickers that were issued 'outside' the collection. Though very rare, these are not as highly sought after because album completists have nowhere to put them. Prices paid for Italian *buoni* coupons, with two blue and red cards, range from £200 to £500 each pair. Cut, single blue and red back cards are worth £50 or more. All cards rise dramatically in value for rarer cards, like Didi, Roger Hunt, both of the England team cards, both Brazil team cards, Tommy Wright, Keith Newton, Alan Ball, etc. which tend to sell for around £30 to £50 each. The collections, both Italian and international, were published in large numbers, and they were collected by many hundreds of thousands of people. More cards always seem to show up. Sooner or later you'll get the cards you want, except for the blue and red rarities. Only these are truly rare, and almost impossible to get. All of the other cards show up, sooner or later. It's the stickers that are the killers! Even used, discarded backing papers have been seen to sell for over £100 each! Every time unused stickers come to market prices seem higher than the last time.

Various series of Campioni cards

In 1970 Panini issued its first World Cup collection. *Mexico 70* has become mythic, not least, because of the amount of money spent on it by collectors around the world.

Mexico 70 cards

Mexico 70 cards backs

Panini 1970 cards

Panini 1971 cards

The 1970 collection of sports champions, *Campioni dello Sport 1970-71*, has 522 cards of which 162 are stickers, including soccer cards of Brazil and Italy. Values range from £5 to £75 each, the higher prices being paid for cards like the rookie card of tennis legend Billie Jean King. Values for *Buono* coupons with pairs of attached cards are worth a lot, up to £500!

Panini followed the World Cup with a regular football issue, *Calciatori 1970-71*. Its 586 cards include 86 stickers, some in pairs. Easy to identify, the cards have red and black backs, and dates. Noted clubs include Arsenal and Manchester City, of which there are team cards and stickers, issued in pairs. Arsenal shares a sticker with Bologna, and City with Vasas. Cut singles of these stickers are worthless in terms of cartophily but may make for an attractive addition to a scrapbook page. Intact pairs of stickers are rare and valuable. Values range from £3 for most of the cards in the collection, to over £20 for the British teams, up to £50 for rarer 'valida' prize

cards, and intact stickers. This collection also includes cards of the Welsh wizard, John Charles; the Scottish all-time great, Denis Law; and England legend, Jimmy Greaves. All three are known with ordinary and with 'valida' prize backs.

Panini's *Calciatori 1971-72* consisted of 595 cards including 179 stickers. The series includes an England team card and a metallic foil sticker of the Three Lions. It also includes cards of many British Isles clubs, including Glasgow Celtic, Linfield, Distillery, Limerick, Liverpool, Chelsea, and Hibs of Cork, in Ireland. Most of these cards will cost less than £10 for new, unused stickers, but £25 is about the most to pay for a top quality item. Buyers beware: many stickers are sold used, without backing paper. These are worth very little, about £1 each.

Other than the beautiful World Cup collection, *Mexico 70*, Panini's wares were mostly unknown outside Italy. In 1970 Panini could not simply set up an office outside the EEC. (The EEC was the predecessor to the freedom of movement and

tariff-free trade zone known which is the EU). If Panini did manage to break into foreign markets it was under cover. Panini surreptitiously entered Scandinavia, Iberia and the British Isles using cards made, on the face off it, by local issuers. Before Sweden, Spain and the UK became members of the EEC, or the European Union, getting business in and out of such countries was tougher than it is nowadays. Native businesses within those countries were needed to front the stickers for Panini. A Spanish firm called Vulcano came to publish Panini's Spanish cards, much as FKS published Fher stickers in the UK. A firm called Thorpe & Porter, a distributer, struck a deal for Panini cards in Great Britain. Williams Forlag, a printer, did similarly in Scandinavia. For more on this, see the entries under Top Sellers (a publisher of erotica and horror magazines) and Thorpe & Porter.

British stars were included in one of the first Swedish issues. The Williams Forlag (Panini) series, *Fotboll 1971*, includes 360 cards which feature Arsenal and Leeds United players. The cards are

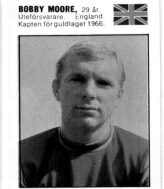

FOOTBALL 72

CARD NO. 16

JIMMY ARMFIELD. A regular England full back in the early 1960's and former captain of the national side. Still a first-class defender who has built-up a name for sportsmanship in the game. Also works as a journalist on a Lancashire paper. Released at end of last season after well over 550 games.

TOP SELLERS LTD
Printed in Italy by Panini 1971

Fotboll 72

157. BOBBY MOORE, fältherre i West Ham och engelska landslaget. Världsmästare 1966. Är liksom Beckenbauer mycket all round. Numera mest libero där hans taktik och fina spelsinne ställer honom i särklass.

157

Williams Förlags AB
Printed in Italy by Ediraf 1972. Prod nr 665

VM-AFFISCHEN

Bild nr 28

BOBBY MOORE, 29 år. Uteforsvarare. England. Kapten för 1966 års guld-medaljörer. Bollsäker extrastopper.

SAMLA BILDERNA I. VM-AFFISCHENS FINA SAMLARMAPP!

VM-affischen kostar bara 4:75 och finns överallt där tidningar säljs!

Williams Förlags AB

BOBBY MOORE, 29 år. Uteförsvarare. England. Kapten för guldlaget 1966.

Swedish and British agency issues

Spanish Vulcano Panini cards

not unrelated to the very similar Top Sellers cards, from Britain, issued one year later. They share a certain look. It's an attractive, generic design that would endure in the United Kingdom until 1977, the year of Panini's great break out. Panini's first British issue by Top Sellers was called *Football 72*. The collection's 422 cards make for a classic series, and no Panini buyer should be without them. Note: the series has two extra cards, primarily of interest to Manchester City and Chelsea collectors but essential for a complete set that includes all varieties. The cards of City's Young, and Birmingham City's Cooke have two varieties each. Further, the wrapper from the cards, and the album cover from this series are both essential acquisitions for a Panini aficionado. Both the packet and the album cover feature Arsenal's Frank McLintock. Initial copies of the albums were given away with a free sheet of six cards, to separate and glue down. As for values, regular cards are worth £5 to £10 each but values rise to £30 for rarer types. The wrapper sells for over £50, and an uncut sheet of half a dozen cards makes more than £100. A full album is worth over £500.

In 1971 Panini opted for Olympics instead of general sports champions. Its series *Olympia*

(1896-1972) [sic] contained 287 cards of which 76 are stickers. It was to be the first of two Olympic Games releases by Panini in a year. French and Italian versions of this collection are known. Values for the cards and stickers range from £5 to £50 each, top price usually being paid for Cassius Clay. *Olympia (1896-1972)* was followed immediately by *München 72*, a collection with 265 Olympic Games cards and pan-sport stickers. Values for these cards range from £5 to £25. The collection has half a dozen football cards. They include West Germany, France, Hungary, Malaysia, Mexico and Yugoslavia. Many foreign editions of this collection are known.

Notwithstanding back-to-back Olympics Games series, Panini had not abandoned football. *Calciatori 1972-73* was well received in autumn 1972. The cards and stickers include British and world teams, including Derby County, Celtic, Leeds United, Liverpool and Tottenham Hotspur, whose clubs emblems are included on stickers containing a quad of miniature crests of various teams from around the globe. You may have to pay over £30 for a complete foursome.

The *Football 1972-73* collection sounds, on the face of it, like it's an English language

TOTTENHAM Inghilterra

CAGLIARI Italia

FIORENTINA Italia

INTERNAZIONALE Italia

Panini quad stickers

collection, however, the series was Panini's first Benelux release. George Best, Bobby Charlton and a host of other internationally recognised stars are included in this Flemish and Wallonian collection. Prices paid for such stars often exceed £75 each.

In 1973 Panini issued a cartoon series called *OK VIP*. Today some of the stickers, if unused, fetch prices of £50 each. The cartoon caricatures feature many footballers, both British and world stars, including George Best, Lev Yashin, Eusebio, Pelé, Bobby Moore, Bobby Charlton, etc.

Later in 1973 Panini returned to the pan-sport generic series it had created in 1966. *Campioni dello Sport 1973-74* included Cassius Clay and many hall of fame footballers including Johan Cruyff, Eusebio, Bobby Moore, Gerd Muller, etc. Values for unused stickers range from £5 to £75.

Panini's 1973 series of football stickers, *Calciatori 1973-74*, marked a departure from earlier Italian issues. For the first time there were no foreign stars, nor teams, nor emblems of anything other than domestic Italian interest. Of more interest to non-Italians, and to most readers of this book, is Panini's third Top Sellers issue, *Football 74*. It included 420 cards of English league clubs and world stars. The value for such cards

and stickers starts around £3 and rises to £25 for rarer types. Wrappers are worth £50 each, and uncut sheets of six cards, as given with the album, are worth £100. A full album would sell for around £500. Note: the second Top Sellers series, *Football 73*, had been printed by a firm named Ediraf, and not by Panini. This has made many collectors believe, wrongly, that the two firms Ediraf and Panini had no connection. The former is a printer. The latter is a publisher. Hand in hand they were, but the motivation for using the Ediraf imprint, and not Panini, has been lost in the mists of time. The 1972 Ediraf Top Sellers series comprises mostly cards but also a selection of self-adhesive stickers, notably puzzle sets, and also a card that had no place in the album, an England World Cup card. It was meant to be a World Cup diviner, a predictor of England's success in a future cup. As an oracle it was defective.

Panini's 1974 World Cup collection, *München 74*, included 400 cards and stickers whose values start at around £5 each. Certain players, notably Kenny Dalglish, make far more! Buyers beware: reprinted cards, reprinted packets, reprinted albums and even newly printed point-of-sale display boxes are on the market. Be very careful about spending big money on this collection. Many unopened packets and display boxes are recent,

very good copies, made in France. In 1974 Panini issued two pan-European versions of the album: the regular album and a Serbo-Croat edition, in former Yugoslavia. This is by far the rarest edition. It's called *Minhen 74* [sic]. If you are going to spend a lot of money on the *München 74* issue, then the Yugoslav version ought to be considered. Also worth buying, if you can get them, are partial, or complete sheets of stickers. Expensive, yes, but guaranteed genuine, obviously off the roller presses of yesteryear, and not hot off computer printers. Copies of the stickers are obvious but packets and boxes are not so easy to distinguish.

At the end of 1974 Top Sellers released the fourth British football Panini collection, *Football 75*. The wrapper and the album cover feature Liverpool match action. An empty wrapper is worth £50 while an album, complete, would be worth around £500. The 420 cards and stickers are mostly available for less than £5 each but rarer types will cost £25. See also: Top sellers.

Sport Vedettes was an early pan-European issue by Panini. It's a general sports series that's well worth looking for. Its 400 cards and stickers include sporting greats, like Muhammad Ali, and also a selection of 10 soccer stickers, one of which is a foil emblem. Others feature Franz Beckenbauer and Johan Cruyff! Here's a tip for

Benelux Panini stickers

Panini 1973 Campions

Munich 74

Panini OK VIP

GIANCARLO ANTOGNONI
ITALIA

EDDY KRIEGER
ÖSTERREICH

JAN TOMASZEWSKI
POLSKA

OLEG BLOCHIN
SSSR

FABIO CAPELLO
ITALIA

JOSE ANTONIO CAMACHO
ESPAÑA

CLAUDIO SALA
ITALIA

GIACINTO FACCHETTI
ITALIA

FRANCESCO ROCCA
ITALIA

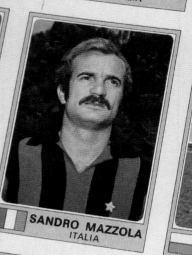
SANDRO MAZZOLA
ITALIA

RAOUL LAMBERT
BELGIQUE - BELGIE

JULIEN COOLS
BELGIQUE - BELGIE

FRANCO CAUSIO
ITALIA

PAOLINO PULICI
ITALIA

ESPA

FRANJO VLADIC
JUGOSLAVIJA

DRAGO VABEC
JUGOSLAVIJA

ULRIK LE FEVRE
DANMARK

Panini Sport Vedettes

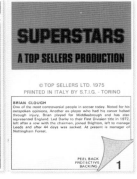

Top Sellers Superstars stickers

Panini Football Clubs

Italian Panini, 1975 Kevin Keegan

buyers: when you are seeking these online, search using numbers. The soccer stickers are numbered 108 to 117. Motorcyclist Barry Sheen, boxer John Conteh and equestrian David Broome feature among the Brits.

Panini issued a stunning football series in 1975. *Football Clubs* was a pan-European, multi-language collection of club badges and maps of European football grounds. Like the World Cup collection, *München 74*, it was distributed in the UK by Thorpe & Porter (they of the T and the P of Top in Top Sellers), a firm conservatively based in foxy Leicestershire, far from smutty Soho, the den of iniquity where Top Sellers flourished. In the 1970s the business of imported cards was much like that of publishing soft porn magazines. It was a business with a Jekyll and Hyde sensibility. While conservative countryside headquarters were removed and respectably far away from the sleazy front line, the shop front would do the dirty work in grindhouse alley. Soho was the business end of operations, where publishers like FKS and T&P would do deals with distributers, in earshot of Jeffrey Bernard sipping at just the one, in the

bar of The Coach & Horses. Note: Panini also issued the *Football Clubs* collection in Serbo-Croat, in the former Yugoslavia. The Yugoslavian edition is the rarest version available. It may cost more to acquire but it will probably out-price the regular version in years to come. See also: Top Sellers; Thorpe & Porter.

During 1975 a fabulous series of Top Sellers postcard-size stickers hit the newsagents' shelves. *Superstars* were ostensibly printed by a firm called STIG, in Turin, in Italy. Though the Panini connection is not overt these are Panini issues, just like the Top Sellers cards. Most of the super-size stickers sell for about £5 but some have exceeded £100! The collection includes boxers, like Ali and Frazier; film and TV celebrities galore, and a handful of soccer stars, including arguably the best English football manager in the last half century, Brian Clough.

The Italian editions continued throughout the late 1970s. Panini kindly included British players in many of them. Kevin Keegan was guest of honour in the 1975/76 collection. Panini also continued the foreign agency collections, by firms like Vulcano; and its Benelux editions ran yearly. From

1976 it added newly appointed, annual domestic collections in countries like France (Football 76, and so on), the UK (Football 78, and the rest) and West Germany (Bundesliga 79, etc.) The first French, domestic league collection, *Football 76*, includes stickers of Billy Bremner and Johan Cruyff. Such stickers, unused, sell for premium prices. A complete album is worth around £200.

Top Sellers cards were phased out as Panini made bigger moves in the UK market. *Football 76* (with a wrapper and an album that feature Derby County) and *Football 77*, (with Tottenham

French Panini

In 1977 the Italian firm issued what would come to be classed as a seminal collection: *Euro Football*. It helped to break the British market for Panini, and it helped break FKS!

Panini silks

Hotspur artwork on the packets and the album) were the last of the much loved collections. Today the cards sell for about £3 each, and complete albums fetch hundreds.

In 1977 the Italian firm issued what would come to be classed as a seminal collection: *Euro Football*. It helped to break the British market for Panini, and it helped break FKS! The timing and the distribution of the release was the secret. It was issued early in the year, when children were down with school blues, and needed a ray of hope. A football magazine called Shoot! gave the *Euro Football* album, as a free gift, along with a packet of stickers to boot! It was a very welcome distraction and life would not be the same again. *Euro Football* reached the parts *Football Clubs* had failed to find. Distribution was the key, and Panini had unlocked the invisible door to the secret garden, much to the delight of many British children playing there.

In 1978 Panini issued three collections in the UK. The year started in the same way as the previous year, with a new collection in January, yet *Football 78* was not about internationals, it was a Panini collection dedicated to the English and

Scottish Leagues. Values today are around £2 for unused, regular stickers, and some collectors have paid more than £20 for so-called *shinies*. Early in the year Panini also issued *Euro Football 78*, a collection of pan-European stickers with plenty of British Isles teams. This collection is known with both blue backs and with black backs. The third Panini collection issued in the UK that year was *World Cup 78*.

Panini's second British leagues issue, *Football 79*, is a collection that's notable for the silky feel of its sleek self-adhesives. The club emblems were made of a satiny fabric. The touch of the stickers lured both young and old. Lust for silk caused school playground stand-offs. Today, the plush stickers are rarely found with their original backing papers. If they are rediscovered, unused, prices soar. *Silks*, as they are known in cartophily, are collected not only by football card collectors but also by genteel cartophilists of yesteryear, who seek that certain satiny satisfaction. Silk cigarette card collecting has been a cartophilic category in itself for 100 years. The cross-over interest, having two groups of collectors seeking the same material, nudges prices higher. This writer remembers

elderly gentlemen pushing kids aside, making their way to the front of the queue to buy packets of *Football 79* – just for the nephew, of course. Collecting cigarette card *silks* they hadn't had much to look forward to since the 1930s. 1979 was a boon! Happy times for young and old alike.

Euro Football 79 was issued in the same year, a year which also saw Panini's first West German issue, an alliance with Bergmann Verlag: *Fussball Bundesliga 79*. By the turn of the decade *Europa 80* and *Football 80* followed. The annual Panini pattern was one at home, a domestic collection; and at least one for abroad, an international collection, or two. Readers will know that many Panini collections were printed in Great Britain and Ireland after 1980, and since that time many hundreds more have been published in lands as far afield as Mexico, Turkey and the African nations. Panini stretches from South America to Asia. These are outside the focus of this volume. More in the future.

A last word on Panini, for now, is reserved for *Sport Superstars Euro Football 82* [sic], a pan-sports issue, with plenty of soccer. World greats like Maradona and Socrates feature alongside Scottish legends such as Kenny Dalglish and Graeme

Souness. Erstwhile Liverpool lad Kevin Keegan is given a spot too, albeit in Hamburg colours. The British Isles teams on stickers are many: Aston Villa, Liverpool, WBA, Spurs, Swansea, Dundalk, Rangers, Celtic, Arsenal, Glentoran, Southampton and Ipswich are all here, as are some of their stars, like Steve Archibald, Gary Shaw and Paul Mariner, not to mention great sides of Euro and world football, and star players from abroad, like Liam Brady of Juventus.

The collectability of certain top boxers and tennis players in this series adds considerable value to the collection.

Due to the broad range of Panini's collections after the 1970s, and because the focus of this book is on rarer cards and stickers from before the time of such multinational dominance, later issues by Panini, those after 1980, will not be covered in this edition. For Panini issues after 1980 this writer recommends Greg Lansdowne's book, Stuck On You, by Pitch Publishing. Many rare images of Panini stickers can be seen on www.footballsoccercards.com

Pattreiouex issued tobacco brands like Casket, Critic, Senior Service, Illingworth and Trawler cigarettes. Its earliest cards did not show the name Pattreiouex, and they are listed in this book under its brand names, such as Casket, where readers will find the firm's earliest and rarest soccer cards. During the late 1920s, through until 1936, Pattreiouex made cards bearing the firm's own name. The first of these was issued in 1927, with 100 soccer stars, called *Football Series*. Some of the 100 cards are known with both blue and also with brown titles. Most can be found for less than £10 each.

A year later Pattreiouex issued a series of 25 cards, *Photos Of Football Stars*, which were very similar in nature to cards issued by sweets manufacturers, Lovell, and also by Tuckett. Finding the same player in all three issues is quite a task but having the trio of cards increases the values of the cards overall. Lovell cards tend to be the easiest to find, and cost least, with Tuckett cards proving very elusive, and far more costly, yet, it is the Pattreiouex cards that are the hardest to acquire, and worth the most, being priced at around £100 each.

A series from 1930, *Celebrities In Sport*, includes half a dozen footballers, including Dixie Dean. The 1934 collection, *Footballers in Action*, has 78 cards and one error card.

Italian stickers, British subjects

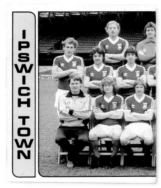

British subjects on Italian stickers

Pattreiouex Action

Pattreiouex Celebrities

People's Journal stickers, 1914

Perfetti Forza Goal

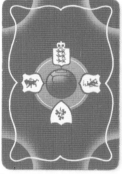

Pepys cards

The People's Journal made the first football stickers in the world. In 1914, it issued a colourful collection called *Gallery of Famous Footballers.* The stamp-like stickers feature Scottish football stars of the day.

Look out for card number 37. It comes in two variations, one ascribed to Stockport County and the other to Huddersfield Town. The set of 54 *Sporting Celebrities* cards of 1935 included almost 20 footballers, while *Sporting Events And Stars* of 1936 includes 96 cards, of which two dozen show footballers or teams. Generally, all Pattreiouex cards from the 1930s are quite easily available, mostly for less than £5 each.

Paulton's of Wolverhampton issued Wolverhampton Wanderers players, and club staff, on cards via the Wolves match programme. Readers would collect tokens for a set of cards. From 1923 onwards various series of cards were issued in both colour and in black and white. Their values are around £50 each card.

The People's Journal made the first football stickers in the world. In 1914, it issued a colourful collection called *Gallery of Famous Footballers.* The stamp-like stickers feature Scottish football stars of the day. An Everton player is known among them, but, otherwise most of the players are from Scottish teams, like Rangers. Values are around £500 for bigger team players though finding any example from this series will cost hundreds!

Pepys cards were issued in boxed games by a firm called Castell Brothers. Some years before World War Two Pepys-Castell issued *It's A Goal!* The game included four dozen cards showing football team colours. Registered at Stationers Hall, in 1939, this is the earliest version of a game that would be republished after the war. It has cards with red backs showing flags, goals and the FA Cup, which are worth £5 to £10 each. The first reissue of *It's A Goal!* came out in 1959. The reissued cards have green backs, with a ball. The game was reissued yet again, in 1962, with the ball flying off in the opposite direction. Whichever green version you have, individual cards from the post-war game are worth £2. Complete boxed games are beautiful and few remain intact thanks to decades of sales of single cards.

Pepys issued another soccer game, by the name *International Football Whist*. It was a game of 44 cards showing football players from the home international teams. Values for these cards start at £10 each. Complete games are rare, for the same reason; few remain intact.

Pequeno Artista (*Little Artist*) children's cards came from Spain, circa 1920. Paint your own

football club colours cards came with a basic, colourless design, showing football action, with small blobs of paint affixed to the card. The little artist would dilute and brush the pigments into the design. It was a simple but ingenious idea. Find a fine paintbrush, get some water and within a moment your monotone footballers become radiant in the colours of your choice. Unused cards have sold for as much as £100 each.

Perfetti is one of the greatest names in Italian gum cards. The firm is not only known for *Forza Goal!*, a series of football cards of the 1980s (with Joe Jordan, Gordon Cowans, etc.), and for its waxy, paper gum inserts of 1970s soccer teams. Perfetti goes much further back. In the early 1950s it issued monotone photographic cards. Back then it was known as Dolificeria Lombardo. The firm is best known to international soccer card collectors for a set of 1967 international footballers and pop culture celebrities, including Rossana Schiafino, Verna Lisi and Claudia Cardinale. Cards of whom? How quickly the world moves on from forgotten famous people of yore. Not so with soccer legends of yesteryear. The score of soccer stars in this series consists of about 10 players with Serie A connections, and 10 from elsewhere. Many of the players are seen wearing Milan, Inter, Torino and Bologna colours. They include English and Scottish stars (Denis Law and Jimmy Greaves). There is a card of Beckenbauer, misspelled as Bekenbauer. This card has been wrongly dated, by some, as 1965. This is bad because it gives value to a card that is actually from 1966/67. It gives the card a rookie status that it ought not to have. Dated wrongly, 1965, it's worth a lot more money than a 1967 card. Its true worth is around £50. Some sources erroneously claim the cards are by a Dutch firm, Monty Gum. They are not. The Italian firm Perfetti made them. The three Inter players, Corso, Mazzola and Suarez, all wear the 1966/67 yellow star jersey. This was not worn before autumn 1966. Knowing how slowly photos were disseminated, and how laboriously sets of cards were made, in the 1960s, suggests to this writer that 1967 is the earliest year of issue. Perfetti was based in Lombardy, near to Milan. The inclusion of so many Italian celebrities and the 10 Italian football-related celebrities, of whom six played in Milan, says it all. It may have been syndicated elsewhere, or excess, unsold stock may have been bought and resold elsewhere, but it is by Perfetti, and it is Italian. These are the footballers [capital letters show how their names appear on the cards]: Florian ALBERT, wearing the red tracksuit of Hungary, photographed in a public park, in England, in summer 1966; José ALTAFINI, in the blue and white of Napoli, whose photograph is similar to that on the 45rpm single record "La Rosa", released in 1967; AMANCIO Amaro Varela, in the white of Real Madrid; Georgi ASPARUKOV, wearing Bulgaria's national away red jersey. The same image was used on the Panini *Campioni dello Sport* sticker from 1966/67;

BEKENBAUER [sic], in a green, West Germany away jersey; B. CHARLTON [sic] seen in blue England squad tracksuit top; Igor CHISLENKO, in red Russia national team jersey; Néstor COMBIN in Torino red jersey; Mario CORSO – and not Uruguayan *Walter Corbio* as some sources claim – wearing the yellow-star Inter jersey of 1966/67; EUSEBIO, in a casual, light blue shirt; Jimmy GREAVES, in a photo re-tinted to show him in a red and black tracksuit, the colours of his former club, AC MILAN; Helmut HALLER, in a Bologna jersey; Denis LAW in a Torino jersey; Sandro MAZZOLA in the yellow star Inter jersey of 1966/67; Bobby MOORE in a blue tracksuit, without a club or team badge; PELE wearing a Brazil first team jersey; Gianni RIVERA, wearing an AC MILAN jersey; Karl-Heinz SCHNELLINGER wearing AC MILAN colours; Luis SUAREZ Miramontes, wearing the yellow-star Inter jersey of 1966/67; and Paul VAN HIMST wearing Anderlecht white. See also: Dolcificio Lombardo.

Perry Books issued football cards in a typical cigarette card format, on pull-out sheets attached inside children's books. A 1949 series was illustrated by an artist named Kerr. A fold-over sheet of cards – made of card, not paper – was designed to be pulled out, and cut apart, resulting in a collection of colour cards. Buyers beware: paper copies are known. If you buy one of these, or a sheet of them, and you get paper, not card, you have been sold a copy! In 1950 Perry Books reproduced the little cards as larger, full page paper images, about the size of large bubble gum cards. They were issued in three little books with various titles, for example, *Stars of Football*. The paper pages from these books, removed and sold as single cards, are not cartophilic but they do appeal to card collectors. Don't pay too much for

them. The value is in the smaller cigarette card size cards from the earlier books, or in complete booklets. A full sheet of cards from 1949 would fetch £750. Single cards sell for around £100 each. The later paper pages are worth but a few pounds each. Complete booklets from 1950 are worth £50 each.

Phillips is a name that goes back to the beginning of cigarette cards. Godfrey Phillips & Sons issued football cards as early as the 1890s. A general interest series of cards, issued in 1896, includes 13 cigarette cards with a pair of footballers, one from Aston Villa and the other from WBA. They are worth about £200 each.

Phillips issued its next football cards more than a decade later, in the *Sporting series* of 1910. The blue cards were re-issued in 1923 with black backs, re-named simply *Sports*. The 25 cards in each set include but a single football-related card. Its typical value is £25 for the 1910 issue and a lot less for the later reissue.

Just before World War One Phillips issued tobacco inserts made of silk. The series of *League Colours* silks have no maker's mark, nor brand name, but some of the backing papers issued with the silks do have identifying information. The unbranded silks from 1914 are worth about £10 each, and a premium £20 for certain teams like Spurs and Woolwich Arsenal. Silks that still have original backing cards are worth much more than those without. Note: these are all small size silks, with dimensions up to 70mm x 50mm. Later issues, from 1920, came in large and small sizes, with brand names (BDV). Values for larger silks are higher. Apparent variations in lettering colour (brown and black) may be due to 100 years of daylight erosion. Premium values may be applied if the silks come with original thin card backing

Perfetti 1967 cards

Perry clipping

Phillips silks

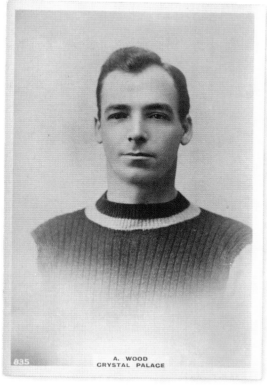

Phillips Pinnace cards, four sizes

papers but, generally, the smaller silks from 1920, without papers, are worth around £5 each, and larger, paperless silks are between £5 and £20. Backing papers add premiums to prices.

Phillips Pinnace cards come in four sizes, with many variations to the backs, and to the fronts. They were first issued in 1919, as small size cards with brown ovals on the backs. Values for such cards start at around £10 for rugby players and £20 for most of the round ball footballers. Buyers can expect to pay a lot more for rookies of the game and for hall of fame legends, with which this series is replete.

In 1920 a second Pinnace series of small cards was issued. They have black oval backs. The cards are much more readily available than the brown cards of 1919. Values kick off at £5 each but much higher prices are paid for rarer cards. Medium size cards, about the size of gum cards, were also issued with black ovals on the rear. They are worth £10 for rugby players, and much more for soccer cards, with premium prices often paid for popular players, and bigger teams. Later in 1920 a new type of small size card appeared. It had double frame lines on the rear. Values start

at £3 each, with premium prices paid for some cards. A medium size set of cards, without ovals, with double frame lines on the back, was also issued. They can be very rare. Prices paid range from £10 to £100 per card!

Between 1921 and 1923 there were two more issues of small size cards. Some have the word *photo* on the rear; whereas others mention, simply, Pinnace. The cards with numbers in three figures are worth £3 to £10 each, with premium prices for rarer variations. Note: many variations exist for Pinnace cards. You may have a dozen small cards of the same player and find all of them to be different from one another. For cards numbered in four digits, a good rule of thumb is to quadruple the price! Footballers of well collected teams, with high numbers, can sell for up to £50 for just one, small-size card.

Large, postcard-size cards of players are available. They were known as cabinet cards and were redeemed, one at a time, in exchange for a large quantity of small or medium-size cards. Few people seem to have gone to the trouble to acquire the large player cards as they remain very rare. Values for such postcard-size cards start at around

£20 for rugby players, and may exceed £100 for cards of famous soccer players and stars of the bigger teams.

The rarest Pinnace cards are the so-called cabinet cards of teams, which were redeemed for 100 small cards – that's 100 packets of cigarettes! They are about twice the size of postcards and show football teams. They all have plain backs. About 100 team photo cards are known. They are found dated, 1920-1921, and undated. Such cards are almost impossible to find. They are the ultimate in Pinnace redemption cards. Their values are around £500 for one card! Few were redeemed, due to the enormous amount of small, medium and large cards needed to get them, which is why they are so rare.

Phillips released various series of packet-issue cards from 1932 to 1934. The cut-out cards are known as BDV issues because of the type of tobacco used in Sport Cigarettes, a leaf called Boyd Dibrell Virginia. Both paper and card BDV packet issues include footballers, boxers, jockeys, tennis players and other notable sports stars of the time. They include lots of variations! The paper

Phillips 1930s cards

Phillips Spot the Winner

Phillips BDV variations

cut-outs were issued on cheaper packets of five cigarettes, whereas bigger boxes, of 10 or more cigarettes, were made of card, from which came the card cut-outs. It's a fascinating series. Some images are slightly larger than others, some have single frames, others have double frames; some have greyer printing, others are more colourful; and some photographs differ, not just in scale. One year to another, different photographs were used. The captions also differ: in names, in team names, and in punctuation. Cards that remain uncut, on a fold-out paper packet, or on a card slider, or on a complete box of cigarettes, are worth far more than cut cards. The trim of cut cards also affects values, so the wider the border, the better. Though prices start low, at about £5 each, rarer examples and uncut boxes may push costs as high as £100 for some cards. Helen Wills-Moody, Dixie Dean and Matt Busby drive buyers wild!

Phillips produced many more series of cards until the hiatus of World War Two. *In The Public Eye*, from 1935, consisted of 54 cigarette cards, of which 5 are footballers. *Famous Footballers* was a series of 50 cards without a logo or a brand name. They are recognisable by the goal net at the top, and the FA Cup, corner flags and football boots at

the bottom, on the back of the cards. In 1936 Phillips produced two series, a collection of 50 footballers in *International Caps*, and *Spot The Winner*, which included 11 footballers. Values for these cards are around £5, for superb quality examples. If you are prepared to take lower quality cards you'll pick them up for £1 each.

After the war Phillips resumed production of cards with *Sportsmen*, a series of 50 packet-issue cards, and *Footballers*, a series of 25 similar issues cut from boxes of Sports brand cigarettes. Cut cards are worth £10 to £25, while uncut packets start at £25 and exceed £50.

In the 1950s Phillips pressed on with cigarettes where the card was part of the packet. Between 1950 and 1952 it produced three annual series of *Footballers*: 50 cards, then 25 in 1951, and 50 again, in 1952. These issues are known printed on both paper and on card. Values for the cut-out paper issues are £15 to £30 each. Uncut paper packets are worth £50 upwards. Cut-out issues on card are worth £10 to £25, though a completely uncut card slider would fetch much more. An entire card box with a notable star would exceed £50.

The final football cards series issued by Phillips – and one of the rarest of Phillips series – was made in

1954. *Sportsmen* comprised 25 packet issue cards, including a handful of soccer players. Cut-out cards sell for as much as £50 each – and some are almost impossible to get at any price. Uncut card slides are worth over £75 each, and entire card boxes top £100.

Phoskitos confectionery, from Spain, issued a series of footballers and club badges, on folding cards, in 1976. Values for these fascinating little triptychs start at £5 each. In 1979 the same firm issued *Liga 79-80 Juego De Fichas*. The token cards have push-out circular discs of famous players. Un-used cards with tokens are worth £20 each. Used, single player discs are worth £2.

Pinguin of Dortmund, West Germany, issued *Spieler des Deutsche Fussball-Bundes* in 1964. The series consists of 18 large, montone photo cards

of players. Values are around £20 each, with a premium price paid for Max Morlock.

PK Gum issued *Football Facts* in 1983. The series of 32 cards shows football colours for English and Scottish clubs. Values have risen to over £20 each.

Planta of the Netherlands published 80 large cards called *Olympische Spielen 1952*. A handful of these relate to soccer, some of which are worth £20 each.

Platin of Spain issued two series in 1954. *Seleccione Campeones* is known in blue and also in red. It consists of 11 small sticker stamps obtained from the packaging of Platin's household dry goods. An album was issued. The stamps were collected then returned to the firm for redeemable prizes. Few remain. Values start

at £30 each but big premium prices have been paid for Kubala and Di Stefano.

Player tobacco issued two series of footballer caricature cards in 1926 and 1927, called, *Footballers Caricatures by RIP*, and *Football Caricatures by MAC*. The two series each have 50 cards, and they are easily available, as are many issues from this period. During the late 1920s and 1930s cigarette cards were produced in the millions, whereas trade cards, from children's sweets, comics and other products, are often far rarer, and can be worth far more. Player continued with the soccer theme with *Footballers 1928* and *Footballers 1928-29, 2nd Series 51-75* [sic]; and, in 1930, the firm also issued *Association Cup Winners*. Player cards from these series are readily available and may cost as little as £1 each.

Phillips c.1950 variations

Platin sticker

PK Gum

Platin of Spain issued two series in 1954. *Seleccione Campeones* is known in blue and also in red.

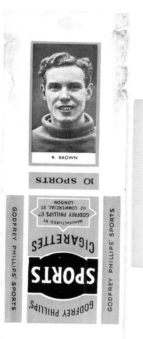

Phillips c.1950 packets

Phoskitos cards

Player tobacco cards

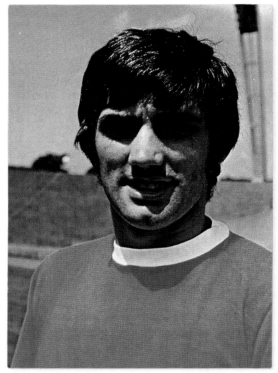

Swiss Poly card

Poolette card

Pluck was a comic of the 1920s, and collectors often have fun with its cards. During the 1922/23 season Pluck issued *Famous Football Teams*, a collection of 34 cards, of Scottish and English clubs. The cards are valued at around £5 each for the regular English cards but they sell for much more if they feature Scottish teams, or, if they are English teams from the Scottish series. How will a collector know this? Well, other than researching the hard way, the quick trick is: check the back of the card. The more valuable English team cards, from the Scottish series, can be identified by the back, where next week's team is advertised. A Scottish team the following week identifies the set as Scottish. Some of the cards were exactly the same, fronts and backs, both north and south of the border, including that of Rangers. The other Scottish teams were only issued in Scotland. They have premium price values and are worth up to £50 each. Also, look out for these teams: Blackburn Rovers, Barnsley, Oldham Athletic, Darlington, Swansea, Leicester City and Huddersfield Town. They were issued with both Scottish and English backs. Scottish back on English cards mean higher values. They are worth over £25 each.

In 1970, Poly, of Switzerland, issued a football card series in three languages (because the Confederation of Helvetia is trilingual). Thus, *Grosse Stars Des Runden Leders* and *Les As du Football* and *Gli Assi dei Calciatori Internazionale* are German, French and Italian versions of the same Swiss collection. They feature George Best and plenty of British players, including Gordon Banks; as well as world greats like Johan Cruyff and Pelé. Values range from £10 to £20 for such stickers. The publisher also issued a collection called Golden Goals, or *Goldene Tore*, featuring similar world greats, whose values are similar.

Poolette was a boxed game made by Sphinx Products. *The Great Football Pool Card Game*, of 1938, included 52 game cards, with many British teams among them. The cards bear no maker's mark, nor brand. These were stated only upon the box. The team cards have black and white illustrations of running soccer players, a football and a divisional title. All 1938 cards have red and white backs. The set was re-issued in 1946 with blue backs. Values are around £5 per card.

Poppleton & Sons made chocolates. In 1922 the confectionery was issued with cards showing famous footballers. The cards show no series title,

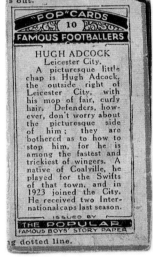

Popular pop-card

nor maker's mark. They are known in both sepia and in black and white. They have plain backs but cards have been seen with a Poppletons rubber stamp impression. The cards are also associated with Clarnico (Clarke, Nicholls & Coombs). The mystery remains why a London based firm, such as Clarnico shared a series of cards with Poppleton's of York, far away, in northern England. Values range from £50 to £500. Early VCC cards have also been found with Poppleton's rubber stamp cancels. See also: Clarnico; VCC.

The Popular was a comic. In 1930 it issued football cards to cut out, fold around and glue together. *Pop Cards Famous Footballers* consist of 12 such folded, and glued paper cards, cut from The Popular comic. They are very rare! Values for cut cards start at £50 each. Uncut comics containing unspoiled cards start at £100 each.

Poulain, the French chocolatier made obliquely famous globally by the success of a certain film, Le Fabuleux Destin d'Amélie Poulain, issued 3615 Poulain *Sportsmen*. The series was released in the early 1980s, with chocolates. It contained many sportsmen. Values start at £5 for footballers, but premium prices are paid for sports legends like Pelé.

Prescott Pickup Chewing Gum issued *Famous Football Club Flags* in 1974. A very similar series had been issued in Italy, by Panini, in 1964, called *Bandiere Nazionali e Sportive*. The Prescott flags look, to all intents and purposes, just the same. They unfurl from around a plastic flagpole that has a top, in a contrasting colour, and which plugs into a plastic base. Values for the Prescott flags range from £10 to £15 each. A packet is worth around £30. Panini issues of the same would be worth triple such figures.

In 1975 Prescott followed flags with *Famous Football Pennants*. The collection consists of 40 European soccer club emblems, with holders. Values range from £15 to £20 each. A packet is worth £30. Things went downhill in 1979 [for many reasons] as Prescott sacrificed its creativity and joined the cards bandwagon, to produce the awful *Sigma Sports Silhouettes*, a series of 60 action portraits of famous footballers, with tasteless 1970s graphics. They looked like something from a lino printing class in secondary school. Values are mercifully low.

Priddy cards deserve a mention in this guide because Bill Priddy's sports cards are unique. Bill's cards also have a very funny story behind

them. The inspiration for a generation of home-printed cards, they were created in a very stressful night without sleep, in Bill's attic. He'd been owed money from a printer. The printer was going bankrupt and could not pay back the money but he offered Bill the chance to print some cards in lieu of the loss. The only thing was the cards had to be printed the next day, the very last day the presses were available. Bill worked all night drawing an idiosyncratic series of sportsmen, and he succeeded in submitting 1,000 designs the next morning! They went off to the printer and the rest is history. What most collectors don't know is that when Bill asked for publicity for his cards from the editor of a, now defunct, cigarette card journal in the south west of England, he got more than he bargained for. The snooty fellow threw the cards back at Bill, and wrote a damning review, warning collectors not to buy Bill's cards, which he said were the worst cards he had ever seen. So, of course, most of the magazine's readers went and bought a set from Bill, out of curiosity. Other readers pestered the editor for the cards and, finally, he had to eat humble pie and buy 50 sets from Bill. The cards were soon sold out and Bill had to print more, just to keep up with demand.

Pulgarcito Bruguera, 1949

A cut PS card

Principe card

Provincial Sports Publications (also known as PS Publications) issued cards of footballers in 1948. Two cards were given with the first two issues of Soccer Stars journal. The cards each feature 30 different footballers. Sadly most are found cut to singles. Uncut cards are worth £75 upwards.

Bill told this writer that he'd never made so much money from cards, as he did with his ugly, little sportsmen. They are in a class of their own!

Primrose Confectionery made *Famous Footballers FBS1*, a set of 1961 cards that consisted of 50 soccer stars. They look very similar to the 1960s cards by Barratt. They can be had for less than £1 each. Primrose's later issue, *Cup Tie Quiz*, in 1972, has 25 trade cards. Values are similarly low.

Principe means prince, in Italian. Principe made chocolates. The firm also produced some stunning trade cards. From 1932, a series called *Cine-Sport* includes various photo trade cards of footballers, actors and athletes. Typical values for footballers are around £35 each.

Progresso Foods, in the USA, issued Pelé, and pals from the New York Cosmos, in 1978. The series, *Meet The Cosmos*, consists of 20 black and white stickers. They were sold in strips. Uncut strips sell for £30 and single stickers for £5, with a premium price for Pelé.

Provincial Sports Publications (also known as PS Publications) issued cards of footballers in 1948. Two cards were given with the first two issues of Soccer Stars journal. The cards each feature 30 different footballers. Sadly most are found cut to singles. Uncut cards are worth £75 upwards. Photos cut from these cards are worth a mere £1, if that. A Provincial Sports Publications card is also known with Wolves and Leicester City, in the 1949 FA Cup. Its worth is also around £75.

Pulgarcito was a Spanish magazine. Since the 1940s it has issued cards and full colour supplements of cards of players, and teams. Values start at £10 each, with premium prices paid for world greats like Kubala, and Larbi Benbarek. The 1949 yellow bannered, large, coloured paper cards known to be by Bruguera were actually given in Pulgarcito!

Platin Spanish stickers, 1954

Quadriga Laws of Soccer

Quadriga

uadriga was a chariot on square wheels. Planned during a pub vigil, held near Westminster Bridge, the ungainly vehicle was designed by a group of friends who vowed to fight against the invasion of Italian stickers that had destroyed their world of work. They might as well have plotted to avert the sun rising. The four FKS rebels sanctified their scheme in the shadow of the statue of Boadicea's war wagon. Though drawn by only two horses the Iceni chariot gave the foursome their belligerent brand name: Quadriga. Alas, evoking the bested Boadicea betrayed Quadriga's destiny, and yet another British rout.

The Laws Of Soccer was a baleful maiden series. It seeped off the presses and slipped out, in shame, unto a world that wished it ill. The cheap collection of blandly illustrated scenes from an imaginary training ground had no star players, and no famous squads. It was not the ideal winning strategy for a new firm. To go against all of the trends of the day, and issue something that resembled tea cards, given by

Brooke Bond in the 1970s, succeeded only in setting back the charioteers.

The Laws Of Soccer had not been designed as Quadriga's first issue. It was a last minute fall-back, a substitute taken from the archives. A similar series of soccer rules stickers had been designed some years earlier, by an FKS affiliate in South American, a Fher firm called Reyauca. The Quadriga artwork was based upon the equally lame Latin American stickers. Subsequent destruction of unsold stock means the Quadriga *Laws Of Soccer* stickers are now rare and quite valuable. Were anyone to attempt to collect this series, to spend money acquiring it, the 300 stickers should cost a small fortune.

Snooker Kings put Quadriga back in the frame. The snooker stickers of Alex Higgins, Jimmy White, Ray Reardon, Terry Griffiths, and other Pot Black princes of the baize, gave the firm a mildly successful break from the bleak reception its first British soccer collection had attracted.

So, if *The Laws Of Soccer* was not meant to be the first Quadriga series, what was? *Soccer 83*. The unissued, final series of stickers by FKS, *Soccer 83*, was due for release after the

World Cup, in autumn 1982, but FKS stopped issuing and was wound down before the launch. Quadriga planned to release the collection but baulked at selling the FKS stickers in Great Britain. It was feared that such an illicit distribution, and sale, of unapproved produce would land the fledgling firm in the jaws of British courts. So, *Soccer 83* was re-named *English Football Tips 82/83* [sic], and launched only in Denmark and Norway.

Quadriga was on a roll, in Scandinavia at least, but the much larger British market was what mattered to the London foursome. Following the success of *English Football Tips 82/83*, in Scandinavia, and the abject failure of *The Laws of Soccer*, at home, the firm launched *Soccer 83-84* [sic]. It comprised three legions of stickers, and unlike the ascetic *Laws Of Soccer* there was nothing spartan about this 300! The series is stylistically the same as FKS's 1982 stickers. It's considered a rare classic and keeps some collectors awake at night. It's difficult to find missing stickers, to finish collections, and the tariffs exacted for errant numbers are often punishing. Unused stickers have sold for as much

Reyauca 1978 Laws of Soccer

Quadriga snooker

11. JIMMY WHITE (*England*). Born: 2.5.62. Home: Tooting. World ranking: 7. Benson and Hedges Masters winner 1984. Runner-up Embassy World Professional Championship 1984. Youngest ever winner of English Amateur Championship 1979 and World Amateur Championship 1980.

25

PETER WITHE

Quadriga British and Scandinavian types

SOCCER 83-84

26. Peter Withe. Striker. Age 31. Born in Liverpool. Joined Aston Villa from Newcastle in 1980 for a fee of £500,000. Has played for many clubs in the past such as Southport (where he made his league debut), Wolverhampton, Portland Timbers (USA), Birmingham, Nottingham Forest. Has been capped by England and was a member of the World Cup squad. Ht. 6.2. Wt. 12.0.

Quadriga British and Scandinavian types

as £30 each! Tip: it was also released as *English Football Tips 83/84* [sic], in Scandinavia, where it was more easily available. In appearance the stickers are almost exactly the same. If you are collecting for an album the Viking issues fill gaps nicely, though you might need fresh glue. The adhesives of the era tend to dry out, and many stickers have, by now, fallen from albums and from their original backing papers.

Quadriga is associated with two paper manufacturers of note: Torras Hostench and Adestor. The former was a well-known Spanish merchant which was hand in hand with Fher. Adestor was a self-adhesive paper specialist, with offices in London. Quadriga stickers often display the names of both firms, just as the brand name Fas-Print was included on the back of 1970s stickers by Cadbury, BAB, etc.

Quaker Oats issued a series of free gifts with its morning-has-broken breakfast fare, but the American firm did not always appreciate what British kids wanted, first thing, on wet winter mornings before boot camp. 1950s give-away gifts like ink blotters, for school desks, absorbed no junior angst; and cards like *Little Cards That*

Amaze & Amuse did neither! Had Quaker not considered that maths cards over oats, before school, would just add to the misery of a young life? Come 1959 the firm had learned. *Stars of Sport Picture Cards* included cricket, boxing, track and field, and Billy Wright, of Wolves. Such a card is worth £35 today. The series was copied by a firm called Shipton, which issued *Trojan Gencards* [sic], featuring the very same water colour, painterly portrait of Billy Wright, etc.

Quaker Oats followed *Stars of Sport* with *Great Moments in Sport*, in 1960. Its 36 packet-issue cards, cut from cereal boxes, show illustrated scenes of various moments from the history of soccer, including a handful of historic, notable FA Cup finals. Other cards include famous sports stars of yesteryear, like Joe Davis, the snooker king; great boxers, like Joe Louis, and tennis legends like Lenglen. Values for football cards start at around £25 each, and can double that price, in auction.

The curiously titled *Phiz-quiz* Quaker cards, of 1961, consist of 36 packet issues, showing silhouettes of sporting stars and historical figures. The sports subjects from this set can make more

than £50, notably the card of Joe Louis.

Quaker Oats issued a stunning series of unbranded, monotone photographic cards in 1962. Though untitled, the 20 cards have come to be known as *Photos of World Cup Football Stars*. The cards are almost postcard-size in dimension, with plain backs. Values start at about £25 but rise considerably for certain players and teams. One seller priced this set of 20 at £1,000! This writer was told, 'someone will pay it'. That may be true. It may not. Quaker free gifts were printed in the millions.

Question of Sport cards date back to about 1986 and have been reproduced every few years since. The cards come from a boxed game that is based upon a British TV show. A box of 240 cards from 1986, and similar issues 1992, 1996, etc. would contain a score of cards relating to soccer. The football cards are worth around £2 each. These cards are outside the timeframe focus of this book but there will be more on this generic board game, along with thousands of other modern day series, in a future edition of this guide.

Quaker Great Moments

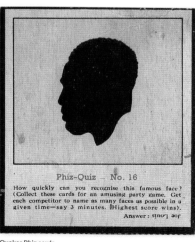

Quaker Phiz cards

Quaker World Cup 1962 card

RE! THE SECOND BIG BUNCH
MOUS FOOTBALL JERSEYS!

NEXT IS
NEXT W

No. 1220—OCT. 2nd, 1948. PRICE 2d

THE
ROVER

CHARLTON ATH.

BLACKBURN ROV.

Radio Corriere

Radio Corriere stickers

Red Star 1933 transfers

Radio Corriere was Italy's Radio Times. It was a television and radio guide magazine. During 1970 the magazine caught cup fever and issued its own collection of stickers: *Coppa Rimet Mexico 70*. The stickers were issued, weekly, in sheets, to cut, collect and stick into an album, also given with Radio Corriere. Few stickers remain in uncut sheets. Complete sheets of stickers may sell for up to £100 depending on the players included. Cut singles of England's stars have been seen to sell for more than £20 each.

Radio Corriere revived the idea in 1974. *Mondiali Monaco 74* sheets of stickers are worth up to £75 each, and cut singles of Scotland players, and world greats, sell for more than £20.

Record issued Italian soccer cards in the 1950s. For identification purposes, many of the otherwise unbranded Record cards, of the late 1950s, feature a quartered red circle, and a match-and-win game. One of the Record collections, from 1954, was never fully released. Only 44 cards from *Goal!* made it out to the street. The rest of the series was left to sink into obscurity, and collectors were left to wonder. Some years later the missing cards were found, being sold in packets by another

manufacturer! Values for these rarities start at £20 each.

The Record Cigarette Company issued cigarette cards unlike any other. During 1934 it gave away miniature, playable 78rpm records – as cigarette cards! The cards, called *The Talkie Cigarette Card*, were made by Dubrico, of Slough. They feature illustrations of famous footballers, with potted biographies; and on the other side there is a miniature record, in shellac. There were 36 *Talkie Cigarette Card* in the series, of which nine relate to soccer. Values start at £200 for most football-related cards, and go skywards!

Red Star footballer transfers, from the 1933/34 season, include the definitive rookie of Stanley Matthews. The coloured illustrations of footballers, on decals, have an enormous value. An intact sheet sold for £1,000 in 2018. Regular single stickers sell at about £40 each, while a Stanley Matthews sticker is worth upwards of £500 based upon a sale price recorded in 2019. There were only 11 complete sheets known. That's 11 of these Stanley Matthews rookies known, worldwide! Some sheets have

Record Cigarette card

Rekord cover cards

44.—DIEGO MARADONA.

Reyauca sticker

FRANK HUDSPETH

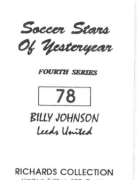

Soccer Stars Of Yesteryear

FOURTH SERIES

78

BILLY JOHNSON
Leeds United

RICHARDS COLLECTION
Limited Edition 500 Copies

Harry Richards cards

been separated, to sell the transfers as singles. The entire known population of these sheets and stickers came from one, unique source. The sheets were stapled together, on to a backing card. The old stock was discovered in a clear-out of a derelict shop, and sold through an internet auction in 2015. Each sheet consists of 31 players and one decal with a logo, a red star on a yellow background. The series has been dated to 1933/34 by the players included, and the strips they wear. The issuer of the decals remains unknown and may never be identified. The transfers are unbranded and have no logos, apart from a yellow decal with a red star.

Until 2015 these rarities had gone unrecorded since their time of publication – not unusual for smaller issues, and local trade cards from before World War Two. Few people, if any, recorded such things, and the war destroyed much stock, and myriad paper records. Old paper, scrapbooks, children's comics, cards, and transfers like these, were given to the patriotic pyre; the paper recycling war effort. Card and paper was collected on every street, to be pulped into propaganda posters like the mythic Keep Calm & Carry On placard. It was not until 1962 that a book on British trade cards was issued, by a wartime British spy, and secret agent, Edward Wharton-Tigar, noted for covert action against German forces.

It's only in recent years that such rare trade cards have been seriously researched and recorded, notably by Alan Jenkins, of the Football Cartophilic Info Exchange. That this series missed the attention of collectors and cataloguers until 2015 is no surprise. It's only surprising that unknown cards from yesteryear don't crop up more often.

Reddish Maid sweets issued *International Footballers of Today*, in 1965. The 25 trade cards are worth around £10 each, though the seekers of George Best and Pelé have broken the chance of making this set. Prices paid for those particular cards are in three figures each.

Regina Chocolates of Portugal made *Rebucados Azes do Football* in 1930. The 130 paper stickers sell for up to £50 each.

Rekord is a magazine that has been published in Sweden since the 1940s. During the 1950s and 60s, small pictures of sportsmen, in pairs, adorned its front cover. The cards were designed to be cut out. Most cut pairs are worth only £10 but very high premiums are paid for world greats like Yashin and Pelé. An un-cut pair, still attached to a front cover, or, better still, a complete magazine would be worth much more than a cut single, or a cut pair. A cut duo with Pelé is worth up to £200. This writer noted an internet auction, in Sweden, during spring 2019, where the final sale price was around £160. Caveat Emptor: reprints of the original magazines were issued. Copies exist!

Reunion was a German issuer of cigarette cards. The tobacconist issued a series called *Fussball Und Ander Sportarten* in 1928. It contains hundreds of sports stars. Values for single, unused cards start at £25 each, and rise sharply.

Reyauca was a South American, Spanish language issuer with ties to Fher and, indirectly, to FKS. It issued many series of football cards during the late 1970s, and onwards, for example, a set of World Cup circular stickers, *Ases Mundial 82*, issued in Portugal, by Francisco Mas, were enlarged and reissued by Reyauca. Values for the Reyauca stickers are around £20 each for noted stars like Maradona, and also for British stars. For more on the smaller *Ases Mundial 82* stickers see under: Mas.

The firm is also known to have made a version of the generic Fher album that was issued in the UK, by FKS, as *Spain 82*. The stickers are similar to those by FKS but show the Reyauca brand name across the upper white borders. Valuable single stickers include Ricardo Villa and Ossie Ardiles, not to mention Maradona. If unused they can exceed £30 each.

Reyauca produced a series of cards for Mexico 1986. There is an unbranded series called, simply, Futbol Mundial. The design of the Scotland, Northern Ireland and England stickers is stylistically similar to the FKS *Argentina 78* collection. They have plain backs, diminutive flags, names and numbers, but they have golden borders, another touch of FKS flair from the 1970s. Prices paid for British Isles players have exceeded £20.

Richards Collection cards were created by a man in a loft, in darkest Dudley. Harry Richards printed many sets of cards in his time, including the *Underwood* sports cards for John Allen FC (football collectibles), in 1995. Typically modern day reproduction cards of players of yore are outside the scope of this book but Harry Richards needs a mention, as Harry, along with fellow caretakers of soccer's yesteryear, Garth and John, of Fosse cards, has done more for modern cartophily than many. Harry was transferring obscure images of footballer caricatures, from

1920s and 1930s comics, on to modern cards long before the era of home computers. By doing so, using Xerox copiers, scissors, glue and his own pen and brush, he rescued thousands of otherwise lost treasures, myriad images of stars of the past. Though many of Harry's earlier cards were monotone blue, his later restorations were in full bloom, hand coloured by himself. He produced one-off sheets of artwork for each series and though single cards can be found for less than £5 each, his colourful art plates of entire sets of cards are valued at over £500 each.

Ripley Brothers had talent! Their 1920s ice cream cards are in a league of their own, and the ice cream has made a name for itself around the world. During the 1920s Ripley's issued *Football Club Colours*. The cards are crepuscular rarities from the dawn of Battock's, and the twilight of Baines. Finding a Ripley's card is akin to discovering an Ormerod oval, or a Schofield shield. The large, delicate trade cards include liveries for both round ball and rugby clubs. Values for these stunners start at around £200 each!

Ritchie & Company made various sets of cards in the 1990s. They have become scarce and sought after. A collection called *Footballers 1994-1995* includes 24 players whose images were also issued, as a set of cards, by South Wales Police. Values are around £10 each Ritchie card. Apparently, most of the rarer South Wales Police cards were destroyed due to... [redacted].

Rizla Chewing Gum issued a glossy set of cards for the 1974 World Cup. The firm's base, in Belgium, required dual language cards, in French and Dutch, hence these cards are known by two titles. Scottish players are included in this rare series. Values start at £20 each. Double that for Scots!

Robinson LTA stickers are actually paper cut-outs, taken from a 1950s magazine, *Football Stars of Today and Tomorrow*. There was a similar, sister series of golden-framed paper players, issued in Spain, around 1954. The Spanish issue would make for a good comparison, side by side, with the British. Values for such clipped cards are in the eye of the beholder but the Spanish Kubala and Di Stefano cut-outs have been seen to sell for about £40 each!

Roche & Company made Rising Sun matches. During 1927 the firm issued a set of 50 little football cards within its matchboxes. *The Rising Sun Famous Footballers* values kick in at £25 each card, except for card number 21. This card is rarer. It

Roche matches

Roche & Company made Rising Sun matches. During 1927 the firm issued a set of 50 little football cards within its matchboxes. *The Rising Sun Famous Footballers* values start at £25 per card, except for card number 21. This card is rarer and features a Sunderland player, for whom premium prices are paid. Expect double, or more for card 21.

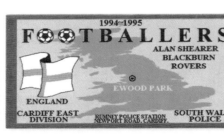

Ritchie South Wales Police cards

Ripley ice cream cards

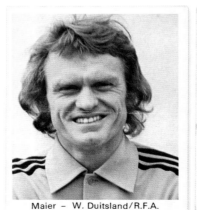

Rizla Gum cards

Rollan card

Rotalfoto cards

Rotopress card

Rover paired cards

Rover stand-up cards

features a Sunderland player, for whom premium prices are paid. Expect double, or more for card 21.

Rogue Donaldson cards have been included in other sections of this book. Valued at £75 to £150 each the cards show player names in red, in contrast to the Donaldson issues of 1946 and onwards, which use various shades of blue. There is no maker's mark on the rear of the cards, which reflects a similar matrix used by Donaldson for its earliest issues. The cards use caricatures with both big heads and with small heads. There is some speculation amongst collectors that these cards are the first Kiddy's Favourites issue. That firm's format was to use a red name on the front of its cards. However, a letter seen by this editor, written by Donaldson to his artist John Barr, in 1947, reveals his concern that Baytch Brothers were copying his cards, or designing very similar cards. See: Donaldson, Kiddy's Favourites, Baytch Bros.

Rollan, from Spain, issued a 1985 series of cards, *Super Futbol 85*, that included British stars, like Steve Archibald. Values for most of the cards are around £5 each but in the British collectors' market cards with Brits make four times that figure.

Rotalfoto made *Fotopropaganda* cards, in 1950. The small, black and white footballer photos were produced to compete with Perfetti's Dolcificio Lombardo cards. They are rare and sell for £30

or more. Rotalfoto produced trade cards, and also commercial postcards, up until the end of the 1980s, under different brand names including series which feature British players, like Gerry Hitchens. Such cards are always sought after by collectors in the UK, as well as Italy, and prices above £20 reflect this.

Rothman's Football Yearbook released *International Stars* in 1984. The series includes 50 cards, one of which is George Best. Easy to find, their values are around £2 each card.

Rotopress, from Sweden, issued *Prärie-Serier & Vilder Västerns Samlarserie*. It's an enormous series of cut-out cards. Among hundreds of Swedish sports stars is a card depicting the victorious Brazil team from 1958. Most cards in the series are worth £10 each, more with unclipped tokens attached, but the Brazil team card fetches over £200. Remember, the cards were printed with tokens. Without tokens they are worth a little less.

Rover was one of a new generation of children's comics issued in the 1920s. Its earliest numbers came with free football cards. Called *Real Photos* by the comic, itself, the cards show pairs of footballers, two photos per card. Cards issued in Scotland were different to those given in England and Wales. The first issue of Rover, in March 1922, came with photos of Bolton

Wanderers and Newcastle United players, in the south. In Scotland it came with a card showing stars from Rangers and Greenock Morton. The second southern issue gave away a card with Aston Villa and Spurs footballers; whilst in Scotland men from Celtic and Dundee were featured. The series went on for many months, and into 1923. Not all issues of Rover gave contrasting cards. Some weeks the players were the same, both north and south of the border. Many if not most of these cards have been damaged, and ruined in terms of value, by being cut into two halves. If you have a single player it means you have half a card. There were over 130 different players issued in all, with at least 47 different cards in England and 18 in Scotland. There were mistake cards issued, and amended cards that followed. With the mostly different cards issued in Scotland – not all, but most – this is a challenging series to complete.

Rover Top Form Footballers

Rover cut-out cards, 1953

Eventually, the issuers found they had photos spare and in spring 1923 they launched an offer where 10 photos at a time were sent to readers. Pairs of players are worth £20 to £100 each, with Scottish couples being the most prized. Cut singles are worth only £1 for English players, and up to £5 for halved cards with single Scots.

In January 1923 Rover issued 11 *Dandy Stand-up Footballers*, as they were called, in the comic itself. The cards are, perhaps, the first free-standing soccer cards in the world. The comic also referred to the cards as *Wonderful Coloured Models of Famous Footballers In An All Star Team*. They would come to influence future Rover designs in the 1960s and 1970s. Values range from £50 to over £100 each, some players and teams being more popular than others. The selection of players includes stars from Celtic, Sunderland, Cardiff City, Liverpool, Rangers, Burnley, Birmingham, Spurs, Huddersfield, Aston Villa and Manchester United. This writer recalls a public auction of collectibles, in Nottingham, where a set of these came up for sale. The interest was phenomenal and the gavel waited an age before coming down on the auctioneer's hardwood sound block. The price paid was enormous, for 1997, and these cards have been seen selling at about £100 each, on occasion, since then.

Rover comic issued *Football Transfers in Brilliant Colours* in 1924. The decals were issued in sheets of four players. Four sheets are known. They are similar to the Boys' Magazine transfers of the same decade but the Rover decals are not inscribed with the issuing comic's name. Values for uncut sheets start at £200, and cut single decals would be worth £50 each. Joe Bradford, for Birmingham; Joe Cassidy, for Celtic; Warneford Creswell, for Sunderland; and John White for Hearts will help identify the unbranded sheets.

In 1925 Rover comic issued a small booklet in the style of a sticker album, called *100 Best Players*. The 32-page booklet includes 100 footballers. An uncut booklet is worth £50. Sadly most have been cut for single images which barely fetch £1 each, if they sell at all! Intact booklets are worth more than cut-up pages.

Rover issued *Team Flags* in 1927. The 22 cut-out paper pennant-shaped flags were to be used on a league ladder, also issued by the comic, but many children ignored the ladder and wore them to school, and to the match – which is why so few survive. The value for an uncut sheet of 22 flags is over £200.

In spring 1927 Rover issued *This Year's Top Form Footballers*, a series of 24 cards, issued in sheets of four. Uncut sheets range in value from £25 to £100, and single cut cards sell for around £5 each. The fact this series includes a card of Dixie Dean, which was considered very common, and easy to obtain, just 20 years ago; a card that's now hard to find, and seen selling for over £100, when it does come to market, is testimony to the rise in value of sought-after football cards.

Rover comic's *The A.B.C. of Famous Football Clubs*, from 1927, is not cartophilic, per se, but the paper cut-outs do appeal to football collectors. Alas, cutting out snippets like these ruins the value of otherwise attractive and valuable antique comics.

Rover comic's last football free gifts before the outbreak of war came out in 1937. *Big Badges [of] Famous Teams* comprised 66 stickers, issued in two sheets, including half a dozen football emblems: Spurs, Queen's Park, Bolton, Rangers, Scotland and England. Anything but big, they are tiny! Values for uncut sheets start at £100.

Rover resumed comic production in the late 1940s. Its post-war cartophilic gifts were initially printed as part of the comic, rather than given away as cards. In 1948 *Football Club Colours*, to cut out and collect, were printed on the front cover. Likewise, in 1950, a series of *Football Club*

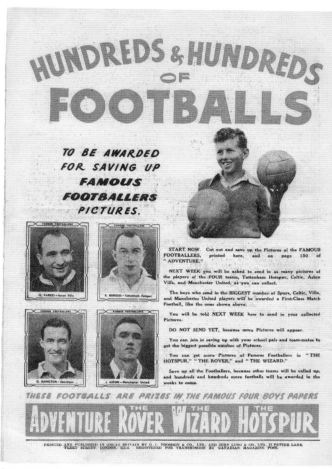

Rover 1951 cut-outs

W. SLATER
(Wolverhampton Wanderers)

J. THOMSON
(Hibernian)

Rover 1950s comic cover cards

BOBBY CHARLTON

FRANKIE VAUGHAN

Rover 1958 cards

Badges was printed on the front cover of the comic. Readers were encouraged to cut them out and collect them. The difference between cutting these and cutting other parts of a comic is that these were designed for scissors, whereas something like *The A.B.C. of Famous Football Clubs*, from 1927, was not. Values for comics with uncut covers start at £20. Cut single badges are worth up to £1.

In 1951 Rover was back with more cut-out football keepsakes. A series called *Famous Footballers* included 200 monotone blue, or black and white pictures. Each week up to 12 were printed within the comic, or on the back page. It was not just Rover. Sister comics Adventure, Hotspur and Wizard also featured footballers from this cut-out collection. Many of the players were issued in more than one comic. In this case the duplicate images may exhibit colour differences and changes in printing style, making for a challenge in finding all of said variations. The aim was to cut, collect and send the full set back to Rover in exchange for a football. No wonder few of these cards remain.

From 1953 until 1956 Rover issued more coloured *Famous Footballers* to cut from its front covers. About 1,000 different pictures are

known. As the footballers were designed to be cut from the front cover, many comics were thus disfigured. The few comics that remain intact are worth £25 to £100 each. Single cut-out pictures sell for about £2.

Rover's autumn 1958 cards, *Stars of Sport and Entertainment*, was a series shared with Hotspur comic. Rover issued 24 of the cards, and Hotspur issued the same amount. The cards were issued in quads. Fifteen cards show footballers, including a rookie card of Joe Baker, for Hibs; and another, of Bobby Charlton, for Manchester United. Finding either player in an uncut strip of four, or in a cut pair, will massively increase the value of such cards. For most cards from this series, values for a pair, or an uncut strip of four cards, range from £25 to £40, but if the Manchester United legend is included you can add £100! For strips with Joe Baker add a premium of £50 extra. For other cards from the series, cut singles are generally worth £2 each, but there are notable exceptions, like Floyd Patterson, Elvis Presley, etc. Fine condition cut singles of Bobby Charlton (Hotspur) are worth £50, and singles of Baker (Rover) are worth £20. Other players in the collection include Brighton & Hove Albion, Scunthorpe United, Hearts, Cardiff City, Bolton,

Blackpool, Linfield, Preston, West Ham, Rangers, Spurs and Wolves.

Rover issued a dozen cards devoted to football in Ulster, in 1960. *Football Teams of Northern Ireland* was only issued in Northern Ireland, hence the cards are rarely seen in Great Britain. Issued as half a dozen paired teams, of postcard size, they are worth £50 if they remain uncut and £15 each as cut singles.

The *ABC Chart of Football Colours* was issued by Rover comic in 1961. The unusual collection was based upon a similar issue by Wizard comic in the 1930s. It consists of four coloured cards, each showing 32 or 33 team colours; and four sheets of many small, black and white stickers, each showing 32 or 33 footballers. The stickers were meant to be cut out and glued to the coloured cards. An unused set of four cards and four sheets is worth over £200. Stickers cut to singles and mounted on cut kits, from the team colours cards, are worth little.

Rover published *The Ace Album of Football Stars* stickers in 1963. A dozen large, gummed stickers were issued in trios. The sheets of three stickers were cut to singles and glued down into an album, also given by the comic. Finding uncut sheets of three is rare, especially since the gum

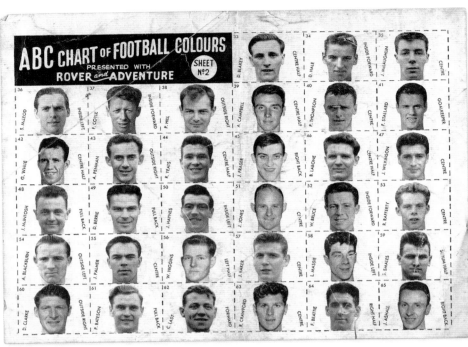

Rover ABC stickers 1961

Rover Ace Album, 1963

on the back of the stickers would become tacky in humidity, so stickers kept in basements, cellars and most places in British climatic conditions can easily get stuck to something and ruined. Values for uncut sheets range from £50 to £75. Unused cut singles, with gum, are worth £10 to £15 each.

In 1961 Rover merged with its sister comic, Adventure. The two comics became known as Rover & Adventure, until October 1963 when it reverted to being called Rover. Adventure's days were done. Within a few weeks, in November 1963, Rover merged with yet another comic and became known as Rover & Wizard. Complicated times for kids and shop keepers!

In 1968 Rover and Wizard comic revived a post-war idea and issued *Famous Football Stars*, cut-out cards, just like the ones printed on the covers of comics in the 1950s. About 1,000 different footballers were so printed, including Pelé and other international stars. An entire, uncut comic is worth £10 to £50, depending on the players featured. One comic is known to feature a certain rookie of Kenny Dalglish. This one cut-out Celtic player pushes that comic's price way up. Most cut single players are generally worth £2 each. The value lies in having the entire comic, or the front cover, at least.

Ruiz Romero was one of Spain's greatest football card producers. For three decades RuiRomer, as the firm was also known, competed successfully with the likes of Fher and Bruguera. It was finally unseated by an Italian lance, and a coup de grace was delivered by bitter rival, Fher, in 1979. This is but a sample listing of a selection of Ruiz Romero's many series. More will follow, in a future book.

In 1962 RuiRomer launched a colourful collection of British, European and mostly Spanish football stickers, in *Campeonatos Futbol 1962 & Copa de Europa*. The collection salutes the Brazilians, and includes a Wolves team sticker, and a Wolverhampton emblem sticker to boot. Values for most stickers are around £5 each, but it costs more like £30 each to acquire the international teams and emblem pairings.

Ruiz Romero commemorated 1966 with an international collection of a different kind. *Futbol Torneos Continentales 1967* included 283 stickers of Chelsea, Manchester United, Rangers, Drumcondra and Juventus to name but a few of the many exotic inclusions. Values for most stickers are around £5 each, but £30 to £50 is typical of sales for British, and other international teams.

In 1973 Ruiz Romero published *Campeonatos Nacionales Liga 1973*. Among its 395 stickers are 60 great European teams. Each is represented by a sticker featuring club colours

RuiRomer Wolves

RuiRomer Manchester United

For the World Cup, in 1974, Ruiz Romero issued a parallel release to the Portuguese firm, Ediguia. *Campeonatos Mundiales Munich 74.* Denis Law and many other Scottish players are included, and typically sell for about £20 each.

RuiRomer 1973 Celtic Spurs

RuiRomer and Ediguia cards, 1974

and crests. British sides like Edinburgh Hibernians, Chelsea, Newcastle United, Glasgow Celtic, Leicester City, Southampton, Spurs, Liverpool, Manchester City, and Manchester United feature. Prices paid for unused, international club stickers start at £20.

For the World Cup, in 1974, Ruiz Romero issued a parallel release to the Portuguese firm, Ediguia. *Campeonatos Mundiales Munich 74.* Denis Law and many other Scottish players are included, and typically sell for about £20 each. See also: Ediguia, and Club do Cromo.

Ruiz Romero's 1977 series, *Historia y Tecnica del Futbol* consists of 162 stickers, including world greats from many lands. British players like Billy Bremner and Bobby Charlton also feature. Values for such legendary players are around £20 to £30 each.

In 1978 Ruiz Romero teamed up with Americana, to issue *Argentina 1978*. The stickers are very similar to those by Lampo Flash, in Italy, and Americana in West Germany. Values for Scottish players start at around £10 each.

Rutherford Cigarettes issued a small series of footballers in the late 1890s. These days a single example of the half a dozen known cards costs about £4,000! Mostly Scottish clubs, the series contains a solitary England club card, with Ned Doig of Sunderland.

 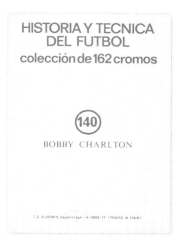

RuiRomero 1977

Rutherfords card

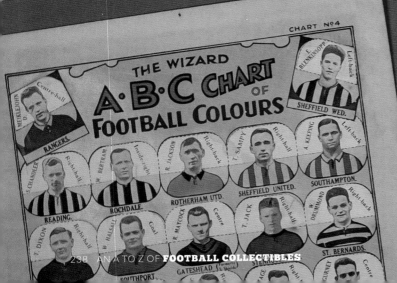

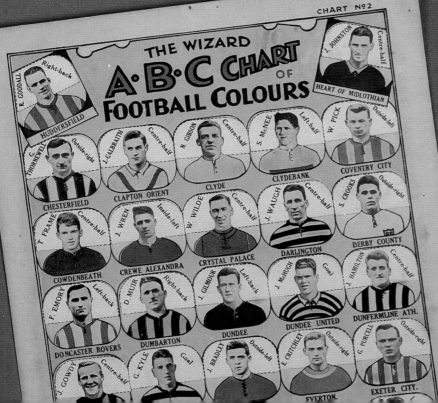

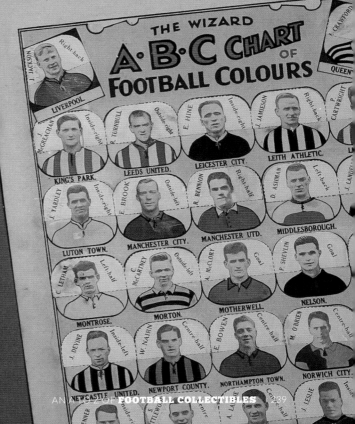

St Petersburg Cigarettes

Sartoni Laporta

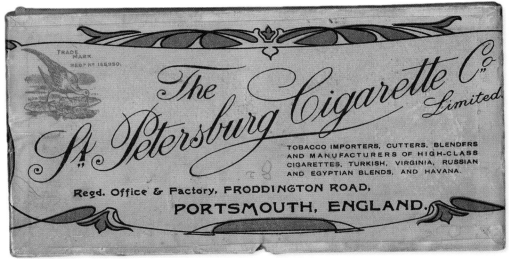

St Petersburg

Saint Petersburg Cigarettes, of Portsmouth, issued a series of card footballers in 1900.

Today they are some of the most sought-after soccer cards in the world. The price for one card is around £5,000.

Sartori Laporta cards were influenced by Donaldson's *Sports Favourites* but that's where the similarity ends. They are more primitive, with colourless black ink, on paper that looks like it was reused from another source (a typical practice of post-war paper users). The images are simple line drawings, caricatures of footballers. Only Tottenham Hotspur players have been seen, to date. The issuers were based in South Tottenham, where they ran a newspaper stand – much like their fellow Italians, in Modena. The publishers were former prisoners of war, who stayed in Great Britain after the conflict ended. The 1950 cards, *Spurs Sports Favourites*, were issued in two batches: *Series 1* and *Series II*. Each consists of 20 cards. Sold in booklets, the cards were stapled together in bunches of half a dozen. The publishers eventually had wider success, having their artwork published in football yearbooks. Values for booklets of cards are around £300. Single cards sell for about £30 each. For similar issues see: Donaldson, Kiddy's Favourites, Junior Pastimes, etc.

S&B Products was an imprint employed by Baytch Brothers. Around 1948 it issued *Torry Gillick's Internationals*, a series of 70, roughly illustrated footballer cards, drawn by a famous footballer – hence the title. The images were the work of Torry Gillick, the Rangers and Scotland star. The cards were issued in booklets of eight cards, stapled together. There are many variations to be aware of. Start collecting these and you may never finish! There are meant to be 69 cards yet five of the numbers are said to remain unissued. Moreover there are at least six cards with major varieties, including changes to a player's name, or differences in wording, contrasts in colouring, altered biographical descriptions, etc. The known variations of print matrix on the backs are bewildering. There are many differences of letterpress, format, and text colour. The colours known include dark green, black, blue and light green. Various graphic devices come and go, for example, stars appear on some cards, but not on others. Collecting just the variations in colour would result in more than 200 cards! Amongst football memorabilia collectors it is a very popular series, having players from England, Scotland, Wales and Northen Ireland. Booklets of cards, unbroken, as issued, are worth £250. Single cards start at £10 each but many sell for much more than this.

S.A.I.M., from Turin, issued two series of cards during the 1961/62 season: *Campionati Nazionali* and *Campionati Mondiali di Calcio*. The latter series

S.A.I.M. cards

Sada stickers

features British stars, and teams from around the world. The cards were issued in three materials: paper, card and also plastic. The cards have wildly diverse values. Pelé can sell for more than £100, and Brazil more than £30. Tottenham Hotspur's Mel Hopkins (wrongly identified as Danny Blanchfower) has a typical selling price of about £40, while Villa's Gerry Hitchens tends to make £20. The England, Brazil, Spain and Russia team cards are all much sought after due to players seen in those lined-up squads. Values for national, Italian league player cards are around £5 each, but international stars of note make between £20 and £40. The aforementioned teams can sell for more than £20 each.

Sada was an Italian publisher whose stickers were beloved of masochists, not least for the name. Completing a set of Three Musketeers stickers, or fulfilling the task of finding all the footballers, were painful experiences, as completion was an impossible task. That said, the 1958 set of Italian footballers offers an attractive selection of images that are still under-priced for their rarity, being worth far more than the £5 that's usually asked.

Salem evokes torture and witch trials. To name a tobacco brand after such bloodletting surely risks profits going up in smoke. Two tobacconists, worlds apart, named their cigarettes Salem. This entry is for the German Salem, from Dresden, not for the American smokes. Salem published many series of cards during the Weimer and Hitler years, notably *Deutscher Sport*

Vorschau Auf 1936, an appetiser for the Berlin Olympics. Many of the 283 paper cigarette cards in this series may be acquired for less than £5 but premium prices are usually asked of footballers and world greats from other sports.

San Giorgio means Saint George, in Italian. In 1962 San Giorgio issued a series of coloured paper stickers called *Le Più Forti Squadre Partecipanti Ai 1962 Campionati Mondiali Cile* [sic]. The title means the strongest teams participating in the 1962 World Cup. It's an unusual series, not least because it includes two stickers of certain players, notably Pelé (stickers numbered 10 and 175). The collection includes England footballers from well known stars like Bobby Moore and Ray Wilson to Alan Peacock, of Boro, and Bryan Douglas of Blackburn Rovers. The series was issued three stickers at a time. Note: some San Giorgio wrappers mention 'two cards, plus a disc'. Such wrappers are from another collection, not the World Cup Football 1962 series. Some of the stickers can still be found for less than £10 but if you see Pelé he's going to cost £150 upwards. The England stars fetch £50-£100 each.

Sanella was a margarine maker of the Weimer Republic. During the 1920s and early 30s the German manufacturer issued many great series of trade cards, including *Handbuch Des Sports*. It includes 112 cards of footballers and great athletes. Values are up to £5 each.

Santi Salvatore, of Naples, issued footballer play money. The toy banknotes, issued for the 1966/67 season, feature soccer players, and

Salem cards

Sanella card

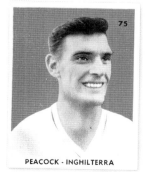

San Giorgio sticker

Santi Salvatore play money

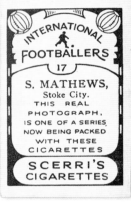

Scerri card

No. 11—Scottish Daily Express Super Sports Postcards.

Front Row—Glen, McMillan and Docherty (reserve). Second row—Hewie, Parker, Reilly, Leggat. Third row—Smith, Johnstone, Younger and trainer Dowdells. At the back—Young (captain) and Evans.

Scotland v. England— Hampden Park, April 14, 1956.

Scottish Daily Express

other subjects. Prices paid for such footballers have exceeded £50 a note. As the issuer cannot print more of this toy money (the plates are lost, the factory is closed) it's not going to fall from the skies cheaply, like real money does for today's central bankers. Play money, like this, suffers less depreciation than the constantly devaluing fiat currency (paper and electronic money) in your pocket, and in your bank account. Collectibles of a certain era, from before the 1980s – and better still, from before the 1970s – are often trusty repositories of worth. More people than ever seem to moving into the rare paper of yesteryear, not trusting so much the paper they print out of thin air today, fiat money. Antique rare cards have become an alternative asset of tangible worth.

Scerri was a Maltese issuer of cigarette cards. In 1936 John Scerri cigarettes came with an *International Footballer* card. There are 25 cards known, including an early Stanley Matthews. Values for most cards exceed £100 each. Matthews is worth more, as is Dixie Dean. As a set this is very difficult to complete and has a premium value for all 25 cards.

Schele of West Germany made a series of football fan stereotypes. The garish national caricature stickers were issued for the 1982 World Cup. The series, *Espana 82 Copa Mundial del Futbol*, has two dozen large stickers of country folk looking stupid. Stickers typically sell at around £50 the set, or singly at £2.

Scoop was a children's football magazine. In 1979 it issued *Soccer Superstars*. The 12 circular stickers came on one sheet of paper. They were meant to be peeled and stuck on to a plastic football-shaped badge, also issued by Scoop. Values for complete sheets exceed £25.

Scorcher & Score issued two series of *My Favourite Soccer Stars*, in 1970 and in 1971. The 132 cards in each series were issued in sheets of eight. The collection was co-released by other magazines, including Valiant & TV21, Buster & Jet, The Tiger, and Lion & Thunder. Uncut sheets are worth £25 to £50. Cut singles are worth little, around £2.

The Scottish Daily Express offered redeemable football postcards with its newspapers, in 1956. *Super Sports Postcards* was a series of 12 black and white football teams. Prices paid for these cards may exceed £40.

In the early 1960s the Scottish Daily Express included souvenir photographs of Scottish teams, in colour, dated 1962/63. The large paper supplements, which are similar to the photo cards issued by Typhoo, have not stood the test of time well. The few that remain are worth over £50 each. The paper issued more souvenir photographs, yearly, throughout the decade.

During the 1970s Scottish Daily Express turned from large supplements to smaller cards. In 1972 the newspaper issued *Scotcards*, a series of 24 Scottish internationals, whose worth is £3 each.

SEIP's *Figurine Sportive* collection was issued in 1954, in Italy. Prices paid for the 198 cards exceed £25. The collection is so rare even reprints sell well. Most examples seen on the market are copies.

Seix & Barral issued stunning, stand-up cards, in Spain, during 1924. The self-standing cards were issued with various logos and brands, for chocolate issuers and the like. The cards are beautiful and delicate. Few have survived the last 100 years. Prices paid exceed £50 per card and major names like Samitier and Zamora command prices in three figures.

Semic Press was Sweden's FKS. Licensed by Fher, in Spain, Semic issued *Fotboll VM 70*, a collection akin to FKS's *Mexico 70*, in which England stars appear on stickers made of card, rather than paper, as in the British collection. The 272 cards are valued from £2 to £25 each, for unused examples. England players, Beckenbauer and Pelé tend to sell for the highest prices.

Seveso Dolciaria was an Italian issuer of trade cards. Its various 1930s photographic issues are sought after, and notable footballers of yore may make over £100.

Seymour Juesbury was an early issuer of football cards. In 1900 the firm published *Football Series Puzzle* cards. Inscribed *W. Juesbury & Son, Birmingham*, the cards feature comic soccer scenes and visual riddles. Such cards have been seen to sell for £50 each.

Sharpe made some of the finest football cards ever seen. Sharpe was active during the later years of Victoria's reign, and into the Edwardian era. Sharpe's earliest soccer cards were oval shaped, and were often printed with plain backs. Similar, shaped cards were issued by other firms, and many of them also have plain backs, so identification of such early cards is problematic. However, most Sharpe cards were branded. The manufacturer's name is often found in very small print, on the front of the cards. The oval cards were followed by *Play Up Football Cards*, a collection of shields and other shapes, featuring quizzes, soccer games, football players, teams and club colours.

Sharpe was, perhaps, Baines's greatest rival. It was certainly the most innovative and creative. Like Baines, Sharpe was a Bradford-based printer, in Manningham. Times must have been rowdy in that there neighbourhood, when the competition was at its hottest.

Sharpe's fancy cards were offered to independent tradesmen, to advertise their wares. For example, a tailor in Derbyshire, John Wilson, distributed Sharpe's cards from its shop. In turn, Sharpe added the John Wilson brand, and business address, to the backs of such cards.

Values of Sharpe cards vary wildly. Whereas small clubs, and church or school squads, tend to sell at prices below £50, bigger teams may sell for many hundreds! So, a card for St. Cyril's School soccer nippers may net a seller a mere £30, whereas a Glasgow Celtic card could sell for £300! A Newton Heath card would very likely exceed that.

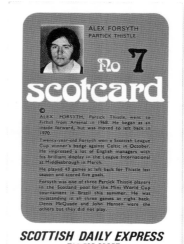
Scotcard

Values of Sharpe cards vary wildly. Whereas small clubs, church teams and other small squads tend to sell at prices below £50, bigger teams may sell for many hundreds!

Seix & Baral card

Semic cards

Sharpe's cards, including backs

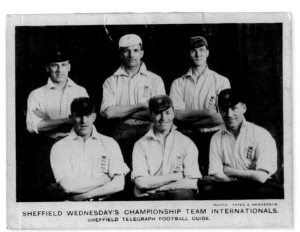

Sheffield Telegraph

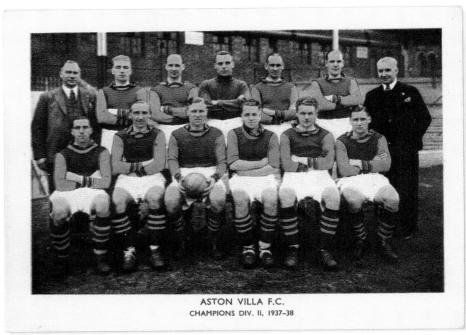

ASTON VILLA F.C.
CHAMPIONS DIV. II, 1937–38

Sherman card

Cards that advertise other trades have a premium value. So, a card with a trade advert on its back is usually worth more than the same card with a standard back.

The Sheffield Telegraph issued cards of soccer teams in 1925. They are exceedingly rare!

The series was known as a *Football Guide*. The various monotone cards, including United and Wednesday, are worth over £100 each.

Shell Petrol issued metal tokens in 1970. The so-called *Top Voetbal* coins were issued in West Germany and in the Netherlands. Values are typically around £5 each coin, except for those featuring Cruyff and Beckenbauer. Expect prices over £50 each for them.

Sherman's Pools issued *Searchlight on Famous Players* and *Searchlight on Famous Teams*. The 76 attractive, colour paper cards, issued during 1937/38, are quite easily available, for around £3 each.

Shoot! magazine issued a series of stand-up footballer cards in 1969. The 32 standing soccer players were made of thick card, sporting a glossy full-colour photo of players in action. They were available in exchange for tokens sent to the publisher. Values today are £25 to £50 each.

Shredded Wheat cards often mentioned the product but not always. Some cards displayed just the manufacturer's name, Nabisco. Shredded

Wheat cards that did not bear the Nabisco name are listed below. For other Shredded Wheat issues see: Nabisco.

In 1958 Shredded Wheat issued *Football Tips From Tom Finney, Footballer of the Year 57*. The set consisted of one dozen packet-issue, cut-out cards. Values for cut Finney cards are around £25. The fact that cereal gift collectors, of whom there are thousands, compete with football card collectors, of whom there are tens of thousands, has an effect on such values. An uncut packet back, showing Finney, is worth over £30. An intact box may sell for over £50.

Bob Wilson's *Soccer Action* was issued by Shredded Wheat in 1972. The 30 stickers published were issued in strips of three. Uncut strips are worth around £25. Most cut single stickers are worth less than £5 but there are notable exceptions.

Shredded Wheat's *World Super Stars And Sporting Trophies* was a series of folding cards, issued in 1976. An unfolded, mint card of Pelé would be worth £75. A folded Pelé is worth £25. Quality counts, especially with contemporary cards.

Shurey's was a publisher of magazines and postcards, issuing sporting periodicals, from the

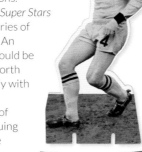

Shoot! stand-up stars 1969

Shredded Wheat strips

time of Victoria through until the 1920s. Its postcards and other football ephemera were often given as free gifts. Suchlike are very rare, nowadays, and much sought after, fetching prices over £50 each.

Sicker was a West German publisher. During the 1960s and 1970s Sicker produced many series of cards and stickers, of which a brief selection is covered here. During 1964 Sicker released *Die Besten Fussballspieler...und aller welt 1964/1965*, a series of 300 stickers, including Denis Law, Jimmy Greaves, Pelé et al. Values for most stickers are around £5, but such world greats sell for as much as £50, if the stickers are unused. Pelé's price may exceed £100.

In 1965 Sticker issued *Die Fussball-Saison 1965/66*, a collection of 500 stickers which includes Bobby Moore, Lev Yashin, Pelé et al. Values for unused stickers range from £5 to over £50 for world greats. This series contains 16 stickers of Liverpool players and the Liver bird club badge, not to mention an early Franz Beckenbauer. The stickers were issued in sheets of nine stamps each.

During 1966 Sicker allied with Fher to produce *Die Weltmeisterschaft 1966 Im England*, with around 300 stickers. The England players, Pelé and other world greats sell for up to £50

each, if unused. Recuperated stickers, used examples removed from an album, are worth less.

During following seasons Sicker released more national, West Germany collections, which included foreign players. These were issued in sheets of eight stamps each. Unbroken sheets with world greats command enormous prices. A sheet with players like Jimmy Greaves, or Bobby Moore, would fetch a very high price, well into triple figures.

Sidam, an Italian issuer, released various series of cards between 1959 and 1962. *Il Calcio Italiano 1959-60* was the first. About 300 gum cards were included in each collection. Card values range from £5 to £10 each but premium prices are paid for rookies, like Gianni Rivera, of Alessandria, and for British stars. Look out for the different series, identifiable by the year. Look out for cards of John Charles, and other British stars.

Sidea was a cards producer of the Mussolini era. In the Italy of 1933 Sidea issued *Calciatori*. The cards are small, square in shape, and can be found with both photographic and illustrative portraits. Values start at £20 each but rise dramatically for world famous names.

Sifta Sam salt was made by Palmer Mann. In 1955 packets of Sifta Sam came with printed cards of *Famous Footballers*, to

Sidam card

Sicker 1967 sheet of stickers

Sicker 1965 sheet of stickers

Sifta Sam cards

John Sinclair cards

Skipper flags

cut out and collect. Complete boxes, with uncut cards, are worth £100, though many cut Sifta Sam cards also sell for such figures!

Simon Chocolates were made in Spain. They were sold with trade cards. During 1964 Simon issued *Album 3 Anos De Vida Mundial* which featured famous footballers. The collection includes Alfredo Di Stefano. His sticker has been seen to sell for £50. An unused Pelé from this collection has sold for over £100.

Sinclair cigarette cards ought not to be misidentified. There were two Sinclair brands, John Sinclair and Robert Sinclair. Both are rare

but cards by the latter sell in the thousands! John Sinclair tobacco cards were issued in Great Britain during Edwardian times. Robert Sinclair cards are Victorian.

In 1906, John Sinclair issued *Football Favourites*, of which there were 51 to collect.

Prices paid for superb condition cards exceed £150 each. The firm's later collections are more affordable. *English & Scottish Football Stars*, *Real Photograph Series*, cost a lot less. The 50 cigarette cards are valued at around £3 each, as are those made in 1938 by the same firm: *Well Known Footballers*, *North Eastern Counties*. A similar issue,

Well Known Scottish Footballers is also available readily, at around £2 a card.

Robert Sinclair's cigarette cards are another matter. During 1898 the firm issued a series of Newcastle United footballers, about 20 cards in all, in monotone mauve, or black and white. A year later, a selection of Sunderland footballers followed. The cards are inscribed, *Rob.t Sinclair's Cigarettes* [sic]. Values for such cards are around £1,500 each!

Singleton & Cole's 1905 series of *Footballers* are worth up to £250 each. There were 50 cards announced but Liverpool's Dunlop comes in two varieties, so let's say there are 51. Buyers should be aware that re-prints exist, however, they are marked as such. The re-prints are worth little but they fill in blank spaces until the real thing can be found, or afforded.

Skipper was a comic. It was issued by the same firm that published Adventure, Hotspur, Rover, and Wizard. In 1931 Skipper co-issued *Football Towns and their Crests & Famous Ships*, with its sister comics. The 32 cards (showing 32 ships and 128 football town crests) are worth much more if they remain uncut. With ships attached, the cards are worth £50, but without ships values stay below £5.

Similarly, Skipper co-issued *Football Clubs*, in 1933. The 64 cards were issued as quartets. Uncut cards are worth £50. Cut singles are worth below £5 each.

The most unusual Skipper series was issued in 1934, called *Winner Football Flags*. Each of the 63 cut-out, fold-and-glue paper flags features a footballer. In their day they were pinned to many a school uniform. Displayed and worn they became ripped, ruined and lost. Few survive. Issued in three sheets of 21, the cut-out flags and players are rare. An uncut sheet would be worth £200. An album and all its 63 flags would fetch a similar figure.

Skipper stickers

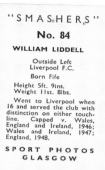

Smasher cards

Smith's 1906 card

Smith's 1912 cards

Smith's 1906 series, *Footballers*, has brown backs. Its 120 cigarette cards are worth around £50 each.

Skipper's 1939 collection, *Football Tricky Tips Show-U-How* stickers was issued as a sheet, to cut and stick. The dozen cut-out, oval-shaped stickers of footballers include Tommy Lawton, of Everton; Stanley Matthews, of Stoke City; Stan Cullis, of Wolves; and Raich Carter of Sunderland. An uncut sheet would sell for £250. Single, unused stickers are worth £25 to £50 each. A complete album of all 12 soccer stars, glued down, is worth £100. With antique stickers, and cards, unused examples are usually rarer, and worth more, than those found glued into albums.

Smashers were issued by Sport Photos, in Glasgow, in the early 1950s. The series includes 96 cards which were published in a trio of booklets, each containing 32 footballers. Values range from £10 a card, for players of teams that are less popular, to £50 for select stars. For earlier cards issued by this publisher, see: Frame.

Smith's cigarettes issued *Champions of Sport* in 1902. The 50 cards have red backs, and are inscribed Glasgow Mixture, or Studio Cigarettes. The series is rare and valuable, and more than £150 is paid for its footballers, if and when they come to the market. Other sports stars sell for around £75 each card.

Smith's 1906 series, *Footballers*, has brown backs. Its 120 cigarette cards are worth around

£50 each. In 1908 Smith's issued 100 *Cup-Tie* football cards. Values start at around £15 each, and rise for more popular teams and players. A 1912 series, *Footballers*, included 150 cigarette cards whose values are, again, around £15 each. These are available with both light blue and dark blue backs, and many brand names!

Towards the end of World War One Smith issued its first series of *Football Club Records* cigarette cards. The 50 cigarette cards are worth around £20 each. A second series of *Football Club Records* was issued in 1922. The later series can be distinguished by the data on the back of the cards. Values are, again, around £20 each.

Smith's Crisps were made by an Irish firm called Smith Food Group. In 1971 packets of crisps came with tokens, to collect, to send away for a George Best Picture Card. There are 20 different cards, each with a colour photo of Best alongside a monotone line drawing, to colour in. Some cards have black backs, others blue. The cards are very rare and sell for up to £100.

Soccer Bubblegum was the trading name of a British gum cards issuer. During 1957 and 1958 the firm issued *Soccer No.1 Series* and *Soccer No.2 Series*. The trade cards are quite easy to obtain and values remain, for the moment, quite low. Most of the 96 cards (two series of 48 cards each) can be had for a couple of pounds each.

Smith's Crisps cards

Soirée Cigarettes is a brand name that enjoys mythical status with soccer card collectors. The Mauritius marque was considered exclusive. The brand sat at the luxury end of the cigarettes trade. Few packets of Soirée found their way into working class hands. In 1958 Soirée issued a series of footballers printed on its packet sliders. They were designed for cutting out. The series of *Famous Footballers* includes 48 packet-issue stars, cut from the slides. Each card featured a coloured painting of a footballer. These were based upon black and white press photos.

It is, without doubt, one of the most beautiful series of post-war footballer cards. The paintings of players are well executed and based upon the monotone photographs used by Colinville for its *Footer Bubble Gum Foto* series of cards, issued during the same season, 1958/59. The Soirée cards are dated to autumn 1958. If they are found today – and they are rarely seen – they tend to be cut out, and often they are cut closely around the image, though occasionally they can be found with entire sliders from the cigarette boxes.

The rarest of the Soirée cards, of which less than a handful are known, worldwide, include:

Brian Clough, Jimmy Greaves, Bryan Robson, Hopkinson of Bolton; Norman, Medwin, and Jones of Spurs; and England's captain, Billy Wright of Wolves. The Bobby Charlton card is a classic, and ostensibly the most sought-after rookie for said star. There are about five known, worldwide. To put this rarity factor into context, consider this: over 20 of the smaller, black and white, Colinville gum cards of Bobby Charlton have been recorded. It was also issued in the 1958/59 season. The Colinville cards have been seen to sell for over £100 each. The Soirée card is many times rarer than the Colinville card. The value of typical Soirée cards start at about £100. Some sell for over £500. Uncut sliders are worth £200 to £1,000. See also: Colinville Gum.

Speranza & Carità, an Italian firm, produced an album and stickers collection, in 1975, called *Goal!* The series includes footballers and action scenes. Stickers issued in strips of six sell for as much as £50. Single stickers are worth £5.

Somportex was a British gum cards issuer, but there was also a Somportex in Malta, run by a man called Xuereb. The two seem to be of the same root. It might explain why certain British produce resembles some Maltese issues of the same era. Somportex traded in Great Britain during the 1960s, issuing lucky bags containing a miniature football magazine and sweets. After a court battle with the mighty Gum Inc., of America, Somportex disappeared in the early 1970s. During its time Somportex was, perhaps, best known for its *Thunderbirds* gum cards but it also issued a very rare series of *Footballer Stamps*. They are similar to postage stamps, but only two sides are perforated, much like the BAB stamps of 1971. Only a handful of examples are known. Age has rendered the print and gum unstable. If you have one you possess a rare but delicate item. They are worth considerable money!

Somportex tended to issue unusual fare. One particular series of Somportex collectibles readily evokes the early 1970s. The series was called *Football Club Badges With Sweets*. Plastic football shield-shape badges were issued in bright yellow plastic packets. The 46 miniature escutcheons sport coloured stickers of club badges. The shields have moulded plastic hooks, just right for piercing woollen jumpers, but ineffective for a lengthy tenure during children's games. Most

Soirée Cigarettes is a brand name that enjoys mythical status with soccer card collectors. The Mauritius marque was considered exclusive.

FAMOUS FOOTBALLERS
A Series of 48

No. 15 Billy Wright
Wolverhampton Wanderers & England

Born in Ironbridge, Shropshire, Billy Wright joined Wolverhampton Wanderers straight from school and signed professional for them in 1941. Captain of the reigning League Champions he has a record number of 96 International caps to his credit. He was nominated 'Footballer of the Year' in 1952 and has won every honour that the game has to offer.

SOIREE CIGARETTES

Soirée cards

Somportex plastic shields

Sorcacius stickers

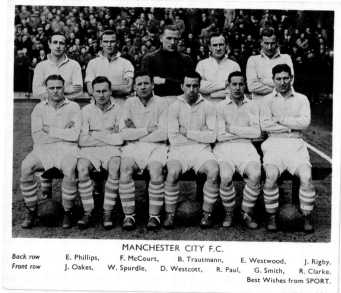

MANCHESTER CITY F.C.
Back row   E. Phillips,   F. McCourt,   B. Trautmann,   E. Westwood,   J. Rigby.
Front row   J. Oakes,   W. Spurdle,   D. Westcott,   R. Paul,   G. Smith,   R. Clarke.
Best Wishes from SPORT.

Sport photo card 1951, Newcastle United

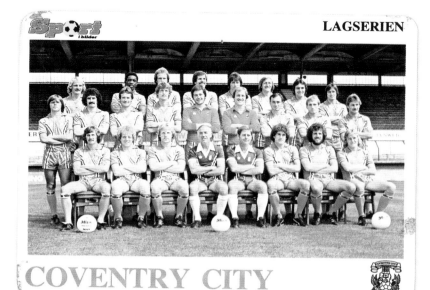

Sport & Bilder Dreyer card

Sport & Adventure strip cards

were lost at play. Values for these emblematic reminders of childhood are around £5 each.

Sorcacius was a Portuguese issuer of stickers. In 1982 Sorcacius issued *XII Campeonato Do Mundo De Futebol*. The 380 stickers include stars from Wales, Northern Ireland and Scotland. Values for players from the British Isles start at £20 each.

Sorcacius followed up, in 1984, with *Campeonato Da Europa De Futebol*. Its 360 stickers again included United Kingdom players from Wales and Northern Ireland but it also included stars from the Republic of Ireland. The value of British Isles footballers in this collection is £20 for unused stickers.

Sports Budget did not issue cards so if you see them for sale know this: they are clippings, cut out and presented as cards. However, in 1927, Sports Budget did give away free gifts called the *Who's Who Of Famous Footballers*. The small booklets are not cartophilic, per se, but they do appeal to collectors of football cards. Paper cut outs from these booklets, and from the magazine, are a small tragedy. They were not intended to be cut up. As these are often

sold cut, as cards, this entry is included to warn collectors not to pay too much! Values speak volumes: cut-outs of players sell for £1 each but entire, un-cut booklets may exceed £50.

Spiro's Mixture tobacco cards were made by Spiro & Valleri. The tobacco cards were devoted to Leeds City FC. The 1906 series, *Noted Footballers*, is very rare and the 11 known cigarette cards, all of Leeds City players, sell for £1,500 each! A set of reprints is known which can be had for about £5, for the set.

Sport & Bilder were issued by a firm called Dreyer, in Norway. The 1980s series of cards, also inscribed *Lagserien*, includes about 80 European football teams, with many British squads to look out for, including Wolves, Liverpool, Stoke City, WBA and Manchester United, to name but a handful. Values are around £20 to £25 each.

Sport has been the name of more than one British football magazine, over the years: The photo cards of soccer teams inscribed, *Presented by Sport*, were issued by a post-war magazine. There are two series of these photo cards known. In 1949 *Wonderful Team Portraits* included 36 coloured pictures, issued in six booklets, with blue

covers, each of six cards. The booklets were not given freely but had to be redeemed for tokens and money. A second series was given during 1951. It is much rarer. The later cards are black and white, not colour. The 36 monotone pictures were also given in half a dozen booklets – with cream-coloured covers. They are worth £35 to £50 each card. By contrast, the easier to find colour cards, from the blue booklets, are worth comparatively little, up to £50 for a full booklet or just £5 each card.

Sport & Adventure was a children's comic of the 1920s. In 1922 it issued a series of coloured football cards called, *Famous Footballers*. The 46 cards were published in 14 strips of three cards each, and two pairs. Values for uncut strips exceed £50 each, but cut cards are worth less than £5. Unbeknown to many collectors, Sport & Adventure also issued a Scottish version of the collection. The *Famous Scottish Footballers* are worth a lot more! The 46 cards were also issued in 14 strips of three, with two pairs, but Scottish uncut strips may sell for £100 each, and cut Scottish cards are worth £20 each.

Sport Pictures issued large, paper supplements of sports stars, in sepia. They are inscribed with the name of the magazine, and dated thus: *1921-*

22, or *1922-23*. The Sportsmen shown include footballers, boxers and cricketers; and football teams. Issued in the 1920s they are very rare. The fact few have survived the years is due, partly, to their size. Many were glued into scrapbooks, and thereby damaged. Others were damaged and discarded, or pulped for the war effort. Values for football supplements are around £100 each.

Sportfoto cards are not just the rarer cousins of Daily Herald cards, they are actually some of the rarest soccer cards ever issued. Unknown to most collectors, at least three series of monotone photo cards was published by the firm. A little like Pinnace, there are the small cards, and there are larger cards, but there are also large cards which were presented in paper folders, including potted histories of players, and these have rarely been seen.

Sportfoto cards were issued during the years 1951 to 1953. The small cards are known with three different legends: *Daily Herald Copyright SPORTFOTO [sic]*; and, more simply, *Daily Herald Copyright*; and also, very simply inscribed, as *Sportfoto*. The large cards show only players' names, and sometimes their team. Neither the paper folder cards, nor the other large cards, mention the firm, Sportfoto, by name. The paper folder series of cards includes Lambert and Liddell, for Liverpool; Cockburn, Carey and

Rowley for Manchester United; Hancocks for Wolves, etc. All of the paper folders feature the legend: *Famous Footballers No.1*

Of the three various types of small cards, those with the simpler legend, *Sportfoto*, are the rarest. They are worth around £30 each. The large cards with player and team name are worth £80 each, and the cards stapled within paper folders are worth £100. See also: Daily Herald

Sporting Mirror issued three series of concertina pictures of footballers. The fold-out series of connected cards was issued tucked inside an envelope, ready for addressing and posting. The idea was to write a letter on the back of the concertina of sport images, re-fold it into the envelope, and post it. The novel stationery was known as a *Letter Card*. Sporting Mirror issued three series of these during the 1948/49 season. They include teams, portraits of stars, and stars in action. Values for complete folders differ, as some series include 12 images, while others have half that. The issues with half a dozen photos are worth up to £50. Those with a dozen images are worth up to £80. These values are all for uncut, complete folders, with all images intact and connected. Cut pictures are worth very little.

Sport-Pics was a northern issue. It featured mostly northern players. Issued in the 1950s, the cards show black and white, photographic heads of players pasted on to colourfully illustrated

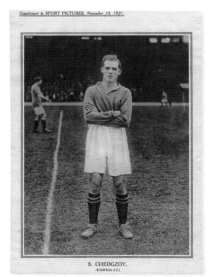

S. CHEDGZOY.
(EVERTON F.C.)

Sport Pictures supplement

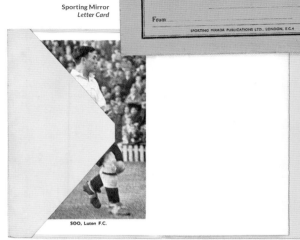

Sporting Mirror
Letter Card

Sportfoto cards are not just the rarer cousins of Daily Herald cards, they are actually some of the rarest soccer cards ever issued.

JIMMY LOGIE
Arsenal

FAMOUS - - -
FOOTBALLERS

No. 1.

A series of booklets containing interesting facts about football and a

REAL PHOTOGRAPH

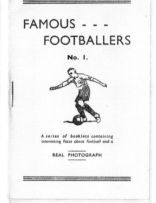

14   JIMMY LOGIE
Arsenal
Sportfoto

Sportfoto cards

SOO, Luton F.C.

Sporting Mirror *Letter Card*

Private stamp 1934

Private issue, football stamps

Football club stamps, 1920s

Test stamps 1950 World Cup

Stenval cards

bodies. There are about 160 cards in the collection. They were issued in 10 sheets of 16 cards each. An uncut sheet is worth £150.

Stamps? Rare, non-postage stamps of footballers and teams decorate, and improve the values of the best collections. Postage stamps are one thing, and that's a subject that fills entire books, but non-postage stamps of football teams, emblems, and players are a little-known collectible of considerable rarity, and, in some cases, great value. Since Victorian times people have used poster stamps (cinderella stamps, as they are known, in philately) to decorate envelopes, to advertise wares, and to seal letters. Football cinderella stamps can be worth hundreds of pounds! The oldest examples are so rare that many have never been catalogued, or listed in price guides. Look out for them. They were typically used on the backs of envelopes, or on postcards, alongside postage stamps. The Eusebio example, shown in this book, is a modern times example. Most poster stamps were issued between 1890 and 1960. See: A&BC Gum.

Regular postage stamps, with football subjects, go back 100 years and are well documented in specialist books and catalogues. Vintage stamps with pertinence to a particular event, like a World Cup, may add a lot of worth to a soccer cards

collection. Especially valuable are stamps made as proofs, made for testing colours, etc., but never issued.

Stenval, from France, issued a series of Pink Panther sports stickers in 1975, called *J'Aime...*

Values are around £25 each for golf, soccer and tennis stickers. Other sports cost less.

In 1978 Stenval commemorated the World Cup, in Argentina, with sticker-card gifts. The gifts were both a sticker, and a card. The sticker would peel away to reveal another image below. The footballers in the series include Kevin Keegan, for Liverpool. Regular cards are worth £5 each but premium prices are often paid for British stars and world greats.

Stella was a card issuer in Italy, sometimes known as Marca Stella. During 1961/62 the brand issued *Raccolta Figurine Calcio*, a series of 24 small cards, each available with different colour frames, including Brazilian stars and Milan players, etc. The Pelé card, which shows him against a dark background, is known with blue, yellow and white edges. Some Pelé variations have sold for up to £100 each. Others from the series are worth £5 to £20 each.

Stella issued a similar series during the 1962/63 season, once again called *Raccolta Figurine Calcio*. The small cards include portraits of Brazilian players but these are different to the first series. There are

Subbuteo cards inscribed with the creator's name, Adolph, were issued in 1953/54.

GEORGE BEST
Manchester United

ROGER HOY
Crystal Palace

Sun 1969 cards

Nº 81. **Sois rapide pour être efficace**
Le bon avant est toujours un bon sprinter. Le plus rapide de ces deux joueurs possédera la balle après le sprint.

DI STEFANO
SPAGNA

PELÈ

Nº 82. **Le regroupement de la défense**
Un attaquant blanc, l'arbitre, et cinq défenseurs rouges pour annihiler l'attaque adverse. La défense est infranchissable.

Marca Stella cards

Suchard stickers, England 1966

Spanish card, 1923 Notts County v St. Mirren

two versions of the Pelé card: one with, and the other without a strange shape behind the player's head. Values range from £20, for Pelé, to around £5 for the others. These images would be re-used as larger cards in 1963.

During the 1963/64 season, Stella's previous series, *Raccolta Figurine Calcio*, grew into much larger cards. Stella added other players not previously included. The cards are decorated with coats of arms, at the bottom. Alfredo di Stefano and Gento also feature in this collection. Values range from £10 to £50 each.

Stockhaus of West Germany issued 250 *Fussball WM74* stickers, for the 1974 World Cup.

Values are around £5 each, with premiums for Pelé and the many world greats included in the series.

Suchard of France published *A La Decouverte Du Sport, Champions, Techniques* [sic], in 1968. The 200 stickers are in the format of large stamps. Mostly they sell at around £5 each but Pelé and England stars carry heftier values.

Subbuteo games, teams and accessories once came with football cards. Subbuteo also issued card games. Some of the various cards issued were inscribed with the issuer's name (Adolph) while others carried the brand name, like *Soccer Market*. Between 1947 and 1964 *Soccer Market* cards were issued and reissued as an ever-changing set of game cards, including different teams. Single type cards from such games are worth £5 each but complete, boxed sets of *Soccer Market* may sell for as much as £300!

Subbuteo cards inscribed with the creator's name, Adolph, were issued in 1953/54. The *Famous Footballers Series Of 50* is now very rare and single cards sell for over £20 each. Shortly after the series sold out, 48 of the cards were reissued as two series of 24 cards each, minus a Bury footballer, and also missing a Notts County player. The cards in the series of 50 are very rare and worth much more than the reissues.

Sugosa issued sweet cigarettes much like its bigger competitor, Barratt, but Sugosa cards are

rarer than similar issues by Barratt. A series of 1964 Sugosa *Famous Footballers* is worth about £30 each card.

Sultana y Americano Chocolates cards are just one brand of typically beautiful Spanish football cards from the 1920s. Many British players and teams were included, from Dundee to Notts County. More 1920s Spanish cards, of British stars and teams, will feature in a future edition. If you can't wait see www.footballsoccercards.com

Sun newspapers issued 22 coloured stickers in 1969. The maiden series was called *Football Strips Of The 1st Division 1969-70*. The cards were issued connected, in a strip. The series was the genesis of the latter day abomination known as *Sun Soccercards* yet the primitive design of the 1969 cards is lighter, more pleasing, and a little psychedelic. Their spawn, birthed in the year of Thatcher's sickening impersonation of St. Francis of Assisi, was a grimmer affair altogether. Values for uncut strips of 1969 cards are in triple figures, and single cards sell for £10 to £15 each.

The Sun's *World Cup Souvenir Wall Chart* of 1970 was a rainbow collection that included 82 stickers of world greats, in all and sundry styles. The Mexico 70 England squad, British footballers of the past, and football flags are just some of the sub-series within this comprehensive mishmash. The Sun was one of the most disdained daily newspapers in Great Britain, even back then. It made one of the least cohesive football sticker collections to boot. It's partly photographic (the England squad stickers), and partly illustrated (stars of the past). It was wholly unwanted when England were dumped out of the competition and many collectors burned the lot.

The reissued Sun *Souvenir Wall Chart* of 1970 included a magic number of *'66 Soccer Calendar* stickers: club captains, emblems and squads. Missing were the earlier images of Johnny Foreigner. Seeing England fall, early on during Mexico 70, the jingoistic newspaper had hurriedly dropped *'World Cup'* from the wall chart's title, and re-issued it, *sans* foreigners. It faded slowly, in the watery British summer sun, and was binned by Christmas.

During the 1970/71 season, the Sun issued its *Scrapbook Encyclopædia 1971* and a series called *Swap Cards*, 134 cards of decent quality. From cards to stamps went the Sun for the next issue: *Football Encyclopædia Soccer Stamp Album 1971-72* had 504 stamps, issued in strips and pairs. A strip of four stamps is worth about £10, trios are worth £8, pairs sell for up to £5, and single stamps for £1. Certain great players, like George Best and Stanley Matthews, increase the worth of these stamps.

The Sun's *Football Encyclopædia and 3D Album 1972-73* included 108 lenticular cards, with the instruction: *'tilt card to and fro'*. These came in both small and large sizes and included sub-series *How To Play*, *Gallery Action* and *Gallery Stars*. They are worth £2 to £5 each.

Sun *Soccercards* included 1,000 ugly and garish pictures that are still worth very little, 40 years later. A full set of the 1979 cards can be had for £50. Many sellers have them in stock, locked away in the basement – not for worth and fear of theft, but for fear of catching a glimpse of them. Sun *Soccercards* are, surely, one of the ugliest sets of sports cards ever printed.

Sunday Chronicle was an Edwardian journal. It issued 40 paper supplements of football teams in 1906. These are worth over £100 each.

Sunday Dispatch printed 20 cut-out cards to stick in to an album provided by the paper. These 1948 packet-issue *Football League Stars* are now priced at £20 each.

Sunday Empire News published *Famous Footballers of Today, Impressions of Sporting Personalities by Mickey Durling* [sic], in 1953. The 48 cards were issued, stapled together, in miniature booklets of eight cards each. Values for booklets of cards are around £100. Single cards sell for about £5.

Sunday Express issued various football postcards, of teams, stars and, notably, a series called *Play Soccer The Matthews Way*, in the 1950s. The various series of postcard-size cards are worth up to £50 each.

Sunday Mail, a Scottish newspaper, issued *Junior Sports Club Scottish Footballers* in 1950. The 34 black and white photo cards have facsimile autographs in white. A year later the same newspaper issued a second series of 34 cards,

The Sun's *World Cup Souvenir Wall Chart* of 1970 was a rainbow collection that included 82 stickers of world greats, in all and sundry styles. The Mexico 70 England squad, British footballers of the past, and football flags are just some of the sub-series within this comprehensive mishmash.

Sun Soccerstamps

Sun lenticular card

Sunday Empire News card

called *Scottish Footballers*. The cards are similar to the 1950 issue but they are without the legend '*junior sports club*'. Values for cards from either series are around £35 each.

Sunday Post *Football Teams 1933-34* are large, glossy supplements, made of card, with two ribbon holes for easy inclusion in a ribbon-ring folder, also issued by the newspaper, in which to collate the set of cards. Values are around £50 each card.

Sunnyvale cards and transfers were issued in the late 1940s. The first series, *Famous Football Internationals*, included a selection of players issued in booklets, of 16. The players were printed in pairs. Note: the series title is *Famous Football Internationals* but the album cover title reads, simply, *Cigarette Card Book*. A complete booklet would fetch over £300. Collectors have paid £100 for a paired card, and £35 is typical for single, cut cards.

Sunnyvale also issued decals, in sheets of 16. Values are around £750 for a complete sheet of transfers, and £45 for single, cut decals. The title of the series, *Cigarette Card Transfer Series*, was printed atop the complete sheet of decals. The decals are printed backwards. They were designed to be cut out and stuck on to things, and like most decals they were cut and transferred, hence their great rarity today. See also: Bailey's Agencies; Barratt, Cadet.

Sweetule made various series of sports cards. They were issued with the firm's confectionery, during the late 1950s. The collections include *Junior Service Quiz*, *Football Club Nicknames*, and *Sports Quiz*. The cards are all readily available and affordable, and worth around £2 each.

Sweetule's most interesting series of cards, also from the 1950s, is *International Footballers*, a packet-issue series. Cut cards are worth £5 each but uncut packets fetch around £30. Note: there are variations of the Mel Charles card. On some cards he is a Swansea Town player, and on others he plays for Arsenal.

Swettenhams Co-operative Society produced a series of *Popular Stoke and Port Vale Football Players*, in 1935. The 50 trade cards are worth between £40 and £100 each.

Sweetule packet

Sunday Express postcard

FALKIRK F.C.—1933-34.
Back Row (left to right)—NISBET, BACHELOR, MURRAY, ANDERSON, THOMSON, RICHARDSON, LOWE, HUTCHISON.
Front Row (left to right)—DOUGAL, BARTRAM, HAMILL, McNAIR, SHANKLEY, GRANT.

Sunday post

Sunnyvale cards & decals

Bespoke Topical Times album, 1940

Tabay

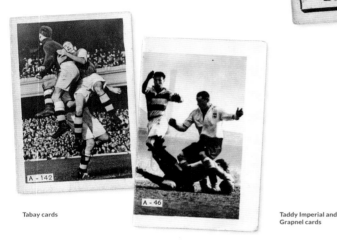

Tabay cards

Taddy Imperial and Grapnel cards

abay was Spain's PK. Like PK gum, Tabay issued miniature packets of chewing gum. The product came with sports cards. Diminutive, to say the least, the cards show photographic highlights of world sporting events during 1948. The *Deportivo Reportages Photograficos* collection consists of 210 small gum cards, including many featuring soccer, whose value is around £25 each. Premiums are added to this price for notable cards. The sports covered include golf, hockey, horse racing and rugby, to name but a small selection. Featured football clubs from the British Isles include Chelsea, Manchester United, Derby County, QPR and Arsenal.

Taddy tobacco included many hundreds of footballers in three sets of *Prominent Footballers* cards, released between 1907 and 1914. Buyers beware: modern reprints look very much like the original cards. Though they bear the 1990s printer's name, it's all too easy to buy one by mistake. Look closely at the backs.

The easiest to find Taddy cards are those issued during 1907/08, the first of the three Taddy series. The cards have either Grapnel or Imperial brands, and they do not mention Myrtle Grove (as do later cards). There are about 600 known, and they are commonly referred to as *Prominent Footballers* 'without footnote'. Cards with southern-based players tend to sell for prices upwards of £20; whereas midlands and northern club players start at £30 each. For some bigger, northern clubs buyers may have to pay over £50 each card.

Taddy issued 400 more *Prominent Footballers* during 1908/09, each having a caption to the foot of the rear of the cards. The caption mentions 'Myrtle Grove'. Values for southern club players start at £30 each, and may surpass three figures; whereas, for midlands and northern teams, values start at about £100 each. Some of these cards are amongst the rarest Taddy cards known.

Taddy's third collection of soccer players was issued in 1914. It includes around 400 cards, each with the title *Prominent Footballers*, and the brand name, London Mixture. Values for cards of London players tend to start at around £50 each; and those from midland and northern clubs may cost over £200 each. Believed to be the rarest Taddy series, it ought to be noted that many of

the 1908/09 cards are just as rare as the London Mixture issue.

Taddy note: there are exceptions to every rule. While cards featuring midlands and northern players are typically worth more than southern clubs, some southern clubs are scarcer than others. Crystal Palace players, for example, are generally rarer than Fulham players, and prices paid may exceed the above guidelines. Millwall

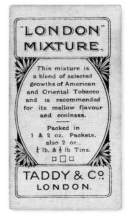
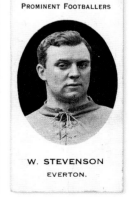

Taddy London Mixture cards

Tavermatic cards

Tavermatic wrapper

cards are, generally, rarer than Chelsea. Most of the Luton Town cards are rarer than many of the West Ham cards. Plymouth Argyle players are seen less frequently than QPR players, and so on. As with all cards condition is a major factor in evaluation. Values in this book are for very good cards, or better, showing no damage, no corner creases, no stains; and no gum marks to the rear.

Tavermatic was an Italian issuer of gum cards. Two series of cards from the early 1960s feature British stars John Charles, formerly of Leeds United, for Roma; and Gerry Hitchens, formerly of Aston Villa, for Torino. Values for these stunning cards are around £30 each.

Teasdale Cigarettes is a name to look out for, though you won't see it often on the firm's soccer cards. Teasdale cigarettes were sweets, for children, in the form of smokes. They were made of white, sugary stuff that dentists made their fortunes from.

Teasdale's best known soccer trade cards are without a brand name, they have no logo, they are made of paper, and they come in black and white. The action scenes shown are copied from a series of cards that was originally issued by Gallaher tobacco. Teasdale's cards show images from the 1928 Gallaher issue, the series with red backs.

Less often seen are football cards by Teasdale which have a brand name: Jigsaw. Values for Teasdale black and white cards (with blank backs) start at over £50 each. Values for cards with Jigsaw backs start at £100 each. For images see: Gallaher.

Tempo means time, in Italian. In 1966, during the decade of Timpo plastic soldiers, Tempo, the Time Magazine of Italy, issued a sticker and album collection to commemorate the World Cup. *Campeonato del Mondo di Calcio* contains many hundreds of stickers. National teams have 22 players each. The stickers were issued in sheets, to cut out. Most stickers have blank backs but some have designs, wording, or pictures of other players (for example, the sticker of Jimmy Greaves has Eusebio on the back). Pelé, Eusebio and other all-time greats, and the stars of England's 1966 squad, can sell for £30 or more. Beckenbauer has a higher price, and if he's found on an uncut sheet a price of well over £100 may be asked for the early example of Franz, Der Kaiser. A complete album is valued at around £250. Remember, a sticker that is not used is nearly always worth more than a glued-down sticker. So, a collection of unused stickers, with an unused album, is worth more. Values for unused stickers from this collection start at

around £3 each, with premiums added to prices for the aforementioned stars. Do not cut stickers from uncut sheets! Uncut sheets have premium values. Some have been seen to sell for as much as £150.

There are very similar images on card, not paper, of Pelé, Jimmy Greaves, and other players. They seem to be from this collection but side-by-side comparisons show them to be different. Some, like the Pelé card, are larger; while others exhibit differences to the paper stickers. The origins of the cards are not clear but it's obvious the collection is different. The Jimmy Greaves card shows the player in a mirror image to the smaller, 1966 paper sticker. The larger image of Pelé uses a different photograph, yet the text matrices are of the same source. These are much rarer than the regular paper images from the 1966 tempo album.

Tennent was a brewer based in Glasgow. In the 1970s it made football beer mats, as well as a certain, very powerful amber ale beloved of serious lager drinkers. In 1974 Tennent commemorated the World Cup with *Are You Ready?* The series of 23 beer mats pictured Scotland's hopefuls. Values are around £5 each, but Dalglish along with other, bigger stars of the squad may cost a lot more.

Tennent's Lager beer mats

Tempo stickers

In 1978 Tennent revived the idea. More table top, ale glass pads were printed to celebrate the Scottish team's journey to Argentina. The 26 glass-shaped beer mats are worth about £5 each.

Tex was a well-known Italian cowboy comic hero of the post-war years. In 1961, on the back cover of the diminutive Tex comics, readers would find a footballer to cut out and collect. The suitably wild west-sounding title for this series is *Navajo Striscia Calciatori*. Values for most, cut-out footballers (cut from the comic) are around £10, but uncut stars, still attached to an intact comic, may net over £25 each. For great players, like Jimmy Greaves, premium interest among collectors ensures that prices paid are double those paid for regular players. As well as Jimmy Greaves, British collectors ought to look out for Joe Baker and Denis Law.

Texaco hit on the coin idea in 1969. *Famous Footballers*, brass coins of 20 British stars, were given away with fuel bought at petrol stations. Values are around £10 each. Like most petroleum collectibles, there were many issued and many collected. The rarest cards tended to come with products that had limited circulation, issued in a particular area of the country, or for a limited

time period. Texaco, like Esso, was visited daily by millions of people during the period in which its free gifts were given with its petrol. Many hundreds of thousands of coins were collected weekly, which is why the values remain low, even today, half a century later.

Texaco's 1971 *Soccer Map of Teams* was very similar to the map and stickers collection produced by BAB, in the same year. For the collection, Texaco produced a large number of small stickers of football club emblems. The idea was to collect them and stick them to the map. Values for unused stickers are high due to the sheer lack of them. Prices paid have exceeded £25. A used, cut-out sticker is worth less than £5.

The Texaco *Soccer Match* challenge of 1972 was a fold-out game consisting of cards showing partial footballers. Match two halves and win. Values for uncut, folded cards are around £20. Opened, halves are worth £5.

Texaco's most attractive collection of the 1970s was a series of silky stickers showing club colours as a rosette. If unused the rare stickers may sell for up to £50!

Thomson published myriad titles in its time. They, in turn, issued free gifts. The gifts rarely, if

ever, showed the firm's name, therefore, all cards, stickers and other free gifts issued are listed under the particular publications with which they were given. See: Adventure, Vanguard, Rover, Wizard, Skipper, Hotspur, Victor, Tiger, Hornet, Ace, Bernard Briggs, Scoop, etc.

Tiger comic joined forces with Lion comic, in 1959, to issue *Football Teams 1958-59*; and anew, in 1960, to issue *Football Teams 1959-60*. The cards were issued in sheets of pairs, or in quads. There are 28 teams in all. Values for uncut sheets are around £50 for quads, and £20 for pairs. Single, cut cards are easy to find and often sell for as little as £1 each. See also: Lion.

In 1963 Tiger comic issued *Star Footballers of 1963*. The 50 cards are perforated, a little like stamps, and were issued in sheets of 12 or 14 players each sheet. A complete sheet would sell for £100. Single, cut stickers are typically available for less than £5 each.

By 1967 Tiger comic had come by a windy companion. As Tiger and Hurricane the weekly children's magazine issued *Roy Race's Album of Football Club Badges*, a collection of 110 stickers. They were issued on half a dozen sheets, to cut up and glue down into an album also given by

The Texaco Soccer Match challenge of 1972 was a fold-out game consisting of cards showing partial footballers. Match two halves and win. Values for uncut, folded cards are around £20. Opened, halves are worth £5.

Tex comic cards

Texaco rosette sticker

Tiger, 1963 card

1967 Tiger, Roy Race stickers

Tiger and Shoot! cards

the comic. Values for uncut sheets of stickers are around £30. A single, cut sticker is worth about £1.

Tiger's 1970 and 1971 collections, *My Favourite Soccer Stars*, consist of 32 cards each. While the earlier series has red backs, the later issue has blue. The cards were given in sheets of eight. The entire issue comprises 132 cards, most of which were issued by sister comics, like Buster & Jet, Scorcher & Score, The Lion & Thunder, etc. Values for uncut sheets start at around £25. Cut, single cards can be found for less than £2.

Tiger merged with Jag comic and issued *Stars of British Sport*, in 1973. The collection took the form of a turn-wheel game, displaying 30 sportsmen. The value for an intact wheel is £25.

Tiger & Jag also issued a collection of stickers and rosettes in 1973. The *I'm A Fan* series consists of a rosette, upon which were adhered sticky letters. The reader of the comic would select the letters he or she wanted, stick them to the rosette and hey, presto! In a recent internet auction, an unused set of stickers and an unused rosette made £50.

Tiger's end came in the early 1980s but not before a swansong in 1982: *World Cup Soccer Cards* included eight football cards, of Scotland, Northern Ireland and England, issued as a sheet of eight cards.

The cards have no series title, nor brand and the comic is not mentioned. The series title was noted on the front cover of issue 20th February 1982. The value is in an uncut sheet, which would be worth £20, or £30 with the original comic. Cut single cards are worth £2 each. Shoot! magazine issued very similar cards of league clubs, at the same time. Three of the cards are seen here. The two Red Devils Bryans are by Shoot! the Three Lions Bryan is by Tiger.

Tiket was a Spanish printer. In 1914 the firm issued a series of 54 cards and an album. The cards are known as *Foot-ball*, after the title of the album, but they've also become associated with Amatller chocolates due to the chocolatier's brand name appearing upon a slightly later re-issue of the collection. Many of the cards fetch high prices due to British players of note, like Gilbert, Gibson, Burnett, Allack, Hodge and the Wallace brothers (the early Brits at Barcelona and Español); and for soccer greats of legend like Juan Kinké Armet and the Irish player, Roma Forns. The cards presently sell for over £50 each, and up to as much as £200. There are very few extant, and prices could go skywards, towards £1,000, for cards from this important and historic set.

Amateur's Internationnal Team

New Cruzaders

1914 Tiket cards from Spain

Tip Top cards

Topical Times
metal cards

Tinghalls are cards from Sweden. Tinghalls issued many and varied types of football cards. They come with a bewildering variety of backs: various colours, different typeface matrices, and brands (Flamingo, etc.). The cards can be seen on sale for hundreds of pounds, though many can actually be had for a lot less, especially with a little patience and some Swedish interaction. Sign up for the Swedish selling sites: www.tradera.se and www.blocket.se where you will find bargains – if you get round the language barrier. If you don't speak Svensk, then ask in English (many Swedes speak it) or use an internet translator. Try searching for well known Svensk brands of cards and you'll soon pick up the lingo used to describe soccer ephemera. This is how the American sellers of the big value, rarer Swedish cards found them in the first instance – and they paid pennies!

Tip Top was a firm based in Malta. During the 1950s and 60s it issued various sets of football stickers and cards, the first of which was a series of photos from classic football matches of the pre-war era. The 25 trade cards show football action of a previous generation, including club versus country matches, like Aston Villa versus Germany! The unusual series of cards was just the first by a business that borrowed images from other manufacturers. Values for Tip Top's 1950s cards start at around £20 each, but some card prices exceed this, and by quite a long way! Arsenal, Villa, Brentford, Chelsea, and other British sides of note feature among the internationals.

Tip Top may have been responsible for variations of A&BC football stamps that are believed to have originated in Valletta. The firm had connections to Somportex Gum and may have been behind other, unusual variations of British-issue football stickers during the late 1960s and early 1970s.

Tobler issued two series of Famous Footballers cards in 1938, and in 1939. The series can be distinguished by the presence of a brand name. One set shows the brand, the other does not. Values start at £100 each for the series with the name showing atop. The second series is the same as the collection issued by Hill tobacco, also in 1939,

and its values are much lower, partly because of the similarity of the cards, and the relative ease in acquiring them. Relative ought to be emphasised! Both Tobler sets are rare but the 1938 cards are almost impossible to find.

Tonibell issued cards from garishly coloured ice cream vending vans, from whose roofs miniature mad cow mascots mooed. The vehicles were known for their pollution, even as far back as the 1960s. Fumes and tunes were part of the ice cream experience back then. Why kids were drawn to the blokes in white, inside, would be scrutinised today. In the dog days of summers long gone, luring children with the sound of a Pavlovian bell and guaranteed dental damage was not frowned upon. Tonibell's men in white were overly optimistic about an England win that never came, and the dozen *England's Soccer Stars* cards of 1970 were soon replaced by a series celebrating heroes of yesteryear: *Team of All Time*. The latter collection consists of 36 circular cards, green on the obverse, pink to the reverse. It not only called on the great stars of the past, it looked like it had been printed in the past. The values for suchlike are between £5 and £10. The earlier set, *England's Soccer Stars*, are better quality cards, rarer and worth a lot more.

Tonibell's 1972 series of hexagonals looks similar to cards issued by its rivals. The *1st Division Football League Club Badges* (of 1972) collection comprises 24 hexagonal cards that are very similar to cards issued by Lord Neilson [sic] and Mr Softee in 1971. Values for the Tonibell cards are around £5 each.

Top Flight made children's cigarettes. The candy sticks came with soccer stars cards, in 1960. *Top Flight Stars* include 25 sports stars of the day. Values are around £5 each, and well over this for certain world greats. Denis Law, John Charles, Joe Baker and Stanley Matthews are the footballers included.

Topical Times was one of the best known football magazines of the last century. Circulation peaked between the wars. In 1924 the journal

G. W. HALL
TOTTENHAM HOTSPUR

Tobler card

Tonibell card

ENGLAND'S · SOCCER STARS
GORDON BANKS
Stoke City

Considered to be one of the finest goalkeepers in the world, Banks was a member of the England team that won the World Cup in 1966 and now has over 50 full international caps. Born in Sheffield, he was first spotted by Chesterfield, for whom he signed in October 1955. During the summer of 1959 Leicester City paid Chesterfield a fee of £6,000 for his services and he rapidly established a reputation as an outstanding goalkeeper. Played for Leicester in both the 1961 and 1963 FA Cup Finals, having previously won Under 23 and Football League honours. Due to the promise shown by young Peter Shilton, Leicester agreed to release Banks in 1967 and he was transferred to Stoke City for a fee of £50,000. Ht. 6 ft. Wt. 12.8.

tonibell

An exclusive series in association with
WORLD SOCCER
magazine

issued metal cards of football teams. The half a dozen cards are worth around £20 each.

In 1928 Topical Times issued what's become one of its rarest series. Paper supplements, about A5 in size, show coloured portraits of footballers, including Dixie Dean. Values for the six football souvenirs are typically around £50 each but the Dixie Dean item is rare and sought after. Its value is over £150.

1928 Topical Times supplement

Topical Times issued so-called *real glossy photos of footballers* in pairs, in 1929. A score of players feature on 10 cards. They are usually found cut to singles, which is a shame. Uncut cards have much higher values. Uncut pairs are worth £30 upwards. Cut singles sell for £5.

Topical Times published *100 Football Stars of 1930*. The 1930s stars are not cards, per se, but a series of miniature magazines crammed full with images of famous players of the time. Today such diminutive journals – in a way they were the sticker albums of their time – are often found cut to bits to acquire single images, which is a pity because they are worth little when cut. Otherwise attractive, antique booklets that would be worth

Topical Times panel portraits

£50 each become fit for nothing more than paper recycling. Cut, single pictures are worth a mere £1 each. As with many rare issues of the 1920s and 1930s, destruction with scissors is an ignominious fate. The upside is that the few remaining, uncut and intact booklets are now worth more than ever.

Between 1932 and 1939 Topical Times issued various series of large, rectangular, photographic cards called *Panel Portraits*. Well over 100 black and white, full-length pictures of players were issued, including Irish stars, issued only in Northern Ireland; and Scottish players, issued only in Scotland. The latter two types are rarest and worth the most. Scottish cards sell for £20 upwards, English for between £3 and £5; and Irish players fetch as much as £50 each. Note: cards with the magazine in which they were issued

Topical Times Scottish special

command double the price. For a magazine that features the accompanying card on the front cover, values may be trebled for such a pairing.

In 1934 Topical Times issued so-called *Special Issues*, which were large, coloured portraits of footballers. The 16 very large supplements are about A4 size and were meant for framing. Different series were issued north and south of the border. Values for English cards are around £5 to £10 each, whereas Scottish cards sell for over £30. Note: the Hearts card of Tommy Walker is not only a stunner, it's his rookie card, and this factor increases the standard value by a factor of three. Cards with original magazines with which they were issued will sell for double the standard value.

Topical Times issued *Panel Portraits In Colour*, in 1936. The 32 large, full-length photographic pictures of players include 16 English cards, which

THE FAVOUS
STORY PAPER

JOE BECKETT.

MIKE HONEYMAN

PETE HERMAN

E. RICE.

"THE CHAMPION"
SPORTS WALLE

BLACKPOOL.

rgh, on
brothers
ue game.
Hibernian's
nd Gibby
drieonians.

Goalkeeper. Born in Wigan.
Joined Preston North End from
local junior side in 1953. Missed
only two first-team matches
during 1957-58 season.

In April, 1945, Tommy Bogan
of Hibernian was playing for
Scotland against England at
Hampden Park. Injured in the first
minute, he was carried off and
didn't play for the rest of the game.

LAWRIE LESLIE

FRED ELSE

The Scottish First Division club,
Glasgow Celtic, played 63 successive
matches without a defeat from
November 13, 1915, to April 21, 1917

PETER DOBING

Inside-right. Manchester born, but
joined Blackburn Rovers from
Crewe Schools, 1956. Played in
all inside positions, 1957-58, and
was top scorer with 25 goals.

oalkeeper. Joined Hibernian
rom Newtongrange Star, 1956.
Played in Edinburgh Select v.
Preston, 1956. Res. Scottish Lge.
v. Irish Lge. and Lge. of Irel'd, '58.

NABISCO

BOB WILSON'S
SHREDDED WHEAT

Soccer
Action

COLLECTOR BOOK

LBUM

Middlesboro

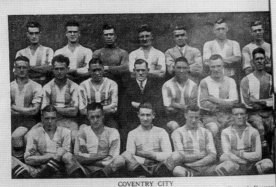

COVENTRY CITY

Back Row (left to right): BAKER, MASON, PEARSON, BOILEAU, Mr. KIMPTON (Trainer), DAVISON
BROWN.
Middle Row: FRITH, BIRTLEY, LAUDERDALE, H. STORER (Manager), JONES, BISBY, WHITE.
Front Row: BROCK, BOURTON, LAKE, LIDDLE CRISP.

CRYSTAL PALACE

Back Row (left to right): BIGG, HEINEMANN, DUNN, HAYNES, PARRY, BROWN, WILDE, OWENS.
Front Row: CARSON, SIMPSON, MANSERS, DAWES, COLLINS, CROMPTON.

In 1937 Topical Times issued *Three-in-One Panel Portraits*. 16 large cards were issued, half being English, and half Scottish. The Scots cards are worth a lot more.

Topical Times Triple card

1938 Topical Times card

are worth between £5 and £10 each; and 16 Scottish cards, which are worth at least double that. Cards with original magazines have premium values.

In 1937 Topical Times issued *Three-in-One Panel Portraits*. Sixteen large cards were issued, half being English, and half Scottish. The Scots cards are worth a lot more. Scottish triple cards may sell for over £50 each, while English trios sell for between £5 and £10 each. Triple cards cut to singles are almost worthless. Cards with original magazines are worth double. Cards with magazines that feature the same card on the cover are worth treble.

Topical Times went with smaller cards in 1937. A series of *Miniature Panel Portraits* includes 48 cards. Their value is about £10 for Scottish cards and around £3 to £5 for English issues. This series is very similar to a second 1937 collection called *Stars of Today*, also of 48 cards.

The last series of Topical Times cards came just before the war, in 1938. *Great Players* includes 48 photo cards of a different format, similar in size to gum cards. Values for Scottish

cards are around £10, and English players sell for £3 each.

Topps *Footballer* gum cards are, perhaps, the defining soccer card issues of the late 1970s. Much though A&BC Gum had been a beloved producer, and, perhaps more enamoured by British collectors, its successor made the cards that became synonymous with six European Cups, back-to-back wins, when the Champions League trophy could only be won by league winners, as British champions Liverpool, Forest and Villa brought the cup back to Britain year after year.

Topps was a gum multinational based in America. It had seen off an erstwhile ally, Britain's A&BC Gum, in 1974. The multinational took over all of the British operations during 1975, and distributed its own cards into a ripe marketplace, developed by the British firm since the 1950s. Much like A&BC Gum, the most sought after issues by Topps are wrappers and point-of-sale display boxes from which the packets of cards were sold. The colourful boxes often show match action from various games, or specific team colours. Those from the 1970s have been seen

to sell for almost £300. Well, how many sales boxes were kept by collectors, in 1977? Very few, if any! It's a miracle that a handful have survived, and that's all there are; just a handful. The later boxes, from the 1980s, are a little easier to find but still command prices in three figures. There are variations too. British boxes differ from Scandinavian editions where gum was not offered, just cards. Wrappers from the various series may fetch over £30 for earlier types. Later wrappers from the 1980s are worth less.

Topps issued yearly sets of soccer cards from 1975 until 1979. Its first English league *Footballer* gum cards, a series of 220 cards, were issued in autumn 1975. The colourful cards are redolent of the era of disco, and many players sport Bee Gees hair. The cards are easily identified by their red and black backs. The Scottish series, of 88 cards, also come with plenty of Gibb Brothers bouffants and beards, and blue and black backs. Values for such cards are around £2, for English issues; and £5 for Scottish cards. Exceptional prices are paid for Celtic cards (why there were only four cards for the Bould Bhoys in green,

1978 Topps wrapper

1979 Topps wrapper

Top Sellers wrapper

no one knows), and for the checklist cards, from both national issues. Clean, unmarked checklists sell for much more than used examples, with pen scribble or other obliterations. The 1975 box has a generic football image and is worth £250.

In 1976 Topps launched its second series of *Footballer* cards. The 330 English gum cards have blue & black backs; and the 132 Scottish gum cards have red and black backs. The English cards are easier to find and have a value of around £2 each. Scottish cards, and checklist cards, are worth more: £5 each. The 1976 box features Liverpool versus Manchester City match action. The box is worth £300.

The 1977 series of Topps cards included 330 English league cards, with red and black backs; and 132 Scottish cards, with yellow and black backs. English cards are worth £2, and Scottish cards are worth £4 each. The box features Sheffield United, Chelsea, West Ham, Newcastle United and Birmingham City action. It's worth £300.

In 1978 Topps issued 396 gum cards for the English league (orange and brown backs) and 132 Scottish cards (green and black backs). Values

range from £2 each, for English, to £5 each for Scottish cards. The 1978 box is worth £250.

In 1979 the 396 English cards had a blue & black back, and the 132 Scottish cards came with red & brown backs. English cards are worth £1 each, and Scottish cards start at £5. The 1979 display box features a 1977 photo of action from an Aston Villa versus Wolves match. Its value is £250.

An American soccer issue surfaced briefly, in 1979. *NASL Soccer Stickers*, by Topps, seemed to be designed to kill American interest in the beautiful game. It's probably the worst series of soccer gum cards ever made. Disappointment is guaranteed for those foolish enough to seek to complete the series of inane puzzles, laws and terminology of soccer stickers. The wrapper and the point-of-sale display box are about the best component parts of the collection, worth around £20 and £80, respectively.

In the 1980s Topps made only English cards. Gone were the Scottish issues. The 1980/81 season saw 198 cards, with pink backs. The *Footballer '81* cards come as trios, detachable by perforation. Single cards are worth less than £1

but complete trios sell for £3 each. The cards came with *Football Posters*. The 18 miniature, folded posters are worth £1 each. An English display box is worth £150; and a Scandinavian version (it's different) is worth £175.

During 1981/82 Topps issued more stars in trios. The 192 *Footballer* cards have blue backs and they are worth £3 for each trio. Cut singles are worth very little. A display box is worth £150.

In 1982 Topps and Jolly Press issued large cards across Europe. The British series, called *Topps Spotlights*, includes 30 footballers whose values are around £10 each. Similar German issues, by Jolly Press, and French cards have also been noted.

For more related to Topps see also: A&BC Gum, Xuereb, Bazooka, etc.

Top Sellers was a British publisher of erotica and horror, run by a firm called Thorpe & Porter Sales (the T & P of Top), which issued Panini cards in Great Britain until 1977.

Top Sellers Limited was responsible for the initial import and distribution of Panini cards and stickers into the United Kingdom before the

1930s transfers

Troman cards

Triumph cards

United Kingdom's membership of the trading block known as the EEC.

Best known for the Top Sellers football cards issued between 1972 and 1977 the firm, under the name Thorpe & Porter Sales, imported and distributed Panini's *Football Clubs* stickers of 1975, as well as the earlier World Cup collections, in 1970 and 1974. By the late 1970s the Italians had put the smut merchants to bed, taking over British distribution themselves. Top Sellers cards have been covered earlier in this book. See: Panini.

Tower Press issued two series of transfer decals between 1966 and 1967. The issues are called *Famous Football Clubs 1st series* and *2nd series*. The 48 water-slide transfers were sold in sheets of 24, each pulled from a hanging point-of-sale display board. Values for single transfers are £1 each. A complete sheet of 24 transfers is worth about £30. Transfers still attached to a display hanger (a picture title card) are worth a lot more.

Transfers have been issued since football stickers have been known. A series of 36 numbered but unbranded decals, from 1930, *Famous Footballers*, is a case in point. The decals show footballers (head and shoulders images) in

club colours, and each is of cigarette card size. Great rarities, they have sold for over £100 each. The series is dated to the 1930/31 season by the inclusion of Harold Blackmore, for Bolton Wanderers; and Hughie Gallacher, of Chelsea. The former was at Bolton until 1931. By 1932 he was a Middlesbrough player. The latter, Hughie Gallacher, was at Chelsea from 1930. Thus, we have a 1930 to 1931 window for this unusual and extremely rare series.

Transimage issued a series of stickers to rival Panini and FKS, in 1979. The collection, called *Football 79/80*, included 528 stickers, mostly in pairs. Values are around £1 each.

Trebor issued sweets, and sometimes gave away football-related free gifts. In 1974, the *All Stars Pop And Soccer Ring* included 12 stickers, of which six showed footballers. Values for complete sheets of stickers exceed £75. Single soccer stickers are worth £10 each.

Having distributed cards by Topps during the late 1970s, Trebor issued its own players for the 1982 World Cup. A set of stickers came inside candy called *Squad 82*. The set includes 26 England stars. Uncut wrappers sell for over £20,

while cut stickers make around £3 each.

Triumph was a comic. During 1926 Triumph issued two superb series of cards: *English League (Div1) Footer Captains* [sic]; and *Famous Footer Internationals*. The collection was collected weekly. Of 22 cards in each set, half were issued with Triumph, while the other 11 cards came with Champion, a sister comic. Values for these fine cards have long been listed way below what they are worth. As a set, the collection scores highly. Making the set was difficult. Children had to buy two different comics, weekly, to get all of the cards. As certain cards from these collections sell for over £10 each, a set of either is worth around £150.

In 1930 Triumph issued *Transfers of Footballers, Historic Events, Peoples and Transport.* The number of individual decals and different sheets of transfers from this series remains unknown. Values for uncut sheets are around £150 each. Amidst trains, planes and… Canadian mounties, are found famous footballers. The issue is very similar to the Boys' Magazine decal images of stars of sport and adventure, also known as *Dazzling 5 Colour Real Magic Transfers*.

Troman cards come from the fin de siècle. *Football Team Colours & Rules* cards originated as an Edwardian table game. There are at least a dozen cards known. The colourful cards show Scottish and English soccer team colours, with rules of the game to boot. Prices paid for these rare cards have exceeded £100 each.

Tuckett sweets issued cards that are very similar to those given with Lovell's confectionery and also with Pattreiouex cigarettes, in 1928. The series, called *Photos of Football Stars*, has a value of £50 each card. Premium values are obtainable for three cards of the same star, with a trio of different backs. For more, see: Lovell, Pattreiouex.

Tudor Crisps issued *Wear'Em, Scare'Em* voodoo masks, in metal, during the 1970s, but it also gave away less frightening fare in the form of *Soccer Fans League* football club rosettes. There are an unknown number of club colours rosettes, for Scottish and English teams. Many Tudor freebies were redemption items sent in exchange for crisp packet tokens, including the rosettes, which are plastic, with golden-coloured ruffles. Their design may have been influenced by the very similar Typhoo Tea plaques.

Prices paid in auction have exceeded £25 each.

Tupinamba, of Brazil, issued a series of stickers in 1960 called *Quigol*. Once upon a time the series was believed to be from 1958. Once upon a time the Pelé sticker was considered as a rookie, but this is no longer so. The series has been re-dated to 1960 by knowledgeable sources in Brazil. Nevertheless, prices asked for Pelé often exceed £1,000. Whether the cards sell is another matter. There seem to be quite a few of them about! Most of the stickers sell for £5 each, with exceptions for better known Brazil national team stars.

Turnwright Toffees were made in South Africa. During 1967 the firm issued *Your Favourite Player's History* cards. There are about 200 bilingual Dutch and English football cards in the series, for which prices start at £5 and rise rapidly, depending on the provenance of a particular player. The better known are a player's previous clubs, the more money tends to be paid for the card.

Ty-Phoo Tea is responsible for some of the most attractive trade cards. As far back as the 1920s it issued the definitive collection of Robin Hood character cards; a series that's delightful. Even if you have no interest in the fables of Nottingham Forest (the wood, that is, not the tales of the immortal Brian Clough) you'll appreciate these cards. In the 1960s Typhoo made more extraordinary cards, this time with football teams and players.

The first series of Typhoo teams was issued in 1963. Initially the teams were printed, in black and white, on boxes of tea but it was also possible to send away for larger, colour versions of the same. The monotone packet-issue cards are titled *Famous Football Clubs*.

Turnwright cards

There are 24, in all. A cut-out card is not worth very much (around £1). An entire side of a tea box is preferred by collectors (£2 to £3), though better still is an intact box (worth over £25 for some teams). The same teams were available, as *Premium Football Clubs* cards. The tea drinker

Tupinamba sticker

Ty-Phoo packet cards

Ty-Phoo Tea is responsible for some of the most attractive trade cards. As far back as the 1920s it issued the definitive collection of Robin Hood character cards; a series that's delightful.

Ty-Phoo Robin Hood card

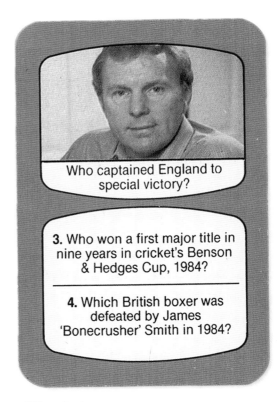

TV Times quiz card

would save up the coupons from boxes of tea, then send the collected tokens to Typhoo, with a little money, and in turn Typhoo would despatch one large team card. In all 24 teams were issued for 1963/64. Values for these cards have been climbing for some years and bargains are hard to find. The average price paid for a top condition card is £20 but some teams sell for much more.

In 1963 Ty-Phoo issued *Football Club Rosettes*. The 16 sew-on, stitched cloth rosettes feature team colours, and they were issued with a dedicated card. Values are around £20 for a rosette and card pair.

During 1965 Typhoo reprised the idea of team cards. *Famous Football Clubs (2nd Series)* [sic] consists of 24 packet-issue cards, printed on the boxes of tea; and the same number of large, colourful redemption cards. Values for cut cards are around £1, but intact boxes sell for over £25. The 24 *Premium Football Clubs* feature teams from the 1965/66 season. Though some teams sell for higher prices, typical values are around £15 to £20 each.

In 1967 Typhoo went for stars, rather than teams. The first series of *International Football Stars* was printed on packets, in monotone, but was available, as had been the teams, as larger coloured redemption cards. Values for the players are

generally less than the teams. Players cut from the packets are worth up to £1, and intact boxes sell for around £20 each. The larger versions, known as *Premium International Football Stars*, are worth £5 to £10 each. Wolves collectors take note: there are two versions of the Derek Dougan card.

Ty-Phoo's second series of players, called *International Football Stars (2nd series)* [sic] came out in 1969. The values are as per the first series. Manchester United collectors take note: there are two versions of the Ian Ure card.

Ty-Phoo opted for something different in 1971. It issued *Football Club Plaques* both as packet-issue cut-out cards, and as premium issued redemption gifts. The 35 packet issues, printed on the sides of boxes of tea, are worth £5 each, while intact boxes sell for around £30.

These packet-issues were used as the tokens to redeem larger, plastic plaques, which are worth between £20 and £50 each, depending on the team.

Very similar plastic plaques, with as many as 40 different clubs, were also issued by the Co-op. A third series of similar plastic shields was mounted on faux melamine – there's an image to keep carpenters awake at night: a plastic version of simulated wood. It's unknown by whom these design atrocities were made.

Ty-Phoo's rarest series of player cards was issued in 1973. Known as the *New Series of Football Stars*, the 24 packet issues, and the redeemable, larger, coloured cards of players are worth more than those of earlier series. Values of cards that are cut are around £3 each, intact boxes sell for over £30, and the large, coloured cards are worth £15 to £50 each, with George Best scoring highest on the values scale.

TV Times, a British commercial television guide, issued sports cards in a quiz game, issued in 1985, and re-issued with different cards in 1988. Single cards are seen for astronomical prices but the game can be bought for a few pounds on well known internet auction sites. You'll get the entire game for a fraction of the prices some sellers ask for a single card!

PLIMENTS OF **Ty·Phoo** LTD., BIRMINGHAM 5
TEA

WITH THE

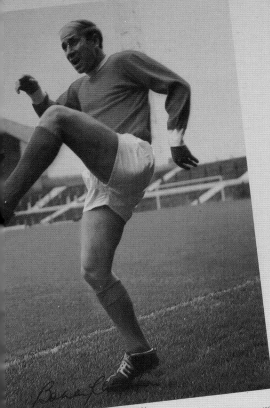

BOBBY CHARLTON
(Manchester United and England)
has been a professional with his present club since 1954 and in that time made over 400
nces. His consistent playing ability has brought an impressive number of honours—
caps and World Cup Winners medal, a European Cup Winners medal, three League
medals and one F.A. Cup Winners medal to date.

GEORGE BEST
(Manchester United and Northern Ireland)
Britain's top candidate to succeed Pele as the greatest player in the world. Packs them in wherever he plays,
and probably the best manipulator of a ball in the business. Has been headline material since making his
first-class debut in 1963. His total of more than 30 caps would have been nearer 50 but for Manchester
United commitments in Europe. Was European Footballer of the Year in 1968. Approaching 200 goals
including six in one match at Northampton.

he and his companions had acto
clear air, sandwiched between two

om **Ty·Phoo**
TEA

am?
can choose from.

NE

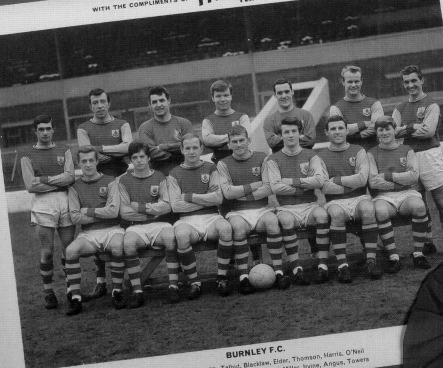

BURNLEY F.C.
Back row, L to R: Smith, Talbut, Blacklaw, Elder, Thomson, Harris, O'Neil
Front row, L to R: Bellamy, Morgan, Lochead, Miller, Irvine, Angus, Towers

Registe
by Eric
Centra
Dept.

E OFFER

Colour prints and rosettes of famous football clubs!

(In response to popular request a new Ty·Phoo football club series starts this season.)

Just collect the 24 different Famous Football Club cards—there's one on every Ty·Phoo Tea packet—and forward them to Ty·Phoo stating the name of your favourite club among the 24 of the series.

In return Ty·Phoo will send to you a colour print measuring 8 inches × 10 inches suitable for framing, and a taffeta rosette in the club colours for you to wear.

Start collecting Ty·Phoo packets NOW—and you'll soon have your colour print and rosette!

Full details are on every Ty·Phoo Tea packet.

Ty·Phoo TEA

TY·PHOO TEA LIMITED,
DEPT. F, BIRMINGHAM 5.

(including Newfoundland) Eagle and Boys' World Magazine with which is incorporated the Merry-Go-Round, printed in Great Britain
hams Press Ltd., Long Act ₂., London, W.C.2. Sole Agents for Australia and New Zealand, Gordon & Gotch (A/sia) Ltd., South Africa,
₀; abroad, including Canada – 12 months 41/2. Dollar rate for U.S.A. $6.25; Canada, $6.50. Please send your order to Subscription

Unela Pam-Pam

Unela gum wrappers

Unela Pam-Pam may sound like a cartoon rock cruncher from The Flintstones but its provenance is a much more serious affair. The United States Near Eastern Laboratory (Unela) was a post-war American outpost in ethnically rearranged Palestine. The outpost was involved in assisting the so-called normalisation of Zion. In 1958 Unela produced Pam-Pam, and Bambi gum, known colloquially as Bam-Bam goes my gun gum, and issued the former wrapped with international footballers to commemorate the World Cup. The wrappers featured players from France, Brazil, England, Hungary and Yugoslavia. The attractive ephemera shows flags, stylised Hebrew lettering, and the names of players in Latin script. Premium prices are asked by sellers for the rookie Bobby Charlton wrapper, whose price will make £300 before the next World Cup; while Pelé, were he available, should fetch well over £2,000. It's not only a rookie, it is probably one of the rarest 1958 Pelé rookie cards on the planet.

The why and wherefore of the value of this series goes something like this: in 1958 Israel

had not taken the Golan Heights from Syria, nor occupied the West Bank, the reduced homeland of the refugee Palestinians; nor had it taken the Sinai peninsula from Egypt. Israel was less than half the size it's become, today. Therefore, the population was much smaller too. The country had less than 2 million people at the time of the World Cup, in 1958. Today it has 9 million. That's partly why these artefacts of Judaica are so rare, and treasured. Relatively few were printed, for such a very small population; and fewer still survived. The wrappers are also highly prized because they are a cross-over collectible. Both football collectors and historical Judaica collectors seek them, and will pay well. British players, like Don Howe, Billy Wright and Derek Kevan are valued at over £100 each. Similarly, values for Brazilians like Garrincha, and French legend Fontaine, will be of three figures. The collection also includes very rarely seen greats of Hungary and Yugoslavia. Generally values for most of the wrappers range from £50 to £200.

Union Zigarettenfabrik was a German issuer of cigarette cards. It produced one of the most beautiful series of cards, ever. In 1938 it issued

König Fussball, a gigantic series of 528 colour-tinted footballer portraits and scenes of soccer match action. The cards employ striking arrays of colour, flags and ornate borders. Collecting cards from this series is complicated by the various tobacco brands that used the images. The cards were shared between Ramona, Solo, Nile Princess and other brands of cigarette made by Union. Thus, it's possible to collect one of each card many times over, each with different backs. The collection includes many foreign players, notably gold-leaf decorated images of various Arsenal stars, the likes of Drake, Bastin and Hapgood; Peter Doherty, for Manchester City; and Tommy Walker for Scotland. Spanish, Italian, Czech and French players also feature alongside armies of Germans. Prices paid for British players have exceeded £100, in many cases.

In the 1930s, United Services Tobacco issued two sets of cards with football interest, which were called *Interesting Personalities*, and *Popular Footballers*. The former set includes over 30 footballers amongst 100 cards. Values are around £5 each, for most cards from both series, though more may be paid for select players. The images on the cards were used by Phillips on its BDV series of packets.

Union cards

Union and similar cards

United Services card

U is for Unknown. Some cards resist easy identification and defy attempts to unearth their provenance. Cards without logos, with no brand, with no manufacturer's legend, are legion. Cards by firms long forgotten, or never known, are referred to, simply, as being by an unknown issuer.

Unknown issuer cards are like a treasure island flying a pirate flag. A staggering find may reward the intrepid explorer, yet danger is ever present, especially when you are handing over sizeable sums of cash. A trophy card which

crowns a collection is usually the card that caused the collector the most anguish, or aroused the most passion, when it was acquired. Risk, loss, reward and future profits are for the individual to weigh up for him or herself, when negotiating the capture of any rare card, not least one that's unidentified. Cards by issuers of whom we know little, or nothing, may be highly alluring. It could be a valuable gem, or it might be a design conceit that was privately made by an enthusiast. It may be worth little. It could be worth thousands. Beauty

is in the eye of the beholder but value is in the expression of the possessor. Notwithstanding the work done by the card cavaliers of last century, there remain unsolved mysteries in cartophily, and bizarre cards of obscure provenance haunt the dreams of card sharks and sticker minnows alike. A newly discovered cartophilic gem awaits you, sooner or later, for there are, as yet, myriad undiscovered and unknown cards out there, just waiting to be found.

1970s stickers

A classic series of cards by an unknown issuer came to light in the 1960s. At some point during the Jazz Age a discrete publisher unleashed the unbranded cards. They have no logos, and they exhibit but plain backs. Half a dozen cards are known.

A classic series of cards by an unknown issuer came to light in the 1960s. At some point during the Jazz Age a discrete publisher unleashed the unbranded cards. They have no logos, and they exhibit but plain backs. Half a dozen cards are known. They feature photographic portraits of footballers. The sepia gravure images of players are printed on beige cardstock. The photographs are accredited to Albert Wilkes, and to an agency called Sport & General. For many years the series was wrongly dated by pioneer cartophilists (as 1928). Recent research, by football fans, has dated the series correctly to the 1921/22 season. These are the stats and football facts that corrected the confusion of the well-meaning, non-sports enthusiasts of yore: Manchester United signed Frank Barson in late 1922. In this series he is shown in Aston Villa colours. Syd Puddefoot departed West Ham, late in 1922, for Falkirk. Herein Syd sits for West Ham. Andy Wilson was with Chelsea by 1923. He's a Middlesbrough player in this collection.

Another series of cards, by an unknown issuer of the flapper years, has had collectors in a flap of their own. The cards were issued paired, two images together, of jockeys, boxers, cricketers and footballers. Identifying the issuer is only part of the challenge. With series like this the year is as, if not more, important. The sports stars feature John Steel, a Scottish striker. Named James in this series, John Steel is with Hamilton Academical. Steel moved to Burnley in 1925. So, the cards are from early 1925, or earlier still. Moreover, why put John Steel into this series, in the first place? An Accies man from the lower reaches of the league was hardly front page news, or was he? In 1922 he was, at least, the club's highest goal scorer. It may be that another achievement of Steel has slipped from the record, after 100 years. Looking towards the boxers on these cards helps to date them. The Australian and French pugilists, Eric Barnes (whose ring name was Frank Burns) and Eugene Criqui, won world championship belts, respectively, in 1921 and 1923. They did little of global note afterwards. Other footballers in the set also help date it. Clem Stephenson and Ben Howard-Baker were newsworthy in the early 1920s. The former starred in the team that won the FA Cup, in 1922; and the latter set a British athletics record, in 1921, in the high jump. He was an Olympian, as well as a footballer. Having competed in the 1920 Olympic Games, for Great

1922 card

1923 card

1930s shield cards

ERIC BROOK
(MANCHESTER CITY)

MANCHESTER CITY

EUSÉBIO

ORIENT

Cards by uknown issuers

N. Lofthouse   Engeland

JUBOLITAN
Cura radical de hemorroides.

Javier Pelaó Olivella Julià Cros Bordoy Serra Vidal Artisus Alcázar Pellicer

C. D. EUROPA
Campeón de Cataluña 1922-23

Urodonal Jubolitan card

Britain, he also donned his first cap for the England soccer team, in 1921, for a victory over Belgium. A noted horse racing jockey, Joe Childs, also appears on these cards. Childs had been at the top of his sport during the Great War. His career quietened down in the 1920s but not before he had won his fourth Epsom Oaks, and his second St. Leger, both in 1921. The weight of such stats may suggest that the series was made no later than 1923.

Before World War Two shield-shaped cards had enjoyed a brief renaissance, but their origins remain mysterious. The enigmatic green shields (see under G in this book) were not the only escutcheon cards known to 1930s collectors. Other, more colourful, shield-shape cards have perplexed collectors for almost a century. The heraldic cards bear illustrations of players at battle, in melee, striving for the ball, charging along green pitches. Occasionally a famous footballer's portrait appears, too. For example, George Vose of United, and Jackie Bray, for Manchester City. Values for these very rare cards are well over £100. Chelsea, Stoke City, Crystal Palace and at least 20 other clubs are known.

Unknown issuers are responsible for unidentified cards as far back as the 1880s, and until the present day. This section will be expanded in a future issue. News of rare cards will appear on this writer's blogs and channels, as advertised on the website: www.footballsoccercards.com Following the social media channels thereon will ensure you miss nothing. Do sign up for updates on this book. See the back of this book for more details.

Urodonal is a name that conjures images of splashed white ceramic and smelly public lavatories, if not pretty and airy Parisian pissoirs. The name is a brand of Spanish medicine. Urodonal's 1922 cards, *Campeones Regionales 1922-23*, were postcard-size trade cards advertising its hæmorrhoid medicine and other unspeakable pharmaceuticals. Jubolitan bottom creams and Poral pudenda remedies are but two of the strange brands found emblazoned on the wince-inducing cards. Values for such extreme and rare additions to soccer card collections start at around £50 each, with premiums paid for bigger teams and all-time greats starring, if not smarting, on the cards.

Maltese Millwall card

Val Gum

J. NELSON, Cardiff City.

VAL „FOOTER" GUM

PRINTED IN HOLLAND

W. MCKAY
Manchester United 16

VAL „FOOTER" GUM

PRINTED IN HOLLAND

R. F. D. ANCELL
Newcastle United 33

Val Gum cards

Presented with " The Vanguard."

J. E. ELKES,
Tottenham Hotspur.

All accidents and unusual happenings barred, the famous Spurs F.C. have on their books the signature of a man who looks like making football history.

J. E. Elkes was born at St George's, Salop. He soon showed signs of promise and was signed by the Spurs as an inside forward.

He is a hefty lad physically, being six feet high and 12 stones 6 pounds in weight.

In season 1923-24 he played for England v Rest, and for North v. South, in the F.A. trials, and in the ensuing season this big athlete in the famous white shirt of the Spurs should go far.

Val Gum was made by Klene Confectionery, in the Netherlands. During the late 1930s the Dutch firm issued one of the earliest gum card series in British history, *Val Footer Gum*. Among the 50 attractive cards are early images of a pair of footballing legends, Matt Busby and Stanley Matthews. There's also Bryn Jones, for Arsenal. Jones had recently moved from Wolves and this card dates the set to 1938/39. *Val Footer Gum* cards typically come with blank backs but are also known with advertising. Two cards from this series are in very short supply. They make it almost impossible to complete a set of 50, unless you pay very highly! They fetch hundreds each, due to their teams, and because of their rarity: Manchester United's McKay, and Newcastle's Ancell are the pair of costly culprits. They are worth as much as £500 each. Other cards in the series are worth around £30, if they are in very good condition, but Manchester United legend, Matt Busby, and Stoke City's Stanley Matthews may sell for over £100

each. Being card number 1, Matthews is what's called an end-number. Such cards, the first and last in a collection, have fanatical collectors. It takes all sorts! It certainly drives up prices.

Valentine & Sons issued postcards of famous football stars and teams from the 1910s until the early 1960s. They were available from street vendors, shops and post offices. Values for the early cards of club colours and grounds are around £70 each. Later issues cost much less. Waddington purchased the firm in 1962. Commercial postcards like these are technically outside the scope of this book but deltiology, as it is known, attracts a vast number of collectors, many of whom also collect trade cards. Books specialising in football postcards and other postcard passions are available. The book by Hunter Davies, on football postcards, springs to mind.

Vanguard was a 1920s comic. During 1924 it gave away a series of elegant and refined cards, with gold-leaf borders. The Vanguard footballers were forerunners of the early gum cards of the 1930s, and the classic gum cards of the 1960s.

F. HARGREAVES, Everton.

Vanguard cards

Vanguard issued cards in tandem with Adventure comic, during the 1925/26 season. *Football Photos* **include 40 photographic cards of famous players. They are valued at around £30 to £300 each.**

Dixie Dean, Tranmere Rovers card

VAV 1940s and 1950s cards

The large, precious cards are rare, and have been long undervalued. Prices ought to be reassessed and this writer puts these cards at between £50 and £60 each. As with all values in this book, prices are drawn from quantities sold over the last 30 years, and prices paid, but quality is also an important key to value. All of the values in this book are based upon the cards being in very good condition.

Vanguard issued cards in tandem with Adventure comic, during the 1925/26 season. *Football Photos* include 40 photographic cards of famous players. They are valued at around £30 to £300 each. This series was hard to complete, even in 1925/26, because of the way it was distributed. Each week a handful of cards were released but only a single card was available in each comic. It was randomly chosen by the printer, or the distributor. A buyer buying both comics would still be short of a trio of cards that week. The series includes an early Dixie Dean card, which typically breaks the set, in terms of costs. You may have to spend £300 for him, unless you get lucky. Though some sellers ask £1,000 for this card, British collectors of

experience know there are many more out there, waiting to come to market. In cases like this, with cards that were once issued across the nation, in their tens, or hundreds of thousands, time rewards the patient buyer. Not that the Dean card is his earliest rookie, but it is the most chased after. A card from his Tranmere Rovers days is in the possession of this writer. After many years it appears to be the only one known. For images of the Vanguard cards, see: Adventure.

VAV of Italy was one of the classic trade card manufacturers. Venturini toffees of Verona, was producing collectible ephemera as long ago as World War Two, and earlier! Today the firm is best known for its football cards, notably those featuring a young Gianni Rivera, of Alessandria; and for six of the Brazilian World Cup winners cards of 1958, showing Pelé, Garrincha, and teammates.

VAV made very attractive cards throughout the 1930s, 40s and 50s, and prices for such rarities can be high. Unlike many issuers it did not cease production during the war, when it was employed to make war propaganda cards for children. After the war it produced football cards every year, until the 1960s. VAV cards are some of the most creative of the post-war era. The firm made circular cards that are highly sought after. It made cards with a playing card theme – that's a cross-over collectible, with appeal to both playing card collectors and to football card fanatics. The annual cards by VAV were often a cut above other marques.

Later VAV cards feature well-known Brits like John Charles, of Wales, the original Welsh Wizard, and the Gareth Bale of his day. Charles was recently voted by Juventus fans to be the greatest ever Juve foreign player! For fans of British, as well as international football, all VAV collections, not just those between 1957 and 1961, are worthy of research. VAV is, naturally, a treat for Italian buyers of Serie A stars and teams, yet Cardiff City, Swansea and Leeds United collectors will be happiest with the many appearances of John Charles. Hibernian, Arsenal and Nottingham Forest fans may want the VAV Joe Baker card. Huddersfield Town, Manchester United and City fans will be interested in Denis Law's appearance, for VAV.

VAV's first series of cards and discs to include the British legend, John Charles, came out during the 1957/58 season. The collection is called *Figurine Calcio*. It consists of 628 cards and metal discs, like pogs. Values are around £10 for most cards and discs but John Charles has been seen to sell for as much as £75.

The next season VAV issued an updated series of *Figurine Calcio*. The 1958/59 release includes 660 items (330 cards and 330 metallic discs) whose values start at £10 each. Prices paid for John Charles cards and discs are, again, around £75 each. The card of Pelé tops that. It has been seen to sell for £1,000! In actuality it's not as rare as the price suggests. £500 is more like a realistic top ask, simply due to the frequency with which these cards come along. One American seller has accumulated more than a handful of the Pelé cards. He's spent thousands but banks on buyers in the future. He may well be proved right. He uses multiple identities, buys under one name, sells as another and asks questions of experts in Europe

using a third pseudonym. That's passion for you! Or, is it obsession?

The 1959/60 collection by VAV includes 341 cards. Prices paid for Gianni Rivera, of Alessandria, exceed £100, though values generally start at £10 each, for most of these cards. The other exception, at around £50, is John Charles.

The 1961 VAV series of *Figurine Calcio* has 246 cards. Over £100 has been paid for cards of Denis Law, Joe Baker and John Charles. Much more on VAV in a future book.

VCC is an enigma. Around 1923 a series of cards appeared with such initials. They feature cricketers and footballers. The cards may well be the very cards that influenced Barratt & Company to issue its own yearly collections of sportsmen but little is known for sure, except that there is probably too much speculation by impassioned enthusiasts and not enough archival research.

It is known that VCC was based on Roman Road, in London, E3. This address is but a few hundred metres from Bunsen's factory (see:

VAV John Charles cards

VCC card

Venlico stickers

210. ARMSTRONG
IRLANDA DEL NORTE

292. ROGER MILLA
CAMERUN

KEEGAN
Inglaterra

Pelé

CALCIOLAMPO

12

HITCHENS GERRY
(ATALANTA B.C.)
Centravanti

EDITRICE VERBANIA
MILANO

Verbania stamps

Bunsen), near Old Ford and Mile End; and it's not too far from Barratt's London base, in Wood Green, N22. No one is sure what VCC stands for but E3 has a large arboretum and lake called Victoria Park, and there was a cricket club based locally until it was devastated by bombs during the 1940 Blitz. 1950s and 60s rebuilding programmes totally reshaped the area, and factories, shops and homes were built over with concrete blocks, highways and new developments.

The VCC cards use overprints. Overprints are additional print markings that are applied after cards have been printed. The VCC cards were, it seems, made with plain backs, then reprinted with various commercial details. A number was also added to the front of the VCC cards. The firm's name, its address, and an offer for redeeming prizes, were also added later. This is certain, because the cards are also known with plain backs; and with and without numbers to the fronts. The cards were also employed by other firms. Cards with the legend, Wilkins Cough Tablets, have been seen. One Wilkins card shows Womack, for Birmingham. Further, many VCC overprint cards can also be found overprinted yet again, by Poppleton's of York!

Though most other VCC cards sell for around £100, a 1923 VCC card of White, an Arsenal player, is known to have sold for £500!

Venlico of Spain made *Los Ases del Mundial* in 1982. The World Cup collection contains hundreds of paper stickers, and includes the Cameroon legend, Roger Milla. Along with many British stars, Milla tops the value league for this series. While British Isles players fetch up to £30 Milla has been

seen to sell for £50. Note: stickers 145 and 146 were never printed.

Venorlandus is an example of a series that was once rare but became easy to get after a trove of unsold stock was found in a warehouse in Hackney, in London. The 1978 *World of Sport Flik-Cards* are now worth little but in the 1990s they were sought after. The series remains attractive due to the 15 very large, poster cards which include stars unissued in the smaller range of cards. The large cards are worth around £20 each.

Verbania is an area of northern Italy. In the 1960s Lampo took the name and used it as an imprint for two series of *CalcioLampo* stamps. The sticker stamps include Gerry Hitchens, Eusebio and Pelé – two versions of the latter, one for each series. Values for unused stamps are around £50 but prices rise for stamps still attached to borders. Note: many of the international stars were also issued in West Germany, in a similar format, by Sicker Verlag.

In 1966 Verbania issued a series of cards and stickers called *Coppa Rimet 1966*. The 256 stars include British players whose values are around £30 to £50 each. The cards feel classy, of a high quality, unlike their paper equivalents issued elsewhere, under licence from Fher. However, some of these were also released on paper, also in Italy. The paper stickers have a token (prize-winning) back. They are just as rare, if not rarer, than the cards. Pelé, from this series, has been seen to sell for up to £100. See also: Lampo, Moderna.

Victor was a comic. Its first football free gift was *Star Teams of 1961*. The 22 teams were issued in sheets. Values for uncut sheets of six start at

SUPER STARS OF '72

DEREK DOUGAN
A tall, strong striker with great ability in the air, Derek signed for Wolves after playing for Portsmouth, Blackburn, Aston Villa, Peterborough and Leicester. Many Northern Ireland caps have been won by this great Belfast-born forward.

Presented with the VICTOR

SUPER STARS OF '72

TERRY HENNESSEY
Captain of Wales on many occasions, Terry joined Derby County from Nottingham Forest in 1970 for £100,000. Exceptional heading ability and great skill on the ground are the hallmarks of this great defender. He was born in Llay near Wrexham.

Presented with the VICTOR

SUPER STARS OF '72

ALAN HUDSON
Born in King's Road just a stone's throw from Stamford Bridge, Alan signed professional forms for Chelsea, in July 1968, after two seasons as an apprentice. Since then this all-action, midfield player has won a European Cup Winners' Cup medal to go with his under 23 caps.

Presented with the VICTOR

SUPER STARS OF '72

MIKE CHANNON
Mike succeeded Martin Chivers in the Southampton team—but he did it so well that Chivers wasn't at all missed. Born near Salisbury, Mike joined the Southampton ground staff at 15 and since then has been picked to play for England's under 23 team for his goalscoring feats.

Presented with the VICTOR

Victor 1972 large and small cards

Victor comic launched a series of stand-up footballer cards in 1965. They were issued in sheets of 8, and in sheets of 4, with name cards. Sheets of 8 players, with name cards, are worth £120 each.

around £35; and a sheet of four cards is worth £25. Cut single cards are worth little, in terms of money, less than £1 each, but they may be priceless for collectors seeking just a token, an image of their own team. Like similar issues by Victor, a plastic wallet was issued for this collection, to keep the cut cards together. It is called *The Victor Sports Wallet*.

Victor comic launched a series of stand-up footballer cards in 1965. They were issued in sheets of eight, and in sheets of four, with name cards. Sheets of eight players, with name cards, are worth £120 each. Sheets of four players, with name cards, are worth £60. Single players with name cards are worth up to £10 each. Combined with comics with which the sheets were issued, prices increase substantially.

In 1968 Victor issued more stand-up footballers, in sheets. The 18 footballers have name cards, so if you are buying these singly, make sure the player also comes with its accompanying name card. Values for sheets of nine players, including nine name cards, are around £120. Single players with name cards are worth up to £10.

Victor issued *Football Challenge Cards* in 1969. They were issued in two sheets of cards. The cards have images on either side. Values for uncut

sheets are around £30, single cut cards are worth £1. There's Celtic interest herein.

Victor's *Football Favourite* was a 1970 supplement. It included a pair of folded sheets, each featuring colour and monotone photos of players and teams. Uncut, such folders are worth £25 each. Cut images are worth little, less than £1 each. These are strictly non-cartophilic items but they find their way into the market because some sellers cut images from the pamphlets. Cutting out pictures from such publications ruins the value of otherwise attractive and often valuable supplements. This entry is included to warn collectors not to pay too much for cuttings.

In 1972 Victor issued *Super Stars of 72*. The unusual collection included cards of two sizes. Issued as a pair of sheets, with 16 small cards each; and, as four pairs of larger cards, the 40-card set is worth little as cut singles. The value is in uncut sheets, which are worth £30 – more with an original comic. Uncut pairs of cards are worth £15. Cut single cards, large or small, are worth £1 each.

Victoria Chocolates sticker

Victoria Vedetien Chocolates, of Belgium, issued *Sport* in 1968. The collection consists of hundreds of cyclists and soccer players. Belgium, being a small country with a small population, produces less cards and stickers, per series, than countries like France, Germany and Britain. Print runs are relatively low. Thus, the stickers of Pelé, Eusebio, Bobby Charlton and others in this series are very scarce. The stickers usually come with glue damage to the rear, due to being adhered within a chocolate wrapper. Prices for noted footballers have exceeded £40.

Victoria of Portugal issued footballers during the middle years of the 1960s. Eusebio is known among the stickers, and his image has been seen to sell for over £100.

Vidall was an Italian cards issuer. Its cards were made for redemption gifts, so most cards were returned to the issuer, and destroyed. Those that remain are very rare. Vidal issued *Calciatori & Premi* in 1958. The series includes British players, for example, Tom Finney.

Values are over £100 each card.

Vittoria—Egyptien Miss Blanche [sic] cards come from the Netherlands. The cards date from 1932. The series called *Competitie Wedstryden 1932-33 Spelfotos* consists of 100 large and colourful soccer match action scenes. Values for un-glued cards of British teams are around £50 each.

Vittorioso was an Italian comic. In 1949 it issued *Concorso Grandi Campioni*. In it there were five footballers, or sportsmen, issued weekly. The cards were published on the back page of the comic, and were meant to be cut out. Premium prices are paid for British soccer stars, or for other sporting greats. The British footballers include Aston Villa youth player, Charles Norman Adcock, who also played for Peterborough FC; and William Jordan of Juve, who also played for Tottenham Hotspur, West Ham, Birmingham City and Sheffield Wednesday, not to mention Bedford Town and Tonbridge Angels!

Vulcano, in Spain, was Panini's outlet in the years before Franco's death and the fall of its fascist government. Spain's application to join the EEC in the late 1970s opened the door to Panini but before that time Vulcano was Panini's key to the relatively closed Iberian market, much as Top Sellers was key to the pre-EEC British market for Panini.

In 1974 Vulcano issued *Munich 1974*, a series of stickers that are, for all intents and purposes, the same as Panini's 74 World Cup collection. They were housed in a slightly different album, with Vulcano brand names and logos alongside those of Panini. For the stickers, values are the same as those for the Panini international issue, but the album is worth much more than the standard

Victoria Belgian stickers

1958 Vidall card

Vittorioso stickers

Vulcano packet of Futbol 76/77 stickers

edition, due to its differences. Following the 1974 World Cup, Vulcano issued *Futbol 75/76*, and *Futbol 76/77*. The stickers from these collections are worth £10 to £50 each, if they remain unused. Premium prices are paid for Cruyff, and for British football team emblems, for example, Liverpool and Leeds United, though being exotic Panini issues prices are set to rise for all and sundry, because many Panini completists have not yet realised Vulcano is out there!

Walker's Tobacco

ISSUED BY THE MAKERS OF THE WAYFARER RAINCOAT.

Wayfarer card

Webcosa gum inserts

Walker's Tobacco produced a series of *London Footballers* cards in the 1920s. This writer's publication, Football Card Collector Magazine, under the watch of its present publisher, Garry Daynes, unearthed the rare cards in 2012. Until that year they had been unknown. The small, monotone cards spent nearly a century in obscurity. Values are around £500 each card. Sadly Garry sold the cards before we could get images of them but they can be seen on the superlative Football Cartophilic Info Exchange, where you may find yourself happily distracted for an aeon.

Wayfarer Tailored Clothes issued large football trade cards in 1937. At first glance the cards appear to be press photographs but the Wayfarer Raincoats legend, afoot the image, confirms the cards are trade issues. The series

includes 30 glossy, monotone cards of football action. The cards are very rare and may sell for up to £100 each, depending on teams involved.

Webcosa was a bubblegum manufacturer. In 1960 it issued a series of colourful gum inserts which have become very much sought after. The footballer caricatures were issued on waxy paper, the inserts coming wrapped around sticks of gum. All known examples are creased. Values range from £20 to £200 each. The series of 48 includes an early image of Denis Law, for Manchester City. It's a stunning series to put together but the rarity factor of the four dozen ephemeral papers may frustrate any attempt to do so.

During 1962/63 Webcosa issued a second series of football

gum inserts. Often mistakenly called wrappers, the *Football Bingo* inserts were themselves issued within wrappers, folded around sticks of gum. The 80 inserts were sold creased and it's not possible to find them otherwise. They show caricatures of players, much like the potato-head men issued by Donaldson, on cards, in 1946. The series came with team check-list cards that double as bingo game cards, each listing 25 teams. The aim was to collect the waxy paper inserts of players, tick off the teams, and when the card was completely cancelled, to return the 25 inserts and a completed card to Webcosa for a prize. No wonder so few are extant today. Values range from £25 to £100 for each footballer, and unused checklist cards are worth £20 to 25 each.

Wilkes photocard

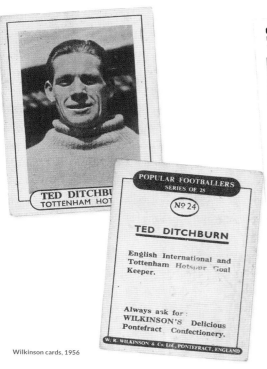

Wilkinson cards, 1956

Williams cards, 1970 Sweden

Williams cards, 1972, Sweden

Wilkes Photography was a Birmingham-based studio, a family firm of photographers, which had been established in Edwardian times by an Aston Villa footballer, Albert Wilkes (he'd also played for Walsall and West Brom). During the first seven decades of last century Wilkes Photography took thousands of photos of footballers and teams. The firm's demise, in 1970, and the digitisation of its archive, by its successor and beneficiary, in the 1990s, meant that the picture library Wilkes had built up, which had consisted of myriad postcards; tens of thousands of archive images; one-off printed photos of footballers and teams; celluloid negatives and glass plates; not to mention ephemera galore, and records going back 100 years, was simply destroyed! During the 1990s most newspaper and picture library collections met the same fate. Photographs were scanned then destroyed. Skips were filled with photos, removed and the images were dumped. Digital copies are all that remain of most picture library stock. Social history on card or paper photograph has been entrusted to electronics and the whims of the sun, its solar moods and the next super solar storm, which will come sooner or later. Private collections of paper will be worth more than gold as digital records across the world come to be lost in the wake of the next Carrington Event. It's due. Print your valuable records and photos now.

Due to the vast array of subjects recorded, values for teams and players photographed by Wilkes vary considerably. Postcards of teams and players from the 1910s may be worth over £100.

Cards from the 1940s and 50s, with the Wilkes rubber stamp on the back, are worth over £50 each in many cases.

Wilkinson of Pontefract issued a very attractive series of *Popular Footballers*, in 1956. The 25 trade cards are known with plain backs and, more usually, with printed backs. Values for unbranded types are around £100, while cards with printed backs are worth about £30 to £50 each, depending on the player and team.

Williams Forlag, of Sweden, issued cards for Panini in the years before Sweden became a member of the EEC. From 1971 it made football cards that were very similar to those issued by Top Sellers (Thorpe & Porter Sales), the British firm responsible for distributing Panini's early Italian cards in the UK. Williams had produced cards before this time but its 1960s fare is devotedly Swedish and outside the focus of this book. Its initial series with Panini interest (under the imprint, Ediraf) was a small set of 40 cards issued with a poster album called *VM Affischen Jättebild i Färg av Sveriges VM lag* (World Cup Posters Giant Pictures in Colour of Sweden's World Cup team). The cards include Bobby Moore, Geoff Hurst, Gordon Banks, Bobby Charlton, Francis Lee and Colin Bell; as well as stars of West Germany, Italy and Brazil, among an army of Swedes. Prices paid have exceeded £50 each card.

Williams issued more cards in the years to follow. Many more! *Fotboll 1971* and *Fotboll 72* have over 300 cards each, including many British players. The same images were used on the Panini

Top Sellers cards but the Williams cards have different backs. Prices paid for unused cards are around £10 to £15 each, with the notable exception of Pelé, for whom collectors have paid much more.

Ediraf, as Edizioni Raf is commonly known, was the publisher of Diabolik comic, a cult favourite among Italian youth and *giallo aficionadi* (horror film fans). As comic collectors may know, Diabolik is a Panini classic. Ediraf, the initial publisher of Diabolik, had its roots in Modena. Williams and Top Sellers cards with the imprint Ediraf can thus be traced to Panini, as can firms like STIG, a printer used on occasion by the Modena mounted man-at-arms knight.

Williams Swedish cards

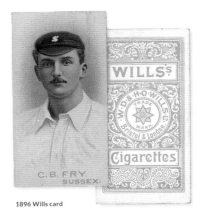

1896 Wills card

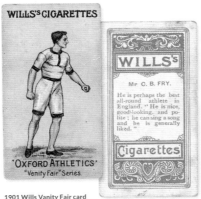

1901 Wills Vanity Fair card

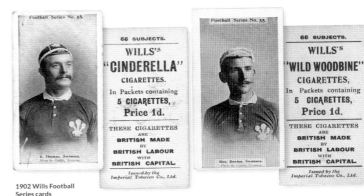

1902 Wills Football
Series cards

Williams Forlag also issued cards in Denmark. As well as issuing collections of cards that are similar to Top Sellers, namely *Fodbold 72/73*, Williams made a very attractive Danish series of cards to commemorate the 1974 World Cup: *Fodbold VM74*. The huge collection of cards includes George Best and John Charles, and many other global names. There are about 340 cards and 16 silk badge stickers, but the silk stickers are impossible to find nowadays. Values for cards range from £5 to £100 each. The national colours, on silks, may exceed even that figure! The series is a variant of the Ediraf collection issued in Italy at around the same time.

Wills produced some of the rarest as well as many of the commonest cigarette cards known.

The rarer end of the scale includes an 1896 series of cards which includes the definitive rookie card of Charles Burgess Fry, the legendary England international footballer. Fry played with Corinthians, as well as Southampton and Pompey. Charles Burgess Fry was also a legend on the cricket field. His 1901 record of six consecutive centuries still stands today! The 1896 Wills card of Fry was issued as part of a set made to celebrate the best England cricketers of the era. The Fry card is the set breaker, due to the many who seek it, and its value. Expect to pay a fee of three figures, even for a poor quality Fry. Note: there are also later Wills cricket cards showing Fry. Do not confound the 1896 rarity with later cricket cards!

In 1902 Wills issued Vanity Fair cards, which also include a fine example of Charles Burgess Fry. In the same year the firma also issued 66 soccer cards in a collection called *Football Series*. The cards are available in both violet and grey. Some players attract large premiums, for example, Smith of Corinthians. Values for the cards vary due to condition, player and team but they are usually quite easily available. Expect to pay £10 for most cards and up to £50 for highly sought-after players.

Wills issued *Football Club Colours* in 1907. The 50 cigarette cards in the series are valued at around £10 each.

In 1910 Wills published *International Footballers Season 1909-1910*. The 67 cigarette cards exhibit various backs: Flag Cigarettes, Scissors Cigarettes and United Services. Some players attract large premiums, for example, Billy Meredith. Cards with red backs tend to sell for around £10 each, but rarer blue back brands may fetch much more.

Wills issued a set called *Famous Footballers*, in 1914. The 50 cigarette cards come with two types of backs: Star Cigarettes, and Scissors Cigarettes. Values are around £10 each card though certain players attract much higher, premium prices.

Wills issued *Homeland Events* in 1932. Of the 54 cigarette cards in the set but a single card features football. It's special to Midlands football collectors. It shows West Brom versus

Birmingham City, at Wembley, in 1931. Club collectors may pay as much as £20 for this single card but patience will reward those who wait. It often comes up for sale in mixed lots, and it can be had for very little in such cases. Buy the lot, take the card and re-sell those you don't want.

The Wills Cigarettes 1935 series, called *Association Footballers*, is easily available. The 50 cards can often be found for £1 each, or less, but there are different printings known, for example, Irish issues, which cost more.

In 1936 Wills made a series called *Irish Sportsmen*. The 50 cards are not easy to acquire. Footballers are included and you will probably have to pay over £10 each for those you want.

Wills issued a series called *British Sporting Personalities*, in 1937. The 48 cigarette cards include some footballers, Ted Drake of Arsenal being one example. Most cards can be had for £2 each but the soccer stars often cost more.

Wills issued *Association Footballers* in 1939. The cards were issued in slightly different formats in different parts of the British Isles but they are easy to find and usually cost around £1 each.

Winston Sporties were issued by S&B Products, an imprint owned by Baytch Brothers. The cards were an earlier version of those known as *Torry Gillicks Internationals*. Issued in 1948, in Scotland, the 64 trade cards are very rare and some cards, like Billy Liddell, of Liverpool, have sold for over £50.

1907 Wills Club
Colours cards

1909/10 Wills International
Footballers Season cards

1914 Wills Famous
Footballers cards

Wills Sporting Personalities card

1922 Wizard cards

1923 Wizard cards

1930s Wills cards

Wizard was a comic born of the 1920s. Its first sports card issue was released in 1922. Wizard announced the cards as *Hand Coloured Real Photos of Footballers* but the cards themselves display the legend: *British Team of Footballers*, *Our Greatest Players in Real Photos*. The 11 cards are worth up to £5 each.

The second series of cards by Wizard was launched in the 1922/23 season. The 18 cards are untitled but they can be identified by the inscription: *'with the editor's compliments'*. Wizard was very popular, and many cards were issued. Sturdy, quality cards like these found their way into adult collections and many have survived thanks to being looked after in that way – unlike many other trade cards from the time. Presently the cards are quite easily available, and £5 each is about the right price to pay, but for how long it remains that way is another matter. It only needs a handful of new collectors on the scene and cards that are presently easy to obtain will become scarce.

In 1929 Wizard launched a series of metal amulets. The miniature shield-shaped artefacts are called *Secret Signs & Footballers*. Individual amulets are known for Arsenal, Leeds and Liverpool (which have sold for over £100 each), and also for Huddersfield Town and Pompey. Rare items indeed, these are cross-over collectibles with comic collectors vying with football fans for them, and this drives up the price. Wizard free gifts from this time, until the Second World War, are much scarcer than cards issued by the same comic in the 1920s.

Wizard issued a fabulous collection called *The A.B.C Chart of Football Colours*, in 1932. The puzzle game consists of four large cards, each featuring many club colours; and 128 stickers of famous footballers. Placing the footballer upon his club colours was the point of the exercise, so sheets of stickers were cut and single footballers were glued on to their club colours cards. Values for uncut sheets of stickers start at £100 each. A complete set of four cards and all stickers, with all eight items uncut and unused, is worth around £500. Prices for single, cut cards, and cut stickers

1929 Wizard Secret Sign amulets

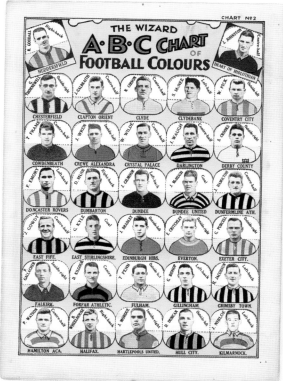

1932 Wizard ABC chart

1955 Wizard Famous Footballers card

1959 Wizard Football Stars cards

(paired) sell for £2 to £5 each. The higher value is in the uncut material.

After the war Wizard launched *Famous Footballers*. The 24 red-back cards were issued in strips of quads. Values for uncut foursomes range from £25 to £50, depending upon the players included. Single cut cards are worth around £2 each.

Similar fare came with Wizard's 1955 series of 25 *Famous Footballers*. The cards were cut from strips. They have backs in magenta and were issued in strips of five cards each. Values for uncut strips range from £30 to £50. Single cut cards are worth £2.

In 1959 Wizard issued *Football Stars of 1959*, yet the cards do not feature the names of stars one might expect. There is no Bobby Charlton, no Jimmy Greaves, and no Brian Clough. However, it's a great series for showing off the lesser seen stars, the less well known names of the British leagues at the time. The cards were issued in strips. Some strips have octets, while others have a dozen stars. The 44 cards have dark blue backs. Values are in the uncut sheets which are worth £40 to £80, the higher price being paid for sheets of a dozen. Single, cut cards are worth £2.

In 1970 Wizard comic issued a colourful set of *Great Captains* cards, which were issued in a sheet of a dozen cards, to cut. An uncut sheet is worth £30 but higher prices are paid for a sheet with the original comic with which it came. Single, cut cards are worth £2 each though all-time greats like Billy McNeill, Billy Bremner and Bobby Charlton may sell for more.

Wizard also issued *The Great Stars of Football* in 1970. The cards were cut from sheets. In all, 16

cards of postcard dimensions were issued, in two sheets of eight cards each. Values for cut single cards range from £5 to £20. George Best tends to attract the top price. Cards in uncut sheets command prices that are much higher.

In 1970 Wizard issued iron-on transfers of *Famous Footballers*. The decals were seemingly all ironed on to something as few have been seen since. Issued in strips of four, used George Best decals (cut from scrapbooks) have been seen to sell for £50 each.

Wizard gave away *Super Photos of Famous Footballers*, in 1971. The stickers were printed in sheets of 12 players, to be cut out. The green paper sheets were issued folded in two halves. The paper was gummed, ready for sticking cut players to a wallchart which was also issued by the comic. Complete sheets are very rare, and may be found with folds that have become glued together. The slightest damp, typical of what accrues after a year in the British climate, never mind half a century, has damaged many of the remaining uncut sheets. Thus, the value for a complete sheet is over £100. Single players, cut out, are worth £8 each, with more paid for George Best and other big names of the day.

1970 Wizard Great Stars card

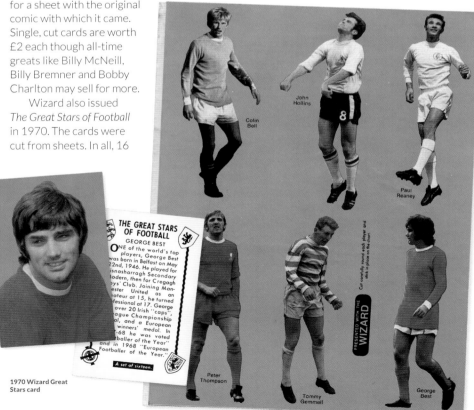

1971 Wizard Super Photos

Wizard All-Stars Ring

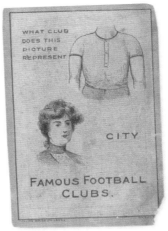

Wood Brothers card.

WS Verlag cards.

1962 WS Verlag cards

In March 1973 Wizard issued *The All-Star Sports Ring* and a sheet of stickers. A similar gift, a set of stickers and a plastic ring, had been issued with The Hornet comic, in October of 1972. The Wizard *Super Stick-on Pictures of Stars of Sport and Show Business* were similarly designed to be peeled and stuck on to the plastic ring. Rarity factor for a complete sheet of stickers and a ring is extremely high. The best chance of finding one is probably through a specialist comics seller, or comics auction. If it comes to a general internet auction chances are the seller won't know they are selling, and it won't be properly described. The collection includes Kenny Dalglish, of Celtic, Allan Clarke, Kevin Keegan, Rodney Marsh, etc. A sheet of stickers with the ring may sell for £150 if ever the set comes to market, and knowledgeable bidders are in place.

Wood Brothers made puzzle cards called *Famous Football Clubs*, in 1900. Values for such exceed £150. The Manchester City puzzle card features a *man*, his *chest*, and a woman (*her*) with a metropolitan centre as the suffix: *city*.

WS Verlag made cards in Wanne-Eickel. The town name is often confused with the publisher. The West German issuer made some of the most notable football cards of the 1960s. Prior to the Heinerle cards revolution WS Verlag had been making football postcards. The *Sportbilder* postcards of 1952 and 1953 consisted of 320 cards made in two series. The earlier cards have white borders, whereas the later issues are golden. Values range from £10 to £50 each, with higher prices often paid for notable football greats.

The firm's 1954 *Fussball Weltmeisterschaft* includes 160 cards. The values for such cards,

unused, are around £5 each, with premium prices paid for world greats. The 1958 issue of *Fussball Weltmeisterschaft* included 128 cards, whose prices start at £10 each, but very high premiums are paid for world greats.

Imitating Heinerle, the Wanne-Eickel producer came to make very stylish alternatives to its competitor. It issued *Fussball Weltmeisterschaft 1962* for the World Cup in Chile. Today the cards are mostly valued at £5 each, but very high premiums are often charged for cards of world greats.

WS Verlag went on to issue many other series of cards but most are devoted solely to German leagues and, therefore, outside the scope of this tome.

X is a secret never to be told

ARBITRO
Equivoco o giustizia?

Xtremely funny!

Xtremely rare!

Xtremely important!
First black professional
player to feature on a card

Xtremely costly!

is a secret never to be told. But they never said anything about writing it down. Card connoisseurs, album buyers, sought-after sticker sellers, rookie card hunters, the top collectors, and all of the people who've amassed the rarest cards, or made money from the scarcest ephemera, enjoy certain, privileged information. The information pertains to finding the rare gems, the how, the where and the when. Locating rare and profitable cards has its secret methods. These tricks were known to but a few – until now. The once jealously guarded secrets, as detailed in Appendix 1, and mentioned elsewhere in this book, will help to bring you prize cards.

Buyers will also find treasures on mercadolibre.com, which represents all of South America! You may need a little time to get used to how it works but it's worth every second spent, and so is every use of internet translators. They'll help you catch a rare card, if not a big fish. Remember: dollar prices on mercadolibre.

com are in local South American currencies. The dollar prices seen convert to as little as 10% of what you'd expect. They're not Greenbacks! In Scandinavia finn.no is Norway's Ebay, and tradera. se is Sweden's internet auction. Most Norsk and Svensk people speak English. If not, use an internet translator. They are easy.

For more card secrets, on buying and selling, and the best places to find treasure; for auction terminology in foreign languages, and bidding tactics, and much more, see Appendix 1.

Xuereb is a name associated with card issuers like Tip-Top, A&BC Gum, and Somportex. A certain Mr. Xuereb issued cards and stickers from his shop, in Valletta, Malta, from the late 1950s until around 1970. His wares were often related – very closely related, it seems – to official products made by the above-named marques. Mr. Xuereb was from North America. His contacts included people at Bazooka Gum, in the USA, and his neighbour in Valletta was a worker at Somportex Gum, in England. Xuereb's

produce bears great similarity to the wares made by those firms, and to that produced by their rivals, however, his first collection of cards, from the 1950s was unique. See: Tip-Top.

Xuereb is believed to be responsible for a series of World Cup footballers on sticker stamps that bear a resemblance to the 1966 stamps made by A&BC Gum. Different types of these Maltese stamps have been seen. Some papers are slightly larger than others, though the images are of the same dimensions. Some have glossy coatings, others not. Prices paid over the last 10 years have topped £100 each, rising to as much as £500, for Pelé, for whom there are two versions known: one with blue rays and one without. The Lev Yashin sticker is worth noting as it is very different from that by A&BC. For an image of a Xuereb sticker on a postcard see: A&BC Gum.

Yanky Bubblegum issued *Popular Footballers*, in 1948. The cards have the legend: *Buy Yanky Gum, It's Best!* They were printed on cardstock of different colours (pink, green and blue cards are

Xuereb stickers
Courtesy of Peter Dunning

Zaini colour cards

Zucconi card

PREMIATA FABBRICA DI CIOCCOLATO
GIULIO ZUCCONI
SESTO FIORENTINO

LE GRANDI MARCHE
SUPERCINEMA
CIOCCOLATO CINEMA
CARAMELLA FILMS

Zaini cards

known). Values start at £50 each. Many variants and errors are known. The cards are believed to have been published by Kiddy's Favourites, in Glasgow.

Zaini was a major Italian cards producer in the 1920s and 1930s. In the early 1930s Zaini issued cards in sepia tones, showing photographs of famous footballers and football teams. The legend, Cioccolato Zaini, can be seen to the front of the cards. The backs are often plain. Values for such Zaini cards tend to kick off around £20 but sellers apply hefty premiums to prices for legends like Meazza, Combi and other stars of the Italian World Cup-winning side of 1934.

Around 1934, Zaini produced cards with footballers and teams in colour, not to mention war cards showing Italian troops in African colonies. The cards have an oval Zaini logo to the rear. Values for these start around £30 but prices rise sharply for cards with Piola and other greats from the two World Cup winning teams of 1934 and 1938.

Around 1934, Zaini produced cards with footballers and teams in colour, not to mention war cards showing Italian troops in African colonies. The cards have an oval Zaini logo to the rear. Values for these start around £30 but prices rise sharply for cards with Piola and other greats from the two World Cup winning teams of 1934 and 1938.

Zuban of Germany made *Torwart* cards in 1928. The 240 stunning black and white photographic cards, with gothic inscriptions, show mostly German players but there are also some internationals. The cards are worth £20 each, for unused examples, and higher premiums will be applied by canny sellers for greats of the game like the Spaniard, Samitier.

Zucconi of Italy issued *Sporting Heroes* in the 1920s. These incredibly rare photographic cards of sportsmen start at £50 each, with much higher, premium prices paid for sporting legends like Jack Dempsey.

Appendix 1 Buying

Tactics and techniques

The regular American buyer opens Ebay.com just as the Brit scans Ebay.co.uk, and the Italian glances at Ebay.it. Yet, the smartest buyers don't only look at Ebay. They also register with Delcampe, and with Todocoleccion. Some also join Mercadolibre, Tradera, Finn and Coisas, and they do well because most non-English speakers sell off Ebay, on national sites like these. The many foreign auction sites are just a part of the secret, though other Ebay sites are important too. Many smart buyers use up to ten different Ebay sites!

Collectors may have up to 100 favourite searches registered on Ebay. They receive Emails when an *A&BC checklist*, or a *Messi rookie* gets listed, or whatever it is they have asked to be notified about. The same is true on delcampe.net and on todocoleccion.net. International collections sites like these have English language interfaces, and you can follow sales, save searches and do all the things you do on Ebay. The difference is you can find rare items, often for less, of things that don't appear on Ebay. Such sites will also send Emails to you when your saved searches bear fruit.

Few buyers know that you can, with a little work and effort, list up to 1,000 searches on Ebay. If you are a serious collector it's surprising how quickly you will fill the 100 slots on your national Ebay page. So, how do you go about getting up to 1,000 saved searches? It's quite easy. There is no Ebay law about having multiple buyer accounts. So, after you have saved 100 searches on ebay.co.uk, go to ebay.ie and open an account there. You can use an actual address, one that's based in Ireland (read on for how) and save 100 searches there.

If you are not registered on a foreign country's Ebay site you won't see many of its items for sale. For example, if you are seeking a Zidane rookie card you may see one or two on .com but if you go to ebay.fr you will see many more. However, if you are not located in France, or, if you don't have an Ebay account in France, you will still not see all of the results available. This is why sophisticated buyers register as users on foreign Ebay sites. You do not need a house in the foreign country. Go to an internet map of a big city in Ireland, select a street and a postcode, pick a number, and you are halfway there. Use an Email address from a portal Email service (there are thousands to choose from) and away you go! You won't be having stuff sent to the mock addresses you used to open foreign accounts, it's just for searching. Once you are registered, with a local address, you will see all of the items that match your searches. If you find something you want, add your real address to your account – yes, it's possible – then, ask the seller to sell to you at your home address. If you offer to pay registered postage chances are he or she will oblige. Foreign languages are easy if you use an internet translator. Keep sentences short and to the point, and use clear language, and the translator will do the trick.

Next, do the same on ebay.de, then to ebay.ph, to ebay.es, to ebay.com.au and so on. If you have trouble with foreign languages then don't worry. Ebay uses similar account structures, no matter what the national site is. So, open an English language Ebay account-opening window page next to the Spanish page, or any other foreign account-opening page, and you can go along step by step, creating a foreign account just as you would in English. Use an internet translator where necessary. In no time you will be ready to search as a Spaniard or as a German. If you really can't deal with languages use the Canadian, Irish and Australian sites, as well as the main Ebay page, ebay.com. With the British site that'll give you 500 searches.

So, with up to 1,000 search results, and being able to scan over 10 different Ebay sites, with the possibility of seeing everything, you will have the edge on other collectors. Note: to easily change from one site to another without opening and closing windows, just click into the URL bar of your browser and change the domain suffix (the .com to a .ie for Ireland, or a .es for Spain, or .de for Germany, and so on). The top buyers and collectors have been doing this for years. It's how they get some of their rarities.

You don't have to wait for stuff to come to auction, to find rarities. Write to sellers directly. Write off the cuff. Send notes to all and any sellers, asking whether they have any cards of such and such, or this type or that kind of collectible. It often results in a yes, and a satisfactory deal. Remember, most sellers have more stuff than they have time to list. A quick message often reminds them of what they have, and knowing you want it many sellers will make you a direct offer.

Some sellers on foreign auction sites only take bank transfers, but most accept PP. Many sellers in Germany have moved to bank transfers, away from PP, due to diminishing postal services, thanks mostly to privatisation. Be careful with bank transfers! In Europe they are free, or cost very little, to EU citizens but outside the EU you will pay £10 or $20 to your beloved bank before you even start!

Words for football card searches, to use when searching foreign language sites

If you are too lazy to open an online dictionary, here are some key terms used in auctions abroad. In Spain: cromo, cromos, tarjeta, futbol, futbolista, pegatina, despegados, etc. Words to use in Portuguese are figurita, futebol, etc. In French try chromo, foot, cpa, carte, vignette, etc.

**Spanish playmoney famous footballers,
1940s & 50s, including Zarra and Kubala**

In German use: sammelbild, sammeln, bilder, fussball, zigaretten, fussball bild, fußball, etc. Use these terms with players names or teams you seek. Remember to use country names in the correct languages. Searching for 'England' in Spanish will result in little. Searching for 'Inglaterra' will retrieve much more. In French, Escosse, Angleterre, etc. In Italian, Scozia, Galles, Inghilterra... etc. Look up names and terms in foreign languages. Use an internet translator. It's never been easier.

Old versus new

Rare cards are not the cards that were made yesterday, or ten years ago, no matter what card producers and collectors of new cards and stickers will tell you.

Rare cards, like some of the cards in this book, are not the recently printed cards with foil-stamped, limited edition numbers, and swatches of material that are claimed to be from player-worn jerseys. Really rare cards may be extant in numbers of less than a handful, worldwide. They are not contemporary cards that shout: *Limited Edition*, or *Mega Rare*! Such newly made chase cards may be brilliant marketing devices, and they may be hard to find when they are new; they may even be hotly collected but they are new, and someone, somewhere has a stock of them. New issues are very effective at making a handful of card executives wealthy but they are not rare when compared to some of the cards in this book, like the Clark's Toffee cards, of which only one or two are known!

Be a little careful of recent cards and ephemera that say, 'collectible' or 'limited edition'. New cards have been made for a market: you. Older cards were merely a sideline, an inexpensive product, a free gift, an advertising toy, and they

were mostly made for children, at children's pocket money prices. Few, if any, cards from before 1970 were advertised as limited editions, or collectibles.

For some, buying rare cards is a way of sharing risk. They buy cards partly due to concerns about the value of fiat money, which is devaluing daily. Fiat money is value that is created out of nothing, out of thin air. Fiat means to be decreed, to be created without effort. Money is created in this way by central banks, and the top bankers get rich from it, by acquiring securities for their bank's balance sheet with such money. Greenbacks and other paper folding stuff, like pounds Sterling, Euros, and so on, are all fiat money. There is no gold standard. It is literally created out of nothing and you cannot take it to your bank and ask for the gold equivalent, as you could do once upon a time. You may have heard of Quantitative Easing. It's banker babble for printing cheap money. Well, for free, actually. Free if you are a central banker, that is. Billions of notes are printed, at no cost to them. The new paper is loaned, at real cost, to regular people, for whom 25 years of life is the typical payback (for a mortgage). The bank gets a sworn security – your home – in return for ... not much cost to them, really. Bankers earn commissions on this. The bind of fiat money has made even them look to alternative assets, and some bankers now collect rare and valuable football cards!

Please note, this is not investment advice. This writer has never lost a penny with cards but it's a road of risk, and you can lose as well as win.

Italian cards, and packet of game cards, 1960s - 1980s

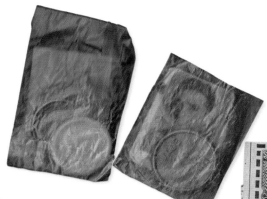

Italian packets of plastic coins and football cards, c.1949

Appendix 2 **Selling**

Strategies for the sale of cards on internet auctions

You can't just list your cards for sale on an internet auction and have success. You need to work them, and you won't get far without a little marketing. You need to make your cards visible, to be seen, and to be shown elsewhere if you want buyers to find you on one in a million auction pages. You need to ensure buyers buy from you and not from other sellers with the same cards. There are plenty of sellers selling the same cobwebbed cards. Research what's already for sale. Find out what other sellers are selling their cards for before you take the time to list your own. It's daft to spend hours photographing, editing images, writing listings and uploading if you are just putting more of the same into the market, and at higher prices. You'll sell nothing.

Try to list cards other sellers do not have. Contact other sellers to announce your cards. They may not be happy to hear from you but they won't forget you and it creates glances. On internet auctions glances mean more chances. More chances of selling! This is because Delcampe, Todocoleccion and Ebay, to name but three internet auction sites, show your glances to other punters. Everything you look at gets shared with people looking at similar stuff. If no one is looking at your cards you won't get third party glances either. If you only have cards that other sellers have, then list them for less. Lower prices mean more looks, and more sales.

Use auctions, not 'Buy It Now'. This is because only auctions get shared a lot. Internet auctioneers do not show 'Buy It Now' sales in as many search results. Less people see them, so fewer glances are generated. Put a low starting price on your auction. It leads to more glances, which lead to more bidders. More bids means more shares. Ebay shares items with bids. Watch and get your friends to watch your sales. The more looks an item attracts, the more Delcampe, Todocoleccion and Ebay share that item.

Strategy, allying with other sellers, and doing deals between you both, so that you are not offering the same cards, is productive. Looking at each other's cards for sale, as well as 'watching', or 'following' (as it's called on Todocoleccion) will increase the number of glances that internet auction sites share.

Use top photography, high quality scans, and nicely edited pictures for your sales.

Pictures sell!

Some sellers use inflated prices followed by reductions to shift stock. No matter that an inflated price is laughable, a price reduced by 50%, and advertised as such, will appeal to someone or other, sooner or later. It's a good tactic.

Word of mouth moves material. Tell, share and blog about your sales.

Italian Gazza banknote, Spanish England team and coin, Perfetti wax paper gum insert of Napoli

Sun token for Sun Swapcards, John Toshack

Appendix 3 Bidding

The esoteric stuff

Wilkins and Barnes on Italian and Spanish cards;
Terry Butcher on an Italian sticker

Bidding is an art. It is a black art. Bidding should be secret and your bids unknown to others but there are ways of revealing what others have bid, and how they do it. If you haven't played poker the following advice may pass you by: keep a poker face (even on the internet), don't give away *tells*, and make them pay! Basically, it means be like an assassin. You can't kill them but you can bid up your auction competitors quite legally. It's part of the fun. Try it! This is not the same as a seller bidding up his buyers using shill bids. That's not right, and it's a crime.

Bidding up a competitor, whether you want something or not, is not only satisfying, it is effective. It is not personal, it is business. It is about making sure another buyer pays through the nose for outbidding you, or just for being there at the wrong time. Your time! In impoverishing an opponent you pay less for other things. The less cash he has the less he will bid for. The lower she is forced to bid, due to depleted cash reserves, the less you have to pay to outbid her. Some bidders place the same bid on a dozen items. Once you know their typical top bid it's easy to bid up all 12 bids.

Let's say there is an internet auction which interests you. Go to the bidding history. Look at the bids. If the top bidder has placed two bids then he or she is daft, and you can make the most of it. Bid them up incrementally, using the minimum bid amount. You will know when you are closing in when you see you have placed a bid that comes between their two top bids. Stop now or risk going too far. Unless you like a thrill! Remember, you don't want to buy something you can't afford, but can you resist adding £50 to a competitor's bill? Some bidders leave artificially low, lower bids. Their upper bids may be much higher. Is it worth going

on? That's up to you. Alas, this exciting feature is no longer possible to exploit on delcampe.net but Ebay still allows it.

On Ebay careless bidders may leave a bid that's an unusual figure. This gives away their top bid. Let's say, for example, that you bid £20.00 for an item. If you see the top bidder's bid is now £21.00, you may want to bid £22.00. You do so. Next, you see the top bid has risen to £22.44, an odd figure. This tells you that it's your opponent's top bid! You only need bid £23.45 to outbid them!

Another way of doing things is to use an unusual bid increment yourself. Let's say the top bid showing is £42.00 and you want to find out how high the top bid goes, do not try £43.00 but try £43.17 or £43.62. If the top bidder's maximum is a round figure you will know, sooner or later. Yes, it can be a little risky but it's only cards, not houses. Bidding up competitive collectors is useful because it depletes their funds so they think twice about future bids, and that means you are more likely to be able to buy other cards for less. It also serves to increase the value of a card you may have for sale. If you can show that a card sold for a very high price, then your example of that very same card may seem to be a bargain, when you offer it for less. That's always attractive.

Todocoleccion extend the time of a sale if late bids are added but it allows anonymous bids. Did you know that Sunday traders get many cards from Todocoleccion? They do. Then they turn them around on Ebay and make profits. Get in there!

Delcampe has automatic limits for bids, so you cannot use colourful figures to freak out competitors, nor to mislead them. However, Delcampe is a site that's worth scouring for the profits that bloom on Ebay often budded on Delcampe, for a lot less. It's possible to meet some

of Ebay's top sellers on Delcampe. They won't be happy to see you there!

Spotting shill bidding

On Ebay you can often tell which sellers use a friend to bid up their buyers, because they keep the auction bidder names hidden. This way they can bid you up without you knowing a thing about who is doing it, whether it's a genuine bidder or a shill. Clicking on a user's name allows you to see their history, how many bids they have with a certain seller. You cannot do this if the seller hides the bidders. They are probably up to no good. A no good called Shill. Report suspected shill sales to the auction platform you are using. When Ebay receive a handful of reports they take action against crooked sellers.

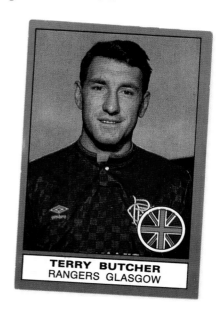

TERRY BUTCHER
RANGERS GLASGOW

Appendix 4 Recommended and Reliable

The right people for rare cards, the best auctioneers, and a list of exotic auction sites

Garry Daynes runs Football Card Collector Magazine, which he took over from this writer 20 years ago. He issues it yearly.

Send £5 for a sample back copy, to the following address: FCCM, PO Box 234, Capel St Mary, Ipswich, IP9 2DZ, and please mention Carl's book when writing to him. Garry knows more about rare football cards than most, he has plenty for sale, and he has a decent knowledge of modern cards too.

Tim Davidson's internet, postal and public auctions are held monthly. With Tim you can buy and sell cigarette cards, trade cards, postcards and other collectibles and rarities (records, posters, matchbox labels, beer bottle labels, and so on). Tim and his delightful staff, Julie and Rachel, run public auctions at select venues in Nottingham, and they are based at New Market House, Meadow Lane, Nottingham, NG2 3GY. Write to them there.

Email: **timdavidsonauctions@hotmail.co.uk**
Website: **www.timdavidsonauctions.co.uk**

Loddon Auctions are based in Arborfield, Berkshire and are long-established specialists in the sale of cigarette and trade cards and all other forms of collectibles including football programmes, match tickets, postcards, and much more. Bi-monthly sales of 1,200 lots and entries always invited. Competitive commission rates and all sales are featured live on the internet. Contact auctioneer and valuer, Gary Arkell. Please mention Carl's book when writing to him.

Email: **info@loddonauctions.co.uk**
Website: **www.loddonauctions.co.uk**

Alan Jenkins does not sell cards but he has all of the info about them! He runs the Football Cartophilic Info Exchange. One visit to his incredible website and you'll probably never leave. Please mention Carl's book when writing to him.

Email: **alanjenkins1899@gmail.com**
Website: **www.cartophilic-info-exch.blogspot.com**

Internet auction sites that will repay your interest:

www.delcampe.net is a Pan-European collectibles site, with English language

www.mercadolibre.com is a South American collectibles site

www.coisas.com is a Portuguese collectibles site

www.todocoleccion.net is a Spanish collectibles site, with English language

www.tradera.se is a Swedish website where those American dealers get their rare 1958 Pelé cards!

www.footballsoccercards.com is where you can stay up to date with cards research and news

Appendix 5 Storage

Storage, slabbed cards and card populations

Storing cards is down to personal taste. A garage full of 1,000s of blocks of plastic may bring happiness to some but this writer prefers less plastic and more contact. Not touching a Da Vinci, and seeing it through a protective plastic plate is understandable. But a rare card you paid to own? It's an artefact to have in the hand. When you touch plastic you feel 2015. You don't feel the card's age. You paid for it but you can't touch it? A relic at home deserves personal contact. You would not put your Victorian ornament in a plastic box. Would you seal your antique flintlock, or your old medals in plastic? None of the antiques at an antique fair are sealed in plastic. Touch is a vital human sense. You can tell a lot by touch. Not being able to take out a card and have actual physical contact with a treasure you own, is sad. Just looking at it inside a plastic slab seems a shame. It dampens the pleasure in collecting arcane ephemera. However, it is acknowledged that some people are happy with a spare room full of plastic slabs, each containing but one card.

Some collectors defend plastic no matter what environmentalists say. Maybe they have invested heavily in slabs, or maybe they sell cards that are slabbed. Maybe they are indirectly involved in the plastics business. Maybe they just like plastic! Other people prefer a modest number of attractive albums with polypropylene pouched pages, or paper and card pages which are a lot better for the planet.

Most American and European collectors use polyurethane storage albums, like those made by Glen and Ultra Pro. They contain polypropylene pages. They are not great for the environment, to say the least, but such albums contain less plastic than the same number of cards sealed in plastic slabs would contain, that's for sure. Albums do the job of showing off a lot of cards very well.

Some collectors now prefer stamp accessories, like display cards, paper stock books and stamp albums with mounts. Prophila and Wessex make these. Stamp stock cards are another easy way to collect older paper ephemera, though modern sports cards need something sturdier than philatelic supplies. Until an eco-friendly alternative is available, polypropylene pages in polyurethane albums may be the best bet.

Work is being done on developing an environment-friendly storage alternative. For more news on such things, as and when they are available, please follow this writer's social media and websites for updates (see appendix 7).

The history of slabbing, in the shake of a snow globe, is this: once upon a time there was a seller who wanted to make more money. He advertised a service he'd dreamed up. [The result of a pact with Mephistopheles?] For a little money from everyone he encouraged collectors to send their rare cards to him. He said the cards would be worth more money if he sealed them inside blocks of plastic. For some reason a few people believed him and paid. People being people, before long, more people copied the example set by the first. In the plastic coatings he included a note, on which he printed data about the card. In no time at all he made himself quite wealthy, thanks to other people's cards. One of today's most respected intellectuals, Noam Chomsky, calls this kind of thing the 'manufacturing of consumers'. Selling something no one needs. It's an art. It's a black art. Slabbers sing that slabbed cards are protected from handling. So are cards in albums. A collection of 1,000 cards, each slabbed, would fill a small car.

Many collectors have collections of 10,000 cards, or more. If you don't have a spare garage to fill, you'll have a viewing problem with a lot of slabs. To see one card will need a lot of lumping, moving boxes full of heavy plastic, whereas an album can be taken off a shelf and hundreds of cards may be looked at immediately.

Moreover, do not take it for granted that everything you see written on soccer card slabs is correct! No doubt it's well meant but it may be wrong. Soccer cards and other antique football ephemera have been made in Europe since the 1880s, and in South America since the 1900s. The slabbers are based in North America, a continent where baseball, gridiron, hockey and basketball rule. Slabbers are experts in American sports cards, without question, but Old World football cards from Europe; and Spanish or Portuguese language cards from Latin America, often defy correct evaluation in the New World.

The informative and highly educational book, *The Card*, by Michael O'Keeffe is an entertaining shocker! It explains how little time slabbers give to cards they grade – all but a few seconds each – and how easily mistakes happen. One example of a mistake in slabber grading is the flashy series issued by Raven. The supposedly Spanish imprint issued cards sometime during or shortly after the Millennium. The cards celebrate Manchester United, Fergie's Fledglings, the amazing youngsters of the 1990s. The cards are similar to the Futera cards of the late 1990s, but a little more developed. They include David Beckham, Paul Scholes and pals. These cards are a classic example of soccer card slabbing that's gone wrong. They have been wrongly graded by slabbers as being 1995 cards. This has caused years of exaggerated prices and many losses to buyers who believed the erroneous grades and dates on the slabs. The Raven cards are a little misleading. Raven used old photos and erroneous info, like Beckham's first cap being in 1995. Rubbish! Were the cards actually made in 1995 no one would have missed that preposterous fact. His first cap came in autumn 1996, after the 1996 Euros, which he played no part in. But the real give-away, the evidence is the technology. The print finish is 2000, at the earliest! Cards from 1995 (Merlin Gold, Premier Striker, etc.) were good but they were not of such high quality. The tech was not available in the mid-1990s to make cards like the Raven cards. Yet slabbers fell for the con. A gallery of wrongly graded slabbed mistakes is available at **www.facebook.com/rarecards**

Card populations versus demographics

Since slabbers started sealing cards in blocks of plastic, so-called population reports have been compiled on certain websites. These stats may be useful for baseball cards, hockey cards and other American sports cards. Most European collectors, and many South American collectors of soccer cards do not speak English, or know of the American sites that run the card populations tables. They do not send away to slab their cards nor do they have their cards included by the census takers at slabber central. The card population tables are a good idea, and they may

work for baseball cards, but they reflect soccer card reality through a skewed set of data.

Further, most Italian collectors have never heard of slabbing, or card population tables. Among the 60 million Italians there are many thousands of rare cards. Few, if any, of these are recorded on card population tables. The same goes for France, Germany, Argentina, Brazil, and even Britain and Ireland. Most very rare cards in the British Isles are in the hands of retired gentlemen of a certain sensibility. They do not, typically, pay to send their cards to be slabbed and recorded in the USA. So, do not take it for granted that a card showing as very rare on a league table is quite that rare. Conversely, cards not showing on such league tables, and seemingly non extant, may actually exist, and in some numbers. Most Baines cards do not show on league tables.

Real populations are, however, very useful in giving pointers to what cards are rare. Countries with small populations tend to issue cards in smaller amounts, so Greece, Portugal, Finland, Ireland and Malta should be the focus of searches. Chile, Paraguay, Uruguay, Peru and Bolivia, too. Countries with bigger populations had more cards issued. So, more cards from such lands remain extant. Wartime destruction is also a factor to consider. In Germany the 1930s population was huge but large areas of Germany

were fire-bombed. West Germany, the smaller country that emerged from the French, British and American zones after World War Two, was only half the size of what Germany once was, and is today, so West German trade issues in the 1950s are often rarer than 1920s Weimer cigarette cards, or 1930s Third Reich trade cards.

Languages play a big part in rare cards collecting. Contacting Greek merchants, Russian retailers, Arabic vendors, and Serbian sellers is a challenge. They not only speak little, if any, English, they don't use the Latin alphabet. Internet translators are only part of the solution. The best bet is to find such sellers on **www.delcampe.net** (many Balkan vendors and former Soviet bloc traders use Delcampe) and let them find the cards for you. Buying an inexpensive postcard, picture or stamp permits you to contact the seller (Delcampe otherwise forbids contact, unless you join its gold club). Ask, offer and encourage the foreign seller to find you cards from their country. It saves a lot of work! The same applies for Latin language sellers in Argentina, Brazil, and Peru. They are often to be found on **www.todocoleccion.net** and **www.mercadolibre.com**

Contact, contact, contact. The more you write to sellers in exotic lands, the more rare cards you will find come your way. Really rare cards!

Various European trade cards, 1910s - 1970s

Appendix 6 **It's not just cards**

And it's not only soccer cards. AWOL and MIA

Football collectibles of worth range from badges to boxed games, from pennants to match tickets and pre-war programmes. The time is ripe for buying such antiquities and quality wares, if the prices are fair. The coming World Cup tournaments in Qatar and North America will see costs for such vintage fare rise. The inevitable passing away of great footballers of yesteryear will see spikes in prices of cards showing the stars of the past. If you seek to buy something of quality, that does not cost a lot, but will increase in value, choose older material. You can be sure it's no longer being made, and that there are not containers of it, in storage, sitting on the quayside, awaiting their moment.

As well as cards, boxed games from the 1950s and 60s are undervalued. World Cup collectibles from the tournaments before World War Two are rare and costly – even a poster stamp can cost hundreds of dollars – but those from the World Cups in the 1950s, through until the 1980s, are often under-priced. Football cards and stickers from before 1980, but especially from before 1970, are the ones to go for. Older badges and key fobs too. Items with players seem to do better than ones with just club emblems. Beware signed material! A lot of signed material is faked. Unless you saw a photo or a card being signed how do you know it's not been signed by the seller, or one of his mates? You can see reams of signed cards on internet auctions. Isn't it funny how those long-gone players all used the same broad-nib, coloured ink marker pens? And how did the seller get those 20 young billionaires together to sign his creased cards? Did they have nothing better to do with their time? Try getting one of them to sign anything! Have you noticed that the dodgy squiggles of ink are often on cheap cards, or home produced photos? *Pro-Set* and *Shooting Stars* cards, which can cost as little as pennies, are cost effective for forgers; almost cheaper than the photos they print at home. Signed shirts? Some are, yes, but many are not genuine. Old cards are best!

It's not just football

Other cards are a wonderful way of not only enjoying the past but of appreciating its artists and designers. Very few creative people become famous, like Salvador Dali or David Hockney, but many artists and designers were employed by trade cards issuers of the past. There are many diminutive works of art out there, waiting for you to discover. Though unsigned, and not recognised as artists's cards, many trade cards were designed by celebrated artists of the 20th century. They can be had for almost nothing.

The legendary cartoonist, Robert Crumb, designed many of A&BC Gum's 1973 *Hip Patch Stickers*. Until this mention they had been selling for a few pounds each. After this announcement they'll be up to £25 each, if they are available at all! Crumb's not the only one. Seek and you shall find! Collections of well-designed cards are like miniature art galleries. They cost little to collect and can be had quite easily by scouring collectibles websites, ephemera fairs and antiques markets. Values have been steadily upwards for decades, and they seem set to continue in that direction. The bigger the sport the more there is to choose from, and the more buyers there will be. Invest in croquet collectibles at your peril!

Absent Without Leave

There are only so many cards that can be included in one book. Some cards went AWOL just as publishing time came around, others are in reserve for next time. Absconding from this issue were pictures of Clevedon Confectionery cards. Ironically they are some of this writer's favourites, and many cards by Clevedon are rare and valuable, especially its quirky 1950s series of *Football Club Managers*, a series of monotone photos, on blue or lilac, of middle-aged blokes in trilbies and duffel coats.

Other brands, from Galli to Guillen, from Sims to Stanley Hotel, to name but four of a thousand types which were not included in this issue, will be part of a new edition, in an updated and expanded guide sometime in the future. A brief selection of MIA cards includes the following:

Missing in action:

Bartola, 1920s Maltese cards, Sleima Wanderers, packet issue cards £10 each

DEA, Italian metal discoid football cards from the 1920s & 30s, £30 to £200

Domanitalia, Italian celluloid cards from the early 1930s, various issues, £50 to £100

Film Stips, English transparencies of football action issued in the 1950s, £10 to £50

Football King Gum packets (advertising BAB Shooting Stars) from 1973, £50 each

Imsa Soccer Pops, early 1970s British football stickers from bottles, £20 to £40

Picciarello, 1973 Italian stickers of quads, packet issues, £50 to £100 each

Quieta Coffee, 1949 to 1952 West Germany cards of footballers, £10 to £20

Sims Tango Toffee, 1920s cards issued in Paisley, Scotland. Worth £100 to £200

Swinton Brewery shield-shaped cards, c.1880s, £100 to £200

Varesina of Varese, chocolates cards from the 1930s, £30 to £150

Wellington Hotel of St Helens, shield-shaped cards, 1880s, £150 to £200

These cards are just a sample of what could not be included this time, and of what's to come, next time, in the not too distant future. Look out for news of the next book on Pitch Publishing's site and this writer's own channels, blogs and website.

A&BC Hip Patch stickers, 1973, drawn by Robert Crumb

Appendix 7 **Contact**

Below you will see this writer's blogs and various internet channels and addresses where you can follow updates on new books, articles on rare cards, and other news.

Send your wants lists, cards for sale, and letters by post to:

Carl Wilkes
BM A to Z Football Cards Book
London
WC1N 3XX

New E-shop with newly listed cards:
www.footballsoccercards.com

Olde Shoppe, with different cards:
www.rarecards.co.uk

The old website at **www.rarecards.co.uk** is based upon the first football cards website in the world, from 1996, which was run by this writer. There are thousands of cards, not just players and football teams but also other sports, from tennis to rugby.
Contact the author at: **cards@rarecards.co.uk**
The new Eshop at **www.footballsoccercards.com** opened in 2019.
Facebook: **www.facebook.com/rarecards**
Twitter: **www.twitter.com/rarecards_fcc**

1880s Stanley Arms Hotel Blackpool card, 1930 and 1938 World Cup stamps, 1973 Picchiarello stickers

Select bibliography

Books and magazines about cards, and collecting cards

The Card. Collectors, Con Men and the True Story of History's Most Desired Baseball Card, by Michael O'Keeffe and Teri Thompson. Published by It Books, 2008.

This book is a must-read! It's not to be missed. It's for all and any card collectors, buyers, sellers and dealers. Biblical in its exposure of secrets you need to know. Don't believe any bad reviews about this book, for they are almost surely written by the people exposed in it. The book reveals dodgy dealings in the multi-million card slabbing and grading business, and tells a tall tale of the card that came to sell for over $3million in 2016. Don't be put off by baseball, if it's not your sport, for this book could be about a soccer cigarette card, or any tobacco card. It's entertaining, eye-opening and a warning! It's also inexpensive. You can pick up a copy on Amazon marketplace or Ebay for a couple of pounds. Five star entertainment!

Stuck On You, The Rise & Fall & Rise of Panini Stickers, by Greg Lansdowne. Published in 2015, by Pitch Publishing.

Essential reading for collectors of Merlin, Match and modern era Panini stickers. Greg's book was made into the TV documentary, 'Stuck on You', by Fosse Films, 2017.

The Pinnace Collection. Published by The Association of Football Statisticians, 1986.

The best starting point for understanding the scale of collecting the definitive tobacco soccer cards of the period after World War One. And this book is just the tip of the iceberg. A pinnace, by the way, is a small boat that sits above deck upon a larger vessel. It's a tender craft, or, in the case of an iceberg, a lifeboat.

The Beautiful Badge, by Martin Routledge. Published by Pitch Publishing, 2018.

One of the most beautiful football books ever! Bedside, for endless sweet dreams.

Cromos Para Recordar, by Juan Ral. Published in Spain, in 2007 by Graf.

Though not about football cards, this is a most elegant book of cards. The focus is on Spanish trade cards from Edwardian times until World War Two.

Deutsche Cards und Tütenbilder, band 1 und 2, by Gerd Päsler. Published in Germany, in 2014, by Fodito Verlag.

For the most reliable information on German trade cards, these books are not only the standard reference guides, they are biblical in scale and in scope.

Köberich's Reklame und Sammelbilder Katalog, 1946–2001. Published in Germany, in 2002, by Lumdatel.

A price guide for post-war German cards. The same publisher also issues a book with an earlier frame of reference, for tobacco cards.

Half-Time, by David Thompson. Published in Great Britain by Murray's, 1987.

In its day this was the best book on soccer cigarette cards. Though dated it still fires on some cylinders. Alas, it does not include post-war issues, like Phillips Sports packet issues, or cigar cards of the 1960s and 1970s, but it does cover the better known cigarette cards and it includes checklists too, though many are not complete. For example, the Taddy cards listings lack many cards that have since been recorded. The book lists absolutely no football trade cards nor trading cards, so it's Capstan all the way, and for Navy Cut lovers only.

Reklamekunst um 1900, by Detlef Lorenz. Published in Germany, in 2000, by Reimer.

Das Reklamesammelbild Sammlerträum, by Evamaria and Erhard Ciolina. Published in Germany, in 2010, by Battenberg.

Figurine e Menù Liebig, Calalogo Illustrato. Published in Italy by Sanguinetti.

The Card Scene, a magazine edited by John Devaney. Issued every few months.

Write for details to: John Devaney, 10 Yelverton Road, Whitley, Reading, RG2 7SU.

The Card Scene, a journal about card collecting and cards with all sorts of subjects, took the spot that was vacated by the demise of Card Times. It is Great Britain's only printed card collecting journal, other than FCCM.

Nigel's ... should be a book but it's not, it's a website. It's included here as it might encourage him to write it, and use all the supporting documentation he has ably assembled over the years since he was a client of mine, in the 1990s. Compliments to him and well worth looking at, for cards of the 1960s and 70s:
www.cards.littleoak.com.au

Football Card Collector Magazine was issued between 1997 and 2018, firstly by Carl Wilkes (until 2000) and then by Garry Daynes. Back issues are worth collecting for the articles, checklists and other features on rare football cards.

This writer's Facebook and Twitter channels have hundreds of pictures and articles on rare cards, as does the website
www.footballsoccercards.com

Find the cards channel at: **www.facebook. com/rarecards** and card news tweets at: **www.twitter.com/rarecards_fcc**

Glossary

Mira, 1968 sticker of the women *tifose* of Verona

A key to select names, marques and brands.

Adolph: Subbuteo
Albosport: Didasco
Ali Erzeugnisse: Jean's Fussball
Altenberg und Stralsunder: Kwartett; Quartett, Ravensburg; Happy Families
Amalgamated Press: Champion, Pilot, Lot-o-fun, Triumph, Comic Life
Anglo-American Chewing Gum Ltd.: Bell Boy Gum
Baldini & Castoldi: Castoldi
BDV: Phillips
Buste ed Affini: BEA
CBT: Kane Products
Cedip: Nuzzi
Coda y Cia: Fher Disgra
Circus Girl Cigarettes: Cohen, Weenen & Co.
C.L. (silks with a horseshoe logo, and the letters "C L"): Cigarillos Londres
Clarnico: Clarke, Nicholls & Coombs
Cornish Match Company: Jay Dees Newsagent
C.S. Ltd.: Comet Sweets
Daddies Sauce: Danone.
Danckleman & Schrader: Cigarillos Londres
Dawber: fake cards created on a PC, an antique rubber stamp added after printing
Disgra: Fher
Drapkin: Major Drapkin

Dreyer: Sport I Bilder [sic]
Dubrico: Record Cigarette Company
Edis: Motta
Fleetway: Champion, Jag, Eagle Swift, Lion, Tiger, Hurricane
Francesca: Carsel
Genescambi: Maple Leaf
Glasgow Evening Citizen: Evening Citizen
Godfrey Phillips: Phillips, Pinnace, BDV
Goudey Gum: British Chewing Sweets
Grapenuts: All Sports Illustrated Weekly
Islanders Cigarette: Bucktrout Tobacco
Hannah's World Cup: Monty
Jubolitan: Urodonal
Kent Police: Copcards
Kinnear: Marcus
Klene: Val Gum
Kurmark: Garbaty
Liverpool Weekly Courier: Football Favourites
Longacre: Charles Buchan Football Monthly, Eagle
Lotus Toffee: Filshill
Maple Cigarettes: Murray's Cigarettes
Merry Sweets Ltd: Soccer Bubble Gum
Napro: Barratt
Nilprincess: Union

Northern Trancessories: BAB
Oh Boy Gum: British Chewing Sweets
Oliman: Maga
Palirex: Dipul
Palmer Mann: Sifta Sam Salt
Panama: Ladbroke
Park Drive: Gallaher
Paytelco: Mercurycard
PG Tips: Brooke Bond
Pinnace: Phillips
Shoot Gum: Miroir Sprint
Sifta Sam: Palmer Mann
Solo Cigarettes: Union
Sphinx Products: Poolette
State Express: Ardath
South Wales Police: Ritchie
Three Nuns Tobacco: Bell
Tonka: Kenner
WHC: Barratt & Co.
Wilkins Cough Tablets: Barratt, VCC
World Distributors: FKS

1920s German card of Uruguayan strikers from Peñarol; and Faas Wilkes, on a 1950 card by Leeuwenzegel Margarine

31. D. MEIKLEJOHN, Rangers
32. F. A. CUP
33. W. McCLEERY, Linfield
34. SCOTTISH CUP
35. ALEC JAMES, Arsenal
36. IRISH CUP